Johnny Pail Face Becomes a Human Being

John Jarvis

Levellers Press

AMHERST, MASSACHUSETTS

Johnny Pail Face
Becomes a
Human Being

Published by *Levellers Press*, Amherst, Massachusetts

Printed in the United States of America

ISBN 978-1-937146-45-0

Book Agent and Manuscript Editor: Sandra Abbott Chmiel
Editorial Assistant: Ivery Stakley
Front Cover Photo: Kelly M. MacIntyre
Back Cover Photo—Johnny Pail Face, Kelly MacIntyre
Back Cover Photo—the Author, Bay Path College File Photo

Dedication

For my mother, who taught me how to learn.
For Uncle Mike, who taught me how to teach.
For my sister Neena who swam upstream
in our River of No Return
for a lifetime.

Together we have come to know
the eddies of ugliness and beauty
that we form even when we do not mean to,
and then call them
Our Lives.

Contents

Part III: A Prayer Looking to the West

Part IV: Prayer to the North (The Last and Longest Road)

Acknowedgments

APPENDICES

Note to Reader

I speak of many hard things in this book. I speak of things that you may not have known about even though they happened to people around you and in places right here in your land and mine. My story and stories about people like me have waited a long time to be told. I am 94 years old. It is not wise to wait longer. As I tell of my life, I wish to be clear about one thing. The U. S. Government, my government, may not be the best in the world. But I have been through most of the world in service to my government and it is the best government that I know. The U. S. Government has allowed me to earn equality. Equality is something that cannot be given. It must be earned. I believe that I have earned my right to be who I am. I believe I have earned my right to be a proud citizen of the United States of America. I don't ever want to give a negative impression of my country. Whatever I have done in the last 93 years, if I have done anything wrong or bad, I did it on my own. I do not blame my country or my beloved government. I take responsibility for my actions.

—Johnny Pail Face
October 18, 2010

Johnny (foreground), brother Raul (back left), and brother Pete (back right), circa 1920 on the Navajo Reservation near Gallup, New Mexico.

Part One

Morning Prayer Looking to the East

Oh Lord, Creator of Mother Earth and the Universe, I have opened my eyes to another day. Please help me by taking away all that is negative. Take away my Impatience, Intolerance, Resentments, Denials, Anxiety, and any other things that are negative within me.

CHAPTER I

New England Refuge

*Everything I've ever done in my life
has been for the wrong reasons.
Everything I have received from it has turned out just right.*

JOHNNY PAIL FACE IS 96 YEARS OLD. He is Navajo. For the past nineteen years, he has slept in the guest bedroom of a dear friend in Western Massachusetts. At the start of each new day he prays in four directions from a quiet spot behind his friend's home. The first time that he let me observe his morning prayer, I drove through the mists of a cool morning in early May to where he resides.

My route led me north along the Connecticut River from a suburb just south of Springfield, Massachusetts. That morning the full foliage of spring was greening the maple and elm forests that blanket this part of New England. It is normally a twenty-minute drive to Johnny's home on the north side of the small town of Granby, but I hit Interstate 91 during morning rush hour. A truck would not let me merge. I slowed almost to a stop and squeezed my small van in behind him. The driver behind me honked in impatience, but let me in. I knew that I was going to be late for my appointment with Johnny. Johnny doesn't like it when I'm late. He doesn't have time to waste.

I moved into the fast lane and sped up. It wasn't fast enough. Cars behind me were jamming up. The speed limit signs posted 50 miles per hour. We were doing 70. The cars behind me were on my back bumper. I pushed it to 75.

I was relieved to reach Chicopee, where the freeway divides and most of the traffic stays with I-91. I followed I-391 North and things got more peaceful. I took the slow lane where there were large spaces between the few cars in sight. When I exited at Holyoke, the traffic dropped off further.

I crossed the Connecticut River at the edge of Holyoke, just below what used to be a magnificent natural falls. Peoples of various Algonquin tribes once caught fish there in abundance. In those days, millions of salmon returned from the ocean some 70 miles to the south to leap upward through 58 feet of tumbling water on their annual run to spawning beds tens of thousands of years old.

Now there is a concrete dam in the place of the falls. It was completed in 1900 to provide electricity and water for the endless rows of paper and other mills that, for a few decades, made Holyoke "The Queen of Industrial Cities" during the American Industrial Revolution. But when there was more money to be made elsewhere, the revolution left Holyoke faster than it came.[1] In recent decades, federal and state agencies have spent upwards of two hundred million dollars to reestablish a salmon run on the Connecticut River. Thirty-four salmon were counted in the most recent run.

However, it is not recommended that you or I should try to catch and eat one. The State of Massachusetts warns on its website: "Children younger than 12 years of age, pregnant women, women of childbearing age who may become pregnant, and nursing mothers should not eat any fish from this water body."[2] The river remains too contaminated by industrial pollution and sewage for children and expecting mothers to eat any fish that are able to survive. One is left to speculate what might happen to anyone else who dares to indulge.

As we see in countless other cases across our land, the City of Holyoke has fared the same as the river that runs through it. It is now a thriving center of violence and despair that is made noteworthy by the sheer number and size of the large, empty, brick factory buildings that rise up on the "turf" of competing gangs.

The factories once fed off of waterwheels that ran the machinery of capitalism before capitalism left town. Today, tens of thousands of immigrants, mostly from Puerto Rico and the Dominican Republic, have taken the places of previous generations of poor newcomers to Holyoke. They came looking for jobs that no longer exist.

Now mothers do not let their children play outside of tenement apartments in Holyoke because of drive-by shootings. I learned how desperate things have become from a friend who works with teens in the town. The weapon of choice for girl gang members at the local high school has become the 9mm Glock pistol. It is not only a survival tool. It is also a status symbol showing that the girl's "man" has money, power, and prestige to pass on to her.

For the last few miles to Johnny's house, the road winds through increasingly rural countryside. Here and there middle class homes cluster between cultivated fields and maple forest. The morning mist shrouds them in a calming cover. I find myself relaxing as I escape the main thoroughfares of America for back roads where a few people still find ways to live quietly.

I roll my window down to let in the fresh air. I hear birdsong on the breeze rushing past the open window. I hear the call of a robin. I catch the melody of a red-winged blackbird. There are other calls that I do not know, all blending together with the sound of the wind as it blows in my open window. I smile at the thought that nature has its own radio frequency and its own playlist for those who pause to listen.

When I turn into Johnny's driveway, I have made the transition from the mainstream world of the United States of America to the world of a 90-year-old mixed-blood Navajo who no longer seems to care what year it might be.

Johnny's world is also noisy, but it is different from the cacophony of rush hour on the freeway. Johnny runs a food kitchen of sorts in the back yard of the home where he lives. His food kitchen serves animals. He has a collection of bird, squirrel, and rabbit feeders placed in assorted locations around the half-acre yard.

As I step from my car and begin to walk toward the house, I am surrounded by a symphony of bird song and squirrel chatter coming from the back deck where most of the feeders are clustered. There are wrens and jays and chickadees squabbling for places at the feeders. A red cardinal wings away as I approach. Robins are scattered across the lawn harvesting worms. Red-winged blackbirds sing back and forth in the trees that ring the property and keep it secluded. There is a mid-sized brown rabbit feeding quietly near the barn at the back of the property where Johnny puts out rabbit food. Occasionally, a black bear wanders through and cleans out all the feeders high and low. Johnny's eyes dance with delight when he recounts such events. He doesn't seem to care which animal gets his food as long as everyone gets something.

As soon as I ring the doorbell, I hear Johnny coming. He is no more quiet than the loudest of the jays.

"Where you been?" he calls out as he makes his way down the back stairs. He is wearing black cotton sweatpants and a red, short-sleeved shirt. I have never seen him in anything but a red shirt. It is his trademark. He has a black baseball cap clamped down over unruly hair. On the black cap are the words "Native Veteran" in white letters. The visor is decorated with a brightly colored Native war shield.

"The traffic was bad," I offer half-heartedly. I know Johnny always waits in anticipation for my visits and it makes him grumpy when I am late.

"No excuses. That's what I always used to say to the people who worked for me. I don't want excuses. I just want results." All the time he is speaking, his eyes are dancing and he is smiling. When he reaches me, he grabs my hand and gives it a firm shake. "How you doin' today, anyway, J.J.?" he asks, looking at me closely.

"I'm good, Johnny," I smile. "Thank you for letting me come today. I'm looking forward to the prayer."

He looks at me an instant longer, and then responds, "C'mon then. Let's go pray."

Johnny takes his ritual position in the back yard just beyond the birdfeeders and in front of the parked motor home that he uses to travel to weekend powwows and Native festivals throughout New England. He always begins his prayers facing East, looking into the rising sun. Today, there is no sun.

"Uh oh, looks like it's gonna rain on my head," he observes. Indeed, as he begins to address his Creator, a light rain starts to fall. By the time he finishes his prayer to the East, then to the South, and is halfway through his words to the West, the rain stops. I hear the wind rustling the leaves in the maple trees nearby as a background to the sound of his voice. A small U.S. flag that he has attached to a post beside the barn moves with the wind. Finally, Johnny turns northward and brings to a close the extended prayer with which he starts each new day.[3]

We are quiet for a few moments. I note that he is standing on a round cement slab that fits neatly into the green of the lawn. As he walks toward me, I ask, "Johnny, did you put that slab there just for doing your prayers?"

He turns and looks back at the slab, as if noticing it for the first time. When he turns back to me, a broad smile is warming his rugged features. "Nope. That's just the cover to the septic tank," he says. "I'd stand on the grass, but the dew makes it slippery and if I fall at my age, I'll break my ass for sure."

This mix of heavenly aspirations and earthy reality is at the core of Johnny Pail Face. Although his words and actions dance constantly between things that seem opposite in nature, his morning prayer reasserts harmony in his world each morning. His four-directional prayer sums up the acquired wisdom of a life well lived. It is life that likewise brings together extremes.

As a dirt-poor Navajo boy born the last of eight children to an aging couple on the eastern border of the Navajo reservation in 1916, Johnny's life did not start out heading in a good direction. At the core of things, he has spent the whole of his life looking for better ways to go. Conquering the many worlds through which he has moved has not been easy. And yet as he speaks of the journey one of the first things to emerge is another intriguing paradox.

After nine decades on Earth, he puts it this way: "Everything I've ever done in my life has been for the wrong reasons. Everything I have received from it has turned out just right."

From the moment that Old Johnny spoke these words during one of our Monday afternoon interview sessions, I knew that I would use them to open the first chapter of this book. They were not merely a passing comment in the aftermath of another of the many interesting stories he had to share. After hours of interviews and many friendly discussions among the bird and rabbit feeders in his backyard, I felt how well these two sentences frame his life. It is not an ordinary life. But then, perhaps there are no ordinary lives. Perhaps lives that seem ordinary are simply hidden.

The hidden things often are especially hidden to the people who have lived them. It takes what Native Americans call "medicine" to make the invisible things visible again, first for the storyteller, and then for listeners and readers. When we work together to bring the beauty of even one life into clearer view, the medicine becomes a force to be reckoned with. A force for insight. A force that can help make things done for all the wrong reasons turn out right.

Johnny was in a good place to tell his life story when I came to know him. He had recently celebrated his 91st birthday. In those years, three wives had divorced him because of alcoholism and he had buried a daughter, also a victim of alcohol abuse. A career soldier, he had fought in World War II, did two tours of duty in Korea, and then ended his years of service to his country with a 22-month stint in Vietnam. He was not an ordinary soldier, however. His work blurred the boundaries between military service and civilian assignments for the Department of Defense.

After World War II, Johnny used the G. I. Bill to get an education. He earned a Bachelor's Degree in weather forecasting and a Master's in climatology. That made him useful to the U.S. Government in ways that he is still hesitant to talk about fully. For the military, he told pilots on bombing runs which way the wind would be blowing as they carried out their deadly work. This was important in the 1960s not just for accuracy, but to know which way the mushroom clouds would drift should we ever need to use our ultimate weapons.

But weathermen are not combatants. Their role is like that of a medic or a chaplain. They are considered neutral and can be easily transferred in and out of embassies, consulates, and situations of conflict. The government has a ready explanation for why they are coming and going. So, Johnny was also useful to the U.S. Government in the messy business of promoting democracies around the world in the 1950s and 60s. He worked on clandestine operations for the National Security Agency in Washington not just to help eliminate human obstacles to American interests, but also to support violent insurgencies that the U.S. favored.

For example, during the Algerian colonial revolution against France in the early 1960s, Johnny was covertly assigned to deliver supplies on a regular basis to the Algerian insurgents. Johnny's plane was filled with heavy boxes. A box broke open one day in transit. Johnny saw guns inside. He closed the box back up. He delivered the shipment just like all the others. He followed orders. He didn't ask questions. He understood. The U.S. Government wanted France to lose its colonies in the 1960s. The U.S. was interested in Algerian independence. The fact that Johnny hauled his cargo out of an airbase that the U.S. was leasing an hour by train east of Paris gives some idea of the delicate nature of the work that he did for U.S. leaders in Washington.[4]

Johnny Pail Face has had time to work through such events from his younger days. His morning prayers are one way he remains at peace with the world. It has been a long journey for a boy born in 1916 to a full-blood Navajo Indian mother and a Navajo/Spanish father in the tiny reservation town of Sheep Springs, New Mexico. It was a hard place to be born. It was a hard time to born. Coming into the world with a red skin did not make things easier. Before the middle of the twentieth century, white Americans were not interested in making peace with the nation's red people. Over the previous fifty years before Johnny arrived on the scene, mainstream attitudes had progressed from "The only good Indian is a dead Indian" to "Kill the Indian, save the man."

U.S. Indian policies followed the same progression, shifting from scorched-earth warfare and extermination to Indian schools that swallowed up generations of stolen red children and force-fed them white language, religion, culture, and values. For most Natives, the noticeable difference over time was that they died more slowly under the second approach. But they still died early, and painfully.[5]

All of this to say, the world into which young Johnny was born was not a hospitable place. It was steeped in the qualities that old Johnny would specifically address in his morning prayers much later in life. It was a whirlpool of "Impatience, Intolerance, Resentments, Denials, Anxiety" and "other things that are negative within."

But, in the end, it was hatred that Johnny found the hardest to get past. He spent most of his adult life fighting that battle. There is wisdom to be gained from such a struggle, if one is able to win it. Now Johnny says things like, "Hate comes from not knowing who you are, what you are, where you are." Spoken by a man in his 90s, these words take on a weight that they might not otherwise have. They have become the bedrock of his life and are etched into the lines of his weathered face. He carries their weight on his sloping shoulders. There are reminders of them in his right hand where parts of two fingers are missing, and in an oddly-shaped left elbow that absorbed the shock of an exploding mortar shell long ago in Northern Italy.

It was not until nearly two years into our work on this book that the significance of Johnny's experiences in Northern Italy became apparent. He spent a year and a half fighting Hitler's troops day after day after day from Monte Cassino south of Rome all the way to the Po River in the North. One afternoon he was retelling a particularly haunting story about a hand-to-hand confrontation with a German soldier so young that Johnny could not bring himself to kill him. In the silence that followed his words, I suddenly understood something that we both had overlooked in all our time together.

"Johnny," I said, "do you realize that you have been involved in two genocides in your life?"

He looked at me blankly for a moment. "I have?" he asked.

I nodded. "Yes, you have. The history books tell us that what happened to your grandparents was genocide. And you were helping to stop Hitler's genocide in Europe."

He thought about this and then said with a slow shake of his gray hair, "Well I don't know which fight wounded me worse. They both were bad. Just bad."

On many levels, it is the effort to deal with two genocides that defines the contours of Johnny's life. He paid a high price in hard living and destructive behavior towards himself and those around him before he worked out who he is, what he is, and where he belongs. Only a profound transformation at the midpoint of his life saved him from self-destruction. "I knew I was wrong," he says. "Something inside was eating me up." And then he adds, "To save yourself, you have to stay within the limits of what you are and you can't lie to yourself about your limits. That's the most important thing in the world. You can lie to the whole world, to anyone, except to one person. Don't ever lie to yourself. That's how the bad stuff begins."

Although Johnny and his family were not in a position to know, a quiet new movement was afoot in the Native American world at the time of his birth. Educated Indians like Sioux Dr. Charles Eastman and Yavapai Dr. Carlos Montezuma were practicing medicine among white patients in Minneapolis and Chicago. A Cheyenne River Sioux woman, Ella Calla Deloria, was working with the renowned anthropologist Franz Boas at Columbia University, where she had earned her doctorate in anthropology under his guidance. Other Native women such as Gertrude Bonnin (Lakota), Tsiana Redfeather (Creek/Cherokee) and Angel de Cora (Winnebago) were excelling in music, dance and art. Redfeather toured Europe in 1918 to entertain the Allied troops with her music. She later had an opera written about her life. It was the first Native American opera to play at the Metropolitan Opera in New York for successive seasons.[6]

In due time, Johnny Pail Face would join this generation of reservation "leavers" that today has become the majority of American Indians. The most recent U.S. census tells us that a full two-thirds of America's four million Native Peoples no longer live on reservations. At the time of Johnny's birth, mainstream Americans assumed that if they could get Indians off of their reservations, they would stop being Indians. They would assimilate into the mainstream culture and cease to be a national "problem" that tied Washington bureaucrats into knots.

The heart of the problem was to find ways to erase from existence great mounds of legal and binding treaty documents that acknowledged the Indians as the previous owners of America. These documents spell out all the rights, privileges and compensation due the Indians in return for three hundred years of deeding over their continent tract by tract, forest by forest, river by river, and mountain by mountain.

In the space of Johnny Pail Face's long life, white America has learned a useful lesson on this topic: When Indians leave their reservations, they do not stop being Indians. While much may be given up, much is kept. They change identities; they do not erase them. In short, the struggle with identity that Indian doctors, anthropologists, artists, and musicians faced at the beginning of the twentieth century has only grown in breadth in the one hundred years since. Johnny Pail Face's life is testament to this ongoing struggle that continues to frame the lives of millions of Americans whose roots predate by thousands of years the arrival of Captain John Smith in Virginia and the Puritans at Plymouth Rock.

As an old man, Pail Face still struggles with who he is. But it is a good struggle. A favorite self-description that he repeats as a touchstone for his life is, "I'm just a poor, homeless, illiterate, alcoholic Indian." (Note that after nearly 400 years of doing so, most Indians continue to call themselves Indians. Well-intentioned outsiders have recently come to prefer the title "Native American.") Johnny usually follows this first line with, "What do I know about anything anyway?"

His eyes dance with merriment as he says these things. Today, he not only has two college degrees from first-rate American universities, but speaks five languages. At one point in his career, he translated the U.S. military's voluminous weather manuals from English to Spanish for weather forecasters in Honduras. He has spent years living and working around the globe in service to the U.S. Government, his government.

Through a very deliberate choice, he has now retired to a refuge off the beaten path in New England. There, he spends much of his time engaged in the "spiritual hobby" of making fine silver and turquoise Navajo jewelry, a craft he began to learn over 80 years ago on the reservation. He spends his summers in a loose-knit and colorful community of New England Indians and whites who come together to celebrate in their own ways the Native "renaissance" sweeping America today. He travels in a comfortable motor home and makes enough money through jewelry sales to pay his expenses.

One day I asked him point blank how he felt about being an Indian in his youth when he really was "poor, homeless and illiterate."

"I hated being an Indian!" he burst out with an intensity that surprised me.

Near the end of the same conversation, I asked him how he feels about being an Indian today, in his 90s.

"I love it," he answered quietly. "I really love it."

But it is a complicated love, as wounded as it is beautiful. In the process of achieving personal autonomy and balance in his life, Johnny Pail Face chose to let go of his birth community and to adopt a new red-white community far from Navajo country. Much was lost and much was gained in the process. He left behind a mother who had learned from the Catholic padres to hate her Navajo self. Johnny's hands now begin to shake and his voice breaks as he relates how, for a lifetime, she prayed fervently to Jesus in a foreign tongue in a vain attempt to find the human dignity that eluded her as a red woman in a white world. He came home wounded from World War II to find her house dark and the front door swinging in the wind. She had died the year before. No one had told him. It took him a year at a mental hospital in Albuquerque to recover from the wounds of war. And from the homecoming.

In time, Johnny chose to bury parts of himself with mother, father, three brothers and four sisters who all now lie beneath the earth in far-flung places across New Mexico, Arizona, California, and south of the Mexican border. With them, he has also struggled to bury self-hatred, burning anger, alcoholism, and similar things that he picked up on the Navajo reservation of his youth.

He chose to replace this inner ugliness with better things, things like self-reliance, dignity, and self-respect. These were hard changes at first to envision, and harder still to carry out. His life shows that the journey of becoming a human being can be long, depending on where one begins. It's hard to imagine a longer journey than one that begins in the human wreckage of a genocide and then crashes head-on into a second genocide. What should surprise us most is that Johnny Pail Face survived the journey at all. In the end, the fact that he made peace with the world is almost beyond our ability as humans to grasp.

Old Johnny's story teaches us that the best we can hope for, Native or otherwise, is to make wise choices about what we will keep and what we will let go, about who we will become and who we will no longer be. For Johnny, such things are all part of the great "circle of life." The most important dimension of the circle for him is the part that reaches into us and sustains us in our deeper places. As he puts it:

> We are born in this circle. It's within us. We can't transfer it to anyone else. Who and what we let into our circles determines our lives. You have to learn to live within yourself, within who, what, and where you are, in order to keep yourself mentally, physically, and spiritually healthy. You have to be responsible for yourself.

Johnny is the fruit of a broken culture. His orphaned Navajo mother survived the devastation of America only because the remnants of her people turned her over to the Spanish priests at a Catholic mission rather than allow her to die of starvation. His father, although born the son of a successful Mexican rancher, was destined to a life at the bottom of American society because his mother was a lifelong servant and sex slave to that rancher.

There is always a balance between self and the group in Johnny's reflections on life. He is a giving, community-oriented person who, nonetheless, constantly emphasizes the role of the individual to improve him- or herself. This emphasis on self springs from the painful reality of his life as it has been lived. "Self" was the only resource that remained in his possession in the cultural chaos that he inherited with his first breath of life in the desolation of an early twentieth-century Navajo reservation. In that chaos, Johnny realized early on that he would only be what he himself decided he would be.

In the complex human process of becoming a better human being, Johnny Pail Face is a guide and a model. He passed through many worlds, cultures, and peoples on his long journey. In the process, he learned first to survive, then to prosper, and finally to conquer those forces within and without that kept him from being the understanding, good, and giving person that he feels it was his human destiny to become.

This path of personal change frames the man's life. A Navajo boy who once loathed who he was now loves who he is. To get from there to here, he did everything for all the wrong reasons. And it has all turned out right. Surely there is what Native Peoples call "magic" and "good medicine" in such an odyssey.

These days, he returns his love and gratitude to his Creator each morning through prayer. He does it with sincerity and gentleness as he raises his weathered face in respect to each of the four directions. He does it while standing on a cesspool cover in the back yard of a safe haven in New England.

Johnny Pail Face did not wait for the collective Native American renaissance that has come too late for most of the people he has loved. He went out and made his own renaissance. He took control of "who, what, and where" he was on the great circle of life, both within and without.

And he has lived to tell the tale.

CHAPTER 2

Sunrise Over Sheep Springs

Nada es verdad.
Nada es mentira.
Todo es asegun el color del crystal
con que se mira.

EARLY IN MY INTERVIEWS WITH JOHNNY at his friend's dining room table, I stumbled across a word that would shape not only my ongoing line of questioning, but the deeper journeys that were waiting under Johnny's surface. The word was "truth." I was attempting to set up the framework for this book and said to Johnny that I wanted to "get at the deeper truth of his life story."

That drew him up short. There was a long silence after I made the statement. I had spent enough time around Native Peoples to have some idea of what it was about. Indians have a natural inclination to duck and cover when a white man starts talking about the "truth." It is born of centuries of trying to hold on to ancient, Earth-centered, and heartfelt ways of living one's life in the face of the soul-chilling indifference of white people's "truth."

After a few moments of reflection, Johnny steered me in a more productive direction. "There is an old Spanish saying about truth that I like a lot," he said. "Maybe we could use that. It goes like this." Then he recited in fluent Spanish the statement that opens this chapter: "Nothing is true. Nothing is false. Everything is according to the color of the crystal through which one looks."

For Johnny Pail Face, this philosophy comes from having been born amid the desperate poverty of an American Indian reservation, which puts one's soul in great need of more hopeful ways of seeing the world. It is also a way of looking backward when you are an old man fluent in five languages and cultures, and you are trying to make sense of the multi-dimensional path into the human experience that you've trod. In short, it is one of those philosophical guides that does not wear thin and slough off with the passing of the years. To the contrary. It becomes more useful for finding ways to account for the complexities of worlds one encounters without and within as the decades slip by.

Johnny's first view of the world came through two quite different "crystals." The first was Navajo and the second Spanish-American. He was born Juan Cecilio Sarmiento in Northwestern New Mexico in November, 1916, at a dusty little cluster of Navajo hogans called Sheep Springs. A half-day drive to the west takes one into the rugged breaks of Canyon de Chelly where Native Peoples have lived in the natural shelters of a fortress canyon for 2000 years. The thousand-foot tall cliffs still harbor the ancient ruins of an Anasazi stone village built 900 years ago. A half-day drive to the East is Chaco Canyon, another Anasazi cliff-dwelling site with thirty large masonry buildings, each one containing hundreds of rooms that once teemed with people. Fifty miles of ancient roadways still lead like the spokes of a wheel to the center of the civilization that once made Chaco Canyon the center of a human world. This all was built by Native American architects, engineers, stone workers, and masons 1000 years ago.

Sheep Springs sits in the high desert between these two ancient sites. It has its own history which is not nearly as old as the Anasazi ruins, but which offers an equally compelling view into the curious twists and turns of the human story. The small town sits in the middle of a historic trail. It is the infamous path that Kit Carson and the U.S. Cavalry followed in 1864-65 when they force-marched nearly 10,000 Navajo people away from their last stronghold in Canyon de Chelly to what bureaucrats in Washington coined the term "concentration camp" to describe. It was the first official use of that phrase in the English language.

The U.S. Government deemed it good public policy in the 1860s to remove the Navajo People hundreds of miles from their traditional homelands in order to teach them civilized ways of living. They relocated the Natives to a place called *Bosque Redondo*, which lies at the center of an expansive alkali flat in what was once one of the most inhospitable parts of the Southern New Mexico desert. To their credit, government leaders in Washington relented and sought less-deadly ways of civilizing them when the Navajos began to die in great numbers in their new home. They allowed the survivors to retrace on foot the hundreds of miles home again while they deliberated what to do next with the Navajo.

In both cases, Sheep Springs was on one of the paths that they trod. In both cases, the tears of the people watered the earth along the trail. At first were tears of hopelessness and despair. Four years later were tears of joy and thanksgiving, as the Navajo returned to the mountains, canyons, rivers, and farms that had provided them homes, sustenance, and meaning for centuries. They returned to the places where their legends, their history, their spirits, their hearts, and the land all blended into a single path of beauty.

The column of survivors that left *Bosque Redondo* on June 16, 1868, stretched for ten miles across the desert landscape. Thousands of survivors walked away from captivity in a strange and foreign land. It was an exodus on a grand scale, a repeat of the Hebrew People's escape from bondage in Egypt that the Whites revered in their sacred book. But white Americans failed to appreciate or even to take note when it happened again right under their noses.

Fifty-six military wagons carried the very old and the sick. A few fortunate Navajo rode horses. And the remaining thousands simply walked the arduous road home again. Trailing behind the people were all that remained of once-expansive herds of horses, sheep, cattle and goats. The animals had been as decimated by life at *Bosque Redondo* as the people, their numbers reduced to barely enough for breeding stock.[1]

Survivors recall that the old people were the first to weep when the column sighted Mount Taylor, the landmark that stood at the southern border of their beloved land. Then through the ranks, people young and old burst into song. One of the songs that carried them home goes as follows:

Ahala ahalago naashá gha.
Shí naashá gha, shí naashá gha,
Sh'naasha lágo hózhó la.
Shí naashá gha, shí naashá gha
Shí naasha, lade hózhóo lá.

In freedom I go.
I am going in beauty; I am going in beauty.
I am going in beauty all around me.
I am going in beauty; I am going in beauty.
I go, wrapped in beauty.[2]

Do not look for this exodus of Biblical proportions in the history books that are used to teach mainstream American children to this day. It has been omitted. Most of the Navajo story, and of the larger Native American story, is only remembered by the victims and their children's children. When the headlines of their victories faded, the victors quickly forgot what they had done to their fellow human beings to get what they wanted as—winners do in all places and in all times.

But, in the end, if nothing is learned, the forgetting is as much a part of the dark side of human history as the dark events themselves. And the forgetting assures that the darkness will happen again. This process, too, is part of what Johnny Pail Face calls the Great Circle of Life. The historians put it a different way as they pass on some version of George Santayana's famous quote, "Those who cannot remember the past are condemned to repeat it." In America, this issue is especially acute. The historians themselves have forgotten what white America did to the Indians in order to take from them an entire continent.

How unfortunate it is that so few remember such things as the tears of the old people returning from *Bosque Redondo*. It is hard to imagine human tears more filled with meaning. How unfortunate that there is no one to let us hear again the songs of joy or the celebration of beauty that erupted spontaneously from a column of refugees ten miles long.

Our mainstream has lost much by forgetting that there are some Americans who love this land enough to weep over its mountains, its canyons, its rivers, and its prairies. America loses again by not re-membering that there are people among its citizenry who once sang with joy as they returned to their heartlands. The Hebrew Exodus has inspired and instructed Judeo-Christian peoples for countless generations. Is it not fair to ask: Have American Christians and Jews nothing to learn from an exodus similar in size and scope that burst forth in joy and renewal in their midst?

In the end, this Navajo story need not be a story of defeat or a dark chapter in America's past. It could be an instructive remembrance of things that matter most for all to pass on to our children.

There is another reason that the mainstream might want to look closely at the Navajo story. It is worth asking in this case as in all cases of human destruction: does it cost the victors less than it costs the victims? How unfortunate that it would be another century after the Navajo Long March before white Americans would begin to love the land enough to sorrow for it. By then mainstream tears would be as much from regret at the strip-mined earth, the clear-cut forests, the devastated fish runs, the polluted rivers and lakes, and the smoke-filled air as from some new-found love of mountains and secret places rich in family memories.

Equally worth considering is how long will it be before the forces of violence unleashed upon the original inhabitants of America subside. How long before mainstream America stops killing large numbers of people in Vietnam, in Iraq, in Afghanistan, in the Middle East...or in its own high schools, on university campuses, in movie theaters, in parking lots, on military bases, and even in kindergarten classrooms? Violence once embraced clings to those who take it in.

White victories have proven costly for all the peoples of this land over time—the Whites included. How we see and make sense of the violence depends upon the crystal through which one looks. As Johnny Pail Face proposes, it takes more than one lens to focus and to see clearly. That is the great secret.

Nada es verdad. Nada es mentira. "Nothing is true. Nothing is false." And so it happened that Johnny Pail Face was born on land watered by the bitter tears of his people. Or by their tears of joy. Or both. Or neither. Johnny was raised among a people who were savages—or beautiful human beings. They were far behind the white man, or a century ahead. More likely they were and remain some-where in the middle. It all depends on how one chooses to look. Or one may choose not to look at all, as so many now do.

For those who might be willing to look at places in American history like Sheep Springs, New Mexico, and at the lives of American citizens like Johnny Pail Face, the first thing that they will note is the seeming emptiness. Sheep Springs is in the high desert country of the American West. It rests on a long, flat, hundred-mile stretch of land that is 8,900 feet above sea level. Many Americans have never been that high in altitude except when flying in a commercial airliner.

When you stand at the edge of Sheep Springs today, you can see for great distances to the North, the East, and the South. To the West, a long ridge cuts off the view after a few miles. The North offers a peculiar vision. Two sharp-edged peaks rise up unexpectedly like desert mirages in the distance. White people call them Bennett Mountain and Ford Mountain, after the first Whites who "discovered" them. To the Navajo, they are different parts of the same extended mountain. It did not occur to the Navajo to name parts of the ageless Earth after such transitory beings as themselves. So they call the awe-inspiring formation rising from the high desert floor Black Streak Mountain because of the lines of dark mineral deposits that run through it.

Sheep Springs, now a small settlement of a couple of hundred Navajo, is surrounded by a broken landscape covered with little more than sparse sagebrush and even sparser clumps of dry desert grasses. In the distance, especially behind the town to the West, dusty ravines and gullies etch their rugged designs into the earth, offering evidence that water does come occasionally to the barren landscape and leaves as quickly as it comes. At 8,900 feet, winters are bitterly cold and summers are swelteringly hot. The high desert is a place of extremes. Johnny Pail Face was born in a world caught between and battered by these extremes.

Summer visitors who stray through this part of New Mexico these days going north or south on the melting blacktop of Highway 491 rarely slow down at Sheep Springs. This is no popular vacation destination. It was and is an example of the "real West" as Indians have lived it since the arrival of Whites. There are no frontier villages, no chain restaurants with kiddy playgrounds, no tourist shops full of plastic tomahawks. There is only one business in the business district, a one-room gas-station-convenience-mart-post-office-social-gathering place.

Behind it sits a half-finished Navajo Cultural and Tourist Center that overran its original building costs and awaits an upturn in the economy to see completion. When it is finished, it stretches the mind to imagine tourists flooding through the large front doors.

On the day that I visited Sheep Springs with a friend, we were the only two non-Navajos in town. We waited in line for gas at the single business in town for nearly twenty minutes. There were four pumps, but only one was working. No one seemed to mind. It gave people a chance to catch up with neighbors and friends. It also gave them an opportunity to ask who the newcomers were and what could possibly have brought us to their sleepy little settlement. When I explained that we were on a pilgrimage of sorts to the birthplace of a 93-year-old Navajo friend, we were treated with kindness and hospitality.

According to the most recent U.S. Census, the population of Sheep Springs numbered exactly 237 persons. Of this, 96 percent were Native American. The remaining 4 percent listed themselves as "mixed race." The annual family income was $11,786 per year, less than one-third of the national average. And so it is not surprising that 73 percent of the population lived below the poverty line. For those over age 65, the poverty rate rose to a full 100 percent.

Life for people who live in Sheep Springs can appear as bleak on the surface as the landscape in which they live. But there are more ways than one to look at a desert and at the people who live there. One does not need a lot of money to live in Sheep Springs. There are very few things to buy there.

And the old people are cared for by their families, helping out day to day with children and grandchildren in meaningful ways until the very end of their lives. There is no expensive "old folks' home" in Sheep Springs. Or rather every home is an old folks' home, if the children and the grandchildren are fortunate enough to have their old people still with them.

All that we saw in Sheep Springs during our visit were very young people and old people. Anyone of working age had gone off to the city to find a job. An old fellow who stopped his pickup to watch me take pictures and then struck up a conversation explained that everyone who lived in Sheep Springs survived on money sent home from those who had left. He himself had spent his working life as far off as Florida and then New York City. But when he retired, he came back to the place he had always called home.

As I stood talking to the fellow, behind me was a Mormon Church. In sharp contrast to Mormon Churches that I had seen in white communities, this one was surrounded by an eight-foot wire mesh fence and a locked gate. The Mormons are aggressive recruiters of new members and are normally eager to welcome people through their doors.

They offer a particularly interesting message of hope to Native Americans. I was surprised to see them fencing potential Navajo recruits out. Straight-laced Mormon missionaries in sharp suits and ties, or in modest skirts and blouses, use their *Book of Mormon* to teach the Indians in poor places like Sheep Springs that they are direct descendants of an extended Hebrew family. Similar to the departure of Old Abraham from Babylon around 1,700 B.C., another patriarch named Lehi left Jerusalem in 600 B.C. with his own extended family. According to the Mormons, they were led by God in sealed-up boats across the ocean to America.

Once in the New World, the evil sons of the family rebelled against their father and his God and therefore were cursed with "dark and loathsome skins." These were chased away from contact with their good siblings, whose children remained faithful to their God and, as a reward, were allowed to keep fair skins. In time the unrighteous children degenerated into the "wild savages" that Christopher Columbus and other Europeans found in vast numbers nearly 2,000 years later. The fair-skinned branch of the family actually fared rather worse in the end. They became increasingly involved in internecine warfare and slaughtered each other to extinction. Even in the Mormon world, bad things happen to good people.

Other than the theme of white-on-white violence leading to extinction, there might appear to be little for a Navajo to hope for in the Mormon story. The positive note comes with the Mormon promise that if the Natives will only return to following the Hebrew God, He will bless them with the same blessings that he gives to good Mormons. These include freedom from the devastation of addictions such as alcoholism and illegal drugs, family harmony, and eternal life with one's extended family once this world slips away.

With this theology, Mormons are sincerely devoted to adopting themselves and others into certain Jewish historical traditions as much as can be done. They have gone so far as to formulate a self-identifying phrase similar to what the Bible uses to describe the early Hebrews as they turned monotheistic. Where the Jews came to refer to themselves as God's "Chosen People," the Mormons now describe themselves as God's "Peculiar People."

The Navajo fellow who spoke to me during my visit to Sheep Springs explained that in such a poor area, the Mormon and other Christian churches offering any form of hope, even a "peculiar" form, often find people willing to listen. He also explained that when Mormon hope faded, all was not lost. A disenchanted Navajo could always carry off anything useable or saleable from church property while waiting for a next promise of better times. Hence the fence.

In such ways, high desert dwellers are habituated to seeing the world from different and often unexpected perspectives. They see a world that alternates between hope and despair as easily as the desert alternates between sun and storm. Their world is always changing and yet, in the long term, that world remains the same.

When spring rains sweep across Sheep Springs, the landscape changes dramatically in a matter of hours. Brilliant red, yellow, and violet cactus flowers burst into view in every direction. The clean fragrance of warm, wet, life-giving earth begins to blow on the wind before the storm has fully passed. Bird song and the humming of insects fill the air from every quarter. Dry bunch grass turns green almost before the eyes. Rabbits, mice, coyotes, snakes, lizards, and insects of every variety come out to drink, to hunt, and to mate. In a matter of hours, one of the most barren landscapes in America overflows with a spontaneous celebration of life. And yet, a day or two of blazing sun returns it to its seemingly barren state.

A similar transformation takes place during the hot summer months when day turns to night. After the sun goes down and the coolness of the high desert reclaims the land, life erupts. Under a full moon, the land overflows with an intensity of animal and plant life similar to the changes brought by the passing of a storm. Mice and other rodents scamper everywhere. Owls swoop and dive to snatch their prey. Bats fill the night air. Bands of coyotes rove the land, singing back and forth in their own language and for their own purposes. Scorpions, tarantulas, beetles, and bugs bring the desert floor to life.

The high desert is a place of extremes ranging from cold to hot, dry to wet, inaction to action, death to life, despair to hope. It is the same for desert people.

To understand such people and to see the beauty of their lives, an observer must be patient. It helps to go back to the beginning with a man like Johnny Pail Face. It helps to look through multiple perspectives as Johnny does.

Todo es asegun el color del crystal con que se mira. According to Old Johnny's philosophy, "Everything is as the color of the crystal through which one looks." And so it was that, from the beginning, young Johnny learned to look through two "crystals" at the world. His mother was Navajo; his father had mixed Navajo and Mexican ancestry. Johnny was their eighth and last child. His mother was nearing the end of her childbearing years when she conceived. It was a difficult birth. Years later, Johnny's older sister Luisa told him the story.

After two days of labor and no baby, Luisa recounts that their mother knew she needed help. So she and teenaged Luisa walked two miles to the midwife's home in the desert outside of Sheep Springs.

The midwife immediately went to work. She was a no-nonsense woman. She had Luisa scrub the table with lye soap and helped Johnny's mother onto it. The rest went quickly. She gave the patient a piece of wood to bite down on against the pain. Then she cut her abdomen open with a knife and pulled the baby out. Just like that.

She smacked his little blue-red bottom and he let out a cry. It was a good, healthy cry. The midwife gave the baby to Luisa to clean, and sewed the mother back up. Refugio remained at the midwife's home for three weeks until she could walk again. Then she walked home with her daughter and new son. She healed fine, but Johnny remembers that she wore a large, wide, leather belt for the rest of her days to hold her stomach in place after the kitchen-table cesarean section.

Little Johnny's first memories are of his fiercely proud mother. Her Spanish last name was Perez. She had been orphaned at birth at *Bosque Redondo*. A Navajo couple who had lost their own newborn took her in. Less than two years later, they were forced to give her up to the Spanish missionaries at a Southwest mission. This was during the starving time that followed the return of the Navajo to their homelands. It took decades to build up ravaged sheep and cattle herds, to replant orchards, and to make farmlands productive again—all of which had been devastated by Kit Carson's scorched-earth warfare.

Johnny's orphaned mother survived these difficult years only because her adoptive parents turned her over to people who always had food—the priests at a Spanish-speaking Catholic mission. The padres there did not ask for her Navajo name when they accepted her. They assigned the small girl a new name: *Refugio*. It meant "Refugee."

The *padres* did not seem to note the irony of the name. Over the centuries, their Jesus and their ways of bringing his message of hope to the people had transformed millions of Native Americans into refugees in their own land from the Atlantic coast to the Pacific. No one was spared, not even little girls. All were made homeless so that white immigrants could have the land and the homes that they wanted.

Refugio learned two things from her years at the mission: to love Jesus and to hate the Navajo in herself. She did both for the rest of her life. It was not a good time to be Indian. It was not a good place to be Indian. Catholic priests and mainstream Americans were on a mission to civilize the Indians in the late nineteenth and early twentieth centuries. They did it in the name of God and Jesus and Manifest Destiny. In the process, they created many orphans like Rufugio Perez. Their ways made sure that it was more than the initial shock of being orphaned that Johnny's mother had to face. Self-hatred made her an orphan and a refugee for life.

Refugio Perez carried a heavy burden from her first breath on Earth to her last. The famous American hero Christopher Houston "Kit" Carson had led the U.S. troops who rounded up her parents and her Navajo people in the mid-1860s. If the rounding up process did not kill them, the subsequent internment in the *Bosque Redondo* concentration camp did. In this years-long undertaking, white America extinguished Refugio Perez's family tree. Everyone who would have loved and nurtured her from birth to the end of her life was killed. By the narrowest of margins, she survived.

It does little good to blame Carson and his men. They only followed their orders. They were ordered to wage "total war" on the Navajo. And they did.

First they killed every person who was not willing or not able to be marched to the concentration camp hundreds of miles away. At the same time, the soldiers burned every field of Navajo corn, every crop of wheat and every vegetable garden that they came upon. They slaughtered the horses, cows, sheep, goats, and chickens. Not even friendly herding dogs were spared. The soldiers knocked down and burned homes, outbuildings, and corrals. Nothing was left standing. Most devastating to the Navajo people, the white soldiers chopped down 10,000 of their beloved peach trees, trees that it would take generations to re-grow.[3]

To this day, when Johnny Pail Face speaks of his mother, his voice turns quiet and fills with reverence. Of her happy days, he will talk on and on. It is difficult, even painful, for him to recall her earliest days. Of these times, he will only speak a few sentences or hesitatingly for a couple of minutes. Then his mind leaps off in a different direction with a ribald joke or a sudden and more cheerful change of topic.

I turned to historical records to fill Old Johnny's gaps. I found more of the truth of what happened to Refugio Perez and her Navajo family from one book in particular. It is by Raymond Friday Locke. Even the Navajo recommend this "white man's book." Later in life, Locke sat on Navajo planning councils and worked side by side to help them continue their rise from the ashes of the past.

Locke does something that few mainstream writers have had the courage to do. He puts women, children and old people back into a story of an American war. Presenting events from the darkest hour of the Navajo campaign in 1863, he writes:

By the middle of December most of the weak and the aged had died. There is hardly a Navajo family that cannot remember tales of an aged grandfather, a pregnant mother, or a lame child that had to be left behind when a camp had to be deserted. The patrols were not interested in taking captives; it was too much trouble to transport them back to the forts. Any Navajos they saw were shot on sight. Mothers were sometimes forced to suffocate their hungry, crying babies to keep the family from being discovered and butchered by an army patrol....[4]

In the larger scheme of things, it is worth pointing out that mainstream Americans did not do to the Indians anything that they were not willing to do to themselves. As General William Tecumseh Sherman did to white citizens in the Civil-War-torn South during his great "March to the Sea," Kit Carson had done the previous year in the American West. Knowing such things brings an element of fairness to the American story. While the U.S. has often been a place of tremendous violence from the arrival of European Whites upon this soil, that violence has not been reserved to a few. Anyone who goes against the American majority takes great risks.

It brought little solace to Indians to learn that this total, wanton destruction was the way Whites treated even each other. Such human beings terrified the Navajo then. They continue to do so to this day. In the end, the metal swords, guns, and cannon of the white man were the weapons that they feared the least. It was the white willingness to kill that most frightened Native Peoples.

Scholars have recently accepted that what white newcomers did to the Natives of America was genocide. The debate today centers upon the kind and degree of genocide it constitutes. Perhaps the most distinguishing feature is that it was an all-encompassing genocide. It did not only target a specific people. Whites systematically destroyed every living and non-living thing that was a part of the world around the people that they wanted to eliminate from the planet.

In short, the Native American Genocide did not target only Native Americans. It targeted beaver, bald eagles, wolves, bears, buffalo, rattlesnakes, trumpeter swans, virgin forests, mineral-rich streams, salmon runs, and coal veins running through mountains. Anything in the natural world of America that could bring money to Whites—or that took money away from Whites—was destroyed. Indians were only one part of this centuries-long rampage. And they were not even the hardest hit. The American bison fared worse.

The bison, or buffalo, was in the unfortunate position of existing in both categories that spurred Whites to destroy the world. On the one hand, this magnificent beast at the heart of life itself for many of the first American communities was an obstacle to White "progress"; on the other hand, quick money could be made from killing it. Buffalo hides sold as fast as eager hunters could cut them off of the millions of carcasses that were left to rot across the plains in 19th century America. Plus, eliminating these magnificent creatures allowed Whites to set up the kind of fenced-in farming communities upon which their version of civilization at the time was based.

This leads to one of the most sobering statistics in American history. In 1492, experts estimate that there were 60 million buffalo roaming from one end of the U.S. to the other. In 1890, there were 30 buffalo still living in America. They were in Yellowstone Park, where federal law made it illegal to kill them. No other full-fledged genocide on record contains such broad destruction that so completely devastated even the fauna and the flora surrounding a targeted people.[5]

This is the white man's "weapon" that broke the Native spirit, tribe by tribe and people by people. Indigenous peoples in any place and at any time rarely killed women and children in their intertribal battles. They never systematically killed the horses, cattle, or sheep of their enemies. They did not destroy enemy crops or cut down peach trees. In the Native American philosophies that have survived, it is not possible for an individual or a group to do such acts and to remain "human."

The newcomers to America continue to see things through a very different "crystal" than these original inhabitants. To this day, mainstream America's greatest heroes include men who participated directly and most effectively in the genocide that made possible, even necessary, the re-peopling of the Americas after 1492 by land-hungry Europeans. For men like Andrew Jackson and William Henry Harrison, killing large numbers of Native men, women, and children paved the path to the U.S. presidency.

In the case of the Navajo, Kit Carson cemented his place in mainstream history by killing everyone and everything in the Navajo world until he brought the survivors in horror to their knees. In the spring of 1864, Carson had his troops herd the survivors into camps on their homelands around Fort Defiance, New Mexico.

Then the U.S. Government chose to carry out a new experiment with the Navajo. Leaders in Washington determined that they would have better success in "civilizing" the Indians if they took them away from their native lands to teach them white ways. In their homeland, they could disappear into the mountains whenever they chose not to go along with U.S. government policies.

With "removal" orders from Washington, Carson and his soldiers gathered approximately 9,000 Navajo at various points in 1864 and force-marched them as far as 450 miles from their homes to one of the most arid, salty, and barren locations in the American West. Some of the troop leaders who were in a hurry to carry out orders systematically shot stragglers along the way. Those most likely to receive a final bullet were the very old and the very young who could not keep up with the soldiers.

At *Bosque Redondo*, the Indians were informed that, with white help, they would build a model community of industry and prosperity. It was a grand experiment in scope and design. And it took new language to describe what was underway. According to the 1863 congressional policy that launched it, the U.S. Government aimed to bring about the "concentration and maintenance of all captive Indians" from the area that was then New Mexico Territory.[6]

In four short years, the U.S. experiment on the Navajo killed off 20 percent of the Navajo Nation. And more were dying daily. They died from starvation, disease, overwork at the hands of their military handlers, bad water, bad food, and attacks by Indians from other tribes who regularly raided their "model community" because the other tribes were likewise starving from the devastating changes in their homelands brought by Whites.[7]

For Refugio Perez and her youngest son, Johnny, such historical events are not simply interesting, if deplorable, trends in American history. They provide the deeper threads of personal and family stories that intertwine over time with strikingly ironic results. Johnny's maternal grandparents were among the thousands who died in the concentration camp at *Bosque Redondo*. Their lives were sacrificed to the great cause of American Manifest Destiny. Two generations later, their grandson Johnny found himself fighting bloody battles in Europe at the sides of American comrades who were willing to die to shut down another people's concentration camps. These Americans fought as intensely in Europe to halt Germany's grand version of Manifest Destiny as their grandfathers had fought back home to build a grand vision of Manifest Destiny. We now know that there is another parallel. At the heart of each vision was a genocide.

Thus it is that Johnny Pail Face and other Native Americans who served their country in World War II find themselves in a most unique position in history. They experienced genocide twice. The first time, they were the victims. The second time, the victors. To this day, Johnny is not sure of which brush with genocide left him the most broken.

It can take a long time to sort out human events of such scale and intensity. However, there is one thing Johnny is sure of from his earliest memories: It was a heavy burden to be "Indian" in America. When he was a small boy, his mother regularly took him to the church where she prayed to Jesus for forgiveness of her sins and for better lives for her eight children. She said her prayers while kneeling at the foot of a cross, her small son at her side. There was no floor, just the bare earth.

Johnny did not pray. Johnny did not like Jesus. By age four, he already understood that his Mother's Jesus did not like it when he spoke Navajo, that her Jesus wanted him to stop being an Indian.

And the small boy already had a response to his mother's Jesus. Young Johnny spent his time gathering handfuls of dirt and quietly throwing them on the cross while his mother's eyes were closed in prayer. "I loved it when some of the other ladies in the pews would see me and get into a tizzy," he says now. "It felt good to fight back even then. God, I was already mad at age four."

Rufugio Perez Sarmiento rarely spoke Navajo to her children, although she had to speak it to everyone in Sheep Springs the minute she left the family hogan. In her own home, she held determinedly to the Spanish that she had learned from her years at the mission, just as she held to Jesus. And yet she had no love for mission life or the "civilized" white people she had met there. Even a brief look at the history of any of the hundreds of Catholic missions among Indians in the Americas serves to illustrate why.

Take, for example, the Franciscan mission at Santa Barbara, California, which anthropologist Jack Weatherford describes as "one of the most lenient and enlightened of all the missions".[8] Following standard Church procedure, once Indians were baptized, they surrendered themselves completely to the good of the mission. This "good" did not apply to the lives of the Indians themselves.

The philosophy of the *padres* was that the best way to civilize the Indians was to make them work. However, the new converts weren't paid for their labor, except with enough food, shelter, and clothing to make more work possible. Their reward was intended to derive from the satisfaction of constructing and maintaining the beautiful mission buildings, fields, orchards, and gardens of their new masters, as well as doing all of the cooking, cleaning, clothes washing, and every other daily task imaginable. This approach served to make life more serene and enjoyable for the priests in the new religion. Life was less serene for the converts.

Some might argue that the work of the *padres* was no less demanding than that of their charges. The priests not only had to work endlessly and to employ constant punishment to keep the Natives at work, but they also felt spiritually compelled to vigilantly safeguard the moral behavior of their charges. For this they evolved a rigid code of rules that governed every aspect of the convert's life, right down to what to do each hour of the day, when to eat, what to wear, when to pray, and, of course, when to copulate.

The solution for regulating sexual behavior at the Santa Barbara Mission was simple. The Chumash Indian men and women who joined the mission were locked up in different quarters each night to avoid the temptation to sin. This kept Indian men from impregnating the women. However, it did not stop, nor even slow, the Spanish soldiers from doing so.

The priests did not hold the same degree of power over their fellow white men that they held over the Natives. Indeed, the Pope himself would have been challenged to keep the lonely soldiers from such a bevy of helpless females. The women were particularly vulnerable prey, according to the account of two early priests who turned whistle-blowers. Their eyewitness reports tell us that the priests kept the Native women so malnourished that they readily prostituted themselves for scraps of food that the soldiers brought as payment for sex.[9]

It was this kind of mission heritage that Refugio Perez joined when remnants of her Navajo people gave her to the *padres* to save her likewise from starving. In another historical irony, at the very time that she found herself entering a mission in New Mexican territory in the 1870s to be civilized by the priests, the Santa Barbara Mission was ending a century of "civilizing" the Chumash. The Fathers had no choice but to halt their work. All of the Chumash had died.

Historical demographics show that at no time in that century of the Church's efforts to "save" the Indians did Native births at any of the California missions equal the number of deaths. The missionaries had constantly to capture and convert new populations because the people they brought in died at alarming rates from white diseases exacerbated by overwork and malnutrition.

Weatherford sums up with understatement his study of the impact upon an entire people of their confinement at the Santa Barbara Mission over a one-hundred year period, writing that the Chumash both "failed to thrive or even to reproduce."[10] Instead, they expired in large numbers in the world that the *padres* made for them and were buried in mass graves. The situation was so dire that the large graves were subsequently dug up and emptied of bones when full so that new generations of dead could replace the old.

The result of this approach to civilizing Native peoples ends with one mind-numbing statistic. In 1870, there were 4,645 Indians meticulously registered by the priests as being resident at the Santa Barbara Mission. However, none of them was alive. They all "resided" either in the cemetery or the ossuary.[11]

On a more positive note, not every Indian who entered a mission died there. Some managed to escape. Those who got away took with them valuable skills for survival in America. Weatherford describes these skills:

> *Those who survived did so by surrendering their native language to Spanish, giving up their religion for Catholicism, and casting off nearly every vestige of Indian culture to become Hispanicized even to the point of disclaiming Indian descent in favor of Spanish.*[12]

And so it was for Refugio Perez at her New Mexico mission. As soon as she was old enough to run, she ran. As a young teen, she fled back to her own people, some of whom had settled at Sheep Springs when they returned from *Bosque Redondo*. But she came back to them doubly orphaned. Her parents had died under the harsh conditions of the prison camp, and her Navajo culture had died at the Catholic mission. She looked Indian, but wasn't. She felt Spanish and Christian, but wasn't. Like her son after her, Refugio Perez was caught in the middle.

Refugio soon met and married Juan Sarmiento in Sheep Springs. She was fourteen; he was in his thirties. Her parents were both Navajo. Juan's mother was a Navajo slave girl. She had been captured by an Indian raiding party in the mid-1800s and sold to a Mexican rancher who lived in New Mexico's Rio Grande Valley. Her owner's name was Sarmiento. Juan was the fruit of this Wild West union between Spanish-speaking rancher and Navajo kitchen slave.

Slavery was an age-old phenomenon among people on this continent as elsewhere, one born in the social upheaval of war and conflict that left vulnerable survivors who needed care and safekeeping. Native conquerors systematically absorbed these individuals over time as full-fledged members of their tribes and their own families as a much-needed way to expand blood lines.

When Whites arrived on the continent, they brought darker twists and turns to the institution of slavery. The Spaniards simply subjugated all Native peoples who survived their coming, creating a vast pool of slaves to help them plunder the wealth of the lands that they declared their own. There was little subtlety or hypocrisy in their approach. They had recently evicted the heathen Moors from Spain and were in the middle of bloody inquisitions to purify the faith of their own people back home.

After the torture and slaughter of the Spanish Inquisition, the Spaniards were not faint-hearted about slaughtering new populations of heathens in the New World. They undertook the business with great enthusiasm and religious zeal. One of the most shocking books ever written in the Americas was penned by the Catholic priest Bartolome de las Casas in the 1540s. The vivid descriptions of creative and endless mass murder led to what de las Casas himself estimated to be the slaughter of twelve to fifteen million Native people in the Caribbean Islands alone in the first 40 years after Spanish Christians "discovered" them.[13] The Catholic Church is not alone in wanting this book to go away. To this day, it remains one of the most earth-shaking books on American history that very few Americans dare to open.

History shows us that, at first, the British colonists were more reticent than the Spaniards about the killing business. Their reformation and new Protestant faith was about getting back in touch with the Bible. Any new resident in America who prided her- or himself on reading the actual teachings of Jesus quickly arrived at an uncomfortable dilemma. It was difficult not to come away from the reading with a sense that the Christian Lord and Savior was generally against killing people—either individually or in large numbers—and this regardless of their skin color or ethnic heritage.

However, taking slaves was another matter. This was a common practice in Biblical times. English-speaking colonists quickly found that trying to keep Native American slaves as laborers in their own lands was neither practical nor profitable. The Indians simply melted away into the vast American forest at the first opportunity and left the white man's work undone.

A better solution was soon found. The colonists began shipping Indian slaves off to sugar plantations in Barbados and other Caribbean Islands where they could not escape into familiar territory. So it was that at the same time that much of America was being built on the backs of vast numbers of incoming black slaves, the places where they would labor were being cleared of less manageable workers by shipping red slaves the other way.

After every major and minor war from the devastation of the Powhatan Confederacy in Virginia, the massacre of the Pequot in Connecticut, and victory in King Phillip's War in the 1600s, through the clearing of the Carolina back country in the 1700s, to the California slave markets of the 1800s, the pattern was the same. Large numbers of defeated Native Americans were auctioned off to eager buyers at home or in the Caribbean to bring additional profits on top of the unimaginable wealth that Whites were acquiring by taking an entire continent for themselves one tribal homeland at a time.

By the time that white America was "civilizing" Johnny Pail Face's grandparents in the 1860s, Native slavery had long been a mainstream American institution. Indeed, under California law, any adult White could "indenture" an Indian for 16 years simply by paying a two-dollar fee to territorial authorities. Permission from the indentured person was not needed. Upwards of 10,000 Indians were legally enslaved before this law was brought to an end in the late 1860s.[14]

An ugly twist in the Indian slave trade in the Southwest was its evolution from a source of labor to a thriving sex trade. As one historian recounts of events in California, "Professional slave hunters raided Indian villages with impunity, seizing women and children for sale to miners and to brothels in the gold rush towns. In the mid-1850s, a pubescent girl sold for about $300 and smaller children for as little as $50".[15]

Unfortunately for the Indians, Abraham Lincoln's Emancipation Proclamation of 1863 did not stop the legal practice of enslavement anywhere but in the Confederate States. Indeed, the City of Los Angeles ran an official Indian slave market every Monday morning until 1869, six years after African Americans had been freed in the American South. Federal relief in this area finally came to the Navajo from a joint resolution of the U.S. Congress in the summer of

1868, which made it illegal to continue to enslave Navajo people.[16] The Navajo were specifically on the minds of men in Washington that summer as the tribe had just been released in June from what had become the *Bosque Redondo* death camp.

But cultural habits, ugly or beautiful, die hard. When Johnny spoke of his boyhood family to me on tape, he described his second-oldest sister Manuela as the one "who was taken." In the early years of the twentieth century, the sex trade was still very much alive in the American Southwest. Just before Johnny's birth, a group of men from another tribe came through on horses and stole Manuela for sale south of the border. It remained a common enough practice that the white authorities did not bother to investigate. She was Indian. That's what happened to Indian girls, especially pretty ones. "And Manuela was a pretty girl, a real eye-catcher," Johnny remembers.

Twenty years later Johnny's family learned the fate of their stolen daughter. In the mid-1930s, a traveler hand delivered a message from Manuela. She wrote to tell them that she was alive. She had been sold to a man in Chihuahua, Mexico. She had given birth to her first baby at age 13. In twenty years, she had birthed fifteen more. Twelve of them were still living. She was leading a life little better than that of her grandmother who had been sold to a Mexican rancher named Sarmiento two generations before. She was in her mid-thirties when she wrote. It had already been a hard and a long life.

And so it was that when young Johnny Pail Face came into the world at Sheep Springs, New Mexico, in the early twentieth century, he inherited some of the most shattered pieces of the American past. His maternal grandparents had both died in an American concentration camp. His orphaned mother had been raised by Catholic priests who were on a mission from their God to erase her Navajo culture from their spiritual universe. His paternal grandparents were a Navajo house slave and her Mexican master who never educated Johnny's father and left him to fend for himself as soon as he was able. His older sister was stolen and sold to a man to be his life-long possession.

From his earliest days, young Johnny looked at the world through these broken bits of culture and tradition, each forming a lens of a different color. Navajo, Spanish, Native Spirituality, Catholicism, freedom, slavery, hope, despair, pride, shame—these perspectives and possibilities swirled around and through this boy born in the high desert of America.

No matter how hard mainstream historians work to whitewash the American past for restless students who are required to memorize only as much of it as necessary to pass high school graduation exams, it will also be a story of extremes for those who dig a sentence or two beneath the surface. Stories with great ugliness and beauty will leap out at these graduates later in life when they ask naïve questions of a stranger of color on a bus or in the next seat on a flight across the country. American history will continue to surprise such Americans when people of different races and ethnicities respond with answers that have been judiciously left out of history books generation after generation.

Perhaps one day the mainstream will find the courage to look at its own past through the eyes of people like Johnny Pail Face. Perhaps then the extremes of what is spoken of openly and of what is kept hidden might begin to come together in America to form a deeper understanding of who we are. Perhaps it is only when mainstream peoples begin to understand what they have done that they will begin to stop doing it, at home and abroad. Then will we all be able to take moral sustenance from the most earthshaking, tragic, and beautiful stories that lie hidden right here under our feet. When that happens, our children's eyes will no longer glaze over in American History classes from one end of America to the other.

But that is a distant story and perhaps one that only a few Americans will choose to explore. There is another story close at hand that beckons to be told now. It is the story of what a man named Johnny Pail Face has done with what he was given from his first days on Earth in a place called Sheep Springs, New Mexico.

For those who have ears to hear, may they hear the goodness of his story. For those who have eyes to see, may they see its beauty. For those who have hearts to feel, may they feel its wonder. And for all who seek understanding, perhaps they will become wiser for listening to what an old man has to say.

CHAPTER 3

Learning to Hate

*And the Whites didn't even know it. They couldn't even see
what they were doing to my mother, to her children, to me.
It just seemed like the natural way of things to them. I'll tell you one
thing, it didn't seem like the natural way of things to me.*

JOHNNY WAS A LIVELY LAD FROM THE START. As soon as he could
walk, he ran. As soon as he could talk, he never stopped. He was alternately inquisitive, troublesome, in the way, out of the way, and on
his way. From first awareness, he was ever testing the limits around
him, ever pushing and pulling at the borders of his world. When
he speaks of earliest memories, it is to his mother that his words
turn. And to big sister Luisa, who was his "second mother." Of his
mother, he recalls, "She was kind and protective. She had compassion. Mostly, she protected me from getting into trouble."

Trouble often came from his father. When he ran out of patience
with his spirited youngest child, old Juan would chase little Johnny
down and tie his ankles together with a piece of rope. Then he would
drag the squirming captive to a nearby tree where he would hang
him upside down. "Stay there until you can behave!" he would growl,
as he stalked back to complete whatever daily task had been interrupted.

His mother came to Johnny's rescue at times like these. She
would free him from his upside down perch with a quiet admonition
to "Stay away from Dad until he cools down." And Johnny would do
so, as best he could.

Johnny never saw his mother angry, at least not at her children. She was a gentle giant at over six feet and weighing 280 pounds. He saw her cry, but he never saw her lash out in fury. Tears were a more likely response. And it was her children who could bring them to her eyes. Johnny remembers one day when she was ironing a pair of slacks for his older brother Pete. Pete was going out somewhere and he wanted to look sharp. His mother was ironing the slacks the old way, with a heavy iron that had been sitting on the stove to heat. The ironing board was homemade and worn. Refugio ended up with two creases in one of the pant legs. When Pete wadded the pants up and threw them into the corner in anger, his mother burst into tears.

There were many sides to Refugio Perez. She ruled her home, but not with an iron fist. She did it with heart. She also made good use of a sense of humor. Johnny remembers a game she would play with his father. Old Juan weighed in at perhaps 140 pounds. He was five feet, three inches tall. Refugio towered over him and weighed twice as much. When he would come into her kitchen and bark an order for coffee or breakfast or something to eat, she would put on an air of mock panic. Holding her skirt gingerly with feigned timidity, she would tiptoe around the kitchen in a rush, from cupboard to stove to table, assuring her husband that everything would be just as he wanted. When she delivered into his hands the requested food or drink, it would be accompanied with a flowery statement such as, "There you are, my wonderful husband. Your obedient and dutiful wife lives only to satisfy your every request." The whole time, her eyes would be dancing with merriment, as would those of her husband.

When Refugio did not wish to play, however, she knew how to make that clear as well. Johnny remembers once when Old Juan came home with several buddies in the middle of the night, hungry and impatient.

"We want food!" he barked at his sleeping wife.

From his bedroll on the other side of the one-room hogan, little Johnny had some idea of how this midnight exchange was about to turn out.

Without rising from her bed, Refugio told her husband that he had until the count of ten to get himself and his friends out of her house. After that, she would bodily throw them out. She assured her husband that he would be the first one she would throw. The men quietly left.

There were other things about which Refugio Perez Sarmiento had no sense of humor. Being an Indian was one of these. She hated the government's Indian allotment system that assigned each member of a Navajo family a number, and stamped it on a round medallion that often would be hung about the neck. Upon presentation of these medallions at the local trading post, Native families received food allotments for their basic necessities of life. Refugio regularly watched at the trading post as Navajo mothers and fathers stood with heads bowed in shame and inked their thumbs to place a print on a blue form, proving that they were still alive to be fed by the U.S. Government. She watched as children followed their parents with their smaller prints on similar forms. She watched, but she refused to do the same.

"My mother was very proud," Johnny remembers. "My mother was the one that said, 'Don't ever accept anything for nothing. You must always work for whatever you get. Always." Her sons took her teachings to heart. They worked hard throughout their lives. Johnny made his career with the U.S. military, serving overseas in three wars. Older brother Raul later retired from a long career as a crane operator in the steel industry for the Kaiser Company. Pete worked a lifetime in the coal mines of the American Southwest. Leo was an auto mechanic. Refugio's four daughters, Concepcion, Manuela, Luisa, and Luz, all married and labored hard to raise families. For sons and daughters alike, their mother's shame at watching Indians take handouts at white trading posts was one of the first and deepest lessons of life.

It was a lesson that hit close to home for a Navajo family that had been broken from its cultural moorings on both sides of the family tree. Perhaps it was as much fear as pride that drove Johnny's mother to turn away from this fragmented heritage. Pride and fear would better account for the hatred that Refugio felt toward the Indianness that was both within and around her. But only fear would explain why she turned regularly with shame to the Jesus that had been given to her by the fathers at the mission.

More than anything, little Johnny remembers Refugio's shame. Ninety years later, he still thinks of a life of shame when he remembers what being an Indian in America did to his mother. When asked about his earliest memories, it is the painful trips to the trading post that come back to him. He recalls, "We were so discriminated against, so persecuted, so much treated like animals that nobody wanted even to look at us. This is why my mother wanted to be Spanish. This is why my mother wanted to be something else. This is why my mother was Christian." He adds, however, "My father didn't give a rat's ass. He couldn't read. He couldn't write. He couldn't give a damn." But it is his mother's shame that her youngest son has carried most intensely from then to now.

Refugio was the only one in her own family of ten who obtained any formal schooling. She was literate, although this, too, was problematic in America. She could read and write, but in Spanish, not English. Still, her situation was significantly above that of her husband. It took Juan a full two minutes to make his "X" on paper for a formal transaction. There was no local school for her children. When the family later moved to the large town of Gallup, Johnny discovered that Indians were not allowed to attend white schools. "There were no written rules against it," he muses now. "But some rules don't have to be written. It was not safe for an Indian boy to try to walk into a white classroom."

The only education available to the red children of Sheep Springs or at Gallup was at a reservation boarding school. In those days, it was several days' journey to the school. Children who were taken there were only allowed to return home once or twice a year and for short stays. Once white school officials got them away from home, they wanted to keep them away. The unapologetic goal at Indian boarding schools was to eradicate the Native cultures of their young charges and to replace them with what was deemed "civilization."

When school children went home, even for short stays, they slipped back into Indian ways. They spoke languages other than English. They participated in heathen rituals. They danced uncivilized dances. They returned to nature and to their traditional ways of living in harmony with the natural world. At the height of the industrial revolution sweeping America, such people were considered enemies of all that was "American." They had to be changed.

At the start of the 20th century, white teachers and school administrators were the front-line troops in a new version of the ongoing war that Euro-Americans had declared upon the Native world. Mainstream America was determined to wipe Native cultures off of the planet. *E pluribus unum* was a more attractive national motto for the "one" that benefited than it was for the "many" that were eliminated.

The story of Native American boarding schools in this ongoing war is another noteworthy topic that has been surprisingly omitted from American history textbooks. I write the word "surprisingly" because of its scope. It involved hundreds of thousands of Indian children over the nine decades that it lasted. It is one more of those pieces of the past that shock mainstream citizens to the core when they stumble across it.

In young Johnny's day, tens of thousands of Indian children as young as ages four and five were being taken away from their parents each year to be "civilized" by well-intentioned white people. Beginning in the late 1870s, an Indian educational system that grew into hundreds of national and regional schools was established by the U.S. Department of War with the help of various churches and other well-meaning organizations. At the heart of this system were boarding schools that isolated Indian children from their Native cultures so that white culture could do its work on them.

From the beginning of the Indian boarding school experiment, one thing is clear. A school set up by a Department of War is a different kind of learning institution than anything mainstream Americans are likely to impose upon their own children. At these schools, Indian children were treated as conquered peoples. They were punished, often brutally, for speaking their native tongues. The same happened if they were caught practicing Native rituals, dancing traditional dances, or engaging in pagan spirituality. They were given Christian names. The boys had their hair cut short. Girls and boys were dressed primly and properly in mainstream clothing donated by benevolent white people from around the nation. It was all part of a national mission to get red-skinned people to look, act, speak, think, and live like white people.[1]

Extinguishing other people's cultures was a first order of business for the young nation in those days. As with outright violence, changing peoples' cultures contained an element of fairness. Newly arriving immigrants of every color and creed experienced a similar "Americanization" process. They were quickly and forcefully integrated into American ways through intense social pressure at work, at school, at church, by the courts, and through every other social institution that touched their lives. But all of these forces combined were not enough to compel most Native Peoples to adopt white ways. So, greater force was brought to bear upon America's first cultures to get them to come around. This greater force can best be described by two words: "cultural genocide."

It must be emphasized that cultural genocide in the late 19th and early twentieth centuries was an improvement in the mainstream approach to the "Indian Problem." As indicated earlier, before the 1870s, the national motto for dealing with the indigenous peoples of the continent had been: "The only good Indian is a dead Indian." After the 1870s, this gave way to the more nuanced "Kill the Indian, save the man." In short, "cultural genocide" replaced outright genocide as the American policy for dealing with the Native peoples toward the end of the 19th century.

There is general consensus among historians and demographers that as many as ten million Indians lived in the continental U.S. in 1492.[2] There were just 230,000 left to be counted on the U.S. census of 1900. The well-intentioned founders of the boarding schools took up a mission to save this small remnant that had survived the coming of "civilization." These are the reformers who championed the new slogan that aimed to "save the man." But it was the youngest of the "red men" that the boarding school proponents set out to save. Their goal was to kill only the cultures of Native children. Their best efforts taught us this above all: If you kill the culture in a child, it can be very difficult to keep the rest of the child alive.

But do not presume that the children went down easily. Surprisingly, it was the smallest charges at the Indian boarding schools who often resisted in the most determined and unexpected ways.

Take, for example, the kindergarten jailbreak at the Fort Mojave School in Bullhead, Arizona, in the 1920s. Large numbers of students had been deserting the school in the night and staff members were spending great amounts of time, energy, and resources catching them and bringing them back to school.

Most persistent in their escape attempts were a number of determined kindergarteners. Their size made them particularly adapted to the business. They could slip out of any unboarded window or opening, however small. Once on the loose they were harder to catch than rabbits and they could hide right in a rabbit hole or behind the smallest of bushes. Only the dogs could find and flush out the kindergarteners once they took to the woods.

Out of exasperation, the headmaster finally locked up the worst of his smallest offenders in the school jail, assuming that nothing could wear down the spirit of a lively kindergartener more quickly than strict confinement. The headmaster and staff made only one mistake. They did not lock up all of the kindergarteners.

A couple of mornings later, as the adults sat down to breakfast, the building shook with several large crashes that came from the jail. By the time that they made their way to the scene, it was too late. All that they found was a log that the rest of the kindergarten class had rigged with ropes and had used as a battering ram to crash through the heavy door.

The administrators could not believe their eyes. As one of them later wrote in a memoir of her year at the school, "At the sturdy jail, there lay the sturdy door, broken from its hinges. There lay the log, a big one, and the many pieces of rope. We were amazed!"[3]

The entire kindergarten class had gone on the lam into the river bottoms adjacent to the school. That day the little people won. It was like a story line taken from *Tom Sawyer* or *Huckleberry Finn*. If we were to scatter such stories here and there through U.S. History textbooks, mainstream children to this day might read them without being threatened with the current equivalent of time in the school jail.

In reality, not many stories of day-to-day life at Indian boarding schools turned out as well as things did that day for the kindergarteners at the Fort Mojave School. No one was more keenly aware of this than Johnny's mother Refugio. She had boarded for nearly a decade at a white man's mission and had attended the mission school. She knew intimately the day-to-day use of force, violence, and brutality that was required to "civilize" the children into white culture. She had no doubts about how her irrepressible youngest son might fare in such an environment. Even his own relatively patient father occasionally resorted to a rope and a tree to deal with his un-bounded energy. Whites at a boarding school would have brought the full force of their harsh ways upon such a lively young spirit.

To this day, it can be a profoundly moving experience to visit a Native American boarding school. Although only four remained in operation at the time of this writing, many have been turned into museums or have plaques out front that sum up the now hidden piece of American history that was lived out on the premises. Even if the buildings have been converted to new uses or have been torn down, there is always one piece of every boarding school that is sure to remain. Each boarding school, by necessity, had a school cemetery nearby. It's hard to convert a cemetery to new uses. It is a particularly sensitive challenge when it is a children's cemetery, even if the children were red.

And so we have many valuable records of the ultimate impact of Indian boarding schools upon large numbers of Native children. The records are neatly organized in rows of small graves across the landscape beside hundreds of former Indian boarding schools. Each gravesite has a marker of some sort that gives us a short record of the child who lies buried beneath it.

One of the best examples of an Indian cemetery is at the first and most influential boarding school of them all. You can still find it in Carlisle, Pennsylvania. The buildings have been converted to new uses by the military. They now make up the Army War College. Americans there devote themselves to study of how best to use war to get what the U.S. Government wants around the world in the same buildings where the U.S. "war" upon Native children was launched. It is sobering to think that new generations of Americans are learning to do to other peoples and to their children things that our textbook writers will likewise hesitate to pass on to new generations of children. And so the great circle of American history cycles forward as we repeat the dark patterns of our past without apology.

As the flagship school for the mainstream assault upon Native children, Carlisle is a good place to see the broad lines of what happened in this last and most heart wrenching Indian war. At a commencement ceremony during the School's peak of operations, the white keynote speaker, Reverend J. A. Lippincott, spelled out the school's "quintessential mission" about as clearly as one could do. He told the graduating class of 1898: "the Indian is DEAD in you. Let all that is Indian within you die!…You cannot become truly American citizens, industrious, intelligent, cultured, civilized until the INDIAN within you is DEAD!"[4]

There was a related observation that Lippincott and others were careful not to make. By 1898, there was a large number of Indians who were quite literally "dead" at the Carlisle school as well. Their graves still sit at the southern edge of the War College just off of a main thoroughfare. At the cemetery entrance is posted a neutrally-worded sign giving a short overview of what happened at the place. It does not prepare the visitor well for what lies behind it. Once you walk through the metal gate, you will quickly find yourself surrounded by what remains of one of the most tragic of American stories.

On nearly 200 identical headstones, in neat rows, you will find eloquent white/red names like "Fannie Chargingshield," "Nannie Little Robe," and "Aaron Tatosis." In some places, the gravestones carry fully traditional Native names like *Kawseh*, and *Zeneke Uh*, or anglicizations like "Young Eagle" or "Friend Bear." Others show mixes of American cultures, through descriptive names like "Abe Lincoln, son of Antelope Cheyenne" and "Dennis, son of Blue Thunder."

Finally are stones with fully Christianized names, such as "Albert Henderson." Whether Native, mixed, or mainstream, above each name you will see a Christian cross as no child was admitted to a boarding school without first accepting Christianity and adopting a Christian name. Because the children arrived from all parts of the nation at ages as young as four, we must apply a liberal interpretation to the words "adopting," and "accepting." In many cases, beneath the names are the tribal heritages of the deceased. There, too, we find a rich mixture of Native American groups from Apache to Zuni, all comingling into a universal tribe of dead children.

Another common feature on the gravestones is the month, day, and year of death. These appear just below the tribal name. There are no birth dates. Traditional Indian families did not live by Gregorian calendars with the years, months, and days neatly organized into units of time that told them what to do and when to do it. They had indigenous calendars no less detailed that used the sun, the moon, and the seasons of the earth to guide their lives. Such things, of course, were left behind at the doorstep of the white man's school.

The deepest part of the Carlisle story is to be found on a different set of headstones than the ones that first meet the eye. There are some that tell us the most by saying the very least. They are the ones that are marked with the single word "Unknown."

I found thirteen of them in my slow walk through the cemetery. I know the number because I systematically took a photo of each. At first I did not know what to make of them. I had not seen them in pictures, nor had there been mention of them in any of the literature that I'd studied prior to a first visit to Carlisle.[5] I took a picture of the first one I came to because I was concerned that friends and colleagues might think I had been out in the hot summer sun too long if I relied only on words to describe what I'd found. A dozen photos later, I had to sit down.

At that point, my dilemma became more personal because I had my twelve-year-old daughter, Hannah, along on the research trip. She was outraged, as any idealistic young person would tend to be in such a place. Indeed, I would not be able to imagine a better field trip destination for a group of bored high school students. One walk through that place would light a brighter fire to know more about their nation's deeper history than anything else I can imagine. I saw it happening to my daughter right before my eyes as we sat among the gravestones.

"Goddamit," my daughter said. "How could the people who made this place not know the names of the children they killed?" My daughter is a bright human being. She has understood from her earliest years when it is appropriate or not appropriate to swear. When she swears, I always know she is close to the heart of something.

She continued. "It's a school. They have class rosters. They keep records. How could so many children end up dead and the teachers didn't even know their names?"

As a scholar, I knew there was only one thing that could account for most or all of the thirteen unknown graves. As a father, I wasn't sure I wanted to tell my daughter what I knew. In my research, I had come across many journals and interviews where Native peoples refused to speak of what had happened to themselves or to their children at boarding schools. My own Indian friends over the years had often grown distant and quiet when the subject came up in our conversations. Certain topics are deeply taboo in many Native cultures. Things like sexual abuse, especially involving male authorities and young boys, is so unthinkable to most Indigenous peoples that they cannot be put into words. To do so would only wound the listeners and spread the horror further.

Navajo peoples like Johnny Pail Face take the taboo a step further. To speak of the devilish acts that would explain thirteen graves of unknown children would risk calling back the wandering dark side of the deceased children's spirits, or their *chi'indies*. For traditional Navajo, this carries a great risk of leading to bad fortune, hauntings, spirit possessions, insanity, or even death among the listeners.

So there I was, seated in a children's cemetery in Carlisle, Pennsylvania, faced with a serious fatherly dilemma. Beside me sat a daughter in a perfect state of moral outrage demanding answers to some very potent questions. Would my answers trouble her too much, carry her too close to the intense fires of our collective past? Would I raise evil spirits, Navajo-style or otherwise, by speaking the unspeakable? Such are moments that a father either celebrates or regrets the rest of his life. Do you speak? Do you remain silent? In the face of my uncertainty, I took a familiar tack.

"Do you want me to tell you the truth or do you want me to fog you?" I asked. My daughter has often shown herself to be surprisingly prudent when I ask that question. There have been times that she has, in fact, preferred that I gloss over a troublesome issue without painful detail.

But this time she was in no mood to be fogged. "I want to know the truth," she said.

I thought about how to say what I needed to say as we continued to examine the headstone beside us. It was the first in a row of seven stones all marked "Unknown." My brain works slowly in the best of circumstances. I needed time to ease into this not-the-best-of-circumstances.

"Look," I said finally, pointing to a small leather shield on top of the gravestone one over from where we sat. "There's a gift. Someone remembers these children."

Hannah looked.

I continued, "They've been here for a hundred years, maybe more, and yet someone put that gift here. Who do you think would do this?" Without meaning to, I had stumbled into a right way to tell the story. I had seen Indian friends do this sort of indirection. They have intriguing ways of wrapping something ugly inside something beautiful that balances it and diffuses the pain. I thought I saw my way forward.

"Think about it," I said to my Hannah. "If the school administrators did not know this child's name a century ago, it's very unlikely that anyone today knows it today."

Hannah nodded.

"And yet someone has come by and honored this child with a gift. I saw a cigarette earlier," I said. "It was dry. Someone left it since yesterday. It rained yesterday, remember?"

She looked at me and nodded again. "Look, look," she said, pointing at another gravestone in the series of seven. "There is a quarter on that one."

As our eyes traced down the line of unknown graves, we realized that all of them had a gift of some sort either on top or on the earth around the headstone. In addition to the shield, there was another stone with a small dream-catcher atop it. Others had quarters, nickels or dimes on them or a clean cigarette on the ground.

"Isn't it amazing," I whispered. "After a hundred years, *someone* still comes to honor these children. Who do you think comes?'

"Indians," Hannah replied immediately, adopting my whispered tone. "It had to be Indians. White people only leave flowers."

"Maybe the real story here isn't how these children ended up buried in unknown graves," I told her. "Maybe the real story is that there are people on this earth, so beautiful that they would continue to come for a hundred years and put gifts on the graves of children they don't even know."

We both paused a moment to consider the thought.

Then Hannah spoke again. "I still want to know what happened," she said. "How did so many children end up dead and without names?"

By the gentler tone of her voice, I knew she was ready to hear what I had to say. And so I said it.

I explained that in the early days, the War Department relied on reservation employees and sometimes even soldiers to get Native children to go to the schools that it had set up. Often housing, food, clothing, and other supplies promised by federal treaties in exchange for Indian land were not given to parents who kept their children out of schools. They could even be arrested and jailed. Rather than see their families starve or freeze in winter, the parents usually finally gave in and turned over their little ones.

The Whites had orders to take children as young as age four. They loaded them onto wagons and trains, and often sent them as far away from their homes as possible. They did not want the civilizing process to be interrupted by children going home on the weekends or by family members coming for visits.

When such things were done to children as young as kindergarten age, some of them never recovered. During the long days or sometimes weeks that they were in the wagons, the trains, or ships if they came from Alaska, they stopped talking. Even in their native tongue. Even to other children like themselves. They had no way of making sense of what was happening to them. They despaired. They stopped eating. They stopped drinking. Towards the end, they often assumed a fetal position. And then they died. Quietly. Alone.

The biggest problem then was if the identity tags around their small necks had been lost during the journey. When this happened, they arrived at school not only dead but among strangers who had no way of knowing who they were. The Whites had no choice but to bury them in unknown graves.

I told her that I could not be sure that this is what happened to all thirteen of the unknown children around us. Groups of runaways in winter sometimes died in the bitter cold. If they were not found until the spring thaw, after nature and wild animals had had their ways, there were no forensics teams nor dental and medical records with which to identify them. Between epidemics of deadly diseases that swept through crowded dormitories, to the combined effects of malnutrition, exhaustion, and debilitating homesickness, to the perils of life on the road for runaways, there were so many ways to die when the Whites declared war on Indian children. Some were ways that the Whites could not have imagined beforehand and were eager to forget after. And so they have.

Hannah accepted my explanation quietly. It satisfied her immediate need to know what had happened. But, of course, there is much more to the larger story of what happened to so many Native children in America.

As surprising as it may be to most Americans to learn that there are unknown graves of dead Indian children in Pennsylvania, there is another dimension of this story that is equally surprising. Its scope.

In the school year 1900, there were 153 government boarding schools in operation. They had a combined enrollment of 17,708 Indian children. At the peak of the boarding school experiment in 1915, enrollments reached 20,690 per year.[6] In short, during the first fifty years of government use of boarding schools, hundreds of thousands of Native children experienced the cultural devastation of the boarding school experience. Ten thousand alone went to the Carlisle School before it closed in 1918. And there were 200 schools in operation during that time. Indian boarding schools constituted a much larger experiment in social engineering than the one that concentrated 10,000 Navajo at the *Bosque Redondo* camp in the 1860s. In the end, it also gives us the biggest and most shocking children's story that the mainstream has decided, perhaps prudently, not to tell its children.

But Johnny's mother knew the story intimately. She had lived it for nine years of a broken childhood at a Spanish mission. She had learned to read and to write at the Catholic school the *padres* ran there. In those nine years, she learned enough about boarding schools to make her sure of one thing: her own children would never set foot in one.

As much as she hated the way that her offspring were treated at the trading post and in other public places, she hated worse the idea of sending them away to a white man's school. First and foremost, it was a loving mother's way of protecting her children from what she herself had suffered. But the choice extended beyond the short term of their school years. She wanted to shield them for a lifetime.

To do so, Refugio Sarmiento needed to erase their very identities as Indians. This made it even more important to keep them out of Indian boarding schools. To send her children to an Indian school would irrevocably identify them as Indians. According to Johnny, that is why she resisted above all. That is why she made them speak Spanish at home. That is why she had each baptized into the Catholic faith and required that they attend church with her whenever she could go.

Over time, she found other ways to move her family closer to the perceived safety of the white world. The U.S. Census Reports of 1910 and 1920 tell us in concise and fascinating detail how she did so. In both decades, she and husband Juan claimed Mexico as their birthplace. They claimed Spanish as their native tongue. These statements reflected the realities of American history as they had lived them. The U.S. border with Mexico remained in dispute until 1924. Although Juan and Refugio had been living in Mexico territory in their younger years, the U.S. "immigrated" to them when the border shifted.

Refugio, a full-blood Navajo who had learned Spanish, was married to a man who was at least half Mexican and who also spoke Spanish. She used this combined Spanish heritage to the family's social advantage in both 1910 and 1920. When the census taker asked about the primary language that family members spoke, she put "Spanish" for herself and Juan. She left the category blank for her children. No mention was made of the family's fluency in Navajo. She indicated, accurately, that her husband could neither read nor write, but that she could do both. And then, under "Color or Race," she had the census taker mark "W" for "White" for Juan, herself, and each of her children.

On the 1920 Census, the depth of Refugio's determination to shift to the Spanish/white world is more evident. Unlike on the previous census, the questions of birthplace and mother tongue extended from the current citizens to their mothers and fathers as well. Refugio had the census taker write "Mexico" and "Spanish" as the birthplaces and languages for both of her parents and for her husband's parents as well. However, according to the family stories passed down to Johnny and his siblings behind closed doors, three of those four parents were pureblood Navajos living in Navajo communities.

There is one more detail of the 1920 census record that is deeply revealing. In a rare and surprising move, the census taker seems to have questioned the accuracy of some of Refugio's statements. After writing down "Spanish" as the mother tongue of Refugio's children, the census worker subsequently came back and marked a large "X" through the word "Spanish" for three of the five children still at home. It was for the three oldest children that the language was marked out. There is no further explanation, so the meaning of crossing out the words cannot be certain. A reasonable interpretation is that the dutiful public servant heard the older children speaking fluent Navajo before leaving the premises and so crossed out what he or she had reason to believe was false information.

In 1924, Refugio had another significant opportunity to bring her children closer to a safe identity in America. When the U.S./Mexican border was finally established, she was able at last to obtain official U.S. birth certificates for her eight children. She registered them all in the same manner as she had done on the census records. She made them white children whose native tongue was Spanish.

Johnny was a young boy at the time and remembers these details. He remembers also that his mother and family members had very limited experience with the white man's sense of time. No one in the family had been to school since their mother had fled the mission as a girl. None of them had since lived in a white world. None of them knew what it was to live by a calendar or a clock. Johnny smiles now to remember "how bad" it was. "My mother had to ask at the trading post to find out what year it was before she could start filling out the citizenship papers. They were in English, so she had to get the white man at the trading post to help her.

Refugio's approach to the task mirrored her own no-nonsense approach to things. She started with the youngest, Johnny. She put his birth year as 1924 and then worked backwards to estimate the birth dates of her other seven children. Little Johnny's official name was given in Spanish: Juan Cecilio Sarmiento. His birth date of 1924 puts him in the unique position of being able to remember the day he was born. In 1924, he was a busy lad who was helping out daily with family chores by herding their small flock of goats in the desert around their home and helping his father load bread and pies into the ovens at the commercial bakery that he had set up to make a living for his family.

Juan Cecilio was a large and active "newborn." But no official record keepers seemed to notice. Neither did they write in their records that this dark-skinned "white" boy and his siblings all spoke fluent Navajo as well as a homegrown version of Spanish.

In retrospect, perhaps the white workers saw what they wanted to see. They saw a successful white mission to "civilize" savages and immigrants. It must have appeared at the time that the red and brown peoples of the American Southwest were turning into Whites at a good pace. Indians were disappearing. The white population was booming. All was moving forward properly in America. Unless, of course, you were an Indian boy caught in a baffling world high in the American desert.

A poem written around the time of Johnny's birth by Carlos Montezuma, a Navajo doctor living and working in Chicago, sums up the world in which Johnny came of age. It goes, in part:

> *They have taken your country,*
> *They have taken your manhood,*
> *They have imprisoned you,*
> *They have made you wards,*
> *They have stunted your faculties,*
> *You are not entitled to the rights of man.*
> *You are not an American citizen—*
> *You are an Indian,*
> *You are nothing and that is all…*[7]

It is important to note that when Refugio registered the births of her children in 1924, this did not make them citizens of the United States of America. Johnny's people remained "wards of the state" until the 1950s. This meant that they had the same rights and privileges as incarcerated criminals and committed residents of state-run insane asylums. Indians faced this sobering reality each morning when they rose from bed in a white world.

Young Johnny did not need to see a graveyard in Carlisle, Pennsylvania, or to read Indian poetry to know what was happening in his world. He read it in his mother's face. He heard it in her voice as he sat in the dirt beside her while she prayed to the cross of Jesus. He saw it in the eyes of the white people that turned on them when they went to town.

Inside of young Johnny, a response to the red-white reality of America was forming. He felt it burning from his earliest memories. Deep things were coming to the surface. It was not pretty. It did not feel good. Even as it happened, he was aware that it did not feel good. But it would not be denied.

A red-skinned boy in America was learning what it felt like to hate. From the start. From his first memories of a proud, loving mother's head bowed in shame before white men and their white God. From the way white people looked at him and his brothers and sisters when they went to the trading post. From the ways that his dark-skinned family was treated in shops and stores and on the streets in nearby towns. A young red boy was learning to do things for all the wrong reasons.

Johnny, of course, did not think explicitly about such weighty matters as a small boy. When he rolled out of his bedroll in a one-room Navajo hogan each morning, there was breakfast to be had and a busy day beckoning. His blankets consisted of old cloth sewed together to make a quilt plus a couple of sheep and goat hides to stave off the bitter cold in winter. It was not unusual for temperatures to reach 40 degrees below zero in the cold months. The mud hogan's only heat source was an open fire pit in the center with a hole in the ceiling above for the smoke to escape.

Refugio was up early making breakfast over the open fire. She used mesquite charcoal that Juan and the boys made themselves in the warmer months and stored up in an outbuilding. Breakfast for the family consisted either of cornbread or corn tortillas, supplemented with a helping of beans. In good times, fried eggs rounded out the meal.

After eating what was available, little Johnny would be off to take the family's few scraggly sheep and goats out to graze for the day. From the time that he was big enough to walk and to talk, he was contributing to the family economy through hard work. Everyone had his or her role to play. His job was to keep the goats and sheep out of the bitter-tasting chaparral bushes and to bring all of them back at the end of the day. The chaparral made the goat milk almost too bitter to drink or to make good cheese, although bitter or not the family had to depend upon it as part of their daily food supply.

Johnny remembers his early childhood fondly. As the youngest child in a large family, he was surrounded by love and by people who looked after his wellbeing. As there was no television, no radio, and no newspaper available, young Johnny had no way of knowing what day, month, or even year it was according to the white man's way of living.

He also had no way of knowing that his family was dirt poor. When he looked about him, everyone he saw in his little desert corner of the world was equally poor. It seemed to him that they were living exactly as everyone everywhere lived, except for the white trader's family at the trading post.

Furthermore, there was always a meal waiting at home. There was always a warm bed at night in a one-room hogan where everyone he loved slept around him. And the days were filled with laughter that Johnny remembers to this day.

One morning when he was about five, he went out to play in the desert not far from the hogan. He soon stumbled across a pile of cracked corn that had mysteriously appeared during the night. He was too young to ponder the origins of such bounty in a dry, unfertile land, but he knew exactly what to do with it. Chickens eat corn. It makes them fat. And Navajo families eat chicken. It makes them happy.

Johnny scampered home, grabbed a couple of buckets and returned to the moist, steaming mound of corn. He filled his buckets and made straight for the family chicken coop. He spread the mash around and the clucking chickens went to work. Johnny skipped off to play and left them to their feeding.

A short time later, Old Juan came and found Johnny. "Are you the one who fed the chickens all that corn this morning?" he asked.

Johnny nodded.

"Where did you find it?"

"Over by the road," Johnny told him. "I think someone else's chickens didn't want it anymore."

"C'mon," his father said. "I want you to see what it did to our chickens."

Johnny trailed along behind Old Juan back to the chicken coop, feeling increasingly concerned about what must be waiting there. His father was not acting pleased.

When they got to the chicken wire and looked into the coop yard, Johnny's fears were confirmed. There were a couple of hens lying on their backs with their feet in the air. They were not moving.

Old Juan pointed at the hens and said, "The stuff you fed the chickens killed those two hens."

Johnny got ready to run for it.

Just then, father and son heard the strangest rooster call that Johnny had ever heard before or has heard since. They looked toward the roosting shed. Propped against the door on one leg was their big rooster. He was trying to crow, but having little success. Johnny sums up the situation and aftermath.

What I had fed our chickens was the corn whiskey mash that some moonshiner had dumped out by the road. The stuff was too strong for the smaller of the hens and killed them, but the rooster, he got a bellyful of that fermented grain and was feeling pretty good. He was so drunk he couldn't walk. He just stood there leaning against the chicken coop and trying to crow about how good he felt.

My dad got to laughing so hard that he almost fell down. He wasn't even angry about the dead hens after that. Once he could stop laughing, we took the hens out, plucked them, and turned them over to my mother to prepare for dinner.

The whole family laughed all the way through dinner as Dad told the story, trying his best to imitate the rooster's drunken crow as he went. Pretty soon all of us boys were trying to out-do Dad's drunken rooster crow. It was one of the best chicken dinners I've ever had.

Old Juan was patient with his youngest son. Only when the boy was being completely unreasonable and unteachable would the old man chase him down with a rope and hang him upside down from a tree. Most of the time when Johnny did something wrong, his father helped him learn from the experience with a more traditional Navajo approach to parenting.

Johnny remembers another day not long after he found the corn whiskey mash that he found a box filled with a bunch of identical little metal objects. He wasted no time in figuring out what to do with them. He emptied the box into the dirt beside the hogan and began to make a little town by standing the long, thin metal objects upright and side by side. As he was making the outlines of buildings and using his fingers to smooth out the streets between them, his father came by. Old Juan stopped and watched for a while.

After a time, he said, "I don't want to bother you, but can I have one of those? Do you mind?"

Johnny gave him one.

He took it in hand, turned to face a large rock ten or fifteen yards away, and threw the object at the rock. To Johnny's great surprise, when the piece of metal hit the rock, it exploded with a boom. His father looked at him and said, "If you keep playing with those things, that is what is going to happen to you." Then Old Juan turned and walked away.

Johnny remembers scooping up his metal toys as quickly and as carefully as he could and then chasing after his father, begging him to take them.

Old Juan accepted them and said, "These are blasting caps. They are used to set off dynamite in the mines. They are dangerous and they can kill you if you drop a rock on them or put one into the fire. If I had taken them away from you, you would have been mad at me for spoiling your fun. I don't doubt that you would have found a way to get them again, only this time you would have played with them somewhere where I wouldn't see." Johnny learned in this manner to respect dangerous things that were commonplace in his world.

He also learned responsibility at an early age. By the time he was seven years old, he was allowed to take a single shot .22 rifle with him when he went out to graze the livestock. It was not for sport. The rabbits and prairie dogs that he shot were carefully cleaned and brought home for the evening meal. "Prairie dogs are very earthy tasting," Johnny remembers. "You really have to marinate them in something for two or three days before cooking them. It's the only way to keep them down."

There was great variety of cacti growing in the desert around the family hogan when they moved from Sheep Springs to live near Socorro, New Mexico. Johnny remembers the saguaro standing tall with their arms pointing toward the heavens. There were also the turnip-shaped mescal cactus, barrel cactus and flat cactus. He remembers in particular the brilliant colors of the barrel cactus blossoms that transformed the drab desert into brilliant yellow, orange, red, and lavender when they came out.

We ate the flat cactus, Johnny recalls. You have to get the new ones when they are two to three inches in length. With my father and brothers, we would hit them with sticks to break them off and then gather them together on a flat rock. We would use the rock as a cutting board as we got rid of the thorns.

After we diced them, father would wash the pieces and boil them soft. He added in leaves to keep the watery mixture from getting too thick and gooey. Then we would take a big batch of cactus home for my mother to fry up with scrambled eggs. Cactus, scrambled eggs and beans—that was a good breakfast!

The family did not eat the large, stately saguaro cactus but used it in other ways as part of daily life. Johnny remembers his father cutting down big saguaros in the fall of each year to make water storage and ice containers. Old Juan would cut them in half and then hollow out long cactus troughs. In winter, they would fill the troughs with water or snow and freeze them solid. When the ground began to thaw in the spring, his father would have them dig a pit and layer the bottom with weeds. On top of this layer would go the ice-filled cactus segments. Then they would bury them in more weeds and straw, topping it all off with a thick layer of dirt. In this manner, they kept a regular supply of ice and water that would last through the summer despite the blistering desert heat.

Although Johnny's father worked much of his life as a laborer, he had picked up a skilled trade as a young man that he returned to in his later years. He was an old-style baker. "Old-style" means that he had learned how to make his own ovens as part of the trade. In his earlier years, he had even baked at Indian boarding schools in the region.

Some of Johnny's earliest memories of his father center around the large outdoor oven he built behind their hogan in Sheep Springs. It was round and made from weeds and straw mixed with mud to form its adobe hive-shape. The oven had to be large because Juan used a car hood for his bread pan. On it he would place multiple loaves, as well as the occasional meat pie or other item to bake, using large wooden bread paddles that he had also made. His home baking helped the family survive. They always had bread to eat and regularly traded extra loaves to other families for food items and things that they needed. Occasionally, someone would show up with money and buy a few loaves, bringing in much-needed cash.

Old Juan had one other way to make money. He knew how to make cactus whiskey. Over the years, his "cactus juice" had always been a part of day-to-day life for a poor family with little means to buy alcohol at the trading post. Johnny was initiated into the practice as soon as he was old enough to be useful. When it was time to make a batch of juice, Old Juan would wake up his sons before dawn and take them into the desert. They would carry with them a bag of sugar and a sack of onions. Once they found a location with lots of healthy cacti, they would cut bowl shapes into specific plants picked out by their father. Into each bowl they would pour a cup of sugar and place a few slices of onion. That was the end of their work for the first day

They would return the following day before sunrise and ladle out the juice that had formed around the sugar and onions in each cactus bowl. This they would take home and put in a crock jar, which was placed at the back of the baking oven where it would stay warm and begin to ferment.

Within 24 hours they would have to begin cooking the fermenting juice or it would start to rot. This they did in Old Juan's still. It was a simple distilling system made out of odds and ends of things that Johnny's father was able to scavenge from around the reservation. There was a copper tub, a wooden cover, a section of hollow log, copper tubing, and a copper pan filled with sand on the top of the whole affair once it was assembled. Johnny's job was to climb up on the brick walls Old Juan built up around the still and to pour cold water into the sand so that cactus alcohol would condense onto the bottom of the copper pan. It was not elegant, but it worked.

Johnny remembers that the first juice that came out was powerful stuff, but it got weaker as the boiling process went on. Old Juan and adult family members treated the resulting cactus juice as a staple of life over the years. During the prohibition era, it was a valuable commodity in the neighborhood that increased the family cash flow.

Old Juan regularly kept a cup of this home brew near his bed in the hogan. Now and then, little Johnny would get into it. The family would subsequently find him passed out under the table or in a corner. He remembers hearing them say, "The poor little guy, he must be tired." As Johnny reflects back on the epic battles he was later to fight with alcoholism, he fears things had an early start with his father's homemade cactus juice.

But it was Old Juan's baking skill that became the mainstay of the family. His ovens gained him a good reputation for bread baking around the region. In the early 1920s came an offer he could not refuse. He was asked by a man from the town of Socorro, New Mexico, a hundred miles to the south, to come there and to set up a commercial bakery. Juan accepted. Johnny remembers the drive to their new home. There were five of eight children left at home at that point, Lucy, Pete, Leo, Raul, and Johnny. They rode the whole way in a big, black automobile with a cloth top. It was a grand adventure for reservation children who rarely saw a car let alone rode in one.

Once arrived, Juan went to work. It was not easy for the family's illiterate father to set up and to run a busy bakery. The hardest task was ordering baking supplies to keep the place running smoothly. Johnny remembers how Old Juan did it. He used a variety of small rocks, corn kernels, beans, and other items as a sort of abacus. Each time that he used up a bag of flour or a box of salt, he would place one of that ingredient's symbolic stones or corn kernels aside to remember which supplies and how much of them would be needed when the distributor came round again. As rude as his system was, Johnny recalls that it worked without fail.

Young Johnny and his brother, Raul, often helped out in the Socorro bakery. It was a good place to be for a couple of hungry young boys. When they were unloading the ovens at the end of an early morning bakery run, a pie or pastry or bread loaf would invariably slip off a bread shovel and end up on the floor. And two boys would immediately jump to salvage it in a manner that left no tasty morsel wasted.

There were many good memories for young Johnny in Socorro. But there were an equal number of bad memories, memories of how he and his mother and his brothers and sisters were treated when they left the refuge of home to venture into public places. He remembers going into grocery stores where both he and his mother would be told by a white merchant not to touch any fruits, vegetables, or other merchandise "unless you are damn sure that you are going to buy them." He noted that this directive was not given to white mothers and to white children.

He remembers the timid air with which his large, imposing mother approached the counter to pay for whatever supplies they had picked out. He saw that she never looked into the white man's eyes. Her hands trembled as she offered payment. She always hurried him out of the store as if their very presence there was an offence. Such memories stain his thoughts to this day, nine decades later.

And so it is that hatred is born in the youngest of hearts. Johnny hated the Whites because the first crystal through which he looked at life was a foreboding one. When he looked out at the world through red eyes, he saw the dark, destructive side of America. He saw how white people with their light skins, their English language, their bloody-cross religion, and their sense of superiority over all other living things were able to make his loving mother hang her head in shame. The sound of a white voice or the sight of a white person crossing the street ahead of them would silence her laughter and bring a troubled look to her eyes.

Because of Whites, she scolded her children for speaking Navajo at home and did all that she could to steer clear of Indian beliefs and rituals and seasonal festivals. Because of these light-skinned people with "white eyes," she claimed to be Spanish and followed the white man's Jesus to her dying day. White people made Refugio Perez hate herself. It was as simple as this to her youngest son. Johnny Pail Face began life by hating the people who would do this.

And the Whites didn't even know it, he says now. *They couldn't even see what they were doing to my mother, to her children, to me. It just seemed like the natural way of things to them.*

I'll tell you one thing, it didn't seem like the natural way of things to me. Not even when I was a little guy. I hated it and I knew from the start that I was going to do something about it.

It sure took me a long time, though, to find something good to do, something that worked. For a lot of years, I was just an angry fool filled with hate who was going to make the 'white eyes' pay every chance I got.

Johnny's early embrace of hatred may have continued unabated for a long time, even for a lifetime, except that his world was soon to be turned upside down. At the center of a seismic shift in his life would be a white man. A good one. The man was an undertaker. His name was R. C. Ritchey. He would soon take Johnny into his home and set him on a path toward understanding the white world. It would be a long path. Decades long.

Mr. Ritchey and his wife would not see where that path would lead their young Navajo charge. They would only see a young man who seemed determined to do everything he did for all the wrong reasons. They would not live long enough to witness how things turned out for young Johnny. They would not know how fondly he thinks of them now, or how warmly he speaks of their influence when he looks back to the people who have made a difference in his life.

Mr. and Mrs. Ritchey were white. They were good human beings. They were the kind of people of any color or creed who are able to make a positive difference in this world. But in particularly difficult cases, it can take a long time for the good to work its magic. By age eleven, when he first met the Ritchey family, Johnny Pail Face was already a particularly difficult case. It was going to take some time for the good to take hold in this mixed-blood Navajo boy. It was going to take some time to chart a pathway through the hatred.

Chi'indie

IN 1927, THE SARMIENTO FAMILY PULLED UP STAKES and left the world of their small bakery in Socorro, New Mexico. They had no choice. Old Juan had grown too sick and weak to continue his work there. They moved north to the coal mining camp of Ellison just outside of Gallup. This put them back on Navajo reservation land. The Sarmientos had family at Ellison. Older daughter Luisa's husband, Paolo, worked in the coal mine, and he promised to get the three teenaged Sarmiento boys, Leo, Pete, and Raul, work there too. Even eleven-year-old Johnny might be able to earn a little money sorting coal. So ailing Old Juan and Refugio packed up the four boys and headed north.

The first problem that the family faced upon arrival in Ellison was that Luisa's house was too small to accommodate six more people. Brother Pete went out scavenging and came back with news of a deserted hogan not far away. The family wasted no time moving there and tidied the place up. With a little work, it was made livable.

The next problem to be dealt with was Old Juan's failing health. Johnny now realizes that his father must have had a severe stroke while still in Socorro. He remembers that one morning his father rose from his bed walking with a terrible limp. The right half of his body was partially paralyzed. His face drooped on that side. He had difficulty talking. People did not go to doctors for such things in Johnny's world. They simply waited for life and death to run their inverse courses.

Once the family was settled into the hogan in Ellison, Old Juan announced that he would soon die. This brought up two religious issues, one Navajo and one Catholic. According to Navajo tradition, if a person dies inside of a dwelling, the living must knock a hole in the north wall and remove the deceased through it. This allows the person's *chi'indie*, the evil side of the spirit, to be set free on its northward journey back to rejoin the great circle of existence. Then the hogan must be burned down. If this is not done, the house will be uninhabitable because the dark energy of the *chi'indie* will curse it, along with anyone who attempts to dwell there. In a rare return to her Native heritage, Refugio became concerned that Old Juan must not die inside their hogan or they would have to go through all the trouble of destroying the place and either rebuilding it or finding a new one.

But there was another issue that lay closer to the bone for this mother of eight. Despite their decades together, she and her husband had never been officially married by a Catholic priest. Refugio became obsessed with the sin that this oversight would leave upon her soul should Old Juan die without giving her a proper marriage. Johnny remembers how his mother began to plead with his father for this last concession.

Old Juan would have none of it. He vowed to rise from his death bed and to throw the priest from his house if Refugio brought one in. As the bastard son of a Catholic rancher and his lifelong sex slave, Old Juan had not been well catechized in the Christian faith. The gulf between his father's beliefs and practices gave him a lifelong antagonism to the Catholic way of life. This made Old Juan decidedly unfriendly to the idea of a church wedding on his death bed.

Refugio worked on him for days, bringing the many persuasive skills of her gender to the task. She reasoned. She pleaded. She reminded him of all that she had done over their many years together to be a good wife. She spoke of the sacrifices that she had made as a mother of eight healthy children. All that she was asking in return was one final gift. She knew he would not wish the marriage ceremony for himself, but could he not accord it to her, she who would go on living and struggling to raise the last of his children after he was gone?

In the end, Old Juan relented. Johnny remembers the man in the black robe coming to the hogan and performing the marriage ceremony at the bedside of his father. Even as he left, the priest knew that he would be called back soon. Johnny's last memories of his father are of an invalid shooing flies away from his face as he lay quietly in his bed waiting for the end.

"But there were no flies," Johnny remembers. "It was the wrong season for flies." It was only a matter of days before the morning came that they found Old Juan cold and still in his bed. He would never again open his eyes.

In the end, Refugio had also relented to her husband. She let him die comfortably in bed inside the hogan. Such were their last gifts one to another: a marriage for the one who would go on with life, a comfortable death for the one who would not.

After her husband drew his last breath inside of that weathered hogan in Ellison, New Mexico, in 1927, Refugio moved forward to respect both of her and her husband's cultures. First, she followed Navajo tradition. She asked her sons-in-law and her four boys to open the north wall of the hogan. They took picks and shovels and did as they were instructed. They removed Old Juan's body through a breach in the wall. Then they burned the dwelling down.

Next, Refugio gave her husband a Catholic burial. She had her sons load the body onto the bed of a truck sent out from the R. C. Ritchey funeral home in Gallup. She had engaged Mr. Ritchey to give her husband a proper Christian funeral and to bury him in a cemetery in Gallup. After that, she was going to move the family to Gallup as well. It was against Navajo tradition to rebuild and inhabit a hogan that had been visited by death. And Refugio had no resources with which to build a new one. In the regional town, they would have the best chance of finding a new home. Johnny remembers the quiet in which they gathered up their few belongings and set out on foot behind the truck that bore away husband and father.

They walked the three miles to Gallup. Refugio hoped that they could find a place to live there as easily as they had done in Ellison. This would put them closer to her husband's grave while keeping her three older sons in proximity to the Ellison coal mine where they were now employed. As they walked in that small family processional, Johnny did not cry. He did not resist the passing of his father. He had not been taught to fear death or to mourn and to struggle against its presence.

This is not to say that young Johnny had some profound or mystical insight into death as an eleven-year-old boy living in the margins of the Navajo world. He did not. Rather, as he puts it now, "I had a Catholic mother and a pagan father. That gave me lots of instability. It gave me a lot of bull that I could not decipher. I was confused between Mother's Jesus and the Navajo Great Spirit. This confusion led to me just letting it go when Father died. All I thought about was what we were going to do next without him."

By the nature of things, poor people are often closer to death than rich people. Most obviously, they lack the material means to hide death. It takes money to banish it to an "old folk's home" or to the geriatric ward of a hospital. Poor people also lack large amounts of education. This makes it more difficult to hide death intellectually behind a curtain of eloquent words and high-minded abstractions. Poor people hear death coming. They smell it on arrival. People who seek to understand death would do well to ask questions of the poor.

The Navajo people would be a good place to start. They know a good deal about death, if only because they, along with other Native peoples of America, have seen so much of it. When Columbus set foot on land in the Caribbean Islands in 1492, there were somewhere between twelve and fifteen million Native peoples living just in the region that the Spaniards would declare their own and rename Hispaniola. This figure comes from Fr. Bartolomé de las Casas, a Catholic priest who was confessor to Columbus and then to his son when he followed in his father's footsteps to govern Hispaniola for some 40 years. In 1542, de las Casas summed up decades of observations with a sobering assessment of what his fellow Spaniards had achieved:

> *We can estimate very surely and truthfully that in the forty years that have passed, with the infernal actions of the Christians, there have been unjustly slain more than twelve million men, women, and children. In truth, I believe without trying to deceive myself that the number of the slain is more like fifteen million.*[1]

Despite the willful ignorance of people now living in the continental United States, a similar story unfolded, albeit more slowly, on the mainland north of Hispaniola. The approximately five percent of

Indians who would survive the coming of the Whites to this land know about as much as anyone may ever want or need to know about death.

For one thing, they know how to survive death's passage. When recalling his father's death eight decades later, Johnny is forthright. "I didn't think about death. I don't think about death. I live one day at a time. 'Death'—that word has no feeling for me. I keep a safe distance with death."

The more I came to understand Johnny's Navajo way of dealing with individual death, the more I was keen to know how he had dealt with genocide. He had encountered this extreme form of death twice in his lifetime and had somehow worked through it to become a gentle, kind, and cheerful old man. Logic and instinct both suggested that Old Johnny ought to have something significant to say on this intense topic.

When we were talking about his first encounter with death through Old Juan's passing, I saw an opening to get to how he had dealt with so much death after that. I asked him point blank how he had gotten through not one but two genocides in his life, the first when he was just a boy and the second as a soldier nearing age thirty. His response gave me a lot to think about, as his best answers always did.

"If I had thought about genocide back then," he said, "I would have quit. If I start thinking about genocide now, I would probably still quit. People who start thinking about death soon end up dead. Someone who thinks they are a victim of genocide soon is a victim of genocide. I never let myself think like that when I was young and I don't think that way now."

This response helped me better understand that in Gallup, New Mexico, in 1927, eleven-year-old Johnny was thinking about life. In particular, he was thinking about what he could do to help his family move forward. His summary of the issue was,

"It's not good to think about death. My father had died. He was gone. That's all. My concern was what my mother was going to do."

The fatherless family was walking along the railroad tracks on the outskirts of Gallup as Johnny pondered the situation. They soon came across a railroad employee. After hearing their story, he showed them to a one-room adobe shack with a tin roof where they were welcome to stay until they found something better. It was a simple gesture of kindness from a white man. Johnny's mother accepted. It was enough to keep them going.

Two days later came the Christian funeral for Old Juan. Mr. R. C. Ritchey put him to final rest with a proper Christian sermon and then a burial in a church cemetery. Johnny does not remember much about the funeral itself. What he does remember is the bill. It cost $184 to bury Old Juan in the Christian way. That was a lot of money in 1927. It was a small fortune for a family of no means living in a borrowed shack on an Indian reservation with four hungry boys to feed.

"My main concern was that my brothers and my mother would not have to pay that $184 for Dad's funeral," Johnny remembers. So the eleven-year-old took it upon himself to approach Mr. Ritchey after the funeral. Through a Navajo interpreter, he explained that he wanted to work off his father's funeral bill.

There must have been something about the sturdy young Navajo that Mr. Ritchey liked. As subsequent events would reveal, the man was a kindly fellow and progressive in his thinking. Perhaps it was the sincerity of the boy's offer, or recognition that the young Indian was about to come of age in a harsh world that would give him very few chances to make something of himself. Whatever the motive, Mr. Ritchey's response was positive. He had the interpreter tell Johnny to report to work the following week. The boy did as instructed. And so it was that young Johnny took his first bold steps into the world of white people.

CHAPTER 5

"Pail Face"

THE YOUNG MIXED-BLOOD NAVAJO HAD A LOT OF CATCHING UP to do in his new world. First, he had to learn English. Only one other of Mr. Ritchey's employees spoke enough Navajo and Spanish to communicate with the boy. Johnny could not always count on his being present to translate work assignments around the funeral home. At first, Johnny's tasks were of the most basic sort. He cut the grass, raked the yard, washed the hearses and limousines, cleaned whatever Mr. or Mrs. Ritchey told him to clean, and ran errands. His employer and his wife, Bessie, were good to him. They paid him fairly for his work, giving half of his weekly earnings to his mother for her support and keeping the other half to pay off the family debt. Each Saturday, Mr. Ritchey gave the hardworking lad fifty cents to keep for himself.

There were other benefits as well. At the end of a work day, Mrs. Ritchey often invited him in for a good dinner before he walked home. There grew up a warm friendship between them. She was the one who Johnny eventually allowed to cut off his Navajo braids and to give him his first "white man" haircut. As time went by, he began to sleep at the Ritchey's when he wanted. It became his second home. He was treated with respect and kindness there.

Johnny would continue to work for the Ritchey family whenever needed for the next sixteen years until World War II called him away to serve his country far from home. It was not steady work. He came in only when there was a funeral or the grass needed cutting or some other task came up. But the job at the funeral home and his friendship with the Ritchey family nonetheless formed one of the most lasting touchstones of his early years.

With Johnny's older brothers working in the mines at Ellison and his earnings at the funeral home, the fatherless Sarmiento family soon got back on its feet. It wasn't long before Luisa's husband Paolo and older brother Pete decided to build a house for Refugio on land given to them by a generous neighbor. The men and their friends pitched in and built a sturdy dwelling out of cast-off railroad ties that were abundantly available.

Johnny remembers helping to put on the sod roof. When the first rain came, it leaked like a sieve. Paolo then came up with enough money to put tar-coated roofing paper on it. Johnny devoted himself to collecting fruit skids and loose boards on his daily walks home from Mr. Ritchey's business. In time the family had enough small lumber to put a wooden floor over the dirt in the main room of the house. "It was all very makeshift, very poor," Johnny recalls. But it was shelter. It kept them dry. And they had enough to eat and clothes to wear. They were doing all right.

Under the surface, however, young Johnny was struggling with something that would shape the rest of his life. Every day that he went to work in the white world, he felt inferior. To this day, he retains painful memories of white people coming past the funeral home as he worked in the yard. They would stop and point at the barefoot, dark-skinned youth in blue overalls and black braids and say things in English that he did not understand. Their smiles and finger pointing made him feel like an animal on display.

The anger that he felt came from more than specific incidents in the life of an eleven-year-old boy. The people who stared at him and talked about him in their strange language were the same people who could make his mother bow her head when she met them on the street. They were the ones who had let his grandparents die in an Indian concentration camp on one side of his family and his grandmother live out her life as a servant and sex slave on the other. Whites had created a world in which people like him were treated as little more than animals to be caged and kept away from polite society. With just a word or a glance, they could make his mother look away in shame for who and what she was.

"They made me very angry with their fine clothes and big houses and new cars and their English words," Johnny recalls. "I hated them. So I said to myself, 'If I must learn your language to beat you at your own game, I will." With anger and hatred as motivators, Johnny threw himself into learning all that the white world would teach him. Today, he looks back at this stage of his life with a rueful sigh. "Everything I did, I did for the wrong reasons. I did it out of hatred for others. I did it out of hatred for myself. I was angry at the world for making me feel inferior. I was going to make the world pay for it."

As negative as his motivation was, the outward results were positive to those around him at Mr. Ritchey's workplace. The young Indian showed himself to be surprisingly quick at adopting white ways. At work, he applied himself diligently to learning the English words for everything. He spent his days repeating the new vocabulary of the funeral home over and over as he went about his chores.

He also had great curiosity about the work that was done in the embalming room. "Mr. Ritchey would throw me out of the embalming room sometimes three or four times a day," he chuckles. Mr. Ritchey told the Indian boy the same thing each time he put him out. With time, Johnny was able to understand what he was saying. The words are still burned into his memory, "Boy, you can't climb the tree from halfway up. You've got to start at the beginning if you want an education."

After work, Johnny refused to play with his Navajo friends any time white boys came by. The white boys were permitted to go to school. They did not have to work yet for a living. They could spend their days learning how to succeed in the world.

He felt keenly the disadvantage at which this put someone like himself. He knew that he would have to work extra hard to "beat them at their own game." So he ran off after them to listen to their words as they played. He was determined to spend every waking hour learning the language and the ways of the white boys. He wanted to feel equal. He wanted to be equal. Inside his young breast was a knot of anger and hatred. It was hard on him that these light-skinned boys and their light-skinned world assumed that he was less than them. His soul would not have it so.

One day, after playing with the Whites, Johnny found that one of his Navajo comrades had drawn a picture of a bucket with eyes, ears, a nose, and a mouth on it. Other red friends gathered round and they all began to tease him mercilessly with the rough drawing. They mocked him for trying to be a "pail-face" rather than a Navajo. They laughed at him, telling him he could never be a white. They said he was too ugly to be white. He was even too ugly to be Indian. He was just a boy with a face that looked like an ugly pail.

The mockery did not have the desired effect. Johnny was pleased that they were seeing him in a different light. He was proud to be able to speak English better than they could do. He took their disapproval as a positive sign of his own progress. He laughed at their teasing. To their consternation, he proudly accepted their new title of "pail-face."

> *They stopped calling me 'Pail Face' after a few weeks. It does no good to tease a kid when he is proud of the teasing.*

> *But I kept the name that they gave me. It was right for me. I did have a mug like a bucket. I still do. And back then I was damned determined to become like the pale faces. Only a fool would have wanted to be an Indian where I was living. I wasn't going to spend my life being a fool that the whole world could spit on.*

Still today, eight decades after this childhood event, Johnny Pail Face carries the image of a bucket with a face on it everywhere he goes. He stamps it on every piece of Navajo jewelry that he makes. It is the logo on the business cards, ink pens, and signs that he uses to market his crafts at powwows throughout New England. There is a good-sized mural of it posted on the barn door near the house where he now resides. Pail Face took his new name to heart and has carried it proudly to this day.

Mastering the language and the ways of white boys in New Mexico long ago was the beginning of a lifelong journey into learning. He went on to become fluent in five languages. He lived for years in Germany, France, Korea, and Vietnam. In each place, he took on the ways of the "faces" around him, some pale, some not so pale. He not only learned to speak other people's tongues; he absorbed their cultural ways. He looked inside of their worlds to find out what was there. He worked hard to become "equal" in each place that his life took him.

Mr. Ritchey was at the heart of launching young Johnny on this life-long quest for equality and dignity. When he scolded the boy for trying to "climb the tree from halfway up," it was not out of anger or indifference. To the contrary. Mr. Ritchey soon demonstrated a lasting commitment to educating Johnny the best that he could. Since Indian children were not allowed to attend white schools, Mr. Ritchey made his funeral home into Johnny's "school." In their spare time between the various tasks of running the place, he taught Johnny the alphabet and then moved on to reading, writing, and basic math. This was no small commitment on his part. He devoted years to educating one Navajo boy.

After teaching Johnny the basics, he used his own money to pay for correspondence courses that carried the boy's education to the eighth-grade level. Johnny still remembers the long hours that this kind white man spent poring over correspondence course assignments with him before they mailed them back for grading. A warm friendship grew up between the middle-aged white man and his youthful Navajo employee.

Johnny's devotion to learning white ways extended beyond book learning. He was a lively, healthy boy who was keen for adventure as much as anyone his age. When he turned 14, Mr. Ritchey decided that he needed a driver's license. He had learned to drive the hearses and limousines as part of his daily tasks of cleaning them and assisting at funerals. This brought up an insurance problem. Should he damage one, the insurance company would not cover the repairs for a car driven by someone without a license.

So off they went to the regional state police headquarters where licenses were handled in those days. There, a big police officer who towered over the fourteen-year-old Indian boy explained that a chauffeur's license was needed to drive a hearse or one of Mr. Ritchey's limousines filled with mourners. Johnny would be chauffeuring people, even if some of them were beyond worrying about being killed in an automobile accident. A regular driver's license would not do. He had to have a chauffeur's license.

The officer looked Johnny over and said, "Boy, you have to be eighteen years old to get a chauffeur's license. Tell me that you are eighteen years old or I cannot issue you one of these."

"I'm eighteen years old," Johnny said.

That's all it took. Johnny was surprised. He got not only the license but a lesson in how the things worked among white men. It was who you knew that determined how you were treated. A fourteen-year-old Indian boy could get a chauffeur's license if he had a white friend who needed a driver. The white man had money. Money meant being able to get things to turn out the way that one wanted. Johnny took the lesson to heart. He would need to earn money to beat the white man at his own game.

Mr. Ritchey was a good role model for learning how to earn money. He was a successful businessman on two fronts. In addition to his funeral home, he ran an ambulance service on the side. His hearses were ideal for the task of ferrying injured people to the hospital in Gallup. Johnny knew he could learn from the man's example. Once he had a chauffeur's license, he soon began to assist Mr. Ritchey in both enterprises.

Johnny laughs now to think of rolling up to an accident scene in a black hearse and loading the injured for the trip to the hospital. "You do that nowadays and somebody is likely to have a heart attack on the spot if they are alive enough to have one," he says. "Mr. Ritchey's funeral business name was in white letters on both sides of the hearses. We didn't have many real ambulances in those days. Injured folks didn't seem to mind how we got them to the hospital as long as we got them there."

With his dual driving duties, Johnny succeeded so well that when he had paid off his father's burial costs, Mr. Ritchey asked him to stay on. Before his fifteeth birthday, Johnny was spending his days either helping to save people's lives or to send them properly to the next world when they were beyond saving. It was serious work for a young lad who had come into Mr. Ritchey's employment as a "poor, homeless, illiterate Indian" three years before.

This is not to say that the young man was all business and no play. His bright and lively spirit was up to hijinks as a teen much as he had been back when his father occasionally tied him up in a tree. Once he began driving, Johnny took up the habit of asking Mr. Ritchey for permission to drive his mother to visit her daughters now and then on a slow weekend at the funeral parlor. Her grown daughter Luisa still lived in Ellison and her eldest, Concepion, lived a few miles west of Gallup in Mentmore, another coal mining camp. Mr. Ritchey was obliging of these family requests.

Johnny's remembers how his mother would fill up the entire back seat of the nine-passenger limousine with all of her bundles and gifts destined for her daughter's family. She was proud of her enterprising youngest child who took her on local visits in such a grand manner. When the two of them would sweep into the mining camps in such a large vehicle carrying such a large woman with bundles and packages everywhere, the whole affair made an impression on the local population. Children would skip down the dusty road behind the automobile and stand back with in wonder to watch Refugio and her son unload their brightly packaged cargo.

The freedom and responsibility that came from Mr. Ritchey was sometimes more than Johnny's irrepressible young spirit was able to handle. Occasionally, he would ask permission to take his mother on a weekend visit without any intention of doing so. Instead he would load the big limousine with friends and run off to the mountains for fun. One warm Saturday morning, he packed fourteen teenaged friends into the vehicle and still found room in the trunk for a tub of beer on ice and some bottles of hard liquor. Off they then roared to a not-too-distant National Park for a wild drinking party.

On the way home, the good times took an ominous turn. Everyone, including Johnny, was drunk. One of his male friends jumped on the hood of the car as it set out and gleefully challenged Johnny to shake him loose. They were headed down a narrow, winding road back through the mountains to Gallup. The road was covered with gravel, which caused the speeding car to slip and slide from side to side as they sped along. The inevitable happened on a sharp bend. Johnny could not hold the limo on the road. It skidded down a sharp embankment and hit a tree broadside, bending the frame like a horseshoe.

The good news was that no one was killed. The bad news was that there were a lot of banged up and bloody teenagers. The car was so packed that the bodies cushioned the worst of the crash for each of the 14 riders. Johnny came out of it with a gash in his head and blood all over his shirt. One of the group who was relatively unhurt ran down the road to the nearest dwelling and called the state police. With the police came ambulances. Mr. Ritchey was among the ambulance drivers in his big hearse.

His first words to Johnny were, "Boy oh boy, I could kick you in the ass. If you weren't injured, I'd kick your ass for sure!"

Johnny prudently jumped into a third ambulance hearse. It was being driven by a fellow named Rawley, Mr. Ritchey's competitor from the other side of Gallup. A few hours later when the sobered-up boy returned from the hospital to the funeral home with his head in bandages, he didn't know what to expect. He feared the worst from his white employer. He figured that at the least he would lose his home away from home at the Ritchey's as well as his job. At most, he knew that he might end up in jail, which was standard procedure for drunken Indians. It was all up to Mr. Ritchey.

Mrs. Ritchey met Johnny solemnly at the door and accompanied him in silence to her husband's office. Johnny was surprised by the man's demeanor when he entered. He remembers, "He looked at me with such sadness I just about could not stand it. He was not angry. He asked me if I was sorry about what I did and about what had happened."

Johnny assured him that he was truly sorry.

Mr. Ritchey replied, "Boy oh boy, I have never, ever told a lie in my life. But for you, I told them a lie. I don't know why I did that."

Johnny worked up the courage to ask him what the lie had been.

Mr. Ritchey had covered for him. He had told the state police and the insurance company that he had given the boy permission to take the carload of young people on the car ride out to the national park for the day. Then he added to Johnny, "Don't worry about the car or the hospital bills for all those kids, because they are covered by insurance."

After that, Mr. Ritchey turned businesslike again. He asked Johnny if he was ready to get back to work.

"Yes sir!" was the quick reply.

With a nod, Mr. Ritchey sent him on his way with the admonition, "Get out of here and go back to work, and please stay out of trouble."

With a great deal of relief, Johnny turned and did as instructed.

Whatever one might say about life at the funeral home, it was not boring. For a young man of Johnny's age, every day was an adventure. When he wasn't doing maintenance work or driving a hearse or a limo, he spent his time in the embalming room watching Tony Ferkovitch, the embalmer, do his work. Tony taught him how to use a trochar, the pointed hollow tube used to drain blood out of newly arrived cadavers. They also used the trochar to put embalming fluids of various kinds back into the body cavities. He learned which main arteries were essential to the embalming process and the different ones to use for different body types.

For a woman, they would work through the femoral artery in the upper leg and pelvis so as not to scar the neck. It would not do to scar the neck in case she would be dressed for burial in a low cut dress. This was not a problem for men, who invariably had a collar and a necktie to hide the incision in the carotid artery. For children, they would cut straight through the chest into the aorta coming directly out of the heart. With time, Johnny went from assisting Tony to doing the embalming himself when Tony was away.

One time, Tony and Johnny both were called into action after an accident at the mine where Johnny's brothers worked. Fortunately for Johnny, none of his family members were involved. In addition to three men killed, a large black man had been shot to death the same weekend. Tony and Johnny had their hands full to get the embalming done in a timely manner for the multiple funerals.

As there was only one table on which to work, they had to embalm the dead men one at a time and drag each stiff body to a different corner of the room where it would stand upright on its own. The cabinets with all of their instruments and embalming supplies sat in one of the corners, leaving just three secure places to keep the bodies upright. After they placed the three embalmed miners in their respective corners, they had no option but to lean the 300-pound black man against the wall.

In a playful mood, Johnny began to use the black man's stomach for a punching bag. Why he chose to treat the black man this way rather than the other dead is perhaps a sign of how well he had absorbed the ugly undercurrents of American culture of the time. In any case, his stomach punches threw the cadaver off balance and it began to topple forward. Johnny knew enough to realize that if the big man hit the floor hard, it could bruise his facial features, so he tried to catch the body and to push it back against the wall. Johnny remembers that the man was stiff as a large tree and equally as heavy. The boy just kept going back, back, and back, with the body crushing down on top of him.

Johnny was able to keep the man from bruising his face, but he did it by cushioning the fall. When the fellow was all the way down, Johnny found himself lying flat on his back with a 300-pound embalmed body lying on top of him, face to face. "I was unable to move or to breathe," he shakes his head. "I could barely yell for help."

When Tony turned around and saw Johnny's predicament, he laughed so hard that he was immobilized himself for several moments. Then he helped Johnny work his way out from under the cadaver. It was almost more than they could do to stand the body back up against the wall again.

Another time, they received the body of an elderly fellow who ran a used furniture store in Gallup. He was an unsavory character who people in the Spanish community had nicknamed *Molancho*, meaning "Toothless." His business practices were as unsavory as his character. He would sell old furniture to elderly and poor people on credit. Every week he would circulate through the rough neighborhoods collecting payments. In his truck he always kept a couple of large, aggressive dogs. When he came through, you could hear his dogs barking from blocks away.

He had found that he could greatly increase his profits with a simple strategy. Just as a family or an old couple would be getting close to the end of their payments, he would neglect to stop by to collect for a month or so. Then he would suddenly show up and demand several weeks of payments. Of course the people would rarely have the increased amount that was now required, so he would repossess the property so that he could sell it again.

After collecting a payment one day, he was crossing the street back to his truck when a single mother with two children ran him over and killed him on the spot. The poor people of the neighborhood, mostly Mexican-Americans and Indians, were of the opinion that the woman had done the community a valuable service. But the authorities, all white people, saw things differently. The woman was sent to jail and her children put in foster care. And the *Molancho* went to Mr. Ritchey's funeral home. It turned out to be a most complicated funeral.

The *Molancho* had divorced his first wife and left her and their children so that he could start another family. His second family was the one that called the Ritchey establishment to come and pick up the body. Johnny and Tony did so.

No sooner was the task completed than a knock came at the front door. It was the County Sheriff with a court order that told them to cease and desist what they were doing and to transport the body across town to their competitor, the Rawley Funeral Home. The order came from the man's first family. They wanted control of their father's funeral…and his money.

The Sheriff was a patient man. He did not require them to move the body immediately. In a small town, he knew the parties involved and he had a pretty good idea of how things would work out. He figured that the second family would get a court order to override the one he had just served. He was right. When the second family showed up with the second court order, he gave Mr. Ritchey permission to continue the embalming.

While the legal wrangling was going on, the deceased did not remain peacefully on the sidelines as one might have expected. This was all happening during the hotter part of the year in a New Mexico desert town. While two families fought over control of the deceased, the deceased was busy developing tissue gas. Once they had legal clearance to begin the embalming, Johnny, Tony, and Mr. Ritchey had repeatedly to take the old *Molancho* out of doors and to use a trochar to relieve large quantities of odorific gas from his abdomen.

And this was just the beginning of the troubles.

For the wake, they realized that they would need to put up a partition in the funeral chapel to separate the two families. Otherwise fist fights were likely to break out between the adult male children of the deceased. They worried that womenfolk might do likewise. The two-family band of mourners was clearly a chip off of the unsavory block of the patriarch.

The wake was conducted on two different days to accommodate the two families. It seemed to be working to keep people apart. Afterward, Mr. Ritchey and his staff likewise ran two separate religious services. All proceeded well. Then there was the three-mile drive to the cemetery. Mr. Ritchey came up with a plan for two separate motorcades so that family factions did not visit upon each other the same fate that had put their common father in his untimely grave.

Mr. Ritchey organized things so that one family drove its cars ahead of Johnny's hearse and the other family was firmly instructed to remain behind the hearse. Then what Johnny always feared would one day happen to him happened. "I started to get a thump, thump, thump in the right front tire and we had to stop right there while I jacked it up to change the tire." Fortunately both mourning parties remained in their cars while Mr. Ritchey coached Johnny and Tony through one very fast tire change.

Finally, the extended cavalcade made it to the grave site where the pall bearers placed the dead man's casket on the canvas bands of the pulley system that is used to lower it into the grave. Johnny recounts what happened next.

"When the services were over, Mr. Ritchey nodded to me to release the catch, but instead of a slow, controlled descent into the grave, that casket just went phsht-boom straight down and hit the bottom with a whole lot of dust billowing up. Everyone looked with eyes wide to Mr. Ritchey. His face remained perfectly calm and he said nothing, as if it was the most normal and proper way to send a man to his final resting place."

When it was all over, the gravedigger forgot to show up, so Johnny rolled his sleeves and spent the rest of the day filling the hole in the desert heat. "It was hard work. I preferred driving," he remembers with a shake of his head.

When he got back to the funeral home, Johnny asked Mr. Ritchey what he would do if they had to get the old furniture seller's body back up again. It seems that the two families had nearly gotten into fisticuffs at the cemetery about whether the old man should have been buried somewhere else.

"I wouldn't do that for a million dollars, not at any price," Mr. Ritchey told Johnny. "That guy was trouble in life and trouble in death and I won't have anything further to do with him!"

Johnny does not know if the dissenting family ever succeeded in digging up the old *Molancho* and moving him. If they did, Mr. Ritchey held to his word and had nothing to do with that dead man again.

Although Johnny found the embalming business plenty filled with adventure, it was not something that he wanted to do for the rest of his life. He realized that he would need to become a funeral parlor owner to rise in the world as Mr. Ritchey had. Another option was to work in the mines and to try to rise through the ranks there. From the vantage point of the funeral home, he saw regularly where that trade led. Bodies that did not come in crushed and mangled came in after men coughed their lungs out from years of breathing coal dust day in and day out. Johnny knew he needed to learn some sort of trade or specialized skill if he was going to get anywhere in the white man's world.

Soon, another work opportunity came knocking. Next door to the Ritchey Funeral Home stood the Deluxe Cleaners, owned and operated by a Mr. Flores. One day Johnny came across the man as he was complaining about having to come in every Sunday to clean the large steam boiler at the heart of his dry cleaning business. Johnny offered to come in and do it for him. Mr. Flores was reluctant to pay the young man for something that he could do himself at no cost. Finally Johnny struck a deal in which he would clean the boiler for free as long as Mr. Flores would pay him to press ties on the roller press afterwards. Mr. Flores warmed to the proposal quickly.

Mr. Flores had a contract with a tie maker who shipped in newly made ties by the boxful for him to press prior to retail sell. He paid Johnny two cents per tie. Johnny soon found that he could press four ties at a time on the large roller press. He had to repeat the process on both sides, but still could earn eight cents in a matter of a minute or so. That was big money to the enterprising young fellow.

At the time, Johnny was still paying off his father's funeral with half of his weekly earnings going to Mr. Ritchey and the other half to his mother. That left 50 cents a week for his own purposes. Earning a couple of dollars each Sunday that he could keep for himself was a big boost to his budget.

Besides bringing extra cash, Johnny's work for Mr. Flores gave him something to do on Sundays. Before the pressing job, he could keep busy the other six days of the week, but Sundays always found him restless and bored. The white community would congregate in its Christian churches that day and then come home to rest, in obedience to their God's instructions. But Johnny had no interest either in white man's religion or in his day of rest.

Although the young man was determined to master white ways in other respects, his mission did not extend to white religion. He was no more interested in Jesus as a teen than he had been as a four-year-old watching his broken mother kneel in shame to him. The one thing he never did was to accompany the Ritcheys, Mr. Flores, or any other of his white friends to church on Sundays. After setting himself up to press ties for Mr. Flores, he found himself ideally situated to use every day of the week to move himself ahead in the white man's world. Sunday became his day to earn extra money as well as to devote himself to completing the homework assignments for the correspondence courses that Mr. Ritchey continued to order as fast as Johnny could get through them.

Just as Mr. Ritchey had come to depend upon Johnny at the funeral home, Mr. Flores came to rely upon his regular Sunday contributions to his dry cleaning business. In both cases, the relationships lasted for years. Johnny becomes quiet and reflective these days as he talks about Mr. Ritchey. "I now realize how much love I had for this man," he says. "He was always there for me." After a pause, he adds, "But I was seldom there for him."

As he was reaching his mid-teens, Johnny was moving forward in life. He was gaining the respect of the white men who hired him and befriended him. He was also becoming educated, at least by local standards. With Mr. Ritchey's help, he had earned an eighth-grade equivalency certificate through the American Correspondence Courses Program.

Johnny was young and like young people in any place or time, he was impatient. He wanted more from life than to work for others for a few dollars here and there, even if his employers did come to respect him in the process. He wanted to rise higher. He wanted to accomplish more. Often when he was walking through the streets of Gallup on an errand or going to and from work, he would pass a certain gentleman's clothing store. In the front window were smart suits, shirts, ties, and other items. "I used to slobber over those beautiful suits," he says. "I figured that if I was wearing one of those suits, no one could disrespect me. I wanted one so bad, but I couldn't afford it."

Nowadays old Johnny laughs.:

It wasn't very long before the day came that I could afford those suits. I found a way to get money in my pocket. Then I would go past that same store, look at the suits, and say, 'Now that I can afford you, I don't need you.' It wasn't too hard to learn how to make money in the white man's world. It was a lot harder to learn how to stop hating the white man for loving money so much and people so little.

Just as Johnny was learning how to move forward in the white world, another influential person found his way into his life. It was a man very different from Mr. Ritchey or Mr. Flores. An old mixed-blood Navajo by the name of Victor soon offered young Johnny a radically different perspective on the ways of the world. As it is with many of the best things in a long life, it was a perspective that Johnny would not begin to understand until many, many years later. In the end, it would be Victor's teachings that would bring balance back into the fragmented world of Johnny Pail Face.

CHAPTER 6

Victor's Beautiful Way

VICTOR WAS A BLIND MAN WHO LIVED IN GALLUP when Johnny's family first moved to the area after Old Juan's death. Some people considered him a shaman. A sliver of wood had taken his eyesight in one eye and cataracts covered the other, leaving him very limited vision. He lived in a wooden shed along the route that Johnny would regularly take to go to work for Mr. Ritchey.

As time went by, young Johnny took up the habit of stopping to visit the old man and to share a cup of coffee. Victor ground his own coffee beans. Johnny insists that he has never had a better cup of coffee in his nine decades on Earth than the ones he shared at Victor's house.

Victor had a secret for making good coffee. He soon shared it with his young visitor. "The blacker the pot, the better the coffee. Do not wash the pot if you want it to taste this good."

Johnny remembers looking at Victor's worn, blackened pot and asking, "When was the last time you washed this one?"

"Never," Victor replied.

"So you never wash the pot?" Johnny asked

"Never," Victor said again.

"How long have you had the pot?" Johnny asked.

"Since I was a young man."

"That's a long time," Johnny said.

"Maybe not so long," Victor smiled. "Maybe I'm still a young man even now," he said.

"He was always talking like that," Johnny says. "I didn't understand it then, but I liked his company and I loved his coffee. So I kept coming back."

Victor also played the guitar and sang. It seemed to brighten the old man's spirits when Johnny stopped in and from time to time he would pull out his guitar and play old songs to serenade his young guest.

I was lonely a lot in those days, Johnny says. *'No one seemed to notice that. No one stopped to ask how I was doing or how I felt. The Indian kids didn't like me because I was trying to be white. The white kids didn't like me because I was Indian. Mr. Ritchey was helping me learn things, but he was a busy man. My mother had her own stuff going on with pregnant daughters and new grandchildren.*

I spent my time working and mostly being alone or spending time with Victor. Victor sang to me. I tell you, there wasn't anyone else taking time to sing to me in those days.

Johnny developed a complex mix of awe, fear, and affection for Old Victor over the years that he befriended him. The Navajo people around Gallup whispered that he possessed magic and wisdom. For Johnny, the greatest magic was perhaps the kindness he felt when the old man would pull out his guitar and sing to a downcast boy.

There is a line in the Jewish Talmud that tells us, "Kindness is the highest form of intelligence." It is also a form of knowledge that is available to the least among us. You do not have to have a college degree to be kind. You may not even know how to read and to write. Johnny never saw Old Victor do either. But he had kindness.

The old fellow was gifted in other ways. "He had more songs in his head than would fill a dozen song books," Johnny recalls. "And he could sing them in three languages too. He made me laugh with Spanish drinking songs and Navajo joke songs. When he told me what the English songs meant, I could learn new words."

For a young man struggling with his father's death and a difficult transition into a harsh world, Victor's kindness offered a place of refuge. In it young Johnny Pail Face found a haven where no one was watching and judging and preparing new ways to push his young spirit down.

What Johnny found most intriguing about Victor's world is that there was always something unusual going on in it. The old man rarely left the broken-down shed that he called home, but adventure seem to come regularly right to his doorstep.

"Strange things were always going on with Victor," Johnny says. "There was never a boring day at his house."

Johnny recalls the afternoon that Victor's shack was hit by lightning during a summer thunderstorm. He went racing over as fast as his legs could carry him to see if the old man was still alive. He recalls:

I found him on his back. He was laughing so hard he couldn't talk at first. He had fallen over backwards in his chair by the front door. The lightning had struck right between where his feet had been on the floor. I helped him up and we searched around to see what had happened. The lightening had made a hole in the screen door in front of where Victor had been sitting and feeling the storm outside. He was too blind to see anything much so that is how he did things. He felt them.

He loved to sit at his front screen door. He told me that he felt the day go by as he sat there hour after hour. It gave him time to think. He would call out the name of anyone walking by his house. He would ask them about daily things going on in their lives. I don't know how he always knew what was going on in the neighborhood. I began to suspect that he could see things without using his eyes somehow.

Anyway, as I looked around where Victor had been sitting, I could see that the hole made by the lightning continued down through the floor. Victor had burns on the insides of his legs, like a bad sunburn. I went down into the root cellar below the hole in the floor. A big rock in the cellar was partly shattered.

He was still chuckling when I went back upstairs.

Johnny explained to me that many Navajo people considered Victor a male witch. There were rumors that he had special powers, that he could ask favors from evil spirits and could tell the future. The lightning strike confirmed Victor's reputation for many in the neighborhood. Who but a powerful shaman could dance with lightning and not be destroyed?

Johnny only glimpsed this side of Victor on rare occasions. It kept him in awe at the same time that the generous side of the old fellow nurtured their warm friendship.

In their conversations over coffee, Victor taught the young lad about life. "He spoke to me about who God was and wasn't," Johnny recalls. "He tried to instruct me in what life was supposed to be about. He explained that the Creator was inside of me and having the creator in there made me responsible for things."

Old Victor's lessons were simple statements about how things were in the world. He sent them across the kitchen table to Johnny in a voice that blended with the aroma of good coffee. He taught Johnny that the world consisted of more than what one could see with the eye. "Basically, he had no eyes, so he seems to have found other ways of seeing," Johnny says.

Victor spoke about the world of the spirit, where everything and everyone was connected. He taught his young listener that everyone and everything was responsible for what happened and for how it happened.

"Nothing happens unless we make it happen or we let it happen," he said many times. "We are the things that happen. It's just us that is happening. Once you understand that, you never grow old. And if you even start to think about getting old, lightning might come along and make you young again!"

And then he would chuckle and rub his legs where the burns had been and change the topic to something the boy could understand. The boy never forgot the words.

"He was very wise," Johnny recalls, "and I was hungry for knowledge."

The knowledge that Old Victor passed on did not fit mainstream preconceptions of what knowledge ought to be about. "It wasn't in the books and materials that Mr. Ritchey got for me from the correspondence course institute, that's for sure," Johnny says. Then he adds with a slow shake of his unruly white hair, "I saw him do things a man should not be able to do."

For example, one day as Johnny and Victor were walking along a dusty road in Gallup, the old man nudged Johnny and pointed to two Navajo women walking a few paces ahead. He told Johnny to watch the woman on the left because she was about to fall down. Johnny remembers that the woman took three or four steps and then stumbled to her knees. Johnny looked at the nearly blind Victor and asked, "How did you see that coming? How did you do that?"

Victor smiled. "Magic," he said.

Later, I asked him again to explain it to me. He did the best that he could, or at least the best that I was ready to hear. It was all about remembering that you are not separate from anything else and that you are what is happening around you.

He said that he hadn't wanted to hurt or to embarrass the woman in front of us. He just wanted me to see and maybe to understand what he had told me before.

He said if I ever figured these things out, I might do a lot of good in the world. I had no idea what he meant by that because I wasn't interested in doing anything good in the world at that time in my life.

Another time, Johnny came to Victor with a problem to solve. A new Navajo family had moved in beside his mother's house and they were a wild bunch. They spent the nights drinking, fighting, and generally making it impossible for anyone in Johnny's household to sleep. Their neighborhood disruptions continued in the daytime as well and Johnny's mother was at her wit's end with the situation. Johnny asked Victor if there might be something the old man could do to make them go away.

Victor instructed Johnny that the boy himself could make the family move away. He then described a ritual that Johnny could carry out to make it happen.

Johnny was to go to the local cemetery and to gather dirt from three separate graves that held the remains of people who had died violently. In a place like Gallup, this was easy enough. It would have been hard to locate graves of three people who had died peacefully in their sleep. Johnny's work at Mr. Ritchey's funeral home gave him inside knowledge on where to look.

Once Johnny had the grave dirt, he was to take it to the house of the offending neighbors at midnight and to climb onto their roof.

Victor instructed him to throw each handful of dirt on the roof while repeating, "Even as I never wish to see this dirt again, I never wish to see these people again."

"That will do it?" Johnny asked.

"That will do it," Victor replied.

Johnny did as instructed. Within a few days of the ritual, the chaotic family moved away.

"Magic," Victor assured him over coffee with a smile.

To this day, Johnny is not sure if Victor spread word through the neighborhood of the midnight ritual. It is possible that the trouble-makers got wind of what had taken place and fled because of their own Navajo superstitions and Victor's reputation. Perhaps Old Victor was a shrewd practitioner of human psychology. Perhaps he was a true shaman. Perhaps he was both and more.

Such things are difficult to know for those of us trapped into narrower and more defined ways of perceiving the world. In our conversations over the works and the ways of Old Victor, Johnny and I found common ground. We agreed that Victor possessed what Jewish sages considered the highest form of intelligence. He was kind. That's what brought a lonely young man to his door. That's what kept him coming back.

The last that Johnny heard of Victor took place a couple of years later when the old man became too feeble to live alone. State authorities took him away and placed him in a rest home. After that, Johnny received a couple of vague messages through friends requesting a favor. Old Victor wanted him to go to the root cellar and to retrieve some items there. There seemed to be something that Victor wanted Johnny to have.

At this time in his life, Johnny was a busy, enterprising young man who had thrown himself completely into rising in the white world. In the rush of his days and weeks, he never got around to following up on the favor.

When word came that the gentle old fellow had passed away, local authorities came to clear out and to tear down his dilapidated home. In the process, they came across a canvas bag with some $5,000 in silver dollars hidden in the root cellar. It was then that

Johnny understood what Victor had been trying to communicate to him.

At that point, it was too late, of course. The authorities took the money and a few other paltry possessions left behind by the old Navajo. Johnny now figures that the money most likely went to reimburse the government for Victor's days at the rest home and to cover the costs of his burial.

In the end, Johnny did not need to receive Victor's money to understand what the final message from the old man meant. Victor's feelings for his young friend were sincere. Although he did not particularly value a sack full of silver, he was willing to pass it on to Johnny in a final gesture of friendship. That is what Johnny remembers today at a point in his life when he has earned the status of an old man himself.

Now when I ask Johnny how much influence Victor has had on his life, his response is quick and firm. "Victor?" he asks with a widening of his eyes. "He has always been with me. His teaching has always been with me."

The seeds of that teaching, like any good teaching, took the better part of a lifetime to germinate, to grow deep roots, and to lift their fruit skyward. They rested dormant in Johnny for the right season and the right circumstances to bring them to blossom. They waited until Johnny was ready for them, when he needed them and would value what they had to offer.

So perhaps it is true that Old Victor was a shaman and knew something of magic. Is it not magic when one person can transform another person's life long after he is dead? Is it not magic how kindness given in youth can circle back through the years, bringing knowledge and wisdom with each return? What could be more magic than that a man who never met Victor, is now writing him into a book and has developed respect and affection for him? What could be more magic than readers reading the book and feeling similar connections. If we are what happens, then Old Victor is still happening.

As I listened to Old Johnny's words during many long talks, I saw that Victor's teachings have matured and taken the shape that

Johnny's life needed. Here is how they come out today when Johnny speaks of what he learned from an old Navajo shaman:

Everyone is born within a circle and you take in those that you wish and you reject those that you wish. You're born naked and you die naked. The point is, you must live your life the best that you possibly can. That's why the Creator put you here, to make an impression on those you encounter, on those within your circle of responsibility.

It's the impressions that matter. The impressions can be the source of great ugliness and pain or they can bring great beauty and satisfaction into your world. If you want to return to the Creator with a clean heart and without shame, you have to choose the beauty way. There is no other way but the beauty way.

At age 15, Johnny only saw vaguely and without understanding the meanings hiding in Victor's words. His vision was clouded by a more pressing need. He wanted white people to look at him as an equal. He wanted to feel inside himself that he was, indeed, equal. He wanted to be called "Mr." not just "Hey you," or "The Indian kid." He wanted to own a fine home like the Ritcheys and to have money to spend and to be able to go on vacation, all things unheard of in his mother's world.

To get from where he was to where he wanted to go, he needed more money. As he neared the age of 15, the young man decided that it was time for a career change. The reason that he had gone to work at age 11 was no longer looming over him. The debt for his father's funeral was paid and his mother had enough family support to keep her comfortable. Young Johnny Pail Face was free to seek a white man's fortune. He decided to go into the lumber business. He knew it might be a dangerous line of work, but it seemed like a step up from where he was.

Down the Road and Back Again

JOHNNY'S OLDER BROTHER, RAUL, put him onto the lumber business. When Johnny reached his mid-teens, Raul was living and working in McNary, Arizona, where he had landed a good-paying job in a busy sawmill. One day a friend of the family came by in a small pickup headed for McNary. Johnny had been thinking about a change of work and of scenery for some time. His work for Mr. Ritchey was on an "as needed" basis. When there was a death or the lawn grass got long, he was needed. It was the same with work for Mr. Flores. Much of the time, the restless young man had little to do.

When given the chance to join up with Raul, he took it and headed off to make his fortune cutting wood. He would stay with his brother until he got his feet on the ground in this new line of work. That was ambitious young Johnny's plan.

The plan was simple enough. The goal was clear. There was only one flaw. It seems that young Johnny had more ambition than size. He did not find another Mr. Ritchey or Mr. Flores among the lumber foremen in McNary. Everywhere he went, he was told that he was too young and too small for the jobs that they were offering.

Johnny stayed on a bit anyway, hoping that his luck might change. One Sunday Raul, some Spanish-speaking Catholic buddies, and Johnny were sitting around in their church clothes. Their buddies had been to mass, but Johnny and Raul's Sunday ritual was to dress up and sit around drinking and smoking and passing a pleasant day. On this specific Sunday, two forest rangers came roaring up in a truck and told them that there was a forest fire "burning out of control" south of McNary. The young men all jumped on the truck, still in their Sunday best, and roared off to save the town. They spent the next three days fighting the fire. In the end, the fire was put out and McNary remained untouched.

But their best clothes showed the effects of the hard work. "My clothes were all dirty and my good shoes were ruined," Johnny recalls. "The Forestry Service gave us two dollars a day and that barely paid for one shoe, let alone the cleaning of my Sunday suit."

With six dollars in his pocket, Johnny returned to Gallup disappointed, but pleased to have spent several weeks with his older brother. His old employers were happy to have the young man back and he picked up where he had left off on his part time jobs with them.

Then another opportunity came up that he could not resist. A gentleman from the copper mines at Morenci, Arizona, stopped by the funeral home. After a friendly conversation, he told Johnny about good-paying jobs at the Morenci mine. It was a large, open-pit mine that employed hundreds of workers. Surely he could make some serious money there. The man offered to let Johnny stay with him and his wife while looking for a job.

It was too much to resist. An open-pit copper mine seemed like a big step up from the dirty, underground coal mines where men either died early from falling rock or later from black lung. Johnny knew about such things from his own brush with the coal mines as a sorter and from his brothers who worked there. He accepted the man's offer and off he went to seek his fortune in a copper mine in Arizona.

He hit the same obstacle as with his lumber mill adventure. The people at the mine refused to hire him. They said that he was too young for the backbreaking work of open-pit mining. He was told to try again in a few years. Johnny began to realize how well people treated him back in Gallup. Mr. Ritchey's kindness and Mr. Flores' willingness to give him a chance had led him to believe that it would not be hard to find a foothold in the white man's world of work. He had not expected things to be so difficult.

Life was not easy on the domestic front in Morenci either. Johnny was staying with the man who had brought him to look for work, but things were not turning out well. The man and his wife were nice enough, but he assumed that they must be poor. They only fed the boy once a day. He grew tired of being hungry all the time. At the height of the Depression with no prospects for a job and a stomach that seemed emptier by the day, Johnny turned back once again back to his home base at Gallup.

He rode an ore car down the mountain from the open-pit mine to where the tracks met the Southern Pacific railroad. There he hopped a boxcar headed in a generally eastern direction, towards home. However, when the old-fashioned coal burning train stopped a few miles later to take on water for its boilers, a brakeman saw him and put him off the train.

With nothing else to do, Johnny started walking the tracks eastward. He found some bottles that he could fill with water and carry along as he trekked along under the hot desert sun. "I walked for three days straight," he remembers. "All I had to eat were some discarded orange peels that I found beside the tracks."

Finally, he came to a section gang house. Railroad employees responsible for maintaining a section of the tracks lived with their families in these houses along the tracks. The large house was made of concrete and had apartments for several families. Johnny asked the woman who answered the door if she might give him something to eat.

She was pleased to do so, but asked him to chop some wood in return. The half-starved young man responded with an enthusiastic "Certainly!"

Johnny remembers that while he was chopping the wood, the woman brought him a dish he had hated as a child. "It was a great big platter of boiled rice and onions," he smiles. "But do you know that I finished every bit of it and nothing had ever tasted so good to me."

This time, Johnny had stumbled into another good-hearted white family. He stayed the night with the woman and her husband. The next morning the man drove Johnny 250 miles from southern Arizona all the way across New Mexico to El Paso, Texas. That was the best place to catch a train back up to Gallup.

In El Paso, a couple who looked like tourists stopped Johnny on the street to ask directions. He told them that he, too, was a stranger to the town and that he was just passing through as he tried to make his way home to New Mexico. To this day, Johnny has an exceptional ability to turn strangers into friends in a very short amount of time. If someone stops long enough to exchange a few words with the man, his sense of humor and disarming charm will soon have them chatting with him as if with an old friend. Johnny's engaging young spirit quickly won over the two tourists. Before they left, they gave him a couple of dollars for food and to help get him home.

Johnny thanked them, took the money and headed across the border to Ciudad Juarez. He was savvy enough to know that he could get a lot more with his two dollars there than on the American side of the border. While he was sitting on a bluff looking across the river to Juarez, a U.S. Immigration Officer confronted him and asked if he was an illegal.

Johnny explained in good English who he was, that he was actually headed home to Gallup but that he first wanted to go over to Juarez to get some food and a few gifts for his family. Johnny got a good payoff that day from his hard work with Mr. Ritchey to get an education. The officer turned friendly upon hearing the boy's English and listening to his story. He wished the young fellow good luck and left him alone.

Johnny wasted no more time and skipped across the bridge into Juarez where he bought a good meal and wolfed it down. Then he purchased a carton of rice paper cigarettes for his mother and had enough change left for two of bottles of tequila for his brothers.

He went back over the bridge to El Paso and made his way to the rail yard where he asked other non-paying travelers where he might catch a freight train bound for Vaughn, New Mexico. From Vaughn, he knew that he could ride the Atchison, Topeka, and Santa Fe into Gallup.

Everything went smoothly until Vaughn. There he climbed on top of a refrigerator car carrying fruits and vegetables. Trouble was, the car was locked and he could not gain access to its cargo. This was unfortunate because the young man had worked up a big appetite in his travels. He was thirsty as well. He gave in to natural inclinations and took a drink from one of the bottles of tequila. One has to take what happened then in historical context.

White men have been drinking fermented beverages for thousands of years. Their bodies have had time to adjust. Over hundreds of generations, white people have worked out how to metabolize alcohol at a fairly efficient rate. Native Americans have no such genetic history. They are newcomers to strong drink. Young Johnny's heritage had not prepared him for what would happen when he took a good, long swig of cheap tequila on an empty stomach on a hot day.

When the young fellow woke up a long time later, both tequila bottles were empty and his head was throbbing like it would explode. After he climbed down off the refrigeration car on unsteady legs and got his bearings, he discovered that he was now in Winslow, Arizona. He must have been unconscious for a day or more for he was a couple of hundred miles beyond Gallup. He had ridden the train right through his own town without realizing it. With his head pounding and body aching, he sat down to wait for another freight train to take him back the way that he had just come.

After the initial car ride over to Morenci for job hunting, days of walking rails through the New Mexico desert on an empty stomach, a long car ride to El Paso, Texas, followed by a tequila-tainted train ride all the way through New Mexico back to Arizona, and then a reverse train ride east again to Gallup, the job-seeker finally arrived home again. It had been a weeks-long odyssey for the young teen. Johnny gave his mother the Mexican cigarettes, told her as much of his story as he could over dinner and then collapsed into bed for a long, long sleep.

When he awoke, he found life in Gallup as he had left it. As he walked the dusty streets back to short stints of work at the funeral home and the dry cleaners, his old resolve to do better with his life returned as strongly as ever. Everywhere he went he met other Indian boys who showed no signs of moving beyond the low expectations and crushing discrimination that white America offered them.

As young as he was, Johnny knew instinctively that many of them would live out their lives "poor, homeless, and illiterate" just as he, himself, had faced not long before. That was not going to be his lot in life. He now had an education; he wanted a life to match. He was going to work hard. He was going to make money. He was confident that no one could hold him down and treat him like dirt if he had money.

His two part time jobs left a lot of room to explore other ways of putting cash in his billfold. When he wasn't making an ambulance run, hauling someone to the cemetery, or pressing ties, he was looking for new ways to earn money. It wasn't long before his chauffeur's license opened the way forward. An older fellow by the name of Gregorio had begun a taxi service in Gallup. Gregorio needed drivers. Johnny signed on.

The money was good enough that the young teen was soon able to buy his own "taxi," a 1928 Chevy roadster. He had seen from Mr. Ritchey's example and others how one opportunity could quickly lead to another.

Indeed, it did not take long to find other uses for his taxi. Mexican farmers and herders in the mountains around Gallup were good at making illegal whiskey. What they lacked were efficient ways to get it to town. Johnny had a roadster. It was an "efficient way."

The timing for Johnny's bootlegging business couldn't have been better. Congress had repealed the Volstead Act ending the Prohibition and making the purchase of alcohol legal again. For white Americans, that is.

In New Mexico, Arizona, and Utah, it remained against state law for Indians to buy alcohol for almost two more decades. The New Mexico and Arizona Natives were only given the "right to drink" in 1948—at the same time that they got the right to vote in state elections. In Utah, the state legislature delayed both rights until 1953.[1]

At issue was the legal designation that had been assigned Indians in the U.S. from the time that the nation began destroying tribes and placing the survivors on reservations. This process started shortly after the American Revolution and ended when more than 500 tribes across the U.S. were either extinct or settled onto reservations. In each case they became "wards" of the U.S. Government. As indicated earlier, this put them in the citizenship category of people in jail or in mental institutions.

"Living on a reservation is like being jailed in a mental institution," Johnny says. "If you aren't crazy at the start of your stay, you sure as hell will be by the end." Johnny would know. He was born on an Indian reservation and he would later be committed by the U.S. military to a mental hospital for a year to heal from the unseen wounds of World War II.

Although the federal government gave Natives the right to vote in 1924, shortly after women received it, states were able to withhold the same right until a generation later.[2] States where there were significant populations of Indians put other legal limitations upon the Natives as well, such as making it illegal for them to purchase alcohol and limiting access to the courts to redress their grievances. Other practices, such as banning Indians from attending white public schools, however, were not done through enacting new laws. Social attitudes were strong enough on this issue that there was no need for laws. Segregation of whites and "coloreds" was as complete in the Wild West in the first half of the twentieth century as it was in the Deep South.

As bad as white discrimination against Indians was in Johnny's world, he found it good for his bootlegging business to other Natives. The Whites had created a world where Indians were not allowed to drink alcohol and then gave them endless reasons to do so. With the end of Prohibition, there was suddenly very little money to be made in the illegal whiskey business in places like Gallup…unless you sold to the Indians. With his 1928 Chevy roadster and his fluency in Navajo, young Johnny Pail Face didn't take long to carve out a lucrative corner on the market.

He found that the best corn whiskey was being made by Mexicans out near the coal mining town of Gamerco. He would run his taxi out there to pick up white lightning in quart jars. "It was powerful stuff," he remembers. "Much better than the cactus juice my Dad used to make." To maximize profits, Johnny would cut in a quart of water for every three quarts of the strong stuff. This he would sell to Indians around Gallup at double the price that he paid to the Mexicans in the mountains. Soon he had more money than he knew what to do with.

On the one hand, it must be pointed out that what the entrepreneurial young man was doing was patently illegal. As mentioned earlier, in New Mexico and many other states it was against state law for Indians to consume alcohol. Bars throughout the American

West commonly had signs on their doors throughout most of the twentieth century that said things like, "No Dogs or Indians Allowed."

In fact, such interdictions were rarely enforced. Dogs could often be found sleeping under the tables inside. But not Indians. Until he was 37 years old and a decorated veteran of two American wars, Johnny regularly had to convince New Mexico and Arizona bartenders that he was of Mexican or Italian descent. Otherwise he would be denied a drink and physically thrown into the street.

One could also argue that young Johnny's bootlegging business was an unethical (he was watering down his product prior to sale) as well as an unhealthy way to treat his fellow Navajo for whom white man's alcohol continues to be a health scourge not unlike the one that red man's tobacco has been for white populations.

These concerns did not bother the young teenager at the time. When Johnny set out to adopt the white man's ways, he did not pause to make fine distinctions between "good" white ways and "bad" ones. This was especially true after his unsuccessful attempts to find work in the lumber business and the copper mines. He had seen in the faces of other young Navajo around Gallup and elsewhere what life was like for men who could not find a job. They were poor, homeless, illiterate and often slept in the streets at night in drunken stupors. In the end, Johnny was determined to get his hands on whatever it would take to lift him above the most brutal forms of discrimination that boys like him faced each morning when they got out of bed.

Money brought about the upward mobility the young man was seeking instantly and upon contact. Literally. When a dollar touched his billfold, white men around him altered their outward behavior right there and then. Trading post merchants, used car dealers, grocery store owners, even bartenders forgot the color of his skin and the broad Navajo features of his face when he opened a billfold filled with green. Dollars were his passport to respect and dignity in white America.

Despite the negative legal, ethical, and moral implications of Johnny's entrance into the world of money, he was soon succeeding at it rather well. The young man could take his taxi into the mountains in the afternoon where he dealt successfully in Spanish with

Mexican producers of the product that he wanted to sell. As the evening came on, he would be back in Gallup selling white lightning to Navajo clients who had come to town with a few coins in their pockets and a driving desire to forget their lives. If the sheriff stopped him, he could wiggle and charm his way out of trouble in English. The sheriff and other townspeople knew him as a hardworking lad with the pluck and drive to juggle work at a funeral parlor, an ambulance service, and a taxi business day in and day out.

Alternately in the seat of a hearse, an ambulance, or a taxi, Johnny was at the center of the entrepreneurial world of Gallup, New Mexico, in the mid-1930s. Because he could and did talk regularly with everyone from the bottom to the top of social ladder, he had his finger on the pulse of life and on new business opportunities in the sleepy Southwestern town.

He was among the first to learn that the local brothel was looking for financial backers for a big remodeling job. Johnny was flush with cash at the time. He jumped in for a twenty percent share of the establishment. He still has photos of the business where he came in as a partner. "It was the Angelis Hotel," he tells me with a chuckle, "but no guests were looking for a peaceful night of sleep in that hotel back in the 30s."

Not yet age 15, Johnny was the youngest partner in this new business. It consisted of a two-story building with twelve rooms on one side of an upstairs hall and twelve rooms on the other side. Downstairs was a parlor, a dining room, and the kitchen, as well as Madam's quarters. There was also a bar that legally sold alcohol on the first level, while upstairs, eight to twelve women lived and worked. Their personal quarters were organized efficiently on one side of the hallway with their working quarters directly opposite.

All the women who worked in the brothel were white. They charged $2 a customer. The women kept half for themselves and turned the other half over to their business partners. "That meant that every time a man found happiness, I earned 20 cents," Johnny recalls. "I was learning that it was easy business to make money in the white world once you figured out how to go about it properly."

As the Great Depression wore on, Johnny soon found himself moving in a circle of Americans who were not feeling the financial pinch of the times. This is not to say that it was easy to live in the margins as Johnny, his partners, and the women who worked for them were doing. One of the most interesting cultural twists in the underworld of Gallup is that Johnny never saw a minority woman choose to work at the brothel. I couldn't help but ask him why.

I hoped that the question would elicit an earthy response with a unique view through yet another "crystal" into the cultural world of his youth. It did. Johnny had an insightful answer but he had to dig for it. He told me he had never thought about this topic before.

"Most Mexican girls were extremely religious," he began. "They would go out and give it away, but they wouldn't sell it. Being known as a 'whore' was about the worst thing that could happen to a Mexican girl. It was the Catholic thing. Being a whore would send her to hell, for sure."

Choosing words slowly, he continued. "Indian girls had too much self-respect to work for us, I think. They would only have the men they chose to have. No man was going to walk through the door and tell them that they were going to have sex if they didn't like the looks of him or didn't feel like having sex at that particular moment." In their personal lives, there seemed to be a tendency for Mexican women to live by guilt and Indian women by pride. Only white women seemed to be able to shrug off such cultural and social constraints.

What the white brothel may have lacked in multiculturalism, it made up for in efficiency. Johnny remembers it as one of the best-run businesses in Gallup in its day. At the core of things, the Madam in charge kept good books and everybody got their cut of the proceeds like clockwork. She also brought in a doctor every week and all the women had checkups. The business operated with the unspoken consent of the local police and the city fathers. As Johnny puts it, "The police did not bother me. Everybody knew me and I guess that they thought I was harmless." Never once was young Johnny removed from the premises of the brothel or hampered in his taxi work that brought clients to and from the flourishing business.

Most surprising, or troubling, was that the police turned a blind eye even to his whiskey-running business. "I've always had the gift of making friends in high places," Johnny explains. "I learned early how to get along with the people who had the ability to do me the most harm." In a more somber voice he adds, "Plus I knew that the whites in charge couldn't give a damn about Indians. As long as there were no big fights involving whites and no stabbings or murder, the sheriff could pretend I didn't exist. Dogs barking in white neighborhoods mattered more than what I was up to."

Johnny's assessment of things seems to be accurate. Despite his tender age, despite his dual roles of illegal whiskey runner and brothel partner, the sheriff and his men never bothered him. The same society that would not allow a Navajo boy to sit beside its white sons and daughters at the local high school did not object to him staying up all night at the local brothel or to selling illegal whiskey day and night to his fellow Indians. For his part, Johnny was willing to snatch up whatever crumbs of opportunity that white America would throw his way.

What he found, of course, was that there was a lot of opportunity for an Indian boy in the shadowy margins of life. During the worst days of the Depression of the 1930s, Johnny never once stood in an employment line or waited for a meal at a soup kitchen as hundreds of thousands of whites were doing. With his many jobs, he worked seven days a week and most nights. Even on Sunday mornings when his Indian clients were sleeping off his illegal booze, the prostitutes were resting from a busy week, and the proper citizens of Gallup were bustling off to sing hymns to God and His Son, Johnny was hard at work on upward mobility by ironing box-loads of ties at the Deluxe Cleaners.

By the mid-1930s, young Johnny seemed to have the white world by the tail. In a few short years, he had gone from being a "poor, homeless, illiterate Indian" to making something of himself. He was a hard worker who was liked and trusted by his employers at a funeral home, a taxi service, and a dry cleaners. He was also a business owner in his own right with a twenty percent piece of a brothel and complete ownership of a whiskey delivery service. Everyone who knew him saw an enterprising young man who was on the move. While his brothers sweated for poor wages at a coal mine in work reserved for people at the bottom of society, Johnny was breaking out of that world. Thanks to Mr. Ritchey, he had even snatched up valuable pieces of white man's education along the way. He was, as he puts it, "beating the white eyes at his own game."

If Johnny could be considered a successful young man in some ways, he was not a happy young man. Even now, so very many years further down the path, his face clouds as he remembers this early stage of life. "I wanted to hurt others," he confesses. "I would do anything to make myself superior and the bluer the person's eyes in front of me, the more it was worth to do it. If I could do a job on a fellow and win, if I could get ahead of him, that's what I wanted most in life."

Then Johnny takes a deep breath and lets it out slowly. "You can lie to the world. You can lie all you want to anyone and everyone… except to one person. You can't lie to yourself. You will always see the truth in the mirror."

As a busy young entrepreneur in Gallup, New Mexico, Johnny did not like what he saw when he looked into the mirror. He saw a person consumed by anger and hatred. He saw someone eager to take advantage of others, eager to raise himself up by putting others down.

This was not a particularly good time for the young man to fall in love. It was not a good time to jump into a marriage and to take on the role of father. But as Johnny came to the end of his teen years, he was as susceptible to the charms and the compelling forces of life as is any young person. Plus, as someone who had demonstrated the ability to take care of his father's funeral and his mother's ongoing livelihood at the age of eleven, he was in the enviable position of being able to do pretty much what he wanted. As it turns out, what he soon wanted was an attractive Filipino woman by the name of Virginia who was nearly a decade older than he was. She also had a four-year-old son, Raymond.

With his customary boldness and personal charm, Johnny went after her.

Love and War

*I always wanted to be someone that people could
accept and respect.
But I did not know how to go about it.*

VIRGINIA WAS TWENTY-SIX YEARS OLD THE NIGHT that she met
Johnny. She was a single mother with a four-year-old son. She was
coming home from a job as a cocktail waitress. Her ride fell through
so she hailed a taxi. The driver had intense dark eyes and was friendly
and charming as he drove her across town. Within a few short miles,
he lifted her spirits with his generous outlook and kind words.

As a single mother in 1930s America, she had reason to appreciate such small kindnesses. Life was tough for her son, Raymond, and
herself. She was stretched thin to keep a roof over their heads and
food on the table. She worked long hours in a smoky bar where men
rarely treated her well.

This man Johnny seemed like a different sort to her. He was
gentle and sincere with his compliments. He listened quietly when
she spoke. When his eyes looked into hers, he seemed to understand
what he saw. They drove around and talked for a long time.

Virginia decided to take a risk. She asked Johnny if she could
come to his place for the night. They parked outside of where he was
living at the time and talked some more. Then they realized that they
were not far from Virginia's apartment, so they got out and walked
there. Johnny slept in her arms that night.

To this day some 80 years later, Johnny speaks of Virginia with
great tenderness and great regret. Theirs was a tempestuous relation-

ship that lasted nearly two decades. Near the end, Johnny finally married her. Although other wives would follow in the flow of the years, she retains a unique place in his heart for good reasons and bad.

Looking backward, Johnny sums up the complexity of his years with Virginia. "I fell so madly in love with that woman that it was the most pathetic way of living that I ever lived in my life. I was such a jealous person, such a possessive person."

In the larger scheme of his world, it is not difficult to understand Johnny's intense jealousy. Virginia was an attractive woman with Filipino, Spanish and Euro-American heritage. They made an unusual mixed couple in the largely segregated world of Gallup. Johnny pulled it off by adopting his mother's way of distancing himself from his Navajo heritage. He did not tell Virginia of his Indian roots. He told her rather that he had picked up a bit of Navajo language from childhood friends. He emphasized the Spanish American thread of his family heritage, as his mother had done before him.

Virginia was a woman who immediately caught the attention of men of any background or race. Johnny was proud of that. It also made him intensely jealous. When he took her to work, he knew that she would spend the hours at the cocktail lounge surrounded by men, especially by white men. It became a torturous part of his daily routine. He recalls, "I used to imagine all kinds of things that other men were saying and doing to her, touching her and making dirty suggestions."

As the day wore on, Johnny's ugly fantasies would wear him down. By the end of her shift, he says, "I would sit in my cab, waiting for her to come out, making myself half-crazy with jealous thoughts. By the time we got to her place I had made her completely miserable with all my accusations."

With Virginia, Johnny entered into another period of great change in his life. Some of the changes were good, some were disastrous. The good was that he let go of the jobs that were not making much money and focused upon driving taxi and selling whiskey. This made his day-to-day routine more settled and allowed him more time to be with his girlfriend and her son.

But the dark demons of jealousy and fear of losing the woman he loved would not let him rest. His lifestyle in the margins of society offered marginal ways to cope with feelings of inadequacy and inequality. His bootlegging business in particular brought easy access to an easy answer. As he sums up, "Soon I started drinking the stuff I was selling. When I was drunk, I felt equal to, if not better than, the Whites around me."

In his early 20s, Johnny became an alcoholic. However, he did not mimic the typical behaviors of other drunken Indians who could be found any day of the week ranging the streets of Gallup in search of another drink. He was an industrious drunk. He continued to work hard. He continued to earn good money. He continued to chase after the dream of making it in the white world one day. But when the pressures and anger came to an explosive point, he turned to the bottle and would go on a drunken binge that could last for days.

Other than the bottle, he found solace in intimacy with Virginia. With her, "the only thing that calmed me down was to have sex and fall asleep. I didn't know what I would do if we should ever separate."

Johnny was willing to make sacrifices for Virginia. Largely to please her, he turned his twenty percent share of the local brothel over to his brother Raul. He made an effort to be a responsible partner and father figure to Raymond. He did not try to make her stop working as a cocktail waitress.

Johnny came from a culture where men do not order their women around. Virginia was drawn to this side of him without knowing its source. Navajo people live in a matriarchal and matrilineal society. Women are respected in this world. Women respect themselves because their culture gives them ample reasons to do so. They own property. Ownership is passed down through mothers to daughters along clan lines. Names are likewise passed through the women. Women have power over their lives. They do not have sex with men who they do not like. Not even for money. It was a different world from the one in which Virginia lived. Many of the differences remain to this day.

As much as Johnny distanced himself from his Navajo roots, he was not able to cut the roots off. Good things continued to course through them. He brought into his relationship with Virginia a natural respect and appreciation for her as a woman. When he was sober and not on a jealous tirade, he was kind to her. He listened to what she had to say. He treated her like an equal human being, the way that he had seen his father treat his mother. He did not assert a male prerogative and insist that she give up her work and change her life to please him as other men had done.

These things she found refreshingly attractive, enough so that she stayed with him for two tumultuous years. But, in the end, his jealousy and his drinking drove them apart. In 1940, they agreed that this was not a good way to live, especially for young Raymond, and they parted amicably.

After the end of his first big love in life, Johnny found himself restless. He wanted to get away from Gallup and the bad memories that haunted him there. He drank even harder once Virginia left. He knew that it was leading him nowhere good, but he couldn't stop. When National Guard recruiters came through town in late 1940, Johnny listened carefully to what they had to say. They treated him and the other recruits, a colorful mix of Mexican Americans, Natives, and Whites, with common respect. He liked what they offered. He signed up to become a part time soldier in the National Guard's 200th Coast Artillery, Battery D.

He and others from the region trained once per week. War was raging through Europe and Americans were on high alert. Every few months, they would go away for two weeks to do more intensive training. Johnny was able to get away from Gallup on these excursions, but could still maintain close contact with his aging mother and other family members. He found it refreshing to get away. The dark ghosts of his past haunted him less from a distance. And his natural curiosity made him eager to see the world.

In early 1941, Johnny's battalion went off to a training camp in Mississippi. It was a tense time on the world stage. Europe was engulfed in World War II and Japan was making demands for more control over the Pacific region. Talk of America joining the war was rampant, but American leaders were moving forward with caution. The nation was just digging itself out of the worst depression in its history. There was little eagerness to rush into a costly and potentially devastating war.

While in Mississippi, Johnny hit some bad luck. He broke his wrist during rigorous training exercises. This was before the Japanese attack at Pearl Harbor. America had not yet mobilized for full-scale war. An injury that would later be overlooked was still considered serious enough for the National Guard to classify Johnny 4F and to discharge him. He was sent home to Gallup.

In August of 1941, Johnny's old battalion came through on a troop train headed to a first posting in California. "I was disappointed and kind of jealous that I couldn't be going with them," he remembers. Then he adds, "They are the ones that wound up on the Philippine Islands. They are the ones who were captured and made to do the Bataan Death March. I was lucky, very lucky."

Johnny's comrades in the 200th Coast Guard Artillery Battalion were among the 75,000 American and Filipino troops taken prisoner when the Japanese overwhelmed the Philippines in the spring of 1942. Many did not survive the infamous 65-mile "death march" without food or water to prisoner of war camps on the Bataan Peninsula. Those who did survive spent the next three years and four months in torturous conditions as prisoners of war throughout the islands and then back in Japan itself. Nearly 12,000 Americans would die in captivity.[1]

Of the 1,816 soldiers in Johnny's battalion who marched off from New Mexico in 1941, only 947 would return.[Ibid] A full 46 percent would never make it home again. Indeed, Johnny was "lucky" on his first effort to join the war.

By 1943, when World War II was in full maelstrom, Johnny got a second chance to serve his country. Need for soldiers had grown enough by then that he was reclassified 1A and he immediately enlisted again, this time with the 8th Service Command, Military Police at Fort Bliss, Texas. Once again, he messed up.

While on training maneuvers in the rough country of West Texas, he became separated from his shirt. It was a blistering hot day in the Texas scrub land. Many of the soldiers had taken off their shirts while being trucked into the field for hardcore drill practice. As soon as the truck stopped, the command came to jump off. In the ensuing melee, Johnny left his shirt behind. It was a painful mistake.

The drills that day were practice advances across the rough landscape. Johnny recalls what ensued. "Every time we were ordered to hit the dirt and crawl, I landed on bushes filled with thorns. By the time we were done, I had thorns stuck deep inside the skin of my belly, chest, and legs."

To round things out, Johnny's top side had suffered equally to his underside. The hot sun had given him "a terrific sunburn" on his back. He spent a miserable night trying to pick the thorns out of his body and to get some rest without touching his back to the bed sheets. "This was not easy to do," he says with characteristic understatement. He spent most of the night sitting upright on his bunk attempting to doze. His second attempt to get into the military ended when he showed up for medical treatment the next morning. "I had to report to the first aid station. They sent me back to the field hospital. They sent me back to Fort Bliss where they again tried to get rid of me."

At Fort Bliss, he was informed that he would no longer be allowed to train for the military police. Instead of accepting a second discharge, he lobbied for and won a transfer to the 10th Mountain Division, Ski Troops. "After wrestling with thorns and getting burned to a crisp in the Texas desert, finding some snow to ski in sounded pretty good," he quips. Within days, he left the heat of the Texas scrub country for Fort Carson, Colorado, where his mission became to learn how to ski, snowshoe, and mountain climb.

Johnny was a scrappy young man with a low center of gravity so snowshoeing and mountain climbing came naturally. Skiing, however, was not a popular sport among the poor Indians of New Mexico in his day. He did not know a thing about it.

This was not an impediment to the Army's way of doing things. Johnny remembers how this way worked.

> They put us in a classroom and showed us a ski, the poles for balancing oneself, and the snap binding to release your boot so you wouldn't break your ankle. Then they said, 'Now you know how to ski.'

After that, they took us to the top of a mountain and told us to ski down. With my luck for hurting myself, I thought I was a goner for sure. Many of the guys got hurt. Some of them ended up going home again like I had almost done twice. But I was lucky this time and just got a few scratches and bruises from falling on the ground about every ten feet or so down that big mountain. It was the guys who hit trees that we didn't see again.

On this third attempt to become a soldier, Johnny was successful. As soon as training ended in Colorado, the 10th Mountain boys were loaded on a train bound for New York City. From there, they expected to ship out for Europe to fight Hitler's best. There were many jokes about ski vacations that year in the Alps, with a little hunting for Germans on the side. Spirits were high as they loaded into ships and began the trans-Atlantic crossing.

But the eager young troops were soon to get another lesson in the Army's way of doing things. They would not be going anytime soon to the Alps. They would not even land in Europe. It was to be a long and paradoxical voyage, one that would never involve ski equipment or skiing skill.

Johnny often uses the word "luck" when speaking of his wartime experiences, first in Europe, then in Korea, and finally in Vietnam. It undeniably is a good word for describing how he survived not one but three major American wars in a period of twenty-two years. As his story will show, his greatest luck came in surviving his first war. Indeed, he was lucky, as lucky as any young man in America or elsewhere who fought in the "Great War" and survived the experience.

We now know that 50 million people died in that one worldwide conflict. The Bataan Death March was an early sign of what was to come. In Dresden, Germany, north of where Johnny would soon end up fighting in hand-to-hand combat, 25,000 people would die in a single Allied firebombing of the city. In Japan, ten times this number would die from the testing of two atomic bombs. Tens of thousands more would die from the nuclear after-effects for generations to come. And, of course, there was the systematic genocide of European Jews and other "unfit" members of society by Hitler and the German people. It was a war in which all parties put aside humanity and devoted themselves to killing with great abandon.

After World War II, after Korea, and after Vietnam, it would be much harder for Indian veterans like Johnny to curse white Americans and Europeans for the horrors that they had visited upon Native Americans. In similar fashion to Whites in the American Civil War, Whites in Europe showed themselves willing to kill each other with great determination.

Few Americans are aware that Hitler drew upon the American treatment of minorities in his book *Mein Kamp* for building his own concentration camps for Jews and other "undesirables" in the lead up to World War II. Perhaps this omission from U.S. History books is of little consequence. Hitler could have found similar models of inhumanity throughout human history.

Johnny Pail Face was lucky to survive a world convulsed in slaughter and destruction in the 1940s. But his luck went beyond survival. He was equally fortunate to learn the lessons that the horrors of war would eventually teach him. They were painful lessons that would bring insight into the best and the worst in human nature.

More than anything, Johnny's war experiences would give him a new perspective from which to view his life as an Indian in America. He would have increasing difficulty to feel that history had been particularly unfair in his special case. This lesson would come most intensely at a place called Monte Cassino in Italy and during bloody fighting afterward along the Po River.

He would eventually return from war. He would come home a man feeling lucky to be alive and with time on his hands in a mental institution to think about what would come next.

CHAPTER 9

Baptism in Blood at Monte Cassino

THE TROOP SHIP CARRYING JOHNNY AND THE MEN of the 10th Mountain Division did not sail for England or for any other port in Europe. The Army sent it to North Africa, to the edge of the Sahara Desert. This was the Army way. It made sense to the military planners, of course. North Africa was the staging ground for invading Europe. Hitler and his allies were making it as difficult as they could for anyone hoping to put troops ashore in Europe.

It did not make sense to energetic young soldiers eager to ski down the Alps. When Johnny and his buddies walked off of the ship into the hot, dry North African desert with ski equipment piled high on their backs, they took a lot of ribbing from other soldiers. Never one to be mocked or teased, Johnny quickly put the issue to rest. He went AWOL. As he puts it, "I decided not to stick around. I took off and got on a fishing boat bound for Sicily. I was with a bunch of wild young soldiers looking to get drunk and fool around with strange women." The redeeming factor in this mass desertion was that the men were running towards the war.

Johnny recalls that the restless band eager for military action stopped for a few days in Palermo, Sicily. They had American dollars and all the optimism of youth in their favor. Sicily had only recently been liberated by the Allies, so the citizens of Palermo received the young Americans cheerfully and tolerated their drinking and carousing around.

Johnny remembers standing on the fishing docks and watching the Sicilian men come in with their catch. "The guys on the boats would hold up a fish, bite off its head, and swallow the body whole.

This looked kind of like fun to me. I was half drunk my whole stay on the island anyway, so I tried it."

"Oh, man, was that awful!" he laughs. "That fish wriggled all the way down to the bottom. I thought I was going to throw up. I finally managed to hold it down. I'll never do that again!"

After a few wild days in Palermo, Johnny's troupe got on another fishing boat and crossed the Mediterranean to Southern Italy. Once again on land, they set out on foot and were able to rejoin the 10th Mountain Division without much trouble. In the chaos of war, no one had time to interrogate them about where they had been or what they had been up to. They were back, and fighting troops were needed. That settled the issue.

"This is where the fun really started," Johnny recalls. "I mean this is where the fighting started for us." The 26th Infantry Division had been hard hit by losses and so the 10th Mountain troops were sent in as replacements for them. The good news for Johnny and his friends is that they were instructed to leave behind their skis, snowshoes, and other mountain gear. It was with relief that they learned that they would be fighting as regular infantry, not skiing down the Alps attempting to fire their guns, fight battles, and dodge trees as they went.

At this point, the Americans were marching up the boot of Italy towards an eventual invasion of the German homeland by way of Austria. They were being met with stiff resistance every step of the journey. At the Battle of San Pietro south of Rome in December of 1943, Johnny's battalion was held in reserve and missed the action.

After San Pietro fell in mid-December, Johnny and his comrades began the march to Monte Cassino, which was the next line of defense for the Germans. As they marched, Johnny remembers, "We came across some farm houses that had been abandoned, so we decided to have a look inside. In one, we discovered three barrels of wine that had been hidden away."

One of Johnny's comrades could not resist the sight of so much wine in one place. He announced that he was going to take a bath in one of the barrels. "He broke off one of the covers and climbed right in, uniform and all," Johnny recalls. "He started to drink it and pour it over his head with his helmet and got real crazy."

Johnny and the others helped themselves to some of the wine in another barrel and then the group moved on. But the incident did not end there.

"The trouble started after the second day that we were on the move. He started to smell real bad and he was having trouble walking. We had to stay upwind of him."

Fermenting wine absorbed into the man's uniform was having a bad effect on his skin. An ugly rash soon covered his body and infection set in. Before they reached Monte Cassino, they had to send him back to the field hospital. Little did Johnny suspect at the time that baptism in red wine would prove to be far less damaging than the baptism that he and other members of the 10th Mountain Division were about to undergo at Monte Cassino. It would be their first battle. They had been spared the most brutal reality of war to that point. That was about to change. Here is how Johnny remembers what happened next.

It was December, 1943, if I remember correctly. President Roosevelt had decreed that every serviceperson overseas should receive a Christmas dinner no matter where they were.

The Germans must have gotten this message too because they were aiming their guns at the big food trucks that were bringing the food to the men in the field. They must have wanted to discourage the Americans about ever getting their Christmas dinner.

I remember that one of the cooks came around with the turkey dinners. I was sitting in a hole with mud all around, cold and wet and thoroughly miserable, with tears in my eyes wishing that I was back home. There I was on Christmas, trying to eat my turkey while wiping the mud off of it. I was in such bad shape and wishing that I was back home that I suppose that was the reason I was crying so much.

They told us to get ready for the assault. I was afraid. I pissed in my pants. I shit in my pants. I had to sit in water to try to clean my pants after I'd dirtied them. This is a fact. I wasn't any kind of a brave warrior and I have to admit that I was really afraid.

There I was sitting at the base of the mountain of Monte Cassino, trying to figure out what was going to happen next, when we were given orders to go up and take it. The monastery up on top was being used by the Germans to spot for their artillery to land shells down on our troops.

We went up twice and were forced off twice, so the Air Force was called in and they destroyed the huge, huge monastery that had been there for hundreds of years, I suppose.

Then, for the last time, we went up with fixed bayonets and we mowed everything and everybody down as we went up that mountain.

I can't remember anything about it, really. To be honest with you, all I can remember was starting out up that mountain with fixed bayonets, and that's all. It was very difficult for me.

After having been forced back two or three times, I can't be sure how many, we must have fought our way to the top. I remember walking along a path up there and I thought that I must have gone through some mud because my feet were wet and my boots were squishing. They were going 'quirk, quirk, quirk' every time I took a step.

So, I sat down on a rock that had been one of the stones of the monastery and pulled off my boot and emptied it out. I found it was full of blood, liquid blood.

I got kind of scared and pulled off the other boot and it was the same thing, full of liquid blood.

I was very frightened by then, so I started stripping off my clothes to see where I had been wounded. My helmet, my hair, my whole body was covered with blood, and still today, after going to a psychiatrist to get this history, we could never, ever find out how I came to be covered in blood and not have a scratch on my body.

I was told that we lost 80 percent of our troops in the Monte Cassino fighting. I don't know. But I was still alive and I am thankful to the Lord Creator even though I was scared silly. I have always been afraid when something like this happens, but I guess one has to do what he has to do in order to survive.

The "huge, huge" monastery sitting atop Monte Cassino in the spring of 1944 was older than the "hundreds of years" that Johnny estimated. The first stones had been laid in 529 A. D., some 1,400 years before Johnny found himself pinned down by German artillery in its shadows.

It was the historic site at which St. Benedict had personally established his first retreat for monks and later for nuns. From its hallowed halls, Benedict set down the foundation for the entire monastic tradition in the Christian world with his guidebook to monastic life, *Benedictine Rule.* At his death, Saint Benedict was buried at Monte Cassino, as was his sister, Saint Scholastica. A chapel was built over their tombs. As the centuries went by, it grew into a vast rectangular monastery rising above the mountaintop and covering acres and acres of ground. Its stone walls were ten feet thick, creating a fortress intended to protect peace and spirituality.

Johnny's account of the numerous allied assaults to take Monte Cassino does not emphasize how much time and effort went into the various attempts to wrest control of the strategic site from the German occupiers. The first major attack came on January 20, 1944, and lasted nearly two weeks before the Allies pulled back.

One observer of the men who came down from Monte Cassino after this attack described the condition of the failed assailants.

It was more than the stubble of the beard that told the story; it was the blank, staring eyes. The men were so tired that it was a living death. They had come from such a depth of weariness that I wondered if they would quite be able to make the return to the lives and the thoughts they had known.[1]

And this was only the beginning.

Fearing that the Germans were using the sacred monastery as an observation site for their deadly artillery attacks, the Allies decided to wipe it off the face of the map. On the morning of February 15, they did just that. Two hundred twenty-nine American bombers dropped 1,150 tons of high explosives and firebombs on the monastery, turning the entire top of the mountain into a smoking ruin.

We now know that the monastery was empty except for a handful of monks and civilians when the Americans turned it to rubble. The German occupiers were sheltered in vast numbers of caves and bunkers down the hillsides below it. They had promised not to enter the structure itself out of respect for its spiritual significance and they kept that promise. A Catholic German officer, Lieutenant Colonel Julius Schlegel, took the precaution of moving some 1,400 priceless texts and manuscripts out of the monastery and to the Vatican in Rome prior to the start of the spring offensive. He knew that his countrymen were not going to give up the mountain without a terrible fight. His fear of what was to come was well founded. In the end, everything that he left behind in the monastery was destroyed.

The deeply dug-in German fortifications outside of the monastery meant that the destruction of the sacred site had little effect on the enemy defenders themselves. Furthermore, the Germans were regularly parachuting reserves in at night. During the second Allied assault, which came in the immediate aftermath of the intense bombing of the monastery, the Allies found the German defenses just as impenetrable as the first time that they had tested them. They fought for three intense days without reaching the smoldering ruins that they had made of the monastery. For a second time in two weeks, they were forced to retreat.

The Germans made their ferocious stand at Monte Cassino for an important tactical reason. Rome was a mere 80 miles away. The Germans knew that if Monte Cassino fell, they would never hold "The Eternal City." Without Rome, it would be inconceivable to keep Italy itself. Here lay the importance of Monte Cassino. More than any other strategic site, the war in Italy hinged on this one mountain.[2]

The Allied Forces again charged up Monte Cassino into the German lines on March 15. At that point, the Germans were entrenched in the rubble of the monastery and surrounding areas and fought more fiercely than ever. The Allies sustained the attack for ten bloody days and pulled back for a third time.

At this point, their commanders had a full sense of what would be required to take Monte Cassino. With the dreadful lessons learned from three failed assaults, they waited nearly two months before trying again. They used the time to gather strength and equipment and to launch a deceptive amphibious landing far up the coast of Italy to pull away as many German defenders as possible.

The fourth and final assault on Monte Cassino that ended with Johnny dazed and soaked in blood on the mountaintop began May 11, 1944. It involved some of the most savage hand-to-hand fighting of the war. Nearly 150,000 desperate men clashed in one of the most intensely personal and horrifically bloody battles of the modern era. Among the Allies were troops from the British Isles, India, Burma, Australia, New Zealand, Poland, France, Morocco, the United States, and Canada. On the German side were the Axis soldiers from Germany, Austria, and the occupied territories, including, of course, Italy. All of these peoples and cultures clashed in an orgy of violence that lasted seven brutal days. When daylight came on May 18, the Germans had finally fallen back, leaving Monte Cassino eerily quiet. They left behind only those comrades too seriously wounded to be moved.

On the allied side, Johnny ended that May afternoon sitting on a large piece of stone blasted from the wall of the former monastery inspecting himself. He was not wounded. It was the blood of others that covered his body. The scene around him has been well-documented in photos and film footage. The entire mountain had been reduced to a pockmarked moonscape. Scarcely a tree or bush remained standing for miles. Every building in the nearby town of Cassino had been flattened. The urge to kill that brought the two armies together had destroyed everything in its path—farm animals, wildlife, soldiers, civilian men, women, and children, even the vegetation of the earth.

Men like Johnny considered themselves lucky to be alive that day. Indeed they were. One hundred five thousand Allied soldiers fought in the four-month engagement. Fifty-four thousand were either dead or wounded, accounting for more than one out of every two Allied soldiers in the fray. Eighty thousand Germans had resisted the Allied advance. Twenty thousand were casualties of the fight. The civilian population of the region had been devastated.

And yet, in a testament to the resilience of the monastery, six monks who had taken refuge deep in its catacombs during the devastating bombing by the Allies survived to tell their stories of harrowing escape. The two founding Catholic saints of the monastery had their own story of resilience. The bones of both Benedict and his sister were disinterred from their many centuries of sleep beneath the monastery's original chapel by Allied bombs. But they came through the fray in fairly good condition and were reburied after the warring armies moved on.

However, their fortress devoted to peace and harmony, even with its ten-foot-thick walls and giant interlocking doors, had not been able to withstand the human urge to kill and to destroy. It was no more.[3]

And yet, in the final analysis, the Battle of Monte Cassino can be taken as a tribute on a grander scale to the resilience of the human spirit itself. It was the fourth time in its long history that the monastery had been destroyed. Within seven years, it was rebuilt a fourth time. The treasures that a German officer had taken pains to remove were returned. Today, to look at the magnificent monastery that sits again atop Monte Cassino, one would find it hard to believe that a generation ago it was reduced to a pile of stones.

The people who fought there in the spring of 1944 and lived to tell their stories were not as easily restored.

Johnny was not physically wounded in the final battle for Monte Cassino. The damage he suffered was all on the inside. After the war, he underwent a year of intensive rehabilitation and psychiatric counseling. Doctors tried every means available to get him to recall the suppressed memory of what he did to reach the top of that mountain. Even when put under hypnosis, Johnny's brain refused to reveal the events of the last day of fighting at Monte Cassino.

That day stands as another important milestone in the young man's life. He learned things about the darkness in the human soul that remain too terrible to think about to this day. So he does not think about them. As in the case of his father's passing, he kept a safe distance with death at Monte Cassino. He closed it up in a deep place that a year of intensive therapy could not unlock. And he went on with life.

What Johnny took away from his Monte Cassino experience was not what happened on the slopes of a mountain in Italy. Rather it was something that a psychiatrist said near the end of their post-war counseling sessions back home. "He told me that I did not have a conscience," Johnny recalls. "He said that if I ever got a conscience, I would surely kill myself. That troubled me for years. I knew that it was not right to live without a conscience."

Fortunately, there was one other important experience in his World War II battles that, with time and years of reflection, would eventually give Johnny hope for regaining moral and emotional footing. It came near the crossing of the Po River in Northern Italy, where the war ended for Private John Sarmiento of the 10th Mountain Division just one short week before the war ended for everyone else.

CHAPTER 10

Crossing the Po

AFTER HELPING TO TAKE MONTE CASSINO, Johnny and his comrades came back down the mountain and rejoined the rest of the 10th Mountain Division for much-needed rest. In the immediate aftermath of the battle, they were eager to forget what they had just experienced. "There were some good times and wine and relaxation, which were very welcome in that kind of situation," Johnny says.

Monte Cassino had been the strongest point in a line of defense that the Germans had established across the whole of Italy to prevent the Allies from advancing northward toward the German homeland. When the Axis defenders fell back, it was to yet another well-entrenched line of defense that likewise cut Italy in two, but this time in the North.

It took a full year, until the spring of 1945, before the Allied forces were ready to assault this final bastion of Germany's presence in Italy. During this time, Italy became a more minor front in a war that had spread as far as the South Pacific and into China. In Europe, much larger operations like the D-day landings at Normandy and the liberation of France took precedence.

By spring of 1945, the Germans occupying Italy had mastered the art of defense in the rugged, mountainous terrain in the heartland of the country. They had dug in deeply in three lines that would allow them to fall back as needed while launching withering counter-attacks on the advancing Allied forces. At the heart of these lines was the Po River. South of the Po was the important city of Bologna. To the north lay Verona, Padua, and Venice. If these cities could be taken, all of Italy would belong to the Allies.

By mid-April, Allied troops had broken through the first line of defense in the Apennine Mountains and were pushing under heavy fire toward Bologna. Johnny's 10th Mountain Division was in the thick of things, crashing through the German lines on the night of April 17. Johnny and his comrades raced through the breach, pursuing the Germans who were now racing the 50 miles to their next line at the Po River. In their first six miles of advance, the 10th Mountain fighters captured 2,900 prisoners.[1] During the ensuing seven days, the Allies would take 100,000 more fleeing Germans into custody in the midst of heavy fighting and with a constant stream of casualties on both sides.

It was in this melee of running skirmishes that Johnny had a second experience that has helped to frame much of his life in the many years since. After breaking through enemy lines, Johnny remembers, "We were starting to take a lot of German prisoners. It seemed like they were just kids in overgrown uniforms." After seven years of war, Germany had, indeed, begun to run out of manpower. Increasingly, any boy large enough to carry a weapon risked being fed into Adolf Hitler's war machine. And men like Johnny were facing them on the battlefront. Here is what Johnny recalls of one particularly intense encounter.

At one point the Germans counter-attacked and this German soldier came at me with a bayonet. The poor kid, I guess he didn't even know what to do with it. I shoved it aside and hit him under the chin with the butt of my rifle. I knocked him down and I started to stick him in the throat with my bayonet. I got within a quarter of an inch of his throat. And I stopped. I looked at his eyes and they were real, real big, and his blood had drained completely out of his face. He was just as white as a sheet. He had a little baby face that was very, very young.

I remember this distinctly and I'll never forget it. His arms were up behind him and he was lying on his back as I started to stick him, and all of a sudden something happened to me. I don't know what it was, but, as I looked at his face, those eyes, at that young kid who must have been about fourteen years old, who was completely scared to death, I just reached down and dragged him up by the collar and booted him in the ass and pointed him to get in behind the lines of prisoners that we had taken.

It's the first time I had ever felt sorry for anyone. He was such a young kid to be in that place.

Johnny recounted this story to me more than once during our year-long series of interviews to write this book. One afternoon near the end of our time together, I was probing into his feelings and insights concerning death. At that point I had a good overall view of his life story. One thing that impressed me most deeply was how intimately he had been acquainted with death again and again throughout his many years on Earth. From the loss of family members to his work in Mr. Ritchey's funeral home, to combat on the front lines of three major wars, he had come to know death in ways and on a scale that most human beings never approach.

However, the more I tried to pin Johnny down about what he had learned of death during his years on Earth, the more he seemed to want to avoid the topic. When we spoke of his father's death, he shifted the conversation to his mother's effort to have a deathbed marriage and to the day-to-day events of life after Old Juan was gone. When I asked specific questions about other experiences with death, Johnny continued to deflect my queries.

Finally, I asked him as directly as I could about what death had taught him. His response surprised me. He returned again to the story of the young German soldier who he had spared at the last instant from the blade of his bayonet. But this time, he added something to the story.

"Why?" he asked quietly after finishing the account. "Why did I do that? Was I getting tired?" Then there was a pause. "Was I becoming a human being?" Another pause. "Tell me, J. J. Why?"

At that point, his voice caught and tears filled his eyes. After a moment, he cleared his throat and, in a husky voice, he said, "Ahh, damn, you're bringing back a lot of memories, my buddy." This was followed by an especially long silence that I chose not to interrupt despite my growing inclination to do so.

I've played back again and again his words that day that are captured on my interview recorder. Something important happened in the long silences between his words. Something that had not before been included in his life story surfaced. Right before my eyes and with the recorder running, Johnny opened up and let a detail emerge that perhaps even he did not know was there, at least not in a conscious sense.

After a seemingly interminable pause, he said with surprise in his voice, "I became a human being all of a sudden."

There was another long pause and the insight ends with Johnny heaving a big sigh and saying, "Enough of this bullshit."

This time I let him off the hook. It did not feel right to push any further into his troubled inner landscape. On the recorder, you can hear me chuckle at his choice of words and assure him that this is the very kind of "bullshit" that most people would most like to hear in his story. Then our conversation turns toward lighter things as we wrap up for the day.

Johnny's humanity toward the young German soldier offers a counterpoint to the horror of what happened to him at Monte Cassino. It is important to note that the word "genocide" was not yet in Johnny's vocabulary in any of the three languages that he spoke at that time of his life. In fact, the word was being created at the very time that he was experiencing his second brush with it. Just as Johnny joined the Italian Campaign against Hitler in 1944, Raphael Lemkin, a Polish Jewish lawyer, developed the word genocide to describe the systematic mass murder of peoples the Germans considered "undesirable." Geno comes from the Greek for "race or tribe," and cide is Latin for "killing." The following year, the new word was popularized by the International Military Tribunal as it prosecuted German leaders for crimes against humanity.[2]

With no word to describe genocide, Johnny had very limited ways to make sense of what began to happen in his life with the sparing of the young German soldier. Over six decades later as we worked together to put his story in book form, Old Johnny was still grappling with what that act of kindness meant. It is an intense event that the fourteen-year-old German boy surely carried in his memory to the end of his days. It is the same for Johnny.

These days, genocide has become a thriving field of academic study in which scholars devote their life's work to understanding this extreme form of human behavior.

"Dehumanization" is a key concept at the core of genocidal behavior. One group must dehumanize another group to the point that it becomes psychologically acceptable, even desirable, to eliminate every member of the target group from the face of the earth. In his book *Less Than Human*, Dr. David Livingston Smith sums up what coincidentally happen to be Johnny's encounters with genocide to answer a fundamental question about the effects of dehumanization. Smith frames the issue this way:

> *When European colonists dehumanized Native Americans or Nazis dehumanized Jews, what remained? In their eyes, what was left was a creature that seemed human, had a human looking form, walked on two legs, spoke human language, and acted in more-or-less human ways—but which was nonetheless not human...where it really counts, they [weren't] human at all...They were regarded as insidiously subhuman.*[3]

Smith then makes the link to the acts that become possible once dehumanization has done its ugly work.

> *Dehumanization isn't a way of talking. It's a way of thinking—a way of thinking that, sadly, comes all too easily to us. Dehumanization is a scourge, and has been for millennia. It acts as a psychological lubricant, dissolving our inhibitions and inflaming our destructive passions. As such, it empowers us to perform acts that would, under other circumstances, be unthinkable.*[4]

Smith illustrates how "unthinkable" such acts can become by describing the broad lines of World War II, which he labels "the single most destructive event in human history."

> *More than 70 million people died in the war, most of them civilians. Millions died in combat. Many were burned alive by incendiary bombs and, in the end, nuclear weapons. Millions more were victims of systematic genocide. Dehumanization made much of this carnage possible.*[5]

Johnny Pail Face does not need to read Smith's book. He has lived it. His mother's shame-filled eyes in the presence of white people were the first pages that he had turned to find the same insights. The "No Dogs and No Indians Allowed" signs on businesses in his youth were his primer on dehumanization. He had joined the military in part to escape being treated in such ways. And the military took him into the heart of a storm of dehumanization that left 70 million dead in its wake.

To Smith's list of how people died in the war, Johnny could make a personal addition. Many also died from bayonet and gunshot wounds. He knows because he was the one holding the weapon. In an unguarded moment one afternoon I asked him how many people he had killed in the war. The question popped out of my mouth during one of his war stories before I had time to think about or to censor it. I held my breath in the silence that ensued.

He began rubbing his eyes and face as if a great fatigue had taken sudden hold of him. He ran a hand through his white, unruly hair and gave a deep sigh. "I don't know, J. J.," he said. He shook his head. "I can't remember that. If I ever start remembering that…and his voice trailed off.

It was then that I began to understand more fully the one story that Johnny did remember often. I began to see why he clung to the story of the German boy he had saved as one might hold to a life preserver on a dark night at sea with a storm raging all around. He never tired of the retelling. He mined that story again and again, adding detail, pausing to reflect, asking questions of me about it. In the end, it became clear to us both. Not only did Johnny save the young German's life; the young German saved Johnny's life in return. It just took years for it to happen.

When I wrapped up my interviews with Old Johnny, I had come to understand how deep the hole was that he had fallen into as an American Indian who marched off to fight Hitler. Outsiders dehumanized Johnny and his people in the Native American genocide. Johnny dehumanized himself in the fight to stop Hitler. He did things so terrible to get to the top of Monte Cassino that his brain refuses to remember them to this day. He continued to do these horrific things day after day for another full year of his life. After winning against the Germans, Johnny came home to spend a year in a mental institution. This is why he would later say to me of the two genocides, "I don't know which fight wounded me worse." Losing a genocide left him crazy with anger at what others had done to him.

Winning a genocide left him crazy with despair at what he had done to others. And to himself.

A baby-faced soldier became the life-line that pulled him up and out of that bottomless hole. That one generous act, more than anything else, revealed to him the path out of the soul-chilling dehumanization that had buffeted his life. In it he took hope of finding his own humanity.

Although Johnny could not know it at the time, his kindness to the young German came at the start of his last week in the war. It not only provides a bookend to his combat experience in Europe, it represents the turning point of his life away from the darkest side of the human story toward a brighter side. It promised to be a long and uncertain journey. In the days that followed his capture of the young German, the Allies pressed forward quickly to catch the fleeing Axis troops before they could reach their second line of defense and regroup. Johnny's battalion was among the first to reach the large Po River. Whatever bridges the Germans had not already knocked out had been destroyed by the American and British bombers as they wrought havoc on the retreating Germans.

Within two days, the Army engineers would have operational bridges up and running for the heavy equipment to cross. But the 10th Mountaineers were ordered to cross immediately on light boats and to take out the German artillery and machine gun emplacements so that the engineers could do their work. Johnny recounts what happened next.[6]

> *When we got to the Po, our artillery was pounding the village on the other side to drive back the Germans who were defending it. We were supposed to cross the river in rafts and take it after the shelling had ceased.*
>
> *Well, this commander of ours was some kind of hot shot, so he told us to get on the rafts to cross the river even though the shells were still exploding on the other side.*
>
> *We got across okay. When we were about 150 or 200 yards up the other side, I heard this shell coming over and it was a short round. I knew it was a short round by the sound of it. It's easy to detect*

because they whistle when they go over and they go 'thump, thump,' when they are ready to fall. This one was about ready to come down.

I saw this tree lying on the ground. I dove down beside it and tried to dig my way under it to protect myself. I must have hit my left elbow on a branch or a knot and I raised it from the electric shock. Just at the same time that round exploded on the other side of the tree.

I found that I was hit by shrapnel all over my left arm. It was still together, but it was all cut and part of my elbow was gone.

I didn't know what to do, but I turned back towards the river and I put on a tourniquet as best I could. I took out of my pouch a syringe of morphine and gave myself an injection to counter the pain.

Then I took off my pack, removed the bolt from my rifle, and threw it into the river, leaving the rifle behind.

I hit the river and swam back to the other side.

There were a lot of troops still there and the medics picked me up, and I wound up in a field hospital. After a couple of days, I was transferred to a hospital in Rome, and I stayed there for a long time until I was stabilized, and then they put me on a plane and sent me back home.

There they sent me to the hospital nearest my home, which was in Santa Fe, New Mexico.

Johnny's luck had run out at a most unfortunate time. He was wounded by "friendly fire" from his own artillery on the afternoon of April 24, shortly after the first wave of 10th Mountain fighters crossed the Po River in M-2 assault boats. By the next morning, the entire division was across the river and a full-scale route of the Germans was underway. Six days later, while Johnny lay in a hospital bed in Rome, the war came to an end for Johnny's comrades still in the field. The last of the Axis forces in Italy ceased major combat operations on April 30, and on May 3 the German representative, Lt. Gen. Fridolin von Senger und Etterlin, formally handed over control of all Axis forces to U.S. General Mark W. Clark at Caserta, Italy. Before Johnny could even complete his journey home, the entire war in Europe ended, with VE Day celebrated on May 8, 1945, throughout the Allied nations.

As happy and relieved as Johnny was to return home and to learn of the war's end, he found little cause for celebration back home. His homecoming wounded him almost as much as the war itself had done.

*Johnny (on right) and a friend share a drink at the
enlisted men's club, Frankfort, Germany, 1952.*

Part Two

A Prayer Looking to the South

Oh my Lord, Creator in the South, where the sun never sets and everything grows, please help me by letting me grow in Eye Sight and Hearing, so I can hear and see the beauty you have created. Let me grow in Courage to be able to fight the battles that come before me. Let me grow in strength—not to be greater than my brother, but to fight my greatest enemy, Myself. Please let me grow in Wisdom, so I can pass it on to others. Thank you.

You Can Never Go Home Again

I was full of hatred because I did not understand civilization
at that time. I only lived to get even.

As soon as Johnny was back on American soil, his first priority was to see his mother. Once he was settled into the Bruns General Hospital in Santa Fe, he requested leave to return to Gallup.

It was dusk when Johnny arrived at his mother's house. The place was dark and the front door unlocked. He entered to find the home empty of furnishings. There was dust everywhere. A close family friend who Johnny's mother had helped raise after her children were mostly grown still lived in the neighborhood. His name was Steve and he had married a woman by the name of Rita. Johnny walked to Steve and Rita's house to find out what had become of his mother. Steve met him at the door and welcomed his wounded friend home warmly. When the subject turned to Johnny's mother, Steve's face darkened.

"Didn't they tell you?" he asked in surprise. "Your mother is dead. She died over a year ago. And your sister has moved away." Then he added, "Do you want a drink?"

Johnny did.

He then returned to the hospital in Santa Fe where he stayed for a year.

This detail of his story came out near the end of a long afternoon interview session and my mind was not a sharp as it could have been. "A year? A full year?" I responded, "Goodness, how badly damaged was your arm?"

He looked at me for a moment and then replied with a shake of his head.

I wasn't there for my arm. I was there for shell shock. My head was messed up by the war. At the end, the Germans had nothing but children to fight us with. When a kid with a too-big uniform attacks you with a bayonet you…you . . in the end you can't bring yourself to kill them anymore. And then you come home. Your mother's dead and no one bothered to tell you. I spent a year at the hospital trying to sort all that out.

There was another thing Johnny had to work on during his year at the hospital. It was something as troubling as his mother's death, troubling enough that he would later choose to go back to Europe, back to the very heart of enemy territory in Germany. Johnny came home from Europe a victor.

Like other G.I.s, he was an American hero. He was a winner. As an Indian, this was a most unusual turn of events. It gave him a strange, new perspective to grapple with. In Europe, he had seen white people do to other white people the same things that the Whites had done to his red ancestors. They had even done it on a grander and bloodier scale than his own people had experienced. Whites had killed Whites. Christians had slaughtered Christians. Children, mothers, old people—no one had been spared.

And he had been part of the conquering army. This time around, he had been the victor, not the victim. In the process, he had learned things about himself that he wasn't sure he wanted or needed to know. He had learned early in life to hate being the victim; it was not clear to him how being the victor was significantly better.

Johnny describes his recovery at Bruns General Hospital as "little by little, little by little." One of the first things from his old life that he picked up again was the desire to be educated. Following the example of his old friend and teacher Mr. Ritchey, he sent off to the University of Maryland for more correspondence courses. This time, he enrolled in the high school equivalency curriculum. During the year spent at the hospital, he was able to earn his high school diploma.

After several months of sitting around with little to do but eat, sleep, do therapy, and study, he "conned" the doctors into letting him out during the daytime on work release. Falling back on familiar skills, he quickly found a part time job at the nearby New Methods Cleaners. He had learned how to clean, press, and even alter clothing during the years that he had worked for Mr. Flores before the war. That all seemed a lifetime away for the recovering soldier, but he had retained what Mr. Flores had taught him.

Johnny also took up again other less savory habits from his past. He remembers, "As I started to get better, and I now had a little money to spend from my earnings at the cleaners and my Army pay, I started to jump the fence at night and go out on the town to drink and raise hell."

Johnny is quick to make clear that he was not a pleasant young man to be around at this time in his life. He was not inclined to sit around a hospital and ponder deep thoughts about the paradoxical nature of human existence. He was bitter, lonely, frustrated, full of hatred, and seething with anger. As a newly-minted war hero, what he really wanted was to get drunk—as often as possible and for as long as possible. And to cause trouble before he passed out.

Johnny's hell-raising included getting a young Hispanic girl pregnant. That put him in an uncomfortable position. She was underage. Her Catholic father gave the young man an ultimatum. He could either marry the girl to save her and her family the dishonor of an illegitimate birth, or he could go to jail. "I married her," Johnny says.

The marriage took place in late 1945. Shortly after, Johnny was discharged from the hospital and moved back to Gallup with his young bride. Mr. Flores was pleased to welcome the young veteran back to a full time job at the Deluxe Cleaners.

After about three months in Gallup, Johnny returned home from work one day to find his young wife gone. Johnny recalls:

She left me, filed for divorce, and got $25 a month for child support. The only reason she married me was to give the baby my name. It was born a girl and given the name Lorraine. I was forbidden to ever come to Santa Fe to see her.

So I stayed in Gallup and became a terrible drunk and just raised hell.

These days when Johnny does his morning prayers, there is a key line in his "Prayer to the South" that describes his greatest struggle after returning from World War II. The line reads: *Let me grow in strength—not to be greater than my brother, but to fight my greatest enemy, Myself.* In 1946, Johnny was his own greatest enemy. At the core of this inner conflict was a weakness that has long haunted his people in Navajo country—alcohol.

"I never felt good enough," Johnny explains. "When I was sober, I was introverted and quiet. I only felt equal to or even superior to others when I was drinking."

Paradoxically, at the same time that alcohol offered Johnny a temporary sense of equality, it served as a primary reminder of his inferior status in society. As he puts it, "I hated being an Indian because I couldn't buy alcohol unless I could convince bartenders that I was Italian or Mexican." His years in the military defending his country on the front lines made this old insult more difficult to bear. And so the vicious circle of alcohol went round and round, alternately assuaging and refueling Johnny's anger and his willingness to "raise hell."

If Johnny was fighting his own "greatest enemy" within during the years after World War II, he was also going through a period of "growth." By age 30, many bad seeds had been planted inside of him. It seemed as if the bad seeds had to grow into plants and be pulled out before good seeds could be put into their places.

One of these bad seeds was his love for Virginia. "I found my old girlfriend, Virginia, with whom I was still very miserably in love," he remembers, "and my hell started all over again. And this is how I spent 1946—drunk, working at the cleaners, and living with Virginia. I didn't even know when my little daughter Lorraine was born in Santa Fe I was so far gone."

In 1947 the Army reduced Johnny's disability income drastically. Cutting soldiers off from disability money helped to balance the government's budget. In Johnny's case, it was not a sign that he was better. At the same time that the Army cut his compensation down by 90 percent, "my arm, the muscles of my left arm, had dried up and it was nothing but skin and bone down to the fingers."

Fortunately, he met an elderly lady in his interactions at the dry cleaners who prescribed a regimen to regain use of the arm. She instructed him to get a rubber ball to squeeze and for him to squeeze it constantly throughout the day. "She said to use my other hand to move the fingers around if I couldn't squeeze the ball with my left hand at first. My arm began to grow stronger with this exercise."

A further difficulty was that Johnny was no longer able to bend the elbow to straighten his arm. For this, "she said I should carry some weight around all the time. So I got a little kid's toy bucket and I filled it up with sand. Wherever I went, I carried this little bucket, and when I sat down, I would squeeze a rubber ball."

Following the old woman's "ball and bucket therapy," Johnny was eventually able to accomplish what the doctors in Santa Fe had not. He sums up, "I managed to get pretty good strength and movement back in my left arm." Just as it fell to Johnny in the end to heal himself physically, the same held true for healing his emotional and psychological self.

To move forward emotionally, Johnny proposed marriage to Virginia. She accepted. Once again he found himself with a little family that included her son Raymond, who was now entering his teen years. As a husband and stepfather, Johnny needed more money to care properly for a new family.

The military had provided a decent livelihood for him before his discharge. The military also gave other things that he liked. It took him away from the chaos and bad memories that surrounded him in Gallup. It was a place where he was treated more equally to his fellow man. The Army had never told him that he could not drink alcohol with his buddies or that he wasn't as good a soldier as men with lighter skin color.

After his marriage to Virginia, Johnny turned again to the military to improve his position in life. Despite his withered arm, it worked. "Would you believe that they allowed me to get a waiver from my reduced disability and to re-enlist?" he chuckles.

His re-enlistment strategy had shrewdly targeted the Air Force. "The Army Air Corps had been converted to the United States Air

Force and they were pretty hard up for recruits. They would take just about anyone for this new Air Force."

Johnny remembers specifically an incident one evening when he was out with new soldier buddies drinking beer at the enlisted men's club. He was at Kirtland Air Base in Albuquerque, New Mexico, for his induction and processing of papers. As the new soldiers were standing there looking at a large flag display along one wall of the club, one of Johnny's comrades said, "Hey, look! That's the Russian flag."

Then Johnny remembers, "We all started walking away, but he just stood there scratching his head. Finally he said, 'Hey fellas, that's not the Russian flag. It's the American flag!'"

Johnny sums up, "That's the kind of guys they were letting into the Air Force. Guys like that, and cripples like me."

From Albuquerque, Johnny was sent to Lackland Air Force Base in San Antonio, Texas, for three months of basic training. Johnny's arm had healed enough that, with a lot of hard work, he was able to keep up with the other soldiers and to successfully complete the 90-day training camp. "It was pretty tough," he remembers. It was hard to keep up with the gang when you had gotten soft. It was really, really hard."

Three years after coming home from the war wounded and suffering from what we now label post traumatic stress disorder (PTSD), Johnny was back in uniform. But it was not destined to last.

Before his next assignment, Johnny received 30 days of leave. "I took the train back to Gallup, in uniform now. I was in khakis because it was summer. I was feeling like a big man."

He spent the month with Virginia, who was receiving his military allotment check each month so that she could make ends meet. As soon as he set foot back in Gallup, Johnny returned to his old habits. "I started raising hell, getting drunk again," he recalls with a shake of his head.

Then he was off to Tinker Air Force Base in Oklahoma City for courses to educate him for his new duties. There, his return to military service was brought up short when he reinjured his arm. It was a discouraging turn of events for the young man struggling to return to a productive life after the Big War. "I was discharged and sent back to Gallup, with nothing," he remembers.

However, he kept something from the short-lived Air Force experience. "When I was at school at Tinker A.F.B., I got hooked on education again." As soon as he was settled in Gallup with Virginia and Raymond, Johnny applied for his high school diploma from the New Mexico State Board of Education. He supplied administrators there with his high school correspondence course scores and they awarded him an official diploma.

With this in hand, he applied to the U.S. Government for G. I. Bill money to begin university studies. He received the G. I. Bill and was accepted to study Mining Engineering at Oklahoma Agricultural and Mechanical College in Stillwater. When Johnny walked into a classroom at Oklahoma A. & M. College in the fall of 1948, it was a huge first in the young man's life. As a young person reared in Navajo country, he had never before set foot in a school classroom. It was the first time he had seen one. He was 32 years old.

As one may expect, Johnny's tenure at Oklahoma A. & M. did not last long. "I just didn't have the math skills, the calculus, to become a mining engineer. It was not something that you could slip through quickly," he says. As much as his years under Mr. Ritchey's tutelage and then his own study while at Bruns General Hospital had helped him to pick up a broad education, his knowledge of math remained rudimentary. But all was not lost for the aspiring scholar.

Johnny's academic advisors at Oklahoma asked him if he might like to study weather instead. It was a field with much demand and required less math than engineering. Johnny did not want to waste his G. I. Bill monies. When he told his advisors that he wanted an education no matter what, they helped him transfer to Pennsylvania State University. There he entered a booming new program in Weather Forecasting. "Friends teased me about doing Indian rain dances and stuff," he says, "but that did not bother me. I was going to become a man with a college degree. Boy, would my mother have been proud of that. I was going to make it in the world of the white-eyes. That's what I focused on."

Things moved fast for Johnny at this point. A year later, he graduated with a degree in Weather Forecasting and was hired as a civilian employee at the Weather Analysis Center at the Pentagon in Washington, D. C. A young man who had not worn shoes until he was a teenager and who had never set foot in a school until he went to college, suddenly found himself surrounded by the bustling professional world of educated society in the American Capitol. With understatement, Johnny sums up, "It was a real nice experience."

Johnny teamed up with a couple of chums from weather school and rented a house in Washington as they all jumped into new careers at the Pentagon. Johnny recalls, "I was on the fifth floor of D Ring working in the United States Weather Bureau. We were making and plotting weather maps. We didn't have all those highfalluting satellites and radars that they have today."

As much as Johnny's quality of life was undergoing radical changes as he moved into the world of educated professionals, some things did not change nearly so quickly. His love of alcohol remained at the center of his new life. He remembers, "So here I was, working, raising hell, getting drunk, and partying in Washington D. C."

His wife Virginia was keen to become part of her husband's new life. In letters and phone calls she began to pressure Johnny to bring her to the big city to be with him. After a few months, he relented. She arrived in Washington with her son Raymond, and they found a house together in Arlington, Virginia, that was close enough for Johnny to commute to work each day.

About this time, the government decided to transfer the Weather Analysis Center out of the Pentagon and to move it to Andrews Air Force Base in Maryland. While Johnny's coworkers were all preparing for the move, an unusual offer came his way that would deeply alter his career and life path. For the first time, his personal history in the margins of America yielded something that the mainstream valued.

Johnny's supervisors at the Weather Bureau noted in his military papers that the young man could speak Spanish. Based upon this mention of Spanish, they called Johnny in and offered him a special assignment to go to Teguicigalpa, Honduras, for a year or so where his job would be to translate U.S. weather training manuals into Spanish for the Honduran Air Force.

As he thinks about this daunting assignment, Johnny confesses, "I indicated on my service records that I could speak Spanish because I used to speak a little with the Mexican kids in Gallup when I was a little boy, but I couldn't read or write it." He had communicated with his father in a mixed patois of Spanish, Navajo, and English up until Old Juan died, and he used the language to buy white lightning from the Spanish farmers who made it. This did not add up to the kind of fluent, written Spanish of weather textbooks.

However, never one to turn away from adventure, Johnny recalls, "I said to myself, 'Oh my God, how am I going to do this?'" But to them I said, 'I accept!'"

Virginia did not agree with Johnny's decision and a big fight ensued. Johnny prevailed and sent her and Raymond back to New Mexico while he prepared for his posting south to Honduras.

Virginia had once again reached her breaking point. Once settled back into life in Gallup, she filed for divorce. Johnny knew that he had been treating her unfairly for a long time. He knew that his drinking and wild life was not good for her or for Raymond. He did not contest the divorce and for a second time they separated and moved on with their lives. He heard later that she married again and moved to California. She left no relatives or close friends in Gallup and he lost contact with her.

"I hope her life turned out better than I was able to give her at that time," Johnny says now. "I hope Raymond found a good life. They both deserved better than me. I was a mess in those days. Virginia was a saint to stay with me as long as she did."

Alone again in Washington, the first thing Johnny did was to move into a small apartment in a guest house. Next, he went out of his way to get to know a number of Honduran diplomats and embassy people who lived in the same residence where he was staying. Through them, he gained membership in the Organization of American States, which allowed him to attend parties and social events with a wide variety of Latin American groups in Washington.

It was a period of great freedom and adventure for a young, hard-drinking man in his early thirties who wanted to cut loose. "Washington, at that time," he says, "had eight women for every man, plenty of single women working in the offices, so we had our pick whenever we wanted to go out and have some fun."

As Johnny looks back from the safety and calm of old age, he is able to see that his days of hard drinking and "fun" in Washington were important survival strategies for a young man struggling mightily with dark and deadly currents inside. These currents pushed most powerfully to the surface on his regular trips back home to New Mexico to be with his family.

> *As I would cross the Oklahoma border and head back into Indian Country, my stomach muscles would begin to tighten. I would start to feel like I was going to throw up. In the pit of my stomach was nothing but hatred and anger.*
>
> *I'd stop for gas and some redneck would come out to fill the tank and to wash the windows. I was driving a nice, shiny new car. I was dressed in expensive clothes. And I was an Indian. I'd watch his face for a sneer of disrespect. I'd wait for him to say something.*
>
> *If he didn't try to put me down, I'd begin to taunt him. I'd ask if he liked my car. I'd point out a new feature of the car that was just added to this latest model. I'd ask him to check the tire pressure because I wanted the smoothest ride I could get on these rough roads.*
>
> *I would never insult him. Instead, I'd rub his white nose in my success any way that I could. That was the way I operated.*

Johnny's struggles intensified when he reached Gallup. There he would have to face some of the very people who had tormented him and others like him the most. There is one incident that brought him particular satisfaction.

> *One day I walked into the court house to see if I could find any of the old gang that I knew. They used to work there as janitors and so forth. I looked around and couldn't find any of them, but as I was walking around, I noticed that the sheriff's office was open. So I went in. The sheriff was sitting there. I greeted him by his first name and asked how he was doing.*
>
> *He looked up at me and said 'What the hell do you want?'*

'Not a thing,' I answered. 'I just come in to see some friends. Why do you ask?'

'Every time one of you comes in here it's because you need something or you want something,'

'No,' I said. 'No, I don't need anything. I've got a good job. I've got a good car. I've got good clothes. I don't need anything, but I'll tell you what…'

And he says 'What? What?'

'If I ever need anything, believe me, you'll be the first one I come to see.' And then I turned around and walked away.

Anyone born into a world similar to that of Johnny Pail Face will understand what he was up to with the sheriff. He was making himself equal to a man who was in a position to make him pay for such an affront. So he did it in a way so that the sheriff would not immediately see the affront. He did it in a way that the man would have to think about it. He'd have to puzzle through why Johnny's visit had rubbed him the wrong way when Johnny had done nothing but say pleasant things and show respect for his power.

In the end, what was little more than a puzzling exchange of words for the sheriff of Gallup was perhaps the closest Johnny ever came to reclaiming a sense of dignity and self-respect in his home town. They were shallow victories, made emptier by the broken lives, alcoholism, poverty, violence, and self-destruction that Johnny revisited each time that he found old friends and caught up on their lives. Such were the things that made it harder and harder for Johnny to return to Gallup and easier to leave at the end of each visit.

Back in Washington in the late 1940s, Johnny did his best to forget his Navajo roots in New Mexico. He drank hard. He chased after attractive women. He lived a carefree life on the surface. But the wild life of Washington did not have a deep hold on him. When the opportunity came to take on a special assignment in Honduras, he snapped it up eagerly.

In 1949, he turned his attention to the Honduras assignment. Foremost on his mind was how he was going to translate hundreds and hundreds of pages of weather manuals into a language he had never learned properly and had not used for any extended amount of time in years. He had only one thing to go on: "I really couldn't read or write much Spanish, but I had a letter from Dr. Salas to his mother who could help me get situated down there." Dr. Salas was a Honduran diplomat who Johnny had befriended in Washington. He assured Johnny that his mother had lots of connections in Tegucigalpa who could help his work move forward.

With a letter of introduction from a son and from other Honduran friends, Johnny stepped off the plane in the capital of Honduras at the end of the 1940s and entered a new world where his early childhood skills at crossing cultures and creating a new world would, once again, be put to the test.

Chapter 12

South of the Border

JOHNNY'S BEST PREPARATION FOR ADAPTING TO THE WORLD of Honduras turned out to be the letters of introduction from Honduran friends. Johnny immediately found himself right in "with the cream of the crop" in Honduran society. The families of his friends in Washington "were all high up on the social and financial ladder of Honduras," which is why they had family members in Washington, D. C. representing their country's interests.

The first place that he went was to the home of Dr. Salas' mother. At first, she welcomed him warmly. Johnny had a lot of gifts to deliver to families of his friends and contacts back in Washington. It did not occur to him that this could cause social upheaval in Tegucigalpa, but it soon did. When he asked for directions to the family residences on his list, Mrs. Salas was most gracious in offering him the use of her car and chauffeur to make the deliveries.

The first friend back in Washington for whom he decided to make the house call was a fellow who had darker skin and curly hair. It did not occur to Johnny that the man's African heritage might make a difference to the upper social classes in Honduras. It did.

When Johnny directed the chauffeur to his family's residence, the chauffeur "made a sour face, but he drove me there anyway." From what he observed of the neighborhood, Johnny soon concluded that the man's family lived on "the poor side of town." Johnny was well-received by the family and delivered their gifts. Then he left with the chauffeur and did not think any more of the incident. Until the next day.

When he rose in the morning, he discovered that "Mrs. Salas seemed very cold to me and did not even speak to me. Her chauffeur was acting strangely too."

As he prepared to make another gift delivery, he elected to choose a taxi. This time he went to the home of the mother of another Washington friend, a fellow named Degas. Mrs. Degas' home was in another affluent part of town. As he was having coffee with her, he brought up the change of mood at the Salas home and asked what might be going on.

Mrs. Degas put her finger on things very quickly. She explained that families with the high class standing of the Salases "have to maintain a certain standard" of public behavior at all times. It was a violation of this Honduran code of etiquette for the Salas family car even to be seen on the bad side of town. Apparently Mrs. Salas was feeling that she had made a mistake to invite such a person into her home who would have dealings with the lower classes.

Mrs. Degas showed herself to be of a different cut of cloth. She immediately invited the young American to be a guest in her home. "You can take my son's place and live in his room," she said. "You can be my son."

Johnny accepted her generous offer. They sent a taxi to the Salas residence to collect his things. Mrs. Salas did not protest his departure.

However, it did not take long for cultural conflict to erupt again. Soon the Degas' household erupted because of Johnny.

After he had been a guest there for a week or so, he came home one day to find Mrs. Degas in tears. He asked what was wrong.

"My whole household is quitting on me," she blurted out. All of her hired help had given the standard two-week notice that they would be leaving her employ.

Johnny instantly suspected that he might be at the center of the upheaval. "Wait a minute," he told his landlady and hostess. "Let's do something about this. Let's find out what this is all about. They can't just be leaving for no reason. Can you get everybody together?"

Mrs. Degas seemed relieved to call everyone together. Johnny recalls what happened next.

We got everybody together in the big living room and we sat down to find out what this was all about.

Well, needless to say, I had been right. It was me. I was causing everyone trouble.

The first one to complain was the maid, who I would always tease and try to grab her ass when she came in to make up my room. She was afraid to go into my room because she thought I would try to seduce her.

The butler was upset that I would fix my own drink and not ask him to do anything for me.

The valet was hurt because I would fold and hang up my own clothes and generally keep my own room neat and picked up. He didn't have anything to do and he felt that he was not earning his pay.

The cook was upset because I would go into the kitchen and use her knives and utensils to fix my own sandwich, and I would just leave her things there on the counter when I was done. She said if I wanted anything, all I had to do was ask for it and she would do it for me.

Man, it was a big mess.

Indeed, it was the sort of "mess" that one might expect a poor Navajo boy from a wild west Indian reservation to create on his first foray into the heart of an upper-class world of privilege. It was Johnny's characteristic boldness that got him through the incident. In his best Spanish, which had come back quickly with his immersion in a Spanish-speaking world, he took his turn at speaking.

I stood up at the table there and said, 'Look, I'm not one of Mrs. Degas' class. I'm one of your class. I have brought myself up from a real poor, poverty-level family and I am not of the social standing of Mrs. Degas. I will not bother any of you again, if you will just cope with me. Please do not leave Mrs. Degas.

Johnny's plea proved to be persuasive. The staff agreed to stay on with the condition that he would behave himself and stop acting like he was still poor and backward.

In the days that followed, Johnny worked out a cultural compromise with them. When there were guests in the house, the house staff would treat him with the respect due someone of high social standing. In the absence of guests or special functions, Johnny "would be just like one of them."

Soon things were working smoothly on the domestic front. "It got to the point where I could have a sandwich with the cook and the housekeeper, and whenever Mrs. Degas had a party with her friends, I became her distinguished guest, one of the family. Otherwise I was like one of the help."

With home life in order, Johnny was ready to turn his attention to his big challenge in Honduras—translating voluminous weather manuals into Spanish for the country's Air Force. His friendship with Mrs. Degas and his own entrepreneurial spirit helped him move forward quickly.

Mrs. Degas introduced him to a language professor at the main university in the city who was skilled at English/Spanish translation. Johnny was receiving $25 a day from Washington to cover his meals and lodging. Because he was a guest at the Degas home, he was lucky to spend $5 a day of this money. This gave him a source of cash for paying the translator to help him get the weather manuals written up in Spanish.

"It was the greatest thing," Johnny recalls. "We completed the entire job within nine months. By the time 1949 rolled around, I had learned to read and write Spanish and to translate it." Johnny's feeling of accomplishment had deep roots in his past. "It went right back to the time when I was a kid and I had people talking about me without my knowing what they were saying. I, now, was fluent in Spanish."

Shortly after completing his assignment in Honduras, Johnny said fond farewells to his "family" at the Degas home and returned to the Weather Bureau, which was now headquartered at Andrews Air Force Base in Maryland. Johnny's foray into a foreign country and into a new culture had given him a taste for this sort of work. He was good at it. In the struggle of his early life on the Navajo reservation, he had forged a set of skills that were ideal for moving into new cultures and learning new ways of speaking, thinking, and being.

Furthermore, the pain of his boyhood and continuing discrimination on the reservation served as powerful reinforcements to a natural curiosity that made him want to explore the world. The combined result was that Johnny Pail Face became a happier and more settled human being the further that he distanced himself from the ugliness of his roots.

These reflections help to understand the unusual decision that Johnny made shortly after returning from Honduras. He had no inclination to stay in the U.S., where he had a well-paying job and a carefree life in a city where there were "eight women for every man."

Instead, he chose to re-enlist in the Air Force, where his education and skills as a weather observer were in high demand. He also knew that the Air Force would let him travel again. In the early winter of 1951, Johnny would find himself on a troop ship heading back to a place that he had not quite reached during his first journey to Europe six years before. He was bound for Germany.

It was a paradoxical and emotionally complex return. He had been baptized in German blood at the Battle of Monte Cassino. He had fought and killed Germans all the way to the Po River, where he nearly lost his life when a mortar round fell short just days before World War II ended in Europe. And now he was leaving behind a secure job and a life of ease in Washington, D. C., to return to places and among a people where he had witnessed the most horrific aspects of the human story.

I felt that there must be something deeper at work in Johnny's puzzling decision to return to the same place that landed him in a mental institution after his first tour of duty there. In our interviews, I pushed hard to get to the heart of this. My hunch proved to be right. One afternoon after repeating his standard line about wanting to see what Germany was really like after coming so close during the war, his words took a more reflective turn.

Somehow, I had to make peace with myself. I wanted to be able to live like a human being. When I was young in reservation country, I had always been treated as not a human being, but like something else. I had learned what it was to live as not a human being. It wasn't a good thing, but I didn't know how to change.

Awful things had happened to me over in Europe. I don't know. Part of me seemed to think that I needed to go back to that before I could work things out.

They didn't heal me very well at Bruns Hospital. Not my arm and not my head either. I didn't want to admit it to myself at first, but I knew what that meant. If I wanted to get my life back on track, I had to go back to where it ran off the track.

I didn't know what would happen back in Europe. I just knew that I needed to go there. I would find out. Long ago, Old Victor had told me to follow these kinds of feelings. So I did.

With such swirling thoughts in mind and at heart, Johnny returned to the place where he had been mentally and physically broken. The second time, he made it all the way to Germany. But this time was different.

Johnny Pail Face's mission was to help rebuild a world not to destroy a world. Old Victor had taught him that all things are connected, that we are the things that happen. Johnny had helped to destroy Germany and it had almost destroyed him. Now he would help to heal Germany. But could doing so bring his own healing?

The only way to know was to go.

CHAPTER 13

In the Wake of War

IN THE EARLY 1950s, it took a long time to get to a place like Germany, especially if you were travelling as a soldier. Johnny Pail Face took the first leg of the journey on a U.S. Navy ship across the turbulent North Atlantic to Iceland. The ship let off some sailors at Reykjavik. Then it plowed on through rough seas to England and from there across the North Sea to the mainland, where it deposited the sea-weary soldiers at Amsterdam. It was an old-style Atlantic crossing with winds, storms, seasickness, and the like. For Johnny, the worst part was the ice.

> I remember that everything above decks was covered with ice. So when we went to get something to eat, we'd climb the stairs to the top deck and stand in the doorway and wait until the ship leaned away. Then we would aim for the guard rail and just slide out across the deck and grab it. There we could move hand over hand, wait for the ship to roll the other way, and skid right into the mess hall, which was further down the deck.
>
> You had to stand up to eat. There was just this bar, a thing that was waist high. There were no chairs.
>
> Sometimes, while we were eating our meals, the ship would tilt, and the trays would slide, and you would be picking food off some other guy's tray. Sometimes, that guy had been seasick and threw up on his tray and this would come to you.
>
> Then you would have to leave and go below decks so that you could stay quiet and recover.

At one point, I slipped on the icy deck and nearly went overboard. I dislocated my left shoulder and tore the tendon of my left arm, my bad arm, trying to keep myself from falling into the sea. They managed to pull me back onto the deck, but my left arm was damaged again.

After fourteen days of a harrowing journey, Johnny arrived at Bremerhaven, Germany, glad to be alive. But his travels were not over yet. He took a train for another day and a half to the small town of Sonhoffen in Bavaria. This part of his voyage was no more comfortable than the Atlantic crossing. "You either had to sleep on the floor, on your knees, or up on the baggage rack," he recalls.

Sonhoffen had been a German S. S. training camp during World War II. It was high in the Bavarian Alps. That meant snow in January when Johnny arrived. Lots of snow. When he finally stepped off the train at the end of his weeks-long journey, "There must have been fifteen-foot snow banks all over the place. The snow was so deep that it was up to the second floor of the buildings."

German ingenuity had devised unique ways to keep buildings warm in such inhospitable conditions. "The brick walls of these buildings were three feet thick, with double windows, an outside window and an inside window, set into them. In the space between the windows there were heaters."

To move from one building to another, there were tunnels through the snow, meaning that in winter when people went outside, they remained underground, or at least "under snow." Except one American fellow. One of his first memories of Sonhoffen is of a comrade who found a new way to go out of doors.

There was this black guy there who said he was going to jump down into the snow bank from the ledge of the building. He wasn't in any way prepared to do this because he was only dressed in his underwear.

Well, he slipped off the ledge and went down into the snow about eight or ten feet. He was in there yelling and screaming and thrashing around.

Someone called for help and a truck with a big snow blower on it came up the road. I stood up in the window and directed it in as close to the guy as I could. Then I told the operator to shut off the engine and I urged the man in the snow bank to reach for the blower so he could be pulled out. He made it but he wasn't in very good shape.

During the week that Johnny stayed at Sonhoffen, the shoulder that he had dislocated on the icy ship deck was giving him a lot of pain. So he went to see an elderly German doctor. The old fellow rubbed Johnny's shoulder down with alcohol and began poking and prodding him. He asked Johnny to tell him when he touched the spot with the most pain in it. It did not take long to locate the center of the injured area.

Then the doctor took out a syringe with a long needle. He plunged the needle into the center of the sore spot. Johnny asked him what was in the syringe.

"Novocain," the doctor replied.

"Novocain?" Johnny responded. "That's not going to last very long."

The doctor shook his head. "No," he countered. "If I hit the right spot, you'll not be bothered for many, many years."

Indeed, the man was right. It was 40 years before Johnny's shoulder began to bother him again. "I suppose it is arthritis as a result of the cartilage that grew from the dislocation," he says now.

When he left Sonhoffen, Johnny was assigned to a small American air base in the town of Tulln, near Vienna, Austria. In 1951, Germany and Austria were still occupied by Allied forces in the aftermath of World War II and were divided into four zones. Each zone was controlled by a different Allied power, including the U.S., Britain, France, and Russia. Russia controlled most of Austria and so when Johnny set out for his posting in Tulln, he took a Russian train to get there. Because of growing Cold War tensions between Russia and the other Allied powers, the train was sealed. The Russians had blacked out all of the windows so that foreigners travelling on it could not spy on the Soviet-controlled countryside. Johnny was given a "Gray Pass" to use as he travelled through Russian occupied territory.

In the middle of his first night, the train stopped. Someone began pounding on the door of the compartment where Johnny was sleeping with another man, an Austrian civilian. When Johnny opened the door, he found himself face to face with a Russian officer and a group of soldiers. They asked him for his Gray Pass and the officer took it.

"Hey, that's my pass," Johnny protested. "C'mon, give it back."

The officer responded, "No, no, no! No give back!"

At this point, Johnny began to get concerned. He knew the Russians could arrest him in their territory if they found him travelling without a pass. He was not eager to be charged with spying and to spend time in a Russian prison.

After a short delay, the train continued on to Vienna. When Johnny opened the door of his compartment at another knock a few hours later, there was an Austrian officer in the train corridor. He was holding Johnny's Gray Pass. After a few questions, he returned the pass, much to Johnny's relief.

Johnny got off the train and soon found the American military office in Vienna. The staff there assured him that he was on the right path to get to Tulln. They instructed him to get back on the train and to get off at the Tulln station, which was about 20 kilometers northeast of the city. Johnny followed their instructions.

Once back on the train, he met another Austrian officer and informed him that he was bound for Tulln. At that point, he figured that he must be fairly close to the town and wanted to be ready to disembark.

The officer replied, "No, no. If you go to Tulln, you will go to jail for many, many years. You go to Lagen-Laben and get off there, and from there you go to Tulln." The town of Tulln itself was under Russian control and military personnel there were not friendly towards Americans.

Johnny didn't know who or what to believe. Fortunately, as he was trying to sort things out, the train was moving slowly along a fence. Suddenly, an American flag came into view waving above the barrier fence. As soon as he saw the flag, he had his solution

He grabbed his bags, opened the door, and heaved the bags out into the snow. Then he jumped after them, rolling down the snow-covered embankment. Right in front of the gates to the American compound was a Russian tank surrounded by a group of Russian soldiers. They were laughing and pointing at the snow-covered American. On the other side of the gates, American guards were yelling and hollering at Johnny to make a run for it. They had the gates open enough to let him through. He did as they said, gathering up his bags and scampering through to safe ground. And so it was that he arrived at his new post in the heart of Cold War Europe.

Once inside, he was keen to know "what the hell was going on." The Americans explained that the Russians maintained a perimeter around the American air base to keep the Americans from coming out "to spy on them." He was safe, they assured him, as long as he stayed inside the base.

Relations were officially tense between the Russians and the Americans as the two nations settled into their Cold War positions. But Johnny soon found ways around this standoff with the Russian soldiers. His old entrepreneurial spirit was alive and well and soon began to flourish in a place where the ravages of war had left losers and victors alike in need of day-to-day necessities.

Johnny soon became aware that there was a lot of opportunity in the "currency exchange" business. He quickly devised a way to get into this line of business. Here's how it worked. Because the Americans were confined to their base, the Air Force paid them in base currency, which had no value outside of the gates. The soldiers could only spend this "funny money" at the Base Exchange or at the Club. It didn't take Johnny long to discover that the scrip could also be used at the American Express Office on the base. So each payday, he would go to the American Express office, buy a money order for $100 or $200 and send it to a secretary friend in Washington. She was kind enough to cash the money order and to send large denomination dollar bills back to him wrapped in carbon paper so that no one in the mail service could detect them.

Johnny would then sell the American dollars at a handsome profit to the Russian soldiers, who were eager to have stable currency. They paid him in Austrian schillings. "From the Russians, I was getting about three to one, or $300 worth of schillings for every $100 bill in greenbacks," he recalls.

A final step in Johnny's currency exchange business brought things full circle. Once he had Austrian schillings from the Russians for his dollars, he would turn around and sell the schillings back to his American comrades for more funny money. The Americans were allowed to go into Vienna when they were off duty, but to do so they needed Austrian money. No one in town wanted their base scrip. So Johnny took the habit of going down the line of soldiers on payday waiting to pick up their base scrip and offering to sell them schillings. They were delighted to do so. It meant that they could party in town, where there was an abundance of women eager to help them spend their Austrian money. For Johnny, there was profit to be made at every step of this exchange cycle. As he now puts it, "I had a nice business going by selling money in three currencies. I was really shittin' in tall cotton, as they used to say back in the South."

Despite the tensions between Americans and Russians, Johnny was able to work out a good lifestyle during his time in Austria. His work as a non-combatant weather man brought him regularly into contact with Russian technicians, who he was helping to set up automatic weather stations in strategic locations around the country. The American government was collaborating with the Russians on this project and his constant contact with the Russians facilitated the sorts of interactions necessary to his money-selling business. Furthermore, there wasn't a lot of work for him to do. There was a Pan Am transport plane that would fly weather equipment into the Tulln base now and then and Johnny would be busy for a while getting it into the hands of his Russian counterparts and making sure that they knew how to set it up and do maintenance. Between busy periods, he had a lot of free time on his hands to run his exchange business and to enjoy himself in town.

If he was a shrewd businessman, he was not cold or indifferent to the people around him. In the early 1950s, life was still very difficult for European societies recovering from the horrendous devastation of World War II. In the bars and clubs of Vienna, American soldiers were in constant contact with displaced women who were destitute and struggling to go on with their lives. The deaths of vast numbers of men in the war left such women without traditional relationships and attendant resources for improving their existences. Russian and American soldiers filled this gap.

The soldiers from the Tulln Air Base tended to congregate principally at a club in Vienna called the Klamgalis, where the owner spoke good English and was especially hospitable to the Americans. They called him "Fred." He worked the black market so was able to procure good whiskey and other luxuries for his patrons. Many of the men soon had "girlfriends" at the Klamgalis with whom they would spend their free time. In time, Johnny came to know a woman who was called "Big Annalise," because of her size, another who went by Liesl, and a third by the name of Rosey. Each was a "Displaced Person," or a "D. P." from one or another Eastern European country that had been occupied by Germans during the war. These women soon became a part of his life far from home. It was a difficult and chaotic time for everyone involved, a reminder that the effects of war last long after battlefields turn quiet. But there was also room for things like humor, friendship, romance, and hope amid the chaos.

One of Johnny's early encounters with Big Annalise falls into the category of humor. Here's what happened.

I remember one time I went into the bar and Big Annalise was angry and more than a little drunk. She came over to me and put her arms around me and said, 'Come on, Johnny, buy me a drink!'

I said, 'I will not!'

She said, 'You better!'

I said, 'Nooo! What do you think I am?'

She said, 'You either buy me a drink or I'm going to throw you out!'

I said, 'Aw, c'mon, I don't want to buy you a drink, and don't do this.'

Anyway, she says, 'Wouldn't I?'

And guess what happened. She grabbed me by the collar and by the belt and picked me up over her head and threw me through the plate glass window in front of the bar, into the street. I didn't get cut. I didn't get hurt. So, I shook the glass off my clothes and walked back inside the bar. She was crying because Fred, the bartender, had called the police. And the police were going to arrest her for the job she had done on the glass.

I said, 'C'mon, Big Annalise, everything's gonna be okay.'

Fred said, 'The police are going to be here in a few minutes.'

I said, 'C'mon Fred, I'll give you 500 schillings to pay for the window.'

He said, 'That won't replace the window. It costs more than that.'

I said, 'You've got insurance and it'll take care of the window. You can just put the 500 schillings in your pocket.'

So, I put 500 schillings on the bar and he said, 'Okay, okay, everything's gonna be okay.'

By this time the police had arrived. I bought them a drink, gave them a tip, and they left.

And here's Big Annalise crying and putting her arms around me, telling me how good I was because she had lost her temper, and I saved her from going to jail, and blah, blah, blah.

So, she said, 'C'mon John. I'm gonna take you to my place to bed and…'

'Not me you aren't! I don't want any part of you!'

She said, 'I'm going to pay you for it, and I'm going to pay you with my body.'

'No, no, no, Big Annalise, I don't want any part of you as far as your body is concerned.'

'Well, why? Am I that bad?'

'No. You're not bad. You're probably very good in bed. You're just too big for me!'

I bought her a drink and that was the end of that.

Johnny had good survival skills. He had spent his young life figuring out people different from himself and how to deal with them effectively. He knew how things worked, how and when to give bartenders and policemen what they wanted. He was good at keeping the peace. He also had a nose for opportunity.

One day he returned from free time in Vienna to find the chief cook at the air base stewing about an impending visit by military inspectors. It seems that the man had 1,500 pounds of old coffee beans sitting in the basement of the mess hall that he did not know what to do with. The bags of beans had been there when he first arrived. "He was upset," Johnny remembers, "because he thought that the inspection team was going to get rid of it or dump it in the river, and he would be charged for it."

"Don't worry about it. I'll take care of it," Johnny told the man.

"You will?" The cook was surprised by the unexpected offer of help.

Johnny replied, "It'll be taken care of." And he went to work.

First, he stopped by the motor pool and requested a truck. His duties as a weatherman often required such requests, so it was immediately granted. Johnny loaded some empty helium tanks onto the back of the truck so that he had an excuse to make a run into Vienna to refill them. He regularly used helium in weather balloons. Johnny continues the tale.

> Then I backed the truck up to the rear of the mess hall and we threw the 1,500 pounds of coffee beans in their 50 kilo bags onto the truck. I took this load of coffee beans down to Fred at the bar and asked if he wanted to buy them.
>
> He said, 'Of course I want to buy them!'
>
> So we finally cut a deal that amounted to about $3.50 a pound. He paid me in schillings and I had a suitcase, a two-suiter, full of 100 schilling notes.
>
> I was really shittin' in tall cotton then!'

Johnny gave the chief cook "a couple of hundred bucks to keep him quiet," and then decided to go on a nice spree in Vienna to celebrate his good fortune.

In those days, Vienna was divided into zones, or "berserks," each of which was controlled by one of the four Allied occupying forces. The "first berserk" of Vienna was the most cosmopolitan and upscale area of town where prices were significantly higher than elsewhere in the city. American soldiers rarely went there. Johnny packed up his suitcase of Austrian money and headed for the first berserk.

First on his agenda was to check into an expensive hotel. Once in his room, he pulled a handful of paper money out of the suitcase and stuffed it into his pocket for easy access. Then he headed for the cocktail lounge for a drink. He took the precaution of keeping the money-filled suit bag with him. "I was lucky that no one knew what was in it," he chuckles, "or I might have been murdered for it."

Once at the cocktail lounge, he soon found more than a good drink. Across the room he spotted "this very beautiful, beautiful lady." Johnny went over and offered to buy her a drink. She accepted, and requested champagne, good champagne.

When Johnny heard her British accent, he assumed that she must be a high class hooker from England, one with a taste for expensive champagne. He recalls thinking, "What the hell. What do I care? I've got plenty of schillings. I could buy this hotel."

One glass of champagne led to another and they had a long conversation. When she asked him about his background, Johnny opened up and talked about his Navajo upbringing. She seemed intrigued and had many questions about lives of Native Americans. In the end, they drained "a few bottles," when Johnny finally said, "Well, it's getting late. I think I need to go up and get some sleep."

She indicated that she was going to do the same.

Johnny could not resist asking such a beautiful woman, "Would you like to come up to my room with me?"

"Of course," she responded.

The ease of all of this reinforced Johnny's sense that she was a prostitute, so he asked, "How much do you charge?" It was the wrong thing to ask.

The woman stood up with a look of disgust and responded, "What do you think I am? Who do you think I am? D'you think I'm selling my body? You better apologize, you son of a bitch! Do you think I'm some fucking whore?"

Johnny backtracked quickly and called for another drink for each of them. By the end of the drink, he had soothed her sensibilities with apologies. Then they went to his room. Johnny recounts what took place after that.

She took a shower and then I took a shower, and we both climbed in bed and enjoyed our bodies for quite a while.

I imagine it was around midnight or so when there was a knock at the door. Earlier we had ordered a bottle of cognac and some sauerkraut of some kind and we were just relaxing in the bed, sipping and nibbling.

A man's voice said, 'Open the door!'

From the bed, I said, 'It isn't locked. Come on in.'

It was an American Army lieutenant and he had a couple of guys behind him. In back of them I could see some little guys wearing homburg hats who must have been Vienna plainclothes police.

He demanded, 'What's your name? What are you doing here?'

I told him my name and said, 'We're trying to get some sleep.'

'Well you get up from there. I want to see your papers!'

I said they were in the inside pocket of my coat and that it was hanging up in the closet on the other side of the room. I said, 'Get them yourself.'

He said, 'The reason I want them is in case this 'bitch' has any disease we might have to get a hold of you.'

I said, 'Well, okay. Whatever.'

And he said to her, 'And you, get your ass out of that bed, you're coming with us!'

She said, 'I'm not going anywhere with you, Lieutenant.'

'You will, if I have to drag your ass out of that bed!'

She said, 'No, not necessarily.'

She stuck her hand out to the little night table beside the bed. One of the guys pulled his gun, a .45.

She said, 'Look, Lieutenant, would you tell that young man to put the gun away? I just want to show you something.'

She reached over and pulled out this little book with a leather cover and handed it to him. 'Well, what do you think, Lieutenant?' she said. 'Isn't this the International Zone and don't I belong here just as much as you?'

'Yes, Ma'am!'

'So, why don't you just put these guys out and close the door behind you?'

'Yes, Ma'am,' the Lieutenant replied and shooed everybody out and left, closing the door quietly behind him.

I wondered to myself what the heck was going on. I reached over to the night table and picked up her little book. It was like a card holder. It had four pages. One was in French, one in English, one in German, and one was in Russian.

She was a lieutenant colonel in the Russian Army, a nurse, and I would never have know it if the American lieutenant had not come barging in.

I asked her why she had taken me to bed. She replied that she had never been to bed with an American Indian and she just wanted to find out what it might be like to make love with one. She said that several other men had approached her that night but she had refused them and sent them away.

In the morning when we awoke, we had sex again, and then dressed and went down and enjoyed breakfast together.

I asked her if she needed anything.

She said, 'No thanks.'

We parted and I never saw her again.

Though he spent only one night with the female Russian officer, Johnny speaks of her to this day. Their encounter marked a significant milestone in his life, a marker of how far he had come from reservation life. If he had been born a "victim" in the world of Whites and Indians in New Mexico, in Vienna in his mid-thirties he was a "victor." The "poor, homeless, illiterate Indian" was, in many ways, at the top of society in war-ravaged Europe. In Vienna, one of the most "civilized" and elegant capitals of the world, he moved through society as "equal to or better than" other men. As an Indian in America, Johnny spent every waking moment in the struggle to rise above the lowest levels of society. As an Indian in Vienna, an elegant and highly successful "white" woman specifically chose to be with him.

It is easy to overlook the choices that Johnny, likewise, made in order to be with her that night. He chose to re-enlist in the military. He accepted to return to a part of the world and to a people with whom his battlefield encounters had sent him to a mental institution. He chose to go back to a world that had left him memories so horrific that his brain simply blocked them out for the rest of his life. When Johnny returned to the scenes and settings of World War II, it may have seemed that he was running away from his life in the U.S. Indeed, perhaps he was. But he was also running toward his life and toward whatever shreds of good inside of himself remained.

On this journey into the fires within, Johnny was growing in "Courage" and "Strength" as his daily prayer to the South these days continues to encourage. World War II had not only allowed him to act out the fury of his soul in the blood-soaked assault at Monte Cassino. The War had also shown him a flicker of hope intertwined with the anger seething within. Near the Po River, he had chosen not to kill the German boy-soldier. There was a piece of humanity in that act, however rudimentary or small.

The broken world of Vienna in 1951 gave Johnny more than one-night stands with curious upper-class women. It tugged constantly at his humanity. It gave him a chance not just to help people worse off than himself, but, more importantly, to care for such people.

For example, he remembers the day he met a "beautiful, dark-haired lady" at a restaurant in Vienna. Her name was Rosey. They began seeing each other once a week at the same restaurant. "I just loved to be in her company," he recalls. "We would dine and relax, enjoying just being together like this."

After a few weeks of this, Johnny invited Rosey to go to the opera with him.

"Oh no, I couldn't do that!" she protested.

"Why?" he asked.

It took him a while to tease the answer out of her. She was embarrassed to admit that she did not own a single outfit appropriate to wear to the opera. She was too poor for such luxuries.

"Things were still pretty tough in those days," he recalls. It was just six years after the war and people were getting by as best they could."

Finally, Johnny convinced Rosey to go to the opera with him. First, however, they spent the whole day beforehand getting her ready. "I took her to a beauty parlor and the hairdressers and the cosmeticians went to work on her, making her even more beautiful than before," he says. Then they were off to a ladies' clothing store, where he got her the outfit of her choice to wear that evening, "starting with the underwear, to the dress, and then the stockings and shoes."

That evening, they watched the opera Carmen together. Afterwards, he took her to "our restaurant" where they shared a late supper. "It couldn't have been more perfect," Johnny says to me in an afternoon interview session, his eyes drifting off to a time that still seems close.

"When it was time to go," he continues, "we left and she asked for a cab. I kissed her and held her, and then she was off."

As is often the case in such a troubled place and time, such relationships rarely had a chance to take root and to flourish. Wars disrupt human life long after they cease to destroy it.

His story of Rosey now ends with the words of an old man still saddened by an experience over half a lifetime behind him. "That was the last time I ever saw her," he says.

He sums up the story with a reflection that has not been dulled by the passing of years:

> *She had never taken me to her home. I never knew her full name or anything about who she was. We never made love, and I just let her go. I never knew why. I really could have fallen in love with that woman. She was so beautiful. She had a wonderful heart and a beautiful soul, and then she was gone.*

These are the stories that one does not find in the history books. As sentimental as it sounds, they are stories written mostly in the hearts of those who lived them. It may be that, in some ways, Rosey's "wonderful heart" and "beautiful soul" were reflections of what Johnny was looking for within himself when he chose to return to Europe after the war. If Johnny offered shelter and hope amid the storms menacing Rosey's life as a survivor of war, she seems to have done the same for him. Two troubled, determined souls caught their breath for a few beautiful moments in a broken world and then they moved on.

Although a "survivor" like Johnny could find ways to prosper amid the chaos of war's aftermath, he could not help but see and feel the pain of the people he found there. The victims of war are perhaps more responsible for the silence about this side of history than others. They are often the first to want to forget and to move on. Women like Rosey had everything to lose and little to gain when they befriended a foreign soldier like Johnny. We will never know why she chose not to see him again after their night at the opera. But love itself was at war in the chaotic aftermath of World War II and it was especially at war in the worlds of the conquered people.

Like everything else in the conquered lands, love was devastated by the monstrous forces that brought the war in the first place. In the place of love came hatred, anger, despair, horror, grief, guilt, and other negative forces within the human breast. There was great learning in all of this for a poor young man from Navajo Country in America. He knew from birth what it was to be a conquered people. In a reversal of his life story, in Vienna in 1951 Johnny found himself among the conquerors in a conquered land. From this vantage point, he had a chance to see his own world, his own mother, his grandmother, or his sisters reflected in the eyes of vulnerable women like Rosey.

What he learned is that victors can love the victims. That conquerors can love the conquered. But it is a dangerous game. It can be deadly. In the years after the war, women in Austria, Germany, and other occupied Axis countries were considered to be the "enemy" by the U.S. Government. In 1951, it was still considered to be "fraternizing with the enemy" for an American soldier to be alone with a citizen of an occupied country. There were severe penalties on the books for violating this policy. But, in practice, everyone from the lowest enlisted man to the highest general was taking girlfriends and lovers right and left. Indeed, in Bavaria where Johnny was first stationed on his way to Vienna, one third of all babies born in 1946 were illegitimate.[1] Fraternizing with the female enemy was so common in Germany that by July of 1946, the rate of venereal disease "exceeded one in four among American troops, probably the highest in U.S. military history".[2]

To have a "frat" with a woman quickly became the soldier's way of saying that he had had sex. The drinking songs of soldiers offer stark insight into the realities of life for soldiers and women alike immediately after the war. One went like this:

> *Underneath the bushes*
> *You take your piece of frat.*
> *You first take off your gas-cape*
> *And then remove your hat ...*

The ditty goes on with a half-dozen short verses that describe the soldier's sexual adventure and concludes with the lines:

> *And to your chums relate*
> *The total cost of all of it*
> *Just one chocolate date.*[3]

It is true that women in the defeated countries of Europe were willing to trade sex for chocolate. They were just as willing to do so for the seemingly endless supply of cigarettes and C-rations that the American soldiers carried everywhere they went. There were some very good reasons for this that are not readily apparent to us today. Chocolate, cigarettes and C-rations were the "currency" of the black market in the war zones. A woman could feed her family for a day or more with a single chocolate bar by trading it for dried peas or some other staple that she could take home to hungry children, parents, or grandparents. Or she simply could have traded it for food to keep herself going.

In the postwar world of strict rationing of food, "housewives and maids" were singled out in places like Vienna to receive the smallest calorie portions of any other social category.[4] This put women like Rosey in a double bind. Not only were they kept in a perpetual state of hunger by the rationing system, but, as women, they were simultaneously expected to be the constant source of food for others in their households. Rarely do our history books pause in their recitations of battles, grand strategies, victories, and defeats to tell the kinds of war stories that Johnny learned from women like Rosey. It is no coincidence that she chose to meet him at a restaurant week after week during their simple romance. One young woman of Vienna recalls from this period, "I was 18 years old then and had seen so much suffering. There was not enough food, apartments were without heat, the threat of death hung on every day."[5] Another young German woman recounts the first time that she and a friend were able to get access to a meal at a soldier's club on a military base at Mannheim.

> *As Germans we weren't allowed, so we said we were Polish. They knew better, but let us come in anyway. Sandwiches were served. I always looked for the heel of the bread because it was thicker, and 'Spam' luncheon meat was the first good meal I had in years.*[6]

It is sobering to think of European societies living in conditions where women would trade sex for a chocolate bar or a pack of cigarettes in order to survive and to keep others alive. Equally sobering is that they could obtain an abortion when needed for as little as a carton of cigarettes.[7] While young soldiers composed ribald drinking songs about such conditions, women like Rosey struggled through each day hoping to see another sunrise. The weekly meals that Johnny provided for a time were perhaps enough to give her both the hope and the strength to go on with life.

The other great danger that a "good girl" like Rosey faced was the severe repercussions from her own people for fraternizing with the enemy. These retributions could be far more serious than anything soldiers faced from their military superiors. Women were regularly brutalized, beaten, or outright murdered for socializing with foreign soldiers. A woman who became pregnant by an "enemy soldier" was, of course, especially at risk. At best, her head would be shaved in a public shaming that would haunt her for the remainder of her life in her community. At worst, she would be beaten to death and no one would be held accountable for the act.

Having even scant knowledge of the social forces and underlying dangers that surrounded Johnny's brief romance with Rosey makes his assessment of her more poignant. Had he met her in better times, perhaps her "beautiful soul" would have been less apparent than he had found it against the stark backdrop of war's aftermath.

In the innocence and simplicity of their dinners together, and then one evening at the opera, Johnny was still naïve to the risks that Rosey ran by accepting his generosity. After their relationship ended abruptly, however, he soon learned firsthand how precarious life in Vienna could be for women who fraternized with soldiers. The lesson very nearly landed him in a Russian prison where he would have found little leniency from an increasingly unfriendly Cold War adversary.

CHAPTER 14

Flight from Vienna

AROUND THE SAME TIME THAT JOHNNY MET AND BEFRIENDED ROSEY, he was living through a more intense relationship with a petite and lively young woman named Liesl. Liesl was a "displaced person" from Czechoslovakia who was living by her wits in Vienna. He recalls their tempestuous first meeting.

> *I remember one night I was sitting at Fred's bar having a drink when I saw this beautiful blonde who was there. She was a very short little girl, but she was very, very pretty and well built. Her name was Liesl. I walked over and asked if I could buy her a drink.*
>
> *She said, 'No, thank you.'*
>
> *'Ah, come on,' I said. 'I'll buy you a drink.'*
>
> *She said, 'No.'*
>
> *Well, a few new girls came into the bar and one of them who was wearing a green coat was quite good looking. So I just walked over to where they were sitting to see if I could buy her a drink.*
>
> *When Liesl saw what was happening she came right over to me and said, 'You no go with Green Coat. We go now!'*
>
> *And so we took off. I didn't even have to buy her a drink.*
>
> *She was the cutest thing. She must have been four foot two inches tall, with a body like a brick shithouse without a brick out of place! Well, I'm telling you that you wouldn't believe it! A natural blonde. A beautiful, beautiful girl.*
>
> *We took a cab. When we got out we walked across a bridge and we were in the Russian zone. You could tell because there were two Russian soldiers on the bridge.*

I was drinking at the time. What did I care then?

We walked a few blocks further to this tenement neighborhood. Her small apartment was on the second floor of a huge concrete building that had been put up during the war to house people. So we went upstairs.

I got undressed and crawled in bed. She got in and we started to have one hell of a lovemaking sex match. After a while, I got tired. I had my orgasm, or whatever, and I wanted to go to sleep.

She said, 'No sleep!'

I said, 'Ah, come on.'

I got up and cleaned up in the bathroom and got back in the bed to sleep.

She said, 'No!'

'Why not?'

She said, 'You come for me, not to sleep. No! I want fuck!'

'What?'

'You come with me. You come with me to fuck! Let's go! Do!'

'I can't.'

'Yes you can!'

I'm telling you, I have never had a night like that night, because every time that I would finish and go clean up and get back in bed, she would just start working on it again, trying to get it up, so that I could continue.

Well, by 11 o'clock in the morning, she was still going strong. I was tired and sleepy. I was dead. Believe me, I have never had such a night in my life!

Finally she said, 'You sleep, you sleep, and I wake you at one o'clock.'

And sure enough, I slept, until she woke me at one o'clock in the afternoon, sharp.

She said, 'Let's go! Let's do!'

I said, 'Oh no. This is it. I can't.'

'Oh yes you can!'

So, I did.

Finally at around three o'clock I said we had to go. We got dressed and walked down the street to the American zone. Then we caught the bus to the base at Tulln, and let me tell you, I had a rash. I hurt so bad, I had just about anything and everything because of that night.

We went to the club and I ordered the biggest steak that they had so that I could get my energy back.

While we were sitting there, a guy came over and sat down and asked how I was doing.

I said, 'Fine!'

He kept looking at her and looking at her, because she was one hell of a beauty.

She took off for the restroom.

He asked, 'Where did you pick that one up?'

I said, 'She's a really nice lady. Do you like her?

He said, 'Man! I'd give anything to be with her!'

I said, 'I'll tell you what. You pay the check. I'm going to the bathroom, and I'll sneak out the back door. You can take care of her from now on.'

He said, 'Really?'

'You betcha!'

When she came back, I excused myself and went to the bathroom and slipped out the back door. When I got to my quarters, I went right to sleep.

The next day, this guy starts to come after me, because the same thing that happened to me happened to him.

Despite his unkind ruse, Johnny kept up a friendship with Liesl. He saw her again regularly after that at Fred's bar and he even returned from time to time to her apartment in the Russian zone where he took gifts of food and other things to her. Her English was fairly good and he enjoyed their long talks and banter back and forth. "But I would never have anything further to do with her as far as sex was concerned," he says, "because I thought she was a nymphomaniac. She just couldn't control what she had, but I used to bring her all kinds of things from the commissary because I liked her so much."

Their friendship continued for some time. Occasionally Johnny would take her to the Prader, an amusement park and gardens in Vienna that was popular with off-duty soldiers. Other days, he would drive with Liesl to the Czech border about 60 kilometers away to a place where he was working with the Russians to set up automatic weather stations. Liesl spoke the language and seemed to love the long drives in the countryside back to her native homeland.

During this time, Johnny was dating other women. However, in the evenings when he came across Liesl at Fred's place, he loved spending time with her. Sometimes he would find himself at her apartment too late in the evening to make the long trip back across town and to the American base. So he would spend the night in her arms. "But we would never have sex, because of the way she was with it," he reiterates.

Then tragedy struck the petite blonde. Johnny recounts the story.

One day back at the Base there was a commotion out in front of the gate. A Russian officer, backed up by a detail of soldiers, was demanding that I be brought out and turned over to him for questioning.

It seems that Liesl was found stabbed to death in her apartment and I was the prime suspect because I had been seen going over that little bridge in the Russian zone with her so often on the way to her place.

The Base commander refused to give me up.

When I was called into his office, I told him that I had absolutely nothing to do with that killing and that I would never have done anything to hurt that girl because I liked her so much. I said that I had no idea who had done it, but that he mustn't let the Russians get their hands on me because they would most likely try and convict me of murder.

Meanwhile, the Russians placed two tanks outside the gate, blocking it, and surrounded the Base with troops. They kept making low *passes over the airstrip with their MiG 21^s to keep any planes from taking off.*

It was getting pretty hairy. We couldn't leave the Base to do our work or go anywhere outside.

Then we got a break. A second lieutenant flew in and landed his L-19, a single seat light plane, on our airstrip. He was carrying some documents for the Base commander.

When he was told about what was going on and my situation, he told me that he would fly me out of there, and that he had a way to do it.

We waited until early evening, when there were no MiGs around. Then I crawled into the baggage compartment in the back of the plane, lying on my stomach, and then he got in. We took off and dropped right down to the deck, flying northwest over the Danube. He was trying to avoid the Russian radar.

We flew just above the surface of the river, the wheels almost touching the water, passing under the bridges. Finally, we crossed into West German air space and landed in Munich. I don't know how or why we were not fired upon by the Russian MiGs, but we were glad to have gotten out of Austria.

And so it was that Johnny's time in Vienna ended. To this day, he has no idea of who might have taken the life of petite Liesl. However, he acknowledges that spending time with American soldiers would not have made her many friends among the citizens of Vienna. Defeated soldiers returning from World War II battlefields and prisoner-of-war camps were especially antagonistic toward women who fraternized with their former enemies. It did not help that such men were trapped in the same cycles of poverty and destitution as their countrywomen, which put them at great disadvantage to the freewheeling Americans who had good health and easy access to food, drink, and money.

In the cauldron of defeat, shame, anger, and jealousy that swirled through post-war Viennese society, Liesl became yet another casualty. And Johnny Pail Face lived on, once again a survivor. But his time in war-torn Europe was far from over. Indeed, he had much more to see, to feel and to learn before he would make his way home to Navajo Country. It was in Frankfort that he began to push deeper into the things that lay under the surface of a world where the mainstream had suffered defeat, not the minority, as had been the case in his world. He still had a long way to walk as a victor, rather than a victim, before he would make peace within himself.

CHAPTER 15

The Things You Can't Leave Behind

IN EARLY 1952, AFTER HIS HARROWING ESCAPE by light aircraft under the bridges of the Danube River out of Austria, Johnny was reassigned to the Weather Analysis Center thirty kilometers from Frankfort, Germany. Here he continued much the same lifestyle of work, leisure, and black market trading as he had done in Vienna. Conditions in Germany were similar for the local people as they had been in Austria. For a bar of chocolate or a carton of cigarettes, a young G. I. could readily find female companionship. Johnny remembers, "If you were someone like me, unattached and looking for a good time, this was an ideal place to be. Many of the young German men never returned from the war and the women were just there for the picking."

He quickly got his black market business up and running again, exchanging *deutschmarks* for "funny money" from his fellow soldiers and then into dollars and more *deutschmarks*. With the profits, he took up buying cigarettes and hard-to-get items to sell to German civilians on the side. "Times were still tough in Germany then," he recalls. "Cigarettes, sugar, coffee, and chocolate were selling at good prices."

On the surface, Johnny may have seemed like a carefree and enterprising young soldier. He had money in his pocket and time on his hands. Furthermore, he was the victor walking through a war-ravaged land. This put him in a position to inspire the attention and affections of the opposite sex, and the envy, if not the respect, of the population at large. But on the inside, Johnny was far from carefree. Speaking of this period in his life, Johnny had little good to say about his inner world.

I wish to emphasize that I was filled with anger. I was angry at anything that walked or talked. I was going to get whatever I could from whatever was there. I didn't give a damn about anything at anytime. I was going to get even with the world.

At the core of this fury were the same ugliness and feelings of inferiority that had haunted his life from the first memories of watching his Navajo mother prostrate herself and her life in shame to the white man's Jesus and to the white man's world. In short, Johnny was still "throwing dirt" at the painful cross that white culture had lain upon him as an Indian boy.

Furthermore, very little had happened in his thirty-some years on Earth to ease the anger. By the time he reached Frankfort, he had left behind the Red/White world of his childhood that seemed to care nothing for his existence. In its place he had found a world equally cold and indifferent to human suffering. Things so terrible happened at Monte Cassino that his psyche refused to recall them. At the Po River, he was gravely wounded by friendly fire. Between the two places, he had walked through the ruins of one village after another, where human lives had been more devastated than his own.

He survived war's indiscriminate killing only to return home to find his mother's house abandoned and her own life ended. And now he was back in some of the worst-hit areas of the second great war to sweep Europe in a single generation, observing firsthand what war leaves behind long after the roar of battle has subsided. Yes, Johnny Pail Face was angry at the world. He worked hard at his military job by day. He drank large quantities of alcohol at night. And he didn't allow himself to give much of a damn about anybody or anything between the two.

It was in this dark frame of mind that Johnny arrived in Frankfort in 1952. He brought with him the baggage and the weight of his past, as human beings invariably do. Fortunately, there were some good things hidden here and there in what he carried. For one, he felt anew the determination to learn the language of the people around him much as he had as a young Navajo in Gallup, New Mexico. In Vienna, because of the many refugees from throughout Eastern Europe who spoke English better than German, there had been less motivation to learn the language. However, in Frankfort, there were few English-speakers. It had become a lifelong trait of his that Johnny could not stand to have people around him speak a language that excluded him.

Another personal trait came to his aid in facing this challenge. Despite the dark side of his character, he was always happy to meet new people and had a knack for charming them. Even if he were doing it for all the wrong reasons, he could put on a cheerful demeanor that others found pleasant and engaging. This made something as daunting as learning a new language and making friends in a foreign land considerably more manageable. When a good dose of strong spirits was added to the mix on a daily basis, life itself became rather tolerable for Johnny. Some days, it was downright funny.

For example, there was one of Johnny's first German lessons shortly after his arrival in Frankfort. By this time, he knew basic greetings and a few day-to-day expressions. He felt ready to branch out into more complicated territory. As he recalls, "I wanted to really master the German language." His approach to learning other languages is most basic. "You just have to find a good interpreter," he explains, "preferable one with beautiful legs." If one judges from his ability to hold forth in fluent German and French to this day, while mixing in a smattering of a half-dozen other languages from around the world when he is in a playful mood, it is an effective approach. Here is Johnny's recounting of an early foray into the subtleties of German after arriving in Frankfort.

> *I remember sitting in a bar next to a friendly young woman. I bought her a drink and I asked her if she could teach me some expressions in German.*
>
> *'Certainly,' she said. 'Hallo fraulein. Kummen sie hier mit der hose in der hand!'*
>
> *So I asked her what that meant.*
>
> *She told me it meant, 'Hello young lady. How are you today?'*
>
> *So, I just repeated it over and over until I had it. She kind of giggled every time I said it but I figured it must be my American accent that got her going.*

Later, I was crossing a street near the bahnhoff and saw a young-looking nun approaching me. I decided to try out my new German expression on her. I tipped my hat in respect and repeated the new expression just as I had learned it.

She looked at me with eyes wide, a horrified expression on her face, and turned and ran. I didn't know what the heck to make of it, figuring that maybe German nuns were stuck up and too good for sinners like me.

When I got back to the bar, I asked another woman why that nun should have run away like that. When I told her what I had said, she burst out laughing.

She said, 'Hallo fraulein! Kummen sie hier mit der hose in der hand!' means 'Hello young lady! Come here with your drawers in your hand!'—Definitely something you wouldn't say to a nun!

It was at the club on the American base near Frankfort that Johnny first met Erika Schmidt. She was eighteen years old, he recalls. Another soldier had brought her to the club but he was drunk and they quarreled. When the other soldier left, Johnny volunteered to accompany the young woman safely to her home where she lived with her parents.

"It was not love at first sight," Johnny says. "But her English was good and she seemed to like the idea of teaching me German." Johnny began spending time with Erika and her parents at their home in Stockstadt am Rhine.

I used to pick up whatever I could from the Base Commissary at Frankfort and would carry it with me down to Stockstadt on the train. Times were still hard for the German people then, and I tried to make it a little easier for this family that had opened its door and heart to me. I would go to the Commissary and pick up meat, chocolate, coffee, sugar, whatever. They were very happy to have me come and stay with Erika and had no objection to my sleeping with her.

Johnny spent the better part of a year working at the weather station near Frankfort and finding refuge in his free time with the Schmidts. As the months passed, Erika's father pitched in and began helping teach Johnny German. "It was just like having a family, a real family life."

This is not to say that it was easy for the young soldier to give in to the domestic life that the Schmidts were willing to share with him. The same old tensions and conflicts still swirled around inside of him. As he recalls this time in his life now, his memories show a man alternating between extremes of anger and compassion, between indifference and sudden kindness.

For example, when I asked him how hard it was to learn German from Erika and old Herr Schmidt, he responded:

It wasn't hard. I had already learned some German in Vienna. And the Lord God Creator gave me the ear to listen and to learn foreign languages quickly. It was a good weapon for me. If it takes your language to beat you at your own game then that's what I'll do. That was my attitude.

This attitude was part of the baggage that Johnny carried with him to Germany. The relative warmth and emotional safety of the Schmidt household did not melt it away.

And yet Johnny was capable of unexpected generosity at the same time. He recalls another incident at the Schmidt home.

I remember one evening the 'Mutie,' the 'Mother,' came in all wet and cold and covered with mud.

I asked, 'What in the world happened to you?'

She told me that she had earned five marks working in the potato fields harvesting potatoes.

I pulled out five marks, gave them to her and said, 'Here's five marks for tomorrow so you won't have to do that again.'

She took them, but when the next day came around she was gone again.

When she got home, again dirty with mud, I asked her what she had been doing. Hadn't I given her the money to stay home?

She said, 'Ya! Five marks you gave me. I make five more. Now I have ten!

I just gave up and let her go do what she wanted.

In the autumn of 1952, Erika became pregnant. Johnny and the Schmidts took the news in stride. As he puts it, he and Erika "just figured that we would have the baby and go on as we had been." But in January of 1953, when Erika was well along in her pregnancy, everything fell apart with a shocking discovery.

> *Things were going quite well until one day the parents had gone somewhere and Erika was looking for something in a box. I started to go through the box too and I came across two cards that had her parents' names under the hammer and sickle, the symbol for the Communist Party.*
>
> *I said, 'Oh my God! What is this?'*
>
> *She grabbed them and said that I wasn't supposed to see them. I kept questioning her. I had to know what was going on. Finally she gave in and told me that her parents were members of the Communist Party, and so was she.*

Suddenly, Johnny had a life-changing problem on his hands. The McCarthy era was raging through American society in 1953. People from high-level politicians to low-level actors and writers in Hollywood were seeing their careers destroyed and their lives turned upside down by the Red Scare. People who had done nothing more than attend a Communist rally in the 1930s found themselves facing jail time. In 1953, Ethel and Julius Rosenberg were found guilty of spying for the Communists and put to death. They left behind two orphaned sons, who, in a twist of fate, now live a short distance from Johnny in Western Massachusetts. And Johnny was facing the grim reality that for nearly a year he had been sleeping with a Communist. Worse, he was about to become the father of a Communist baby.

At the core of the issue, his work at the military weather station involved highly confidential knowledge and activities. He held security clearances similar to the ones the Rosenbergs had possessed for their top secret work on the atomic bomb project in New Mexico. Johnny sums up, "I was in big trouble and I knew I would have to report this to my base commander immediately."

Indeed, the penalty simply for not reporting his contact with Communists was automatic prison time. If ever it were found that he had passed military secrets to Erika or her parents, the penalty could have been the same as what the Rosenbergs received.

Johnny went immediately to his commander and reported everything that had happened between himself and the Schmidt family. He was immediately confined to the base. Within two weeks, he was on an airplane back to Washington and a new assignment. "I never saw Erika again," he says quietly. "They would not let me off base even to say farewell."

Nor did he ever meet their daughter "Gabriella" who was born a short time later. A few letters scattered over the years helped Johnny follow the story of the family he had been forced to leave behind. A year later, Erika wrote asking for financial support to help her care for Gabriella. By then, he was working at a top secret site in New Mexico on the Saturn V rocket project. He did not dare answer, let alone send money. He immediately burned the letter.

Nearly a dozen years passed and then a letter came with the opening line: "Dear Father, my name is Gabriella." The young girl wrote to say that her mother had married and had moved with her new husband to Communist East Germany. Gabriella was living with her grandparents in West Germany. This time, Johnny responded, even though it was still dangerous to do so. He and his daughter exchanged several letters. He sent money. Then she stopped writing. That was fifty years ago.

When I ask him how he felt the day he stepped onto the plane that took him away from his life in Germany forever, gruffness edges into his voice. "I didn't care," he assures me. "I was living life day by day and getting drunk every other day. I didn't let myself care about anyone or anything at that time."

And yet the gruffness had not been there just a moment before when I had listened to him talk about Erika and Gabriella. There had been a gentle feel to his voice when he spoke of his "German family." I have gone back through the interview on my recorder. The gentleness is especially pronounced when he says his daughter's name. He does it with a flourish, drawing out the last syllables on his tongue. When I physically watch him say the word "Gabriella," it is often with a smile playing at his lips at the end, face tilted upward, eyes half-closed

So I sit here at this keyboard wondering to myself, can we love someone we've never met? Can a rough-hewn old man love a daughter he never saw, never caressed, never kissed on the crown of her hair as she danced by? After fifty years, could such an ill-fated love still sit quietly in a safe place deep in an old man's heart?

When I listen to Johnny dance the word "Gabriella" down the length of his tongue and into the world, I think I know the answer. Many times since Johnny shared Gabriella's story, I have tried to imagine the aging father's response if he were to pick up the phone some day before he dies to have the words come again, "Dear Father, my name is Gabriella." Johnny often teases these days about wanting to leave this world at the ripe old age of 105 in the arms of a younger woman. Sometimes he throws in the dramatic detail of dying with a bullet from her jealous husband lodged in his heart.

But if I were to write his ending, I would prefer to write about a daughter named Gabriella and about what her return would do to her father's heart. He might still die in the arms of a younger woman as he loves to talk of doing, but it would be the arms of a family member. This would be one way to end a long, hard-fought life with a dramatic flourish to end all flourishes.

But only life can write such stories that blend the angelic with the dirt of the earth in ways that put everything back in balance again. And Johnny had other angels and demons hunting him down as he left his German family behind in 1953. The demons were at work in Korea, and a red-haired angel was already cruising the streets of Albuquerque looking for a broken man to love.

CHAPTER 16

The Devil's Work in Korea and an Angel at Work in New Mexico

WITHIN DAYS OF HAVING FOUND COMMUNIST IDENTITY CARDS in Erika's home, Johnny was back at Andrews Air Force Base near Washington, D. C. It was early 1953. He scarcely had time to take a breath before he was on the move again. His services as a weather forecaster were needed in Korea. This time, his travels took him to the West, into the setting sun. He flew first to California, then to Wake Island far out in the Pacific Ocean, and finally to Korea. In January of 1953, he landed at Pusan, where another war was grinding to a grisly end.

The North Korean and Red Chinese forces had inflicted terrible losses upon the South Koreans and Americans in the months before he arrived. The Communists had attempted to "drive the Americans into the sea." Only an audacious counterattack by General Douglas MacArthur midway up the Korean peninsula near Seoul had saved the Americans and their Korean allies from defeat. When Johnny's plane touched down at a military outpost at Kimpo near Pusan, the Communists and the Americans had fought to a standstill. Here is what Johnny found when he stepped from the airplane.

I remember getting into Kimpo, where furious fighting had taken place at the airfield. Our troops were in the process of disposing of the enemy's dead bodies.

The North Koreans had attacked in a series of 'human wave' assaults. Now there were thousands of their bodies littering the airfield.

Engineers operating loaders had dug deep trenches alongside the runways and had pushed the bodies into them. Then aviation fuel trucks poured fuel into the trenches and they were torched.

Some of the bodies flailed around when the flames got to them and I wondered if they were really dead before our engineers burned them.

This was repeated in layers until the ground was cleared of bodies. Then the trenches were filled in and the place became Kimpo Air Force Base. This all had to be done quickly so that our C-130 transports could land, bringing in equipment and ammunition.

Johnny kept busy during his months in Korea forecasting weather for the air traffic coming in and out of Kimpo. When the stalemate ended in late July of 1953 with the combatants signing an armistice splitting the country in two, Johnny was pulled out and sent back to Albuquerque, New Mexico.

His specialization in weather forecasting landed him a plum job at Kirtland Air Force Base in the New Mexico desert near the Manzano Mountains. In 1953 the Air Force was hard at work on what they were calling the Moon Rocket Project. Johnny was assigned to the "Blockhouse," a tracking station for the Saturn V Rocket. His team was assigned to study air density so as to determine the consumption of energy required by the rocket. It was up to Johnny's team to establish fuel requirements for the rocket as it went through various temperature zones in its journey aloft. Sensitive work of this nature required, of course, high level security clearances.

The tumultuous previous year or so had taken a toll on Johnny. The months had been filled with upheavals, hard drinking, broken relationships, and unexpected relocations from one end of the world to the other. These were less than ideal conditions for a man still trying to pull his life back together in the aftermath of World War II and then a tour of duty in Korea. Indeed, it would be hard to think of a less suitable day-to-day existence for a man seeking to heal from war.

Coming home again to New Mexico was the one thing least suitable of all for Johnny. As he has reminded me many times throughout our interactions, to this day going home to Indian Country brings out his darkest side. This was equally true in 1953 when he returned from his first posting to Korea.

"My drinking was worse than ever," he recalls. "I was hitting the bottle every day and was coming to work hung over and in bad shape. I couldn't see it myself, but I had become a committed alcoholic."

His assignment at Kirtland AFB demanded a lot of math skill, so Johnny elected to take a math class offered on base. The Commanding Officer of the base was taking the course as well. When he saw the hung over condition in which Johnny repeatedly came to class, he took action. "He saw how bad I was. He saw a security risk," Johnny recalls.

Before the course even ended, a letter came from the Commanding Officer's Office informing Johnny that he had lost all security clearances. The only base assignment available to him without the clearances was mailman. So Johnny went overnight from high-level work on the Saturn V Project to the menial tasks of carrying mail from office to office. In his disappointment with himself and in despair with the direction his life was taking, he drank even harder.

Then everything changed. Another woman came into his life. She was different from any woman Johnny had spent time with before. The way Johnny puts it, "It's as if she fell from heaven." He describes their unusual first meeting.

One morning after a bout of all-night drinking, I found myself waking up from a drunken sleep outside the front door of a bar in the Broadway slum area of Albuquerque. I was wandering around looking for my car that I had parked the day before.

A car driven by a very attractive redhead slowed down and stopped right along side of me as I stumbled in the street. This was Mary Elizabeth Powell, daughter of the socially prominent Powells of Williamsburg, Virginia. She asked me if I needed any help.

'No,' I said. 'I'm just looking for my car. It ought to be around here somewhere.'

She said, 'Why don't you get in and I'll take you to my home and we can have a cup of coffee?

And so they did. Mary Elizabeth understood where Johnny was. She seemed to know from the start how to get him moving forward to a better place. When she served him that first cup of coffee, she put in a little rum. She knew that would help Johnny come down more gently from his recent binge.

In the weeks that passed, Johnny learned that he was not the first alcoholic Mary Elizabeth had rescued from the street. She had been married four times. Johnny would soon become her fifth husband. Each one had suffered from addiction to alcohol or drugs. Each time she had worked hard to save him.

Her most recent husband had died tragically. Despite her best efforts, he had returned to the bottle in the end and then put a shotgun to his stomach and took his own life. And Mary Elizabeth had returned to the streets, finding Johnny.

They saw each other regularly after that first meeting, growing closer with each visit. Within three months, they were married. It was Mary Elizabeth's fifth time to the altar and Johnny's third. The violent end to Mary Elizabeth's previous marriage seemed to make her more determined to succeed with Johnny. For his part, Johnny was likewise eager to move forward to a better world. It was driving him crazy to have been demoted to mailman after losing his security clearances.

Education once again offered a way forward. He remembers, "It began to dawn on me that I needed to pull myself up again, so I applied for acceptance into the 'Bootstrap' Program. That was a special program to enroll serving veterans into college, paying their tuition and their military salaries."

Johnny was accepted into the program and, in January 1954, found himself working on a Master's Degree in Climatology at the University of Illinois in Champaign-Urbana. A short time later, he brought his new wife from Albuquerque to join him in a rented duplex on Illinois Street in Urbana. They would stay there for two years while Johnny completed his degree. They were not easy years. Mary Elizabeth worked tirelessly to wean Johnny away from the bottle. But Johnny resisted her best efforts.

I attended school every day, but my drinking was getting worse and now I was drinking vodka. I had been very fond of scotch, Haig & Haig Pinch to be exact. I started drinking scotch when I lived in Washington, but I developed a terrible, terrible allergy to it. It used to give me hives all over my body.

In order to be able to continue drinking it, I would get into a bath of warm water and Epsom salts or a couple of boxes of baking soda in order to stop the itching. I would have my bottle and my cigarettes and just drink myself into drunkenness.

Well, after getting drunk this way and nearly drowning a few times, I switched to vodka, which didn't give me the hives. To this day if I get into the bathtub, I have to leave the bathroom door open because I'm so afraid of drowning.

During his two years of graduate study, Johnny drank a prodigious amount of alcohol. There was a difference in his drinking habits now, however. He no longer drank openly in wild sprees. He sought to hide his addiction as much as he could from Mary Elizabeth and from friends and neighbors. To do so, he stopped putting his empty vodka bottles out in the trash where everyone in the neighborhood could see them. He stacked them out of sight in the basement of the duplex on Illinois Street. Here is what he found after graduation when he went to the basement to clean out the empty fifths.

I had stored, or rather hidden away, the empty booze bottles that I had finished in the basement. They were stacked up like cordwood against the wall.

I rented a small trailer to haul them away to the dump and I kept a tally on the number of bottles I was taking out of that basement. This collection of bottles began in early 1954 and ended in late 1956.

After a while I just stopped counting as I carried them out in baskets to the trailer. I stopped at over 800 fifths that I had consumed while I was going to the University of Illinois. That averages out to two and a half fifths of vodka a day!

A lot of people who I meet today tell me that I look quite young for my age. Well, it's no secret and I wouldn't recommend it to anyone.

Drinking all that vodka for so many years pickled me and I have stayed pickled to this day!

Despite his hard drinking, Johnny was among just 18 veterans out of 40 who completed the Master's Degree Program in Climatology at the University of Illinois in 1956. He remains deeply proud of this singular achievement in his life. It allows him to present himself to old friends and to greet new ones as "just a poor, homeless, illiterate Indian" with a twinkle in his eye and playful irony in his voice. Indeed, for a reservation boy who never set foot in a school classroom until he went to college in his thirties, it was an impressive accomplishment.

But another experience just prior to his graduation from the University of Illinois would have an impact upon his life equal to or even greater than earning a Master's Degree. During a long afternoon with nothing to do in Chicago, he went to see a film. It changed everything.

Johnny and wife Mary Elizabeth in Albuquerque,
New Mexico, autumn 1954.

Part Three

A Prayer Looking to the West

Oh Lord, Creator in the West where the sun sets and the harvest takes place. Let me harvest all that I asked you to take away in the East so that I can serve you better by giving me Patience, Tolerance, Peace of Mind, and all the other things I asked you to take away. Let me have them in the Positive so I can redeem myself in your eyes.

CHAPTER 17

I'll Cry Tomorrow

BECAUSE OF HIS FLUENCY IN SPANISH, Johnny was often given special assignments to help out when Spanish-speaking visitors attended military events in and around the air base at Urbana. One day in 1956 he was asked to act as chauffeur and interpreter for a group of Argentine visitors who needed to go to Chicago. They were scheduled to fly out of Midway Airport at 11 p.m. Johnny got them to the city hours ahead of time and they asked if they might go shopping for goods to take back to Argentina. Johnny was happy to accommodate and dropped them off at a large shopping district downtown in the afternoon, setting up a meeting back at the drop-off point in time to get them to the airport. This left Johnny with nothing to do and hours of time in which not to do it.

I stopped at the first barroom I saw and had a beer. Because I was an alcoholic, I realized that I was going to be in trouble if I stayed there and I really didn't want to disappoint my Argentine friends because they were so nice.

I walked over to the Loop and stopped at the first movie theatre. It really didn't matter to me what was playing. I bought a ticket and went in to watch the movie to pass the time.

Now this must be how the Lord Creator works.

The first thing to come on the screen was the story of Lillian Roth, 'I'll Cry Tomorrow,' the story of her struggle with alcoholism. I must have really identified with her. I cried as I sat through that movie.

When the film ended, Johnny picked up the Argentine group and took them to the airport as promised. Then he went straight home to bed. The next morning, he couldn't bring himself to rise and go to classes. Instead he lay in bed reflecting on the film he had seen.

All I could remember about the movie was a scene where Lillian comes out of a rundown hotel and walks up the street where she sees the open doorway on a building. Hanging above the door was a big sign that said 'A. A.'

She went in and, at the end of a long hallway, there was a room with a man standing at a podium underneath a light.

He was saying, 'My name is John and I am an alcoholic.'

When Johnny rose from bed in the late morning, it was to go straight to the phone. He called the operator and asked, "Is there such a thing as A. A. in Urbana?" The operator said that she would ask her supervisor and then call him back.

After a few minutes, someone called and asked where I was and if I had taken a drink that day.

"Not yet," I told him.

He said, 'Just stay where you are. It'll take fifteen or twenty minutes for us to get over there and whatever you do, don't take a drink!'

'O.K.,' I said.

It didn't take him very long to show up. The doorbell rang and when I opened the door, there stood a tall man wearing a long, dark overcoat and a homburg hat, looking like a funeral director.

He had a buddy with him. The man's name was Nolan and his buddy was named Jim. They came in. They just stayed with me, being friendly, right through the whole day.

After several hours of not having anything to drink after being soaked in alcohol for months, something started to happen to me. I began to see tiny spiders, thousands upon thousands of them, dropping down from the ceiling. They were crawling all over the floor and all over me. There were so many spiders that they were getting in between my toes and tickling me.

Then tiny brown worms began to come out of the woodwork. They began to eat the spiders crawling on the floor and, as they ate, they got bigger and bigger.

When they climbed up onto the bed after the spiders, I panicked and tried to climb the walls to get away from them.

This was the D.T.s or 'delirium tremens.'

My two new friends stayed with me for three days, holding me down on the bed and restraining me for my own protection. When they spoke with me and I was the object of their attention, all the spiders and worms would be gone, but as soon as they left the room to have some coffee or to speak among themselves, the vermin would return.

At the end of three days, after I had gotten past the D.T.s, they said that I would have to come to a meeting.

I said that I would do no such thing. I wasn't going to be among a bunch of filthy derelicts. I was a decent person, employed and attending a college.

They insisted, saying that because they had seen me through my crisis for three days, working in shifts every hour of those three days, the least that I owed them was to come to one meeting and, if I didn't like it, the rest would be up to me.

'Well, if that's the case, okay,' I told them.

So I went to the meeting and what do you know. There were no derelicts or rotten people. The Treasurer was the Chief of Police and the Chairman was the Mayor of the town, and so I thought I was in pretty good company.

There was a dramatic change in Johnny when he joined Alcoholics Anonymous. The changes had been coming for a long time. A better side of Johnny's personality was emerging, a giving side rather than a taking side. A new source of energy began to drive his life. He is very clear about this. Before 1956, hate was at the core of his way of looking at the world when he rose from bed each morning. "If I had to learn your language to beat you at your own game, I would," is the way he puts it. "I was not a pleasant person. I was filled with anger. I was going to be the person to take advantage. Hate is what got me to where I was. Hate got me to be an alcoholic. I used alcohol to my advantage. It made me feel equal to, if not better than, others." And then comes the old refrain that I was coming to understand better and better as I learned more of his story. "I did everything for all the wrong reasons."

In 1956, perhaps for the first time in his forty years on Earth, Johnny started to do a few things for the "right" reasons. He sums up the change bluntly: "I became Mr. A. A." In real life terms, that meant:

I started parading around trying to find drunks that I could preach to. There was one couple, a very nice couple, and both of them were bad alcoholics. He would sober up and she would get drunk. He would try to help her stay sober and finally he would get drunk because she was drunk, and she would sober up in order to take care of him.

It was a real rat race with those two. In the middle of everything, they were raising two kids, a boy and a girl.

One day I picked her up because she was drunk and brought her to the house of a friend of mine. We had to tie her to the bed to restrain her in order to feed her a little bit of booze at a time. We started by giving her a good shot, and later on we added water to it to finally dilute it so that she wasn't getting any booze at all.

Meanwhile, the husband got drunk and was yelling at me to leave her alone. He said that she was a lot of trouble and she would get me drunk if I stayed with her.

I said, 'Look, I'm not doing anything wrong with your wife. I think that she's a wonderful lady and that she's going to be O.K. I'm just trying to help you both.'

He was beyond reason, and in this state he ran out into the roadway to try to get himself killed. He ran out in front of a car, but it stopped in time and didn't hit him.

The driver called the police and he was put in jail. I had to go bail him out. When I bailed him out, he had sobered up. By this time, his wife had sobered up too.

We got them together, both of them sober for the first time in a long time. They stayed sober and started coming to meetings.

He was partners with his brother in a big lumber yard. He sold out to his brother and the couple went to live in California.

Usually recovering alcoholics don't do well when they relocate like this, but I heard from them later and they were still in California and still sober. Their kids were grown and away at college and they were doing fine.

Johnny's life took on a radically new direction with his discovery of the A. A. way of life. It was a hopeful change, but not an easy one to maintain. Upon graduation, he faced the same challenges of relocation as the couple that he had recently helped. His Air Force assignment remained back at the Kirtland Air Base in his home state of New Mexico. So in 1956, he and Mary Elizabeth returned to Albuquerque and Johnny returned to work at the base. As he was still without his security clearances, carrying the mail remained the only job he could do, only now he was doing it with a Master's Degree. It was hard to feel that he had made a lot of progress.

It was an ideal situation for failure for the newly sober Johnny. And fail he did. As he recalls, "I slipped back into my old pattern. I began to look for bottles that I had hidden and proceeded to stay drunk again. I was what they call at A. A. a '75 percenter.' They say that 75 percent of the alcoholics that begin with them return to drinking before they finally quit."

Finally, Johnny's Air Force superiors decided to give him a new assignment that made better use of his advanced education. Because of his fluency in four languages, Navajo, Spanish, English, and German, they chose to send him back to South Korea to monitor communications in a fifth language, Korean. The work had nothing to do with his newly earned Master's Degree in Climatology and Johnny did not speak more than a couple of words in Korean that he had picked up in bars during his first tour of duty there. But he was relieved enough at getting away from carrying mail that he did not question the logic of his new assignment.

Johnny left Mary Elizabeth in Albuquerque and flew off to in Korea in 1957. He would stay there nearly two years. He was posted to the small Island of Chejedo near the coast of North Korea, where he worked with interpreters to intercept and decode North Korean military communications. The work was not demanding and there was ample time for reflection in the remote place that he found himself. He was still drinking, but it was not the wild partying kind of behavior that had been his habit in the past. "I was trying hard to stay sober," he reflects. "In Korea they have some pretty good rice wine. That didn't help me stay on the wagon, but I kept trying."

In his free time, he began an intensive study of religion. He started by reading the Bible from cover to cover. This was no grandiose foray into theology that Johnny was undertaking. His motivation was much more basic. "I wanted to find my Creator," he says. "For the first time, I knew that I was wrong, that hatred was wrong. I had to change my life. So I started looking for that one God who could never appear."

Searching for the Creator, Finding Suko

JOHNNY DID NOT FIND HIS CREATOR RIGHT AWAY IN KOREA, but he did find a very large rat. His first posting was to the Air Force Base at Kimpo, about a dozen miles northeast of Seoul. The place had rough accommodations that put the troops there in close contact with nature. Rats, mice, fleas, ticks, and various other manifestations of the Creator's limitless imagination were a regular feature of daily living. However, there was a certain rat that stood furry head and shoulders above his peers.

Johnny and the bunk mates who shared the "hooch," as they called their Quonset hut quarters, named the rat "Rinty." Although they only caught glimpses now and then of Rinty when he came through at night foraging for leftover food and remnants of care packages, Johnny remembers him as "the largest rat I ever saw in my life, and that's no kidding."

He was a shrewd old creature who always found a quick escape route when discovered, so the soldiers and the rat lived in a low-level state of warfare, much as the Americans were doing with the North Koreans a few miles away. Then one night things came to a head or, more accurately, to a finger.

Johnny's writing desk was situated at the head of his bed so that he often slept with an outstretched arm that placed his hand upright on the edge of the desktop. One night as Johnny slept in this position, Rinty stopped in for a visit. "Maybe my finger was twitching in my sleep or something," Johnny suggests. "Something made Rinty decide I might be worth tasting!"

Johnny awoke to the unsettling realization that the jaws of a furry creature were securely fastened into the meat of his middle finger. He leapt from bed in a state of alarm, cursing and shaking his hand in an effort to dislodge whatever had a hold on him. He was shaking wildly and cursing ever more wildly as bunkmates began turning on lights and diving for guns to beat back a din that sounded like it might be an invading army of North Koreans.

In the yellow light Johnny found himself, between arm shakes, nose to nose with the largest rat that he ever hopes to meet again. Rinty squinted back at him with a fierce determination not to lose his mouthful of Navajo sustenance.

Finally with a tremendous fling of his wrist, Johnny sent Rinty flying. Once the rat hit the floor, it was over. He bounced off the thick rice-straw mats and disappeared out one of his escape routes faster than the men could follow with their eyes, which was probably a good thing, Johnny reflects now. Some of the men were ready to start shooting the place up with pistols and rifles. "One of us could have gotten worse than a rat bite in that shooting gallery," Johnny says.

When he examined his finger, he noted that Rinty had not left empty-handed. "He got most of what he came for," Johnny recalls, "so I hiked off to the medic station to get myself disinfected and patched up."

It was nearly midnight and the medic on duty was sleeping. When Johnny woke him and asked for treatment, the fellow began to fumble around in a medical cabinet, clinking and clanking his way through a variety of bottles. "I'm supposed to give you a shot of some kind," he mumbled. "I don't remember which one of these."

"You know what," Johnny said, "I'll come back in the morning." He left before he got something worse than a rat bite that night and went back to bed.

The next morning, Johnny rose early and returned for treatment. He didn't want to end up with a serious infection and further problems. This time he found a full medical staff at the aid station. Their reaction was immediate.

"They loaded me into a Red Cross battlefield ambulance and took me roaring off to a nearby field hospital."

At the field hospital, Johnny found himself in the company of six other American G.I.s who had also been recently bitten by a furry animal. They were bunkmates who had adopted a stray dog to take some of the tedium out of their isolated lives. Their pet project succeeded admirably in livening up their days when the dog began to act strangely and then proceeded to bite everyone in the hut.

The camp doctor did an autopsy and found the dog's brain cavity in the final stages of rabies. The whole region was immediately put on a rabies alert. Although Rinty was never caught and examined, the Air Force was not taking any chances. Johnny joined the six other rabies victims for treatment.

From one day to the next, Johnny found himself with absolutely nothing to do all day but endure rabies shots. "The seven of us were in quarantine for 21 days," Johnny recalls. "Each morning they gave us a rabies shot in the stomach with one of those big, long needles they use. After a week of that, my stomach looked like one big mass of raw hamburger."

Johnny saw past the immediate pain and mess of his stomach. He took the whole rabies event as perhaps a sign that the Creator wanted him to move along on his spiritual quest. He wasted no time in doing so.

At first, Johnny spent the long, quiet days reading the Bible from cover to cover for the first time. Looking back now, he acknowledges, "I was still very confused about Jesus Christ and the virgin birth and all of that. I wanted to try to figure those things out." He continues:

> Truth is, I wanted to get saved. I wanted something to happen. I wanted to understand God. I was looking and looking. I needed something that I felt I didn't have and I sensed that the Creator had it.
>
> As a boy, I had been a turd-brain throwing dirt on the cross while my mother prayed to it. Now I felt like I ought to work that out. I needed to be more respectful. So, I figured I should read the whole Bible and give the big book a chance.

Reading the Old Testament didn't help Johnny much in his spiritual quest.

I didn't understand it, Johnny reflects. *There was so much violence in those days. Violence is one thing that I already knew too much about. I wanted something different. Take King David, for example. When he went on that journey to destiny, he decided he had to kill an ox every so many miles and offer it to God.*

It's bad stuff to be killing living things like that. I noticed that it didn't take long before those Bible people were killing people just like they did their animals. That's the way things work. And they did it in the name of God too.

I don't think God wants that. I just don't believe that you can kill your way into a relationship with the Creator. I had done plenty of killing and it hadn't moved me forward with God, that's for sure.

It didn't seem that those Hebrew folks had any more success for all the killing either. They spent their time wandering around in deserts trying to figure out which end was up. That was right where I was too after all the killing and violence and stuff. The more you kill, the more you're going to end up lost in a desert. That's what I learned from my own life and that's what I learned from the Hebrews.

With such thoughts pushing him forward, Johnny moved on to the New Testament. He had a better time with the Christian part of the Bible.

It had decent English. I could understand it better. But I wanted something big to happen when I read that book. It didn't work out that way for me.

All I learned is what I already knew. Jesus is the nearest thing to a perfect human being as one can get. But he was 'human.' He had his faults just like the rest of us. When he threw the money changers out of the temple, he was angry. He lost his temper.

Consequently, I did not feel that I could count on him completely. I didn't want to follow another man. I was looking for the Creator. The Creator does not lose his temper. He's above that sort of thing.

However, there is one part of the Bible that Johnny remembers fondly. It is The Book of Revelations.

It had a lot of prophecies. That John the Revelator fellow went off to the Spirit World and came back with a heck of a message. His book is one big vision quest. I liked it because it gave me a lot to look forward to. Armageddon and all that stuff tied in with what I knew about the Mayan Calendar expiring in 2012 and things like that around the world. That's the only book of the Bible that makes sense to me, to be honest with you.

Johnny was out of quarantine and back on duty when he finished the Bible. After three painful weeks of rabies treatments, he was assigned to Jeju-do Island, an even more remote posting than at Kimpo Air Base. Here he launched into The Book of Mormon and a study of Mormonism's prophet, Joseph Smith. After he read a copy of the book that a Mormon comrade passed on to him, he studied a couple of additional books on Joseph Smith and Mormon history. As one might expect, he had his own take on things.

That Joseph Smith was an interesting fellow. He translated a message from God on golden plates, but they were hidden outside somewhere while Smith did the translation. This Joseph fellow didn't want anyone else to see the plates. At one point he did let a handful of fellows hold a gunny sack with something heavy in them so that they could be 'witnesses.' But Smith told them God would have been angered if their faith was so weak that they had to actually open the bag and take a look.

Not me. I would've opened the bag before Joseph Smith could say boo. You have to look in the bag if you really want to know the truth.

At that point, Johnny turned his religious quest toward the Shinto faith. He had learned a few things about this ancient faith from his friend, Suko Matsumoto, who was from Japan.

I did not learn about Suko until the first draft of this book was completed. I was surprised when she came up unexpectedly in a dinner conversation. Johnny and I were having dinner with his dear friend from Granby and two Korean students from my college. We had selected a Korean restaurant because the students were longing to eat some of their own food after months of meals at an American college cafeteria.

Johnny looked across the table at the two young female Koreans and said, "You two are so young and so beautiful. You remind me of my Suko from my days in Korea. She cost me 600 dollars. That was a lot of money in those days after the war. But having her around was worth every penny."

It took me a few seconds to register what he was saying. "Johnny, did you just say that you bought a woman in Korea?" I asked.

"Yes," he shook his head. "Got her from a brothel near Kimpo Air Base. She was good company."

"How long were you with her?" I asked.

"A year or so. During most of my second stay in Korea."

I let out a mock groan. "J-o-h-n-n-y," I said, drawing his name out like a parent might do with an unruly boy, "How is it that this story is not in our book?"

"Oh, I didn't think you would want the racy stuff in the book," he said.

I shook my head in mock despair. "I want the racy stuff," I said. "I want the tame stuff. I want the shocking stuff. I want the boring stuff. I want all the stuff." I reflected a moment and then added, "How racy is it, Johnny?"

"Well, pretty racy by current standards, I suppose, but pretty tame in my time in the military and all."

Both students and Johnny's friend joined in at that point. They wanted to hear this story about Suko. He gave us a short version over dinner and then I came back to his house the following week for a longer interview to get this story into his book.

What it came down to is that Johnny was not the kind of man who needed or wanted to have sex with a different woman every time he went looking for female company. He enjoyed the "company" part as much as the sex. He preferred to have a meaningful relationship with a woman and to let physical intimacy be a part of that.

Brothels were then and remain today a common feature around military bases and army camps the world over. Johnny found that they showed disrespect for women. Disrespecting women is a social practice with which he had never been comfortable in any culture or language. However, from his own experience as a brothel-owner years before, he had a deeper perspective on how such institutions meet more than the needs of males who spend their money there. There is always a reason and a story behind a woman who works in a brothel. Sometimes being there is a step up, not a step down from where she was before.

After Johnny selected Suko from a line-up of women at the brothel, she took him to her private quarters. Johnny recounted in our belated interview what followed.

After we did our business, we had a long talk. Being so close to an American military base, she had picked up enough English to be able to communicate pretty well. I learned that her name was Suko Matzumoto and that she was from Yokohama, Japan. At the age of 17, she had fallen in love with a Korean sailor and ran off to Korea to be with him when he was reassigned back home. She arrived in Korea to learn that her sailor boy was already married and had kids.

That put her in a bad situation of losing face and bringing great shame to her family. To avoid disrespecting her family, she stayed in Korea and wrote home that she had found a job and was doing fine. She didn't mention that the job was in a house of ill-repute beside a military base. She had a sad story, as every prostitute usually does.

So I asked her if she might be willing to leave the brothel and live with me. I told her that I could become her 'job.' I would set her up in a decent place to live and would make sure that she had every-thing she needed. In return, I would want her to be my woman only, and for her to clean my clothes and cook for me as well. She did not show much emotion at all of this, but I could see in her eyes that she was very interested in my offer.

I had met a few women who had become comfortable with brothel life, but she did not seem like that type. She told me that the Mama-san would never let her go, that she might want too much money to go through with it.

I told her not to worry about that. I could handle Mama-san. What I didn't tell her is that I knew how to get things done when I wanted to. I knew what things scare Mama-sans into being friendly and helpful. Things like the threat of weekly venereal disease checks by military doctors and such. I had no doubt that Mama-san and I could work out a deal for Suko's future.

So I went back to see Mama-san right then and told her I wanted to buy Suko. She went through the whole thing about how she had rescued the poor girl from starvation and felt like a mother to her and would have great sadness in letting her go. Some of it was true. Mama-san had rescued the girl from a very bad situation and was offering her food, shelter, and safety in a world that was hard on young girls like her.

I knew that Mama-san's song and dance would go on as long as I let it go on. When she moved to the part about how much men loved spending time with Suko and how much money she brought to the house, it seemed like a good place to break in.

'How much do you want for her?' I asked. 'I'll make sure you don't lose money on the deal.' As I said these things, I pulled the $600 out that I had brought along to get a woman that night. Six hundred is what I was willing to spend and I knew what effect it would have on Mama-san to see that much money right in front of her nose. You can get a lot done by unexpectedly showing the right people a big roll of money all at once.

We closed the deal quickly and Mama-san went with me back to Suko's room. She was all cleaned up in fresh clothes and was waiting for us. Mama-san tried to make a big emotional goodbye out of it, but Suko wasn't playing along. She had things packed and ready to go faster than I would have thought possible for a woman. That told me that she was happy to be leaving. Like other Japanese I'd known, I learned that she almost never let strong emotion show in her face. I had to watch her eyes closely to ever know what she was feeling.

I got her a place to stay in a hotel for the next few days while I went out and found a nice apartment for us. After that, I spent my free time with Suko on weekends and my days off from the base. She seemed very happy to be away from the life of a brothel. She got to play housewife with me, which was a big step up from being with

*a half dozen or more men every night. I gave her money to buy gro-
ceries and clothes to make herself look nice and for things to pretty
up the apartment. We lived like that for over a year. She was good
company. She became a good friend.*

It was in this context that Johnny learned about Shinto from a
Japanese source. Suko shared with him the stories and rituals that
her grandparents had taught her as a little girl. It was a very old religion and seemed in some ways similar to the Navajo spiritual traditions of Johnny's youth. This made him want to learn more about it
as part of his search for the Creator. But he could not find anything
in Korea on Shintoism that had been translated into English.

So after learning what he could about Shintoism, Johnny turned
to Buddhism. He was able to find writings in English on this religion that was a beautiful part of the Korean culture around him on
Chejudo Island. It was easy to find Buddhist temples and shrines
in the woods and quiet places of the island. As he studied Buddhist
teachings, the first thing that struck him is: "Buddhists don't kill
things to connect with God." He liked this a lot. "Just the opposite,"
he adds. "You got to stop killing things altogether if you want to get
anywhere in Buddhism. If you're a monk or a nun, even swatting one
of the Creator's mosquitoes is out. Now that's serious business!"

However, Johnny could not find enough materials on Buddhism
to explore it more deeply at the time. And the people around him
who were practicing this spiritual path did not speak English. Johnny
tried learning Korean. He can still speak enough to buy something
in the market or to show proper hospitality. But he could not get far
enough on his own to explore Buddhism in the local language.

Nonetheless, Johnny retains a deeply positive impression of
Buddhism. "I think they are closest to reaching for what is called the
Creator," he says. However, the Buddhists would be the first to say
that there are many other worthy paths that lead to "the Creator." In
his eagerness to learn, Johnny moved on to explore yet another path.

The final religion that he explored during his time in Korea was
Islam. "I'm still reading about this one whenever I get the chance,"
he tells me and then promptly gets up from our interview and walks
off to the living room. He rustles around for a moment and returns
with a large, voluminous copy of the Koran. He sets it on the dining

room table and goes to the kitchen to wash his hands. "I think I like the Koran the most," he says as he comes back to the table, drying his hands with a paper towel. "Mohammad was true to what he believed as far as Allah was concerned. He wasn't in it for the money. He had to fight his way to establish the Islamic faith and way of life. He was a good man, there is no question."

Johnny sits down and opens the Koran. He turns the pages to where he has placed a bookmark. "Islam is not about a church," he explains as he runs his fingers down a page written in English. On the opposite page is the original Arabic text. "It's about finding God wherever you happen to be."

He points to the page, "It doesn't say anything here about doing holy war to earn yourself 64 virgins in heaven. It talks about the amount of trouble Mohammad had to go through to get people to understand a better way of doing things. It doesn't say anything about killing. It tells people to pray five times a day."

His fingers pause on the page and he looks up at me. "I pray two times a day. I'm lagging behind these guys." He chuckles and gently closes the book.

With a deep breath he says, "Organized religion is not what I believe our Creator meant for us. Organized religion seems to be all about extracting resources from its followers. In my world, you don't need money to worship. The Creator already has all the resources. I do my prayers to work out things I've done wrong."

There are some important things that need to be said about Johnny's spiritual quest that took full bloom in Korea near the midpoint of his life. First, Johnny did not fall into the common mistake that most seekers make at the outset of their journeys. He did not look around himself and decide to examine a couple of other religious traditions that resembled his own in all but a few aspects. He was willing to wander far afield and to entertain the notion that Eastern beliefs and spiritual principles deserved as much consideration as Western beliefs.

His early grounding in Navajo spirituality almost certainly prepared him subconsciously if not consciously to make this geographical leap. Most Americans do not realize that Native American spirituality came across the land bridge from Asia with waves of immigrants tens of thousands of years ago. In all but geography, Native American spirituality remains Eastern, not Western. The organic interconnectedness of all things underscored in Johnny's Navajo spiritual roots is the same interconnectedness taught in Taoism, Shintoism, Hinduism, or Buddhism. In short, Old Victor had been teaching Johnny a spiritual message from the Far East and from the foundations of the human story.

There is a second observation that takes us a step deeper into Johnny's quest. When he set out to find his Creator, he did not automatically divide the world into simple notions of "good" and "evil." In his study of key world religions, he categorically studied the beliefs of his enemies as well as of his friends. He studied first the Judeo-Christian traditions and sacred books of the people either who had oppressed him as an Indian boy in Western America, or who he and his fellow Americans had fought on the battlefields of Europe. The Americans who conquered the Navajo were, of course, Christians, but so were the Germans who Johnny "conquered" at Monte Cassino and after.

Next in his study came interest in the Japanese against whom his fellow Navajo Code-Talkers had fought in the South Pacific during World War II. The Japanese are predominantly Shinto and Buddhist. Buddhism was also a major religion in Korea when Johnny was there in the 1950s, although Christianity has made significant inroads in the decades since. Johnny was also willing to look deeply into Islam, and nowadays, as Islam comes under much negative scrutiny by many believers in the West, Johnny remains unswayed in his positive view of this faith.

There is much that is pure, unbiased, and refreshingly open about Johnny's quest for his Creator. Despite whatever differences or criticisms one might have about his approach, it is hard to argue that it was not sincere. He was willing to look anywhere he had to look. He found a way to put aside historical animosity towards the Christian people who had devastated his Navajo world. He transcended personal differences with enemies he and his countrymen had met in horrific conditions on foreign battlefields. In the end, it is this aspect of his spiritual journey that is perhaps the most impressive and hopeful. There were so many impediments and roadblocks around which he seemed to maneuver almost effortlessly. However, Johnny would be the first to underscore that he did not make the journey alone. There was someone he could turn to. He had a guide. He had a helper. He had Old Victor.

When Johnny went looking for God, the kindness and wisdom of the blind, half-blood Navajo shaman went with him. Spiritual seeds that had been planted in his troubled young heart half a lifetime earlier finally began to take root and to push upward. Victor did not impose himself from beyond the grave any more than he had done in life long ago over pungent cups of black coffee. Rather he walked with Johnny on the journey. He listened as Johnny wrestled with new ideas. His words and encouragement echoed back from a distant boyhood as middle-aged Johnny asked questions and struggled to find his own answers.

Kindness is not only one of the highest forms of intelligence. It may also be one of the deepest expressions of natural wisdom. It was Victor's kindness that kept the old shaman alive in Johnny's heart over the decades. It was Victor's kindness that, in many ways, helped to keep it alive long enough for that heart to turn from bad to good. The old shaman's seeds of wisdom were planted in kindness, and it was kindness that sustained the seeds until Johnny was ready to help them grow.

It is because of what he found in his long, quiet days of study and searching in Korea that Johnny is now able to say without hesitation, "Victor? He has always been with me. His teaching has always been with me."

It is because of the old shaman's teachings that Johnny can now affirm: "If you want to return to the Creator with a clean heart and without shame, you have to choose the beauty way. There is no other way but the beauty way."

Johnny tried many of the other ways. He looked in churches and sacred books and religious histories and theological doctrines in search of his Creator. "I looked everywhere," Johnny says now. "Like my mother, I looked first outside of myself. I looked and looked. It was only later that I came to understand what Victor had been trying to tell me all along. I was looking in all the wrong places for the

Creator. He was waiting the whole time for me on the inside. I am already connected. We are all already connected."

Johnny Pail Face's spiritual quest in Korea ended in May, 1959. He received orders to return to the States for a new assignment back home. When he told Suko the news, she showed no emotion. She said that she had known from the start that he would have to leave one day. Johnny suggested that she try to find a job in a shop or business that was respectable.

A day or two later when the subject came up again, she informed him that she had made other plans. She had thought everything out and had made her decision. She calmly explained that she was going to commit *hari-kari* or "honor suicide" after he left. She had brought shame upon herself and her family by coming to Korea and living as she had. She was grateful that Johnny had lifted her out of that way of life and now that she knew what it was like, she would never return to it. She also knew that she had little hope of finding a job as a foreigner in Korea during a time when many Koreans had no work themselves and were suffering. So the only option left was an honorable suicide.

Johnny thought about her decision for a few days. Death seemed like an extreme way to regain honor. His own life had shown him that there was always more than one way to get what you needed and wanted from others. He had thought about suicide a time or two himself. One night during his days in Washington, he had become so disgusted with his alcoholism that he had gone to bed holding his .44 military pistol to his temple.

Ironically, the alcoholism saved him that night. He passed out before he could get around to pulling the trigger. "It's funny how your greatest enemy can become your best friend when you least expect it," he said as he shared with me this piece of his life.

Before he left Korea, Johnny was inclined to be a best friend to Suko even though he knew that he did not wish to spend the rest of his life with her. So he went back and asked Suko, "Do you need to commit *hari-kari* to make yourself feel better, or is it for your family?"

It quickly became clear that the suicide would be for her family. She wanted desperately to return to them, but the only way that they could honorably welcome her home was if she were dead. Then she could be buried in the family plot and reside among her loved ones forever.

Johnny heard her out and then told her he had another option to consider. What if she came home from Korea looking like a successful employee from a good-paying job? And what if she brought with her a couple of years of money saved up from her hard work? He suggested that she wouldn't even have to lie if she kept details vague. She could just say that she had worked for the U.S. military and that her "boss" had treated her kindly. Taking care of Johnny was, in a sense, a job that served the U.S. military, and he had tried to be a kind "boss" to her.

Suko did not see how it could work. "I have no money saved up, or very little anyway," she explained.

"I'll take care of that," Johnny assured her. "I'll give you most of what I've saved during my time in Korea. It's about 1,500 dollars U.S. I'll need the rest of my money to get settled in once I get home to America"

Suko's voice registered shock as she stuttered, "You would do that?"

"Yeah, sure," Johnny said. "It's just money. Your life is worth a lot more than money."

It was the first time that Johnny saw great emotion show in Suko's face. Tears filled her eyes and she began to sob.

The next day he took her out shopping. First, they bought large travelling trunks for her to take home, then they filled them with beautiful clothing for her and gifts for various family members. They also booked a flight for her to Yokohama.

A week later, Johnny and Suko said their final farewells and he put her on the plane home. That was the second time he saw emotion in her face. Suko was smiling through tears as he gave her a final hug.

"I never heard from her again," Johnny says. "But that's okay. We weren't meant to last forever. We were just a couple of people who met in a crazy place and a crazy time in both our lives. It's great to remember her, though. It was the first love story in my life that had a happy ending. I felt good about that."

A short time later, Johnny made his own return home. As he did so, his head was swirling with new ideas and perspectives that did not fit well into the life with Mary Elizabeth that he had left behind eighteen months before. The brokenness of his past, his alcoholism, and the anger that had fueled much of his life were contradictory to the emerging self that longed to "find his Creator." Johnny Pail Face found a new feeling welling up inside. He wanted to make peace with the world.

In many ways, he was juggling the voice of Old Victor and the wisdom of his own Navajo roots with a troubled world and a personal lifestyle where such things had little room to blossom. He was still struggling with alcoholism. He had a wife waiting for him back in New Mexico. He could not know where his next assignment would be. More than anything, his spiritual searching in Korea seemed to be putting him on a crash course with the "real world" of his own life. Once he was back on American soil, that crash came swiftly.

Last Drink

JOHNNY WAS RIPE FOR A CHANGE OF LIFE when he returned from a second tour of duty in Korea in the late spring of 1959. But he didn't know it yet. It took one more wallow in the mud and the chaos of his roots to drive the message home. Johnny flew into San Francisco, and his guardian angel Mary Elizabeth was there waiting for him. She had driven their 1957 De Soto the 800 miles from Gallup, New Mexico, to meet him. They took their time driving back to Gallup, arriving shortly before the Fourth of July weekend. Johnny had received orders from the Air Force to report to Rochester, New York, but he had several weeks to report for duty there.

Johnny remembers that the Fourth fell on a Sunday that year, which was a problem. He and other male family members had a tradition of getting seriously drunk whenever he was in town on the Fourth of July. The other men were eager to give their brother and uncle a proper "welcome home" ceremony.

However, there was no liquor to be had on a Sunday in New Mexico. So Johnny, his brother, a brother-in-law, and a nephew climbed into his De Soto and drove west to the Arizona border and drank until they couldn't hold any more. With Johnny passed out in the back seat, his nephew drove the band of merry revelers home again.

When Johnny woke up late the next morning in his own bed, Mary Elizabeth was in a fury. She had good reason to be. While Johnny had been off on his wild spree in the car with his brothers and nephew, she had sat at home trying not to think of a previous husband and all of his brothers who had died in a car wreck in the same circumstances. Johnny had not heard this story before. It came out in furious, hysterical bursts as she unburdened things that she had kept inside to this point in their marriage. The dead man who had died in a drunken car wreck with his brothers had been her second husband.

Mary Elizabeth had hit the breaking point. She was packing her bags and loading the car. The marriage was over, she told Johnny. She had not spent two years waiting for her husband to come home from Korea just so that she could watch him kill himself along with a carload of family members as soon as he got home. Then she went off to get her two dogs ready for the long journey back to her family home in Virginia. The dogs were Tina, a miniature terrier, and Smokey, a black cocker spaniel. They were her closest companions during Johnny's long assignments overseas.

While Mary Elizabeth went to gather up the dogs, Johnny hurried off in the opposite direction. He wasn't ready yet either to stop drinking or to be divorced. He recalls with an impish grin. "I jumped up, got dressed, ran down to the bar and bought a fifth of Old Taylor. I ran back and got in the car, saying, 'Okay, I'm ready!' And we took off."

They got off to a bad start. Mary Elizabeth was so distraught that she did not pay attention to the direction that she was driving. Johnny was so wrapped up in his new fifth that he did not notice either. That evening, they stopped to get a room at a motel. Johnny remembers through the fog of alcohol that the motel owner insisted that all his rooms were rented. When Johnny accused him of discriminating against an Indian and made a fuss, the man threw a key at them.

When he and Mary Elizabeth got up the next morning, they realized that they were in Roswell, New Mexico, headed south toward Mexico. They had driven a whole day in exactly the wrong direction. There was nothing to do but turn the car around and to head north. Before they did, Mary Elizabeth wanted to get some breakfast.

At that moment one of the most important and most unexpected events in Johnny Pail Face's long life took place. In a strange town out in the middle of nowhere, surrounded by sky and desert and cactus and heat, and after a long day's drive in exactly the wrong direction, Johnny Pail Face decided to turn his life around.

There was no big fuss. He did not stand up and shout his decision to the world. He did not throw his arms around Mary Elizabeth and make grandiose promises. He just made a quiet assessment of the situation, spoke the truth to Mary Elizabeth, and then stepped back on the path he had been long preparing to take. In Johnny's words, here is what took place.

Mary Elizabeth wanted to get breakfast. I was very hung over and I told her that if the liquor store across the street from the motel opened up before we left, I was going to buy a bottle, but that I really didn't want to drink any more.

So, we just jumped into the car and took off.

It was a rough trip and we had to stop frequently so I could get out. I had the dry heaves.

They drove like this through several states while Johnny worked the alcohol out of his system. He could not know it then, but this would be the last time in his life that he would have to face the physical trauma of detoxifying himself.

Johnny Pail Face had taken his last drink.

During a stop somewhere in the Midwest, Johnny called his superiors at the base in Rochester to let them know that he was on his way. It was good that he called in. They had a change of orders for him. Because he no longer had top security clearances, he was to report to Fort Devons in Ayer, Massachusetts, where his assignment was to set up a weather station for the Army.

Johnny and Mary Elizabeth turned the car towards New England.

Within a few days, they were settled into temporary military quarters at Fort Devons. Mary Elizabeth's dogs were not allowed in the military housing. The unfortunate creatures had to spend the days locked up in the car. They had an established habit of sleeping with Mary Elizabeth, so, at night Johnny would drive the car around to the back of the building and hand the dogs to her through an open window and they would spend the night with their mistress. The untenable nature of this situation was literally driving Johnny to drink.

Once again he made a life-changing choice. He sums up:

After three days of this and not being able to find a permanent place for us to live, I was getting pretty uptight. So we stopped in Leominster, Massachusetts, at a gas station, and I made a phone call to A. A. to see what I could find. After talking to a few people, I was put in touch with a guy named Hockey. He's dead now, but he asked 'Where are you?'

I said that I wasn't sure, but that I was at a gas station in Leominster.

He asked if I had been drinking and I told him I hadn't, but that I was getting ready to.

He said, 'We'll find out where you are. Don't start drinking. I'll get to you as soon as I can.'

He showed up in five or ten minutes and we followed him in our car over to his house. His wife had just baked fresh bread. We sat down with them and had coffee with bread and jam.

While they were eating and visiting, the mailman came by on his daily route. Hockey went out on the porch and asked if he might know of an apartment available for rent in the area. Sure enough, the mailman knew of a home with a "For Rent" sign in the window not far away. The very next day, Johnny and Mary Elizabeth and their two dogs were settling into the second floor of a house on Mechanic Street in Leominster. And life became tolerable again for all of them.

For the rest of 1959, Johnny kept very busy. In his professional life, he had risen far from his days of operating a taxi, running moonshine, and overseeing a brothel. Because of his Master's Degree in Climatology and extensive field experience, he was in charge of the complex work of setting up the new weather station and of briefing pilots at Fort Devons. He would also be responsible for passing on weather information to the civilian weather stations in the region.

The first thing he had to do was to travel to Langley, Virginia, to work out who would be responsible for what in the multi-agency weather station. He pushed through a contract that got the Air Force to be responsible for the actual weather observation and forecasting tasks. The civilian Weather Bureau provided the necessary equipment. And finally, he got the Army to contribute the building, the living quarters for personnel, and the money to keep the office running.

All of this was spelled out in a brochure Johnny had printed called Continental Air Command (CONARC) Memorandum #33. By 1960, Johnny had the station up and running and was carrying out his main assignment, the essential work of briefing pilots on weather conditions prior to take-off.

In terms of his personal life, New England represented an important turning point for Johnny. He was determined to make a clean break with the broken world that New Mexico had represented for him all of his life. He sums up, "In New England, I was working my way into becoming a worthy citizen. It was the first time that I actually had my life together. I was in my forties. I was just getting too old to keep making the same mistakes over and over."

To begin this journey into worthy citizenship, Johnny became active in Alcoholics Anonymous again as he had been in Illinois three years before. With his new friend Hockey, he began making the rounds to help others in their struggles with alcohol addiction.

Johnny, Hockey, and a fellow named Chappy regularly visited A. A. group meetings throughout the region to offer support and encouragement to others. During one of their long drives to an outlying community, Chappy shared with his companions the events that brought him into A. A.

He had been a closet alcoholic for some time when friends asked him to "house-sit" for them while they went away on a three-week vacation. Chappy agreed to stay at their home as a caretaker in their absence. Just as they were leaving, the husband told Chappy that there was a big oak barrel of homemade wine in the basement that was not too bad. He was welcome to help himself if he liked.

Chappy told Johnny and Hockey that he went to the basement and did not remember coming back up for the entire three weeks. He just drank wine until he passed out, slept it off, and then began drinking again. When his friends returned, they took him immediately to the hospital.

Chappy recalled regaining consciousness in the hospital. The first thing that he heard was someone in the other bed in the room crying and moaning. He got up and went over to find an elderly woman who seemed to be in great pain. He put his hands on the bed beside her and gently began rocking the mattress up and down while he tried to cheer her up.

Then she opened her eyes and looked directly at him. Her eyes were strangely red. Then as he watched, horns began to emerge from her head and she began a satanic laugh. Chappy ran for his life. Wearing only his hospital gown, he fled down the hall and out the front door of the hospital. The police finally caught up with him several blocks away. He was not hard to spot. He was the only half-naked man on the street in broad daylight running like the wind with a hospital gown immodestly streaming out behind him.

When the police and nurses escorted him back to his room, he noted that the bed across from his was empty. There never had been anyone in it. He had been hallucinating as he went through *delirium tremens* on his way out of the ugly grip of alcohol addiction.

As part of his personal commitment to the regional A. A. network, Johnny got involved with a rural addiction rehabilitation retreat near Nashua, New Hampshire. He enjoyed going there to hold meetings and to encourage alcoholics through their most difficult times. The retreat was called Alma's Gateway Lodge after the woman who owned the place and who had converted it from a tourist destination to a rehab center.

Johnny was there one weekend working as a volunteer, when Alma asked him if he would make the 50 mile run to Boston to pick up a woman who had been referred to the retreat, but had no transportation with which to get there. He accepted, climbed into his 1959 Chevy convertible, and set out for Boston.

Johnny recalls arriving in the afternoon at the address where he was to pick up his charge. The woman, Alice, opened the door still dressed in her nightgown from the night, or perhaps days, before. Johnny could see that she was on the back end of a serious drinking spree. She was starting to experience withdrawal and no longer was interested in going to rehab.

Using all the charm and persuasion he could muster, Johnny was able to convince her to get cleaned up and to pack a bag. As they started to leave the apartment, she decided she must take her TV as well. It did no good to explain that the lodge already had a nice, big TV. She wouldn't leave without the TV. So, Johnny loaded her large TV into the back seat of the convertible and they set out for Alma's lodge.

Everything seemed to be going as well as could be expected as they made their way through Boston traffic on the way out of town. Then Johnny stopped at a traffic light that had a police station on the corner beside it. Alice's mood took a sudden turn for the worse. She looked at the police station, at Johnny, and then went into a rage. She was cursing Johnny for tricking her into letting herself be taken to the police while simultaneously jerking on her door handle to escape the car.

"She was going to make a run for it," Johnny says. "All I could do was grab hold of her and hang on for dear life. I had no desire to arrive back at rehab with a suitcase of women's clothing, a big TV, and no client.

Johnny was holding onto Alice's arm, speaking as fast as he could to convince her that he was not going to take her into the station, and trying to maintain control of the car. When the light changed and they could move forward, Johnny was able to persuade her that she was not headed for jail. She calmed down.

A few miles into their journey, Johnny could see that Alice was starting into deeper and more painful stages of alcohol withdrawal. He had learned to keep a bottle of bourbon in his glove box for such situations. He pulled it out and gave Alice a few mouthfuls to cut the edge off of the DT's. She cheered up.

In fact, she became too cheerful. A couple of miles later they began driving past signs for the Cloud 9 motel and resort. It was billed as an ideal place for weddings, honeymoons, and romantic getaways.

Alice suddenly had an idea. They should stop. She found Johnny a handsome fellow. Couldn't they stop for a night or two? They could have so much fun. There was a pool and a sauna. They might get a massage. They could go out for dinner and dancing. What a vacation they could have! And she could really use a vacation just then.

The old Johnny, the Johnny of New Mexico, might have stopped. She was an attractive woman, even when drunk. A couple of nights in the arms of a good-looking white woman from far-off Boston could have been an exotic fantasy-come-true for a fellow from Indian Country. But Johnny was on a different path now in New England.

He made a deal with Alice. "Tell you what," he said. "Three days from now, I'll come back to the lodge for you. If you still want to go to the Cloud 9 with me, we'll go. We'll dance and swim and have a nice vacation, everything just like you want. All you have to do is go to Alma's place for three days first."

Alice went to Alma's.

Three days later, Johnny followed up on the vacation offer. He returned to Alma's Gateway Lodge to check on Alice. She was on DT medication, bundled up in a blanket, and sitting quietly in an overstuffed chair. She was sober and in a dark mood.

Johnny sat down across from her and asked, "Alice, how you feeling?"

She looked at him and said, "Go to hell and leave me alone. I don't even know you."

Johnny smiled. "I'm the one who brought you here."

She looked at him again. "Oh yeah, I remember. Just leave me the hell alone anyway."

"What about Cloud 9? I thought we had a date?"

Alice glared at him for a moment, shaking her head.

Johnny smiled again and left her alone. She had come back to her senses. She was in good hands at Alma's. He hoped she was on her way to getting her life back on track.

Another time during one of his weekend stays at Alma's, one of the cook's saucepans kept disappearing. It was one of her favorite pans and she wasn't pleased that someone was running off with it. During a break from working with patients, Johnny went out on the back steps from the kitchen to smoke. While sitting there he noticed something underneath one of the cars. He went to investigate. It was the missing saucepan. He took it back to the kitchen, assuming that the mystery was solved.

The next day, the pan was gone again. Johnny found it in the same place underneath the same car. Johnny got the maintenance man to help him examine the car for clues. When they took off the radiator cap under the hood, they had their answer. It took just one sniff. The radiator of the car was filled with alcohol. They took their discovery to Alma. When they confronted the owner of the car, a man who had committed himself to rehab, he admitted having drained the radiator and refilled it with alcohol.

It was just to help him through the worst of the DT's, he insisted. He knew Alma would not give him any strong drink to help him through the process and he hated the taste of the medication. So he had brought his own "medicine" to help him through the cure. Each night, he would sneak out with the sauce- pan, open the bottom drain on the radiator, and fill up the pan with what he needed. His error was in drinking so much and feeling so good that he forgot to put the pan back in the kitchen afterwards.

CHAPTER 20

A Worthy Citizen

THERE WERE OTHER WAYS BESIDES WORKING HARD for the Air Force and devoting himself to helping fellow alcoholics into recovery that Johnny used to put himself on the path to becoming a "worthy citizen." One Sunday, he and Mary Elizabeth took the dogs and went for a pleasant drive in the New England countryside.

Their wanderings took them well off the beaten path. Driving along a dirt road, they came across a large sign posted to a tree in front of a quaint old farm. It announced that a farm auction would be held the next weekend. Johnny and Mary Elizabeth thought it would be a nice New England "experience" to attend the auction. They might even pick up a couple of antiques to decorate their apartment in Leominster.

A week later, they loaded up the car with the dogs and a picnic basket to attend their first farm auction. After they arrived, they toured the old farmhouse with a couple of dozen other people during the late morning. Then at 2 p.m. the auction began.

Johnny and Mary Elizabeth had found a few items that they were interested in, but quickly learned that there would be no bidding on individual items. Each potential bidder in the audience was given an envelope with a piece of paper and a pencil. They were instructed to write their bids for the farm on the paper and to put it in the envelope. They were also to include a $500 check. The checks would be returned to all the losing bidders. For the winning bidder, the check would count towards the purchase of the farm.

Johnny and Mary Elizabeth conferred quickly about what they should do. Johnny thought that they should at least put in a bid. It seemed like the appropriate thing to do if one attended an auction.

Besides, now that he was no longer drinking and living the wild life, he had plenty of money for their day-to-day needs. It wouldn't hurt them to put in modest bid for the farm. The worst that could happen is that they could end up with a good investment at a great price.

With this line of reasoning, Mary Elizabeth agreed that it would be fun to make a bid. Johnny wrote $11,700 on his bid sheet, put it in the envelope and added a $500 personal check.

A week later, they received a phone call. Their bid was the highest. Their presence was requested at a closing meeting to finalize the sale. At the meeting, Johnny thought to ask how much land came with the farm. He remembers the sales agent being apologetic. "The farm doesn't come with all of its fields," he said. "They are being sold separately. There are only 108 acres that come with the farm buildings."

Johnny remembers that you could have pushed him over with a feather at that moment. A poor, illiterate, homeless Indian from New Mexico had just bought himself a 108-acre piece of New England with nearly as many buildings on it as made up the whole community of his birth at Sheep Springs.

Next the sales agent took Mary Elizabeth and Johnny to the farm site for a new-owner tour of the facility before they signed off on the deal. When they arrived, they were surprised to find that the previous owners had not yet moved out their belongings. Johnny asked the obvious question. When would the former occupants move out their things so that he and his wife could begin moving in?

The sales agent seemed surprised. "It's all yours," he said. "Everything comes with the estate."

"Everything?" Johnny was incredulous.

"The silverware? The bedding? The pictures on the walls?" Mary Elizabeth asked.

"Well, there are a lot of things you may not wish to keep," the sales agent replied. "There's old clothing in the closets and in the dresser drawers. They belonged to the old couple who lived here, but they are now deceased."

And so it was that Johnny and Mary Elizabeth became the owners of a New England farm. And everything in it. They soon separated out the things that they wanted to keep and disposed of the items that they would not need.

"Oh, man, we got a lot of antiques in that deal," Johnny remembers. "There were dozens of wonderful old pieces of furniture and stuff. And the barn and outbuildings were filled with all kinds of old equipment." The main house had been built in 1772. It burned down in 1815, but had been rebuilt on the same foundation in 1820." That was the house that they bought 140 years later. "I swear half of the stuff in that house was from the 1820s!" Johnny recalls.

Besides his work with A. A. and their move into an old farmhouse, there was one other step Johnny took to become a better citizen. He joined the Masons. "Way back when I was a boy working for Mr. Ritchey at the funeral home, there was a well-dressed and educated man who used to stop and talk to me from time to time," Johnny explains.

He walked past the funeral home often on his way to and from work. He must have noticed how impressed I was with him. One time I asked him how I could become more like him. As the youngest child in a big family, I had learned early that you have to be bold to get anything in this world.

He took an interest in me when I asked him that question. He's the one who told me about how to be wise with my money. He told me that if I saved ten cents right off the top from each dollar I earned, I would have all the money I needed to live a good life by the time I was his age. If I wanted to speed that up, I just had to save ten additional cents from each dollar I spent. I never forgot that advice and during much of my life, I followed it.

Anyway, that man had worn a big ring on one hand. I never forgot that ring. Later in life, I saw it again. It was a Masonic ring. In New England, I decided I was ready to wear that kind of ring myself. The ring had come to represent in my mind the kind of person I wanted to try to become.

One of the most enduring characteristics of Johnny's life story is, without question, his inquisitive mind. He was always eager, as Mr. Ritchey put it early on, "to climb the tree" of knowledge. Even during his worst periods of alcoholism, marital struggles, or recovery in a mental hospital from war wounds, Johnny constantly worked to educate his mind. The Masons fed this hunger for knowledge and Johnny threw himself into learning all that his new Masonic "brothers" could teach him.

"It was part of becoming a better person," he says. "I wanted to learn. I wanted to develop a type of life that I had not known before. It's a hard, hard life to be an alcoholic and to do all those things you do that you know you are going to be sorry for later. I had a lot of bad stuff to work myself out of." During his time in New England, he was associated first with the Caleb Butler Lodge of Masons at Ayer, Massachusetts and the Valley of Nashua Lodge in New Hampshire.

It took Johnny about a year to complete the various stages of the educational program offered by the Masons. At that point, he became eligible to join the Shriners Organization, which he did. He has stayed active in the Shriners for the rest of his life. He likes the work the Shriners do to provide healthcare and hope to the poorest children of the world through their hospitals. Years later, he became the sponsor of a Guatemalan boy who had been born without legs. He helped the boy and his mother afford the journey to Springfield, Massachusetts, to undergo seventeen operations over the years and to be fitted with prosthetic legs.

As Johnny devoted himself to being a productive citizen and doing good for others, he soon found that good came back his way. Sometimes in most surprising forms. The one major career limitation that Johnny still faced in his new life in New England was the loss of his high security military clearances. His addiction to alcohol had lost them for him. It was perhaps only fitting that his willingness to help others combat this disease finally earned those clearances back. Here's how it happened.

One day, after I had a year's sobriety, an officer showed up at the weather station. He said, 'Good morning, John! How are you doing today?'

I was shocked when he addressed me by my first name since he was a two-star general staring me in the face, asking for a briefing.

Fine, sir!'

'Let's go have a cup of coffee,' he said.

'I can't. I'm briefing some pilots,' I told him.

'We'll get someone to take over for you,' he replied. 'Hey Captain! Do you mind taking over for John here while we go have a cup of coffee?'

'No sir!' he said. What else could he say to a general?

So we went down to the break room and sat down with our coffee. I was quite puzzled about how such a high-ranking officer could know me and want a briefing from me.

He said, 'I heard you last night, John.'

'You heard me last night?'

'I heard you over at the A. A. meeting.'

'Oh my God! Don't tell me!'

He said, 'Yep, I'm one of the biggest!'

I said, 'Well, I don't know what to do.'

'You've lost all your clearances, haven't you?' he said. 'You've been having trouble.'

I said, 'Yes. That's a fact.'

He asked, 'How would you like to get them all back?'

I replied, 'Come on, sir. Does the bear shit in the woods? I'd love to have them back.'

'Well then, let's just make sure that you have them back in about six months.'

'Come on, General,' I answered. 'There's no way I could get them back in six months, and furthermore, why me? I don't even know if I will stay sober. I've only been sober for about a year.'

He said, 'I don't know, John. All I know is that I owe someone, and you happen to be it.'

Six months to the day after that meeting, I got my clearances back!

The clearances that were reinstated for Johnny allowed him to work at the military's "Top Secret" and "Q" levels of operations. He had first been awarded this level of access upon his return from

Honduras. His superiors had been impressed with his ability to get things done in a foreign environment and to do so in their own language. They saw these as highly valuable skills for more sensitive and dangerous work that the U.S. government, like most governments, often feels it needs to carry out. Johnny had proven both in Honduras and in assignments since that he could "get the job done" despite highly challenging obstacles.

With his clearances reinstated and his proven background as an international operative came another major change in his life. In 1960, Johnny was inducted into the "Special Weather Service" by the National Security Agency in Washington. The induction was accompanied by special training back at Langley Air Force Base in Virginia. At a training center there, military instructors taught Staff Sergeant Johnny Sarmiento the basic skills for carrying out special operations.

Upon graduation, he became part of a network of special operatives with various "neutral" military roles who can be posted to any U.S. embassy or consulate around the world without drawing attention to themselves. They have knowledge and skills needed by local populations and can make valuable contributions to their host nations through their embassy work.

They also have the knowledge and skills to help the U.S. carry out sensitive missions deemed necessary to secure our national interests by the National Security Agency in Washington. Johnny likes to emphasize that he was not a spy. He was much lower on the secret operations food chain. He was just an Air Force weatherman who had been trained to do what he was told. And not to ask questions.

As a member of the Special Weather Service, Johnny's services were no longer needed back at Fort Devons in New England. The National Security Agency elected rather to send him on assignment to one of the worst places in the world for a recovering alcoholic. His supervisors decided that his services were most needed in France. And so off Johnny went, to the heartland of the nation with the highest alcohol consumption per capita in the world. For three years.

CHAPTER 21

Living in No-Man's-Land

THE MAN WHO STEPPED ONTO A PLANE out of Newark, New Jersey bound for Paris in late 1960 was not the same Johnny Sarmiento who had shipped off to North Africa and to Europe at the height of World War II. He was not the same person who had gone to Austria and Germany a dozen years before. He was significantly changed even from the soldier who had been posted to South Korea three years before. Johnny sums up what had changed.

> *By this point in my life, I was beginning to find myself. I had been sober for a year and a half. I had found a way of life that I enjoyed. Despite all the obstacles that came, I still managed to stay within the limits of what life is all about. I was able to treat others like human beings because I was finding the human being in myself. I liked what I found.*

In Johnny's new world, there was less anger. As he puts it, "You don't lose the anger all at once. You just cut it down, bit by bit." Once he sobered up and began living in New England, Johnny began to see things differently. It was not a sudden change nor dramatic in scope.

In his interactions with people on a day-to-day basis, he found himself less defensive. Even on trips back home to New Mexico, he says, "It became apparent to me when I stopped at gas stations and met rednecks and white supremists. I realized that 85 percent of the discrimination was make-believe. It was all in my head. The other 15 percent I could handle."

Once Johnny's vision was no longer clouded by alcoholism and despair, he began to see a different world. It was one where a white undertaker would take in a Navajo boy and give back much in return as that boy worked off the cost of a father's burial. He educated the boy at his own expense, spending long hours tutoring him through correspondence courses. He bailed him out of trouble. He cared for his young friend.

Johnny began to see a world in which soldier buddies treated him as one of them. And the list goes on. A German woman fell in love with him and had his daughter. A wealthy American woman pulled him from the depths of alcoholism and married him. College professors found him intelligent. People in Honduras treated him as an equal and as more than an equal. The Masons welcomed him into their fraternity. The Shriners did likewise. An American general even came personally to his aid. "Whenever I asked for help from Anglo-Saxon individuals all along my career, people helped me when I needed it most," Johnny sums up, "It's hard to keep carrying anger and hatred inside when people do that."

But there is a deeper dimension to the forgiveness that Johnny was beginning to feel towards his fellow inhabitants of the earth. The more he saw of the world, the more his perspective broadened on the ugliness and injustice into which he was born on a Navajo Indian reservation. It became harder to see himself and his people as unique victims in a white world after seeing what white Christians were willing to do to each other in war-torn Europe.

Memories of the bloody battles in which he participated personally, the total destruction of the Benedictine Monastery devoted to peace atop Monte Cassino, the devastated villages he marched through with the stench of dead civilians and burned flesh assaulting his nostrils, the fire-bombings of major cities, the long-term suffering of entire nations after the war, the burning of thousands of dead and not-so-dead on a battlefield in Korea—all of these memories combined to change how Johnny Pail Face perceived the suffering of his own people in the American West. In the end, it became more difficult to take the suffering personally. He says now:

> *We, the entire world, start out as nothing but a bunch of racists. No matter where you are, no matter who you are, you have a prejudice*

against someone. You have your jokes, your slights, your slanders, your hatred for someone.

But this is what happens—you end up finding out that everyone is human. Once you make this realization, you have to start treating them as such. It's hard to feel good about going out and slaughtering human beings.

As he neared the middle point of his life, Johnny also had come to understand that there were many different ways to be a human being. He had been born a mixed-blood Navajo. He had learned Spanish from his parents and from playing with Spanish-speaking children in the towns around the reservation. He had learned how to be an English-speaking human being in order to make his way in a white world. He had become a German-speaking human being during his time in Austria and Germany after the war.

In 1960, Johnny was on his way to put on another human identity, a French one. I asked Johnny if it was not a serious challenge to learn a new language, especially at mid-life. He laughed with a roguish glint in his eyes and repeated one of his favorite observations. "All you have to do is find a good bed-side dictionary," he assured me. "I prefer ones with beautiful legs."

The fact that he already spoke four languages put Johnny in a good place to understand what it means to learn someone else's language. It's about more than picking up a new vocabulary. One doesn't just keep saying the same things, thinking the same thoughts, and being the same person when vocalizing a new language. Everything you are changes. As Johnny puts it:

To learn a new language and culture is to learn a new identity. You become a different person. You become a person of that country's nature, of their attitude. You begin to see things the way they see them, to feel the way they feel. I went to France to experiment with these things. I had met a lot of French during the Big War. A whole sector of Austria was under French control. Everyone in Europe seemed a little in awe of them, and especially of their culture. I wanted to find out what it was like to become part of their culture.

Things did not start well on Johnny's journey into France. He boarded a commercial airliner at 10 p.m. departing from New Jersey and bound for Paris. But first they stopped in Newfoundland to let off some passengers there. This made the crossing of the Atlantic into a fourteen-hour trip, which was better than the crossings Johnny had made by boat earlier in life, but still left him exhausted.

He arrived at Charles de Gaulle Airport at noon the next day. As tired as he was from sitting for so many hours, his first response to France was a positive one: "As I looked around the airport, I was amazed to see so many beautiful women working there."

At this point, he did not speak a word of French. However, he was soon able to find one of the "beautiful women" who was willing to speak English to him. She explained that he would need to catch a train to his final destination, the small town of Vitry-le-François some 60 miles to the east of Paris. To do so, he had to get to the Gare de l'Est, or the East Train Station. He converted some dollars into French francs and took a taxi into Paris and to the station. With a little looking around, he found the right train and started the next leg of his journey.

It was dark by the time Johnny arrived at Vitry-le-François. At this point, he had been without sleep for nearly 24 hours. In all of that time, he had not had food or drink. When he tried to ask people passing by for directions in English to the American military base, they just ignored him.

Then he heard a woman speaking to her children in English. With a good deal of relief he went to her and explained that he was completely lost and needed directions to the U.S. military base.

She wasn't sure which base he was after as things were scattered around a bit, so she said, "Just go over there and get a cab. Tell them that you want the Medical Depot. That's an American medical outfit."

The cabbie seemed to understand what he wanted and soon deposited Johnny at the gates of the depot. The American guard let him in and he went to the Service Man's Club to get something to eat and to ask about a place to sleep. There he faced his first major challenge of life in France. Johnny explains.

I walked over to the bar. There was a guy standing there with seven or eight drinks lined up in front of him. He looked at me and said, 'Thank God you're here because you can help me finish these before the bar closes. It's getting to be closing time and I don't want to leave them. Please help me get rid of them. Please help me!'

I said, 'Nope. Nope! I can't help you there. I don't drink.'

To this day, Johnny marvels that he was able to withstand the temptation to help that soldier finish his drinks. "What gave me the will to proceed?" he asks, and then answers, "I can only say that the Creator must have been right there for me. I was so tired and hungry and thirsty and so far away from my safety net of A. A. friends."

Instead, Johnny asked the bartender if he had some coffee and something a man could eat. The only coffee was left over from the morning and the bartender assured him that it was "awfully strong." For food, all the man had was some peanut butter crackers. So, Johnny's first meal in France ended up being a far cry from an elegant French dinner. But he made do.

When Johnny inquired about a bed, he found that there were no sleeping quarters for visitors at the Medical Depot. The best the bartender could suggest was that he go to the guard shack and ask permission to sleep in their bunks during the four hours that they were on duty. "So this is what I did," Johnny recalls. "I crawled into one of their beds and when the guy came back, I'd get into another bed, and that is how I spent my first night in France."

The next morning, Johnny was able to get the Colonel in charge of the weather station at the main Lyon Air Force Base on the line, despite the less-than-trustworthy French telephone system at the time. When the Colonel started giving him instructions on which trains and buses to take to get to the weather station, Johnny finally hit his breaking point.

"Look, I'm sick and tired of pushing and doing. I'm not moving an inch from this place. You send someone here to pick me up, right now! I'll be damned if I'm gonna stay here. I'll get on the next train back to Paris and catch the next plane back home!"

It was not normally the way a sergeant would speak to a colonel, but it worked. "Okay, okay," the Colonel responded. "I'll get somebody up there, but it'll take a couple or three hours to get there. It's all right, now."

On his second day in France, Johnny again faced his worst enemy as a recovering alcoholic. As he recalls, "A few hours later, two young Americans showed up in a station wagon. As soon as I got in the car with them, they handed me a bottle of Beaujolais and offered me a drink."

Again, Johnny held firm: "I said, 'Thanks! But I don't drink.'"

Finally, three days after leaving Newark, New Jersey, Johnny's trip came to an end with a good meal and a comfortable bed at the Lyon Air Base. Once he got under the sheets, it was nearly 24 hours before he reported back to the Colonel for his orders. And then, Johnny's new French life got into full swing.

Professionally, he had a couple of important roles to play at the weather station. One was an official role that was communicated to the French Government. The other was a role that could have gotten him killed had the French Government learned of it. Johnny provides the details of both.

I was supposed to set up a gunnery range near a little town called Suippes, which was a place that still had a lot of unrecovered ordinance (bombs, mortar shells, mines) in the ground left over from the war. This would be used by the French and U.S. Air Forces to practice bombing and strafing instead of having to fly across the Mediterranean Sea to North Africa, as they had been doing.

The U.S. F100s and F105s and the French Caravels were using a bombing range at Wheeler Air Force Base in Libya, which required that they use wing tip tanks in order to have enough fuel to get there and back. This would leave them with only about twenty minutes of practice time over the target range after they dropped their fuel tanks.

Our weather station was to monitor upper-level wind direction and speed. The fighter bombers would climb to high altitude and then release a dummy black powder nuclear bomb, roll over to their backs, and roar away upwind from the rising explosion, smoke, and shock wave.

Johnny's role as weatherman was not only to advise the pilots on the general weather conditions so that they could choose good days for target practice, but knowing the direction of the wind was also crucial to their training. In the case of a real nuclear bombing, it was essential that they fly upwind or risk dying themselves in the mushroom cloud and attendant shock wave that they created.

Johnny and his small weather station team were quartered at an abandoned World War II airbase that the U.S. had leased for 99 years from the French. It included a large fuel tank farm where millions of gallons of aviation and ground transport fuel were stored. The facilities at Vitry were a main refueling hub for U.S. military convoys carrying goods to bases in Germany from the Atlantic ports. Drivers regularly stopped over for a night of sleep in converted airplane hangars there as they refueled their trucks.

Keeping an American base in the heartland of France fifteen years after World War II made good sense for the reasons above. Americans and French pilots could work together to hone their bombing skills, skills that were especially crucial in the nuclear world of the Cold War with their common enemy, the Soviet Union. At the same time, they were clearing a piece of French countryside from unexploded ordinance left behind by the Germans from the most recent war. Finally, the French were helping their allies by providing a vast facility for storing and using fuel to keep the American military mobile in Europe.

In the early 1960s, the French were happy to share their land and various military undertakings in Europe with the Americans. The French military was bogged down in a violent revolution in their overseas colony in Algeria, North Africa. The Algerians were tired of being a French colony. They wanted independence. Johnny soon learned that the Americans were using the French facilities at Vitry-le-François for another purpose as well, one the French would have been surprised to learn about. A couple of times a month, an unusual shipping container would be delivered by one of the truck convoys coming through on the way to Germany. Johnny recounts.

Occasionally, a fork lift was needed to unload a large crate from one of the trucks, which would be left on the floor of the hangar. When two or three of these crates had been left behind, I would call a certain phone number and a DC3 or a C47, the two-engine military freight version of a DC3, would be sent from Lyon.

We would load the crates on the plane and strap them down. Then I would go with them to a destination in Algeria, not too far away from Onan, that had a dirt landing strip where we would unload the boxes to the nomad Arabs.

They would hand me a small box a little bigger than a cigar box, very heavy, for each crate that we delivered. We would then rest and have something to eat, usually mutton that they grilled on a spit over an open fire. We had a young interpreter there, a Moroccan Arab who could speak English, French, and Arabic, to assist us in dealing with the nomads.

When we returned to France, we would land first at Lyon, where I would take the small boxes to the American Express Office, and I would get a receipt from the man in charge, detailing how many boxes I had given him. From there I would use buses to get back to Vitry. These delivery runs would continue on and on, two or three times a month, as the large crates were dropped off to us.

I was told that if the French authorities were to grab me in Algeria, I would probably be sentenced to fifteen years in a Foreign Legion prison and could expect to live about three. They told me to be very careful because if I was caught they would not be able to do anything but to deny they knew anything about it.

At that time, the Algerians were fighting to win their independence from French control. The French Government, while a U.S. ally, stood as the middle man between U.S. oil interests in Algeria and the oil they wanted. These secret shipments, which were arms and ammunition for the rebels, were the CIA's way of encouraging the Algerians to eliminate the 'middle man.' The small boxes, I later learned, contained one twenty-four carat gold bar each, bearing the markings of the French mint! It must have been gold the Algerians had looted from the French banks.

Johnny had been selected to run guns to the Algerian rebels because of his cover as a weatherman. The official purpose of his flights across the Mediterranean was to help the local people set up a weather station in a peaceful, goodwill gesture from the U.S. Government. Were he to be apprehended by America's French allies, leaders in Washington would have expressed shock and outrage that he had smuggled weapons onto his weather plane.

So Johnny smuggled other things onto his weather plane as well. His commanding officer helped him do so. When he advised Johnny of the serious danger in which each flight put him, he also advised Johnny to make the flights "pay off" for himself personally. And he cleared a letter to the U.S. Exchange Services authorizing Johnny to buy anything he wanted and as much as he wanted from the Base Exchange. With such encouragement from above, Johnny was back in the black market business in a big way.

Johnny knew the business well from his years in Austria and Germany. In France in 1960, here is how he ran his latest operation.

I got cartons of cigarettes for 90 cents each which I sold in Algeria for three and a half or four dollars each. I also purchased cases of vodka that, although the Arabs were forbidden by their religion to drink, I suppose they turned around and made a profit on by trading them to the French. I did the same with blue jeans and anything else I could find for this business. The Arabs paid for all this in American 100 dollar bills, which they seemed to have plenty of. Where they got them, I did not know. These they couldn't have looted from the French in their battles.

During his years in France, Johnny lived in a moral and ethical "no-man's-land." There is a bit of irony for him to look back now and to realize that the U.S. Government was acting as a renegade force much as Johnny had done himself as a young entrepreneur in Gallup, New Mexico. As a young businessman in Gallup, he had used his taxi service to supply Indians with illegal alcohol and to buy into a local brothel. The only benefit to such activities was to put money into his pocket. In 1960, the U.S. Government was supplying Arabs with guns and ammunition so that they could defeat the French. This would give the U.S. a direct source to Arab oil once the French lost Algeria. The benefit to such activities was to put money into American pockets. It's easy to accept living in a moral no-man's- land when your government is doing likewise.

Johnny followed his commander's advice to make a tough assignment "pay off" for himself in other ways as well. In 1960, the French population was still on a form of gas rationing from the war period. The U.S. was assisting the French with this problem by making gasoline available at gas stations that displayed U.S. Military Quartermaster signs out front. Gas station owners could purchase coupons from the U.S. that they in turn would sell to their customers, allowing them to purchase U.S. fuel.

Johnny and his fellow soldiers got all the gas they needed for free from the tank farm by just helping themselves. According to proper procedure, they were supposed to buy gas coupons from the Base Exchange and to use those to purchase gas off-base the same way that the French did. They did, indeed, buy gas coupons at the Base, where they got a significantly reduced military rate of 20 cents a coupon. They then took the coupons to the gas station owners who cheerfully paid the soldiers up to six times their 20 cents per coupon and everyone involved made a handsome profit.

Between running a thriving one-man black market of cigarettes, vodka, jeans, and other items in Algeria, and selling gas coupons in the villages around the base, Johnny never lacked for cash during his three years in France. He also learned a good deal about two new cultures.

Johnny's culture-crossing skills were seriously tested in his interactions with the Arabs he met in Algeria. As a gun-runner from a country that was turning traitor on one of its own allies Johnny hardly represented a figure that the rough fighters of North Africa with their honor codes and Islamic sense of justice were inclined to respect. As Johnny recalls:

> *The nomad Arabs, who were not particularly friendly, did a couple of things that never stood well with me. They were very jealous people, dirty, cynical and intimidating.*
>
> *They would have an attractive young girl walk past the place where you were sitting having your dinner and would watch your eyes to*

see if you were looking at the girl so that they could take that as an offense of some kind. If you did, they would cast the 'evil eye' on you.

I wasn't about to be intimidated. I just didn't give a damn.

Another thing they did was to wipe the mutton grease from their hands into their hair and all over their long shirts as they carved pieces of the meat from a spit over their camp fire. As you can imagine, they did not smell very good with all that rancid grease on them.

One time, the young Moroccan interpreter with whom I spoke English and was friendly with was wearing a beautiful knife on his belt. It had a bone or ivory handle studded with semi-precious stones. I asked him if I could see it.

He said 'No. I don't want to take it out.'

I said, 'Oh come on. We're friends, aren't we?'

He then drew it from its sheath, placed the tip of the blade on his thumb, and sliced a deep cut into it. He proceeded to wipe the blood from his thumb all over the blade before holding it out for me to take it.

I asked him, 'What the hell are you doing?'

He said that if he ever drew that knife, his customs required that he draw blood with it. Since I was his friend, he did not wish to draw mine.

I learned a lesson from that. You've got to learn the local customs before you start barging into people's lives.

With time, Johnny did learn a few things about how to "barge in" to the lives of the rough men he met in the deserts of North Africa. The knowledge may have saved his life at the end when the insurgents no longer needed him. Johnny retells what happened on the evening of his final gun delivery.

At about dinner time, my Moroccan interpreter overheard the Algerian nomads, while they ate their mutton, discussing how they would cut my throat in my sleep and hijack my plane and goods. He came over to me and warned me about their plans.

I put my food down and walked over to the Algerians with the interpreter. I told him to tell the nomads that if they wanted to find me to cut my throat, I would be sleeping right over there, under the nose of the plane.

The pilot and the copilot got no sleep that night. I was not disturbed by anyone and had a good sleep.

Perhaps it was because of his own roots in another desert warrior culture that Johnny knew instinctively how to deal with the Arab fighters in Algeria. He met them on their own terms and in a manner that brought, however reluctantly, their respect.

Had he been posted to Algeria rather than to France, it is entirely possible that Johnny would have learned the Arabic language and would have integrated into the local culture. To this day, he retains a deep respect for Arab peoples. He was able to distinguish between the unsavory nomads who he met in less than ideal circumstances on lonely, isolated airstrips and the larger cultures of the Arab world. He now keeps a copy of the Koran on his reading table. He does not hesitate to express admiration for the Prophet Mohammad and all that he accomplished in his lifetime. But Johnny Pail Face's experiences with Arab culture were only the backdrop for much deeper cultural crossing that occurred simultaneously in this period of his life. Back at his home base in France, Johnny was making a place for himself among the French.

CHAPTER 22

Le Fou Américain in France

JOHNNY KNEW THAT THE BEST WAY TO INTEGRATE HIMSELF into French culture was to find a good translator. He found one about a month after arriving in Vitry-le-François. Her name was Madame Rolande DuPont. He met her when he and a couple of other soldiers decided to go exploring in the villages around the base one day.

Johnny had been looking for a place off-base to rent and so he welcomed the invitation by two friends at the club to go for an afternoon drive. In a nearby village called Pogny, they came across what had once been either a very large, elegant home or a small castle. The structure was mostly in ruins, but as they poked around, they found that a few enterprising French had fixed up one wing to make it livable again. They had made apartments for themselves and were squatting on a piece of property that had not yet been reclaimed by the owners, who had likely perished in the war. They met one of the squatters. She was a woman in her late thirties who introduced herself in broken English as Rolande du Pont.

The soldiers chatted with her for a bit and then invited her to spend the evening with them back at the club. This was a time when American G. I.s were still considered national heroes by many of the French for having helped to chase the Germans out of their country and for ending Hitler's reign of terror. Plus, the French were still living through hard times nearly a decade and a half after war's end. Mme. DuPont would have known that there was no place like an American military base for a woman to get a good meal, one with meat and side dishes and coffee and dessert, maybe even a cigarette or two afterwards. She cheerfully accepted their invitation.

The foursome had a good dinner at the club, followed by drinking and dancing. Johnny held true to his abstinence from alcohol, drinking only Schweppes tonic water. This meant that by evening's end, he was the only one sober enough to drive Mme. DuPont home. When he stopped the car in front of her castle apartment, she said, "I no sleep with you."

As a healthy, confident career soldier who had been around the world and back, Johnny took this statement as a challenge. He turned on his charm, using all the words that he knew in both English and broken French to soften her resolve. Finally, she agreed that he could come in to see the interesting and creative ways that she had fixed up her piece of the castle.

Johnny recalls what happened next. "We went in the door, immediately got naked, and spent the night together." It was the beginning of a three-year relationship that Johnny remembers these many years later with much fondness. "I called her my little French dictionary," he sighs now. Johnny soon moved in with Rolande at the broken-down castle in the small village of Pogny. The French woman seemed happy to welcome Johnny into her life and into the life of her small village. She devoted herself to helping him learn French and was surprised at how quickly he did so. For his part, Johnny devoted himself to making life better for his new French friend and tutor.

> *The chateau was in ruins. Rolande occupied one large, long room. Her bedroom was at the back of the big room. Her kitchen was on one side near the front. She had a makeshift living room between the two. In the back yard was an outhouse. The back yard was big with a high stone wall around it. The good part of her living arrangement was that she occupied the place for free, with electricity and running water included. The bad part was that it was not a place many people would want to live.*

So Johnny decided to fix up their "castle." Not far away was an abandoned Canadian Air Force Base. It had a number of trailers in which the Canadians had housed troops and their families during the early rebuilding of France. On his days off, Johnny began spending time there salvaging things to fix up Rolande's apartment. He took out all the kitchen fixtures in one trailer, including sink, countertops, and cook stove. From another trailer, he pulled a bathroom sink. Then he salvaged some plywood in good condition and put a wall across Rolande's one big room, giving her bedroom some privacy from the living area. Last, he went out and bought a good kerosene heater to keep the drafty, high-ceilinged apartment warm in winter. At the bombing range 40 kilometers north where he worked during the days, he picked up a 55-gallon barrel and filled it with diesel oil. This provided the apartment with an ample supply of heating fuel for the year.

As the months went by and Johnny's French improved with Rolande's constant help, he found himself slipping deeper and deeper into life in Pogny. At the core of things was his natural cheer and generosity to the people he met each day. One story helps to illustrate how this friendly Navajo wanderer began to break down the doors of cool French reserve.

Every morning at the bombing range, the U.S. Air Force supplied the staff of twelve to fourteen men with breakfast. The cooking staff always brought a five-gallon supply of fresh milk for the men to drink. And every day at least four gallons of it went unused and was thrown out. This bothered Johnny. So he instructed the cooks to put the leftover milk in the back of his car each day. He then took it back to the village and put it out on the edge of the street in front of the castle with a sign in French that announced "Free Milk." Rolande spread word in the neighborhood to reassure her fellow citizens that the milk was good. Soon, wives and mothers came to count on Johnny's generosity as part of their daily routine of feeding hungry families.

Rolande was grateful for the unusual new dimension her close American friend brought to her life, but this did not mean that she gave up her independence. She continued to work at a local box-making factory and to live her life the way that she chose. Her job at the factory was to bundle completed cardboard boxes into shipments. The hard physical labor provided a modest salary, but it was honest work and Rolande was content to live simply.

In her relationship with Johnny, she also kept things simple. From the outset, she made clear that she was not interested in marriage.

She had tried that once and didn't like it. Rolande even expressed relief at the news that Johnny was married. That kept the matrimony issue at a safe distance. At one point in her relationship with Johnny, Mary Elizabeth came for a three-week visit and husband and wife toured Europe. Not only did Rolande accept this inconvenience, she gave Johnny some of her savings from her meager earnings at the factory so that he could treat his wife the way a woman ought to be treated in the capitals of Europe. It was the sort of gesture that is not uncommon among French women who take on the role of lover.

Rolande didn't talk much with Johnny about her previous life either. As is common among the French, she was a private person. This is something that Native Americans tend to understand and to respect. In Native parlance, she "kept her secrets." In many Native cultures, to give up one's secrets to another person means giving that person power over you. There has to be a deep level of trust and a good reason to do such a thing. So it was that Johnny only learned that Rolande had a daughter who was in her twenties when he was preparing to be reassigned back to the U.S. near the end of their three years together. Rolande's daughter longed to immigrate to America and Rolande came to Johnny for advice and support to help her.

In order to understand and to appreciate the cultural "mentality" of women like Mme. Rolande du Pont and other French people living in and around Vitry-le-François, it is essential to know something of their history. Vitry is one of those towns with the great misfortune of always being "in the way" of armies. It was built on a major crossroads between great cities and nations. To this day, two of France's most important north-south and east-west routes *nationales* meet nearby. The east-west highway links France to Germany. National train routes do the same. Three canal waterways come through the region.

For a thousand years, Vitry-le-François has seen a constant stream of people and goods flow through their lives. The unfortunate part of this ebb and flow is that all too often the people and goods coming through have been warring armies and their supply trains. This gives Vitry a uniquely painful history.

In 1142, King Louis VII of France invaded in a dispute with the powerful Catholic bishops of the region who had the audacity to excommunicate him. He taught the religious leaders a lesson about who was in charge by burning alive all 1,300 citizens of Vitry. This mass burning was accomplished by locking men, women, and children in the village church and burning it to the ground. Despite such "scorched-earth" tactics, Louis still lost his fight with the Church. The Pope in Rome then required him to carry out a two-year crusade to the Holy Land and to slaughter more people as he had done in Vitry in order to be reinstated as a good Christian in the faith.[1]

In 1544, armies fought their way through again. This time they belonged to France's King François I and Germany's Emperor Charles V. It's not entirely clear who burned Vitry to the ground that year. It may have been both sides in their attempts to destroy the cover of the opposing forces. However, it seems that some of the local citizenry survived this time by fleeing the battle zone. And King François, perhaps feeling some remorse for his people's misfortune, rebuilt the town not far from its original site and lavished a good deal of attention on it, calling upon the best skills of his chief military architect, Girolmo Marini, from Bologna, Italy. By the end of the 1540s, Vitry had become a strikingly elegant rural town for the people who were still alive to admire the changes.

In 1814 during Napoléon Bonaparte's final campaign through Europe, the slaughter took place between French troops and Napoléon's European enemies, the Tsar of Russia, the King of Prussia, and the Austrian Generalissimo Schwartzenberg. The people of Vitry who survived this third campaign have two reasons to be cheerful. First, their village has the distinction of being the site where Napoléon narrowly missed capturing all three of his rivals in a brilliant rear-guard raid. This has fueled two centuries of "what if's" among scholars of military strategy and politics, as Napoléon went on to lose because of the missed opportunity at Vitry. The other positive outcome of the war from the perspective of the locals was that most of the town's buildings remained standing at war's end.

The twentieth century was a mixture of bad and worse for Vitry. During World War I, the town served first as the headquarters of the French Army under Marshall Joffre. His troops were routed early on by the Germans, but then a vicious counter-attack brought the place back under French control. After that, things weren't so bad. The town became a hospital city for the rest of the war and neither side burned or bombed it to the ground.

World War II made up for the forbearance shown in World War I. Vitry was completely leveled twice. In quick succession in 1940, the Germans bombed a quarter of the town and its inhabitants into oblivion and then the French counter-attacked and destroyed all but about ten percent of the buildings that the Germans had missed. An amazingly resilient population soon threw up huts and shanties on the town site and continued on with their lives as best they could. Four years later, the Allies came to their rescue and chased the Germans all the way back to their fatherland. The downside of this final rout was that some 500 citizens were killed by the friendly fire of their Allied saviors. And the entire city was leveled one more time.

Outsiders who do not know anything of the history of French towns like Vitry-le-François often are put off and even offended by the coolness and cynicism that characterize the outlook on life of the local populace. People like Johnny Pail Face who take time to listen and to learn about such things tend to be more understanding. Because of its strategic location on the highway to war, this French community of 17,000 people today retains only a single house and a couple of parts of the city walls from the beautiful town that François I built in the 1540s. The original inhabitants fared about the same.

With this dark background in mind, it is easier to understand the difficulty that citizens of the region had to make sense of Johnny's cheerful, "good-neighbor" approach to life. He, like them, had been constantly in the way of war in his own life. And yet he chose a different response to the ugliness of the human experience. The French were constantly surprised by this. Another story illustrates.

One hot day in early summer, Johnny came across a stalled car about three kilometers from Pogny. He stopped to see if he could be of service. A well-dressed man was looking under the hood. His wife was sitting in the car fanning herself. Johnny and the man tried for a time to get the car running but with no success. He then offered to tow the car back to town. The Frenchman seemed shocked and suspicious. With an air of independence, he assured Johnny that he could walk to town and send a tow truck back for the car.

Johnny agreed that was one option that would work. However, he added, that his concern was mainly for Madame who was sitting in the hot car. It would make a long, unpleasant wait for her and she did not seem to be dressed properly to take the long walk with him. Johnny told him he'd be happy to drive both of them on into town. As that was the way he was going anyway, it would be no trouble to him. The neat, well-dressed gentleman gave in to Johnny's logic with warm expressions of gratitude. Johnny assisted husband and wife into his American-made Nash Rambler and soon deposited them at the front door of their home with both thanking him profusely.

The next winter, Rolande came down with a bad cold and called her doctor for an appointment. The appointment was in the afternoon at a time when Johnny could stop at the doctor's office and pick her up on his way home from work. When Johnny drove up to the doctor's home and office that afternoon, he recognized the place. It was where he had taken the well-dressed couple home the previous summer when their car broke down.

There was no place to park legally so Johnny sat in the car waiting for Rolande to come down. When a woman came by heading into the doctor's office, Johnny asked her from the car window if she might inquire for a Madame Rolande DuPont in the doctor's office. If she were there, might she inform her that Johnny was waiting outside to take her home?

The woman scowled and went into the doctor's office without responding. Johnny knew French culture well enough to understand that he had overstepped the boundaries of proper etiquette between strangers. He shrugged it off and kept waiting. Understanding the French did not mean that he was going to stop being himself.

A couple of minutes later, Rolande came out and got in the car. She was laughing.

"What is so funny?" Johnny asked.

"You have made quite a name for yourself in this village," she replied, still chuckling.

"Why? What happened?"

She explained that a woman had just come into the doctor's office and had asked everyone in the waiting room if there was a Madame Rolande du Pont there. Roland had been saying goodbye to the doctor. When she indicated that she was Rolande du Pont, the woman informed her that an American "pig" was outside waiting for her in his car.

When the doctor heard the derogatory reference to Johnny, he became indignant. "In this office, you will never say anything bad about that man," he told the woman firmly. "Last summer my car broke down and he helped my wife and me through a very difficult situation. He did not require money or even a thank you for his kindness."

Johnny's interactions with the villagers of Pogny ranged from big things like helping the doctor and his wife to the mundane. On his days off from work, he took up the practice of riding his bicycle to the bakery shop on the village square each morning for fresh bread and croissants while Rolande got a hot pot of French coffee going. Rolande soon learned that there was no need to hurry in preparing the morning coffee. Johnny's trips to the bakery began to take longer and longer as he made friends in the community.

It was his practice to greet everyone he met with "bonjour" and a cheerful comment on the day as he rode by on his bicycle. If he met someone he knew, he would stop and chat. At the bakery, he would do his best to make the baker's wife laugh with his teasing. Soon, the whole village came to call him "le fou américain" or "the crazy American." But Rolande assured him that they invariably smiled and shook their heads in wonder when they spoke of him this way. It was an affectionate title that they had bestowed upon him, one acknowledging that they didn't quite know what to do with this strange fellow from America. It also suggested that they could not bring themselves to dislike him, hard as they might try.

Johnny remembers going to the grocery store one day with Rolande. As they were entering, an older woman with two large bags was staggering out. Johnny immediately helped her down the steps leading out of the market and carried her bags to the bus stop. The store owner watched as this was happening and then turned to Rolande. "Is he always like this?" he asked.

Rolande smiled. "Yes," she replied. "He is always like this."

Another source of goodwill for him in Pogny was Johnny's willingness to work the black market to the benefit of his fellow villagers. On the military base, he had ready access to goods that the villagers both lacked and longed for. In time, neighbors began to come to him regularly with orders for meat, cigarettes, vodka, shampoo, toothpaste and other items that were not available at the local markets. One time he even came up with a movie camera for a grateful contact. All of this was in addition to his regular traffic in gas coupons and free milk.

Reflecting back on this period in his life Johnny sums up:

> *In France, I never got into trouble because I got to understand the language, the culture, and the people. For example, whenever I got the chance to stop and chat with a gendarme, a policeman, I would do so. The French are scared to death of their police. Those fellows have a lot of power to make your life miserable if they want. So I would always leave them with a friendly handshake and a pack of cigarettes.*

Not only did Johnny's "good will" gestures keep him out of trouble for his black market work in the village, but he made friends with the police. One day Johnny was looking for City Hall. It wasn't very big and was easy to miss. He stopped to ask a policeman for directions. He couldn't remember the French term for City Hall (*hotel de ville*), so his brain switched to Spanish and the word came out in that language.

The policeman looked at him in surprise. "Do you speak Spanish?" he asked.

"Yes, sir," Johnny replied in Spanish.

The policeman smiled. "Well then, ask me in Spanish. I'm Basque."

From then on when Johnny came across that officer, he spoke Spanish and the fellow seemed delighted to do likewise.

Johnny chuckles now at how well he got along with the police in Pogny. One day as he was driving to work, he did not notice that a little French "two-horse" pickup had stopped in front of him. He reacted too late and hit it in the rear. A policeman was directing traffic and witnessed the accident. He immediately came over and began yelling at the driver of the pickup. "What's wrong with you?" he shouted. "Look what you have done to Monsieur's car!" The accident was Johnny's fault, but the policeman was one of his "cigarette friends." Fortunately the damage was minor and the French driver was too intimidated by the policeman to protest the reversal of responsibility.

The village of Pogny opened its doors to le fou américain to a degree that rarely happens to outsiders in France. This acceptance is nowhere better evident than when Johnny was called to testify in a capital murder case that took place one autumn in the village. Next door to Rolande and Johnny in the castle complex lived the Tiertre family. Madame was a German woman married to a wiry little Frenchman who regularly abused her. People of the village called her "La Bosche," or "The Kraut," and as a German, she was on the bottom rung of local society in the aftermath of the most recent war. Her back yard bordered on that of Johnny and Rolande.

When Johnny found out that she was German, he took up speaking German with her from time to time across the back yard fence. She seemed to appreciate this simple gesture of friendship. She had a son from a previous marriage and to assure the survival of them both, the German woman had married a Frenchman by the name of Tiertre. As one might expect, he was not the "cream of the crop" in terms of French manhood.

Johnny describes Monsieur Tiertre flatly as "a no-good drunk." As a recovering alcoholic himself, Johnny was in a position to know. "He was a first rate son-of-a-bitch," Johnny adds.

At one point, the man had thrown a frying pan of hot grease on his wife, leaving ugly scars on her neck and chest. Johnny had been next door when the woman came home from the doctor's office after the incident. Her husband was not around and he helped her to get settled back in her home. That's how he came to know the details of the abuse that she regularly suffered at his hands.

Many months later, Monsieur Tiertre came home one morning drunk and in a typically foul mood. He got into an argument with his stepson that quickly escalated. The man knocked the young boy down and was in danger of doing serious damage to the lad. Madame Tiertre grabbed a claw hammer and, as Johnny recalls from court testimony, "stuck the claw part of the hammer in Monsieur's head." The man died on the spot and Madame Tiertre was charged with murder.

When her case came to trial six months later, Johnny had his first and last up-close encounter with the French justice system. "It was really something," he recalls. "They didn't have a jury. The case was decided by three professional judges who do this sort of thing day in and day out. I was asked to testify on behalf of Madame Tiertre by her lawyer. He wanted me to tell the court what I knew about the way that Monsieur Tiertre treated her, about how he abused her. So I did."

"La Bosche" may have been near the bottom of French society, but Johnny found that French justice still applied to her in equal measure as to everyone else. The woman was acquitted by the judges. They found that she had acted in self-defense and in defense of her family. It was justifiable homicide. Johnny knew from his own youth what it was like to live at the bottom of society. This gave him added appreciation for what he saw at Madame Tiertre's trial. He felt that she received the kind of justice that was often lacking in New Mexico for people like himself.

"I think it was the fact that there were three judges instead of a jury of French people," he says. "Those fellows seemed to be able to put their prejudices aside. They knew the law in and out. They knew the French Constitution and their Bill of Human Rights. Their job was to listen to both attorneys and to assure that justice was done. There was no messing around, no big song and dance by lawyers playing games with people in the jury who had lots of reason to hate Germans. The judges did their job and justice was the result. It was great to watch."

Madame Tiertre came home from the trial and she and her son picked up their lives without a drunken husband to torment them anymore. Johnny and Rolande remained their friends and did what they could to help the mother and son get their lives back on track.

There was a deeper reason that the French justice system impressed Johnny. As a foreigner himself, he was often in a position to see and to feel the prejudices of French society. As a soldier who had been through two wars and who would yet see one more, he had few illusions left about human nature. As he says when the topic comes up, "We are all racists and bigots. We all find someone or some group to hate and to put down."

It did not take him long to find where French prejudices erupted to the surface. In the open country around the military base at Vitry-le-François, people kept herds of sheep. Johnny came across a Basque fellow one day who was herding sheep for a wealthy French landowner. The owner's land bordered the base. Johnny struck up a conversation in Spanish with the Basque shepherd and soon learned that the biggest problem the fellow faced was getting adequate water for the sheep. He explained that if he lost any of the sheep to dehydration, he would be in big trouble with the owner. Such encounters generally brought out the best in Johnny and this one was no different. He soon found a way to provide water for the shepherd from the base's abundant supply. He made a new friend in the process.

A few days later he was stopped beside the road talking with the Basque fellow when a shiny, big French car came roaring up.

"That's my boss," the shepherd said nervously.

The French landowner stopped and got out to check on his sheep.

Johnny greeted him and started to exchange pleasantries.

"You're American," the Frenchman said, cutting him off.

"*Oui, monsieur,*" Johnny acknowledged.

"The Americans, they are a bad lot," the landowner said.

"That's not true," Johnny countered.

"The Americans are dirty racists. The way you treat your black citizens is criminal." This was in the heyday of the American Civil Rights Movement back in the U.S. The bus boycott in Selma, Alabama, was still in the forefront of French consciousness. Martin Luther King was making headlines almost every day in the Paris papers. The French were on the side of John F. Kennedy and their beloved Jacqueline, who they saw as champions in the White House fighting the ugly scourge of racial hatred that was tearing America apart.

Johnny was aware of where the wealthy Frenchman was coming from. He couldn't help but note the irony of an Indian in France defending the same white society that had devastated his own people. If one lives long enough and pays attention, such ironies are inevitable. Johnny did not bother to bring up his ethnic identity. He suspected that he might have a rich Frenchman slobbering all over him in pity for his "noble savage" heritage that was so tragically lost. That was not the direction he wanted the conversation to turn.

When the Frenchman began lecturing Johnny on how everyone was equal in France, he saw his opening.

"Is that true, then?" he responded.

"Yes! *Oui!*" the Frenchman insisted.

"If we are all equal, would you invite me, an American, to your home for dinner?" Johnny asked.

"But of course!" the rich fellow assured him.

"How about this Friday?" Johnny continued.

"Sure, why not." The Frenchman was sounding a little less enthusiastic at this.

"Good." Johnny said. "And since we are all equal, I have a friend to bring. May I bring a friend?"

"Okay, okay, bring a friend. I have room for two."

"He's an Algerian," Johnny said.

There was a long pause at this.

Then the Frenchman blurted out, "What? No, no, monsieur… everyone is equal in France *except* the Algerians. No Algerian enters into *my* home!"

"What about the Germans?" Johnny pushed on. "My next door neighbor is a German. Could I bring her and her son for dinner?"

"Oh, *les Boschs,* they are all pigs! No good French person would have anything to do with them.

"How do you know this?" Johnny asked.

"My father fought the Krauts in the big war. He told me to stay away from them. He told me that they are all pigs and are not fit for good company."

"Yes, that's how it all begins," Johnny said.

The landowner started to protest, but then he noticed the twinkle in Johnny's eye and saw that his employee was trying hard not to chuckle. He took a deep breath and then his features softened into a smile. He knew he had been beaten.

"You are right," he said, with an embarrassed laugh. "You are absolutely right. Now I understand what you are saying and I apologize, *monsieur*." Then he added, "You are not like other Americans I have known. I am pleased to meet you."

Johnny smiled and they shook hands. Johnny thought for an instant to mention that he wasn't, in fact, like most other Americans. For an instant there was an opening in which he could have explained that he was an American Indian, but held his tongue. He was a human being. That was enough. He gave a final wave as the busy Frenchman climbed back into his big car and roared away. And Johnny Pail Face continued his morning conversation with his Basque friend.

For all their foibles, shortcomings, and troubled history, the French impressed Johnny as an essentially good people. He remembers in great detail the day that news of John F. Kennedy's assassination swept the country. Late in the day on November 22, 1963, he and Rolande were dressing up to go out for the evening to celebrate his birthday. They had reservations at a first-rate restaurant and wanted to look their best. Rolande was listening to the radio as she got ready. Suddenly she came rushing from the bedroom to exclaim that President Kennedy had just been shot.

Both forgot about their evening plans. They glued themselves to the radio as the news from America took over the airwaves. Twenty minutes later the announcement came. John F. Kennedy was dead, cut down in his prime by an assassin's bullet. Rolande began to sob. Johnny took off his dress clothes and climbed into bed. Then the battle-hardened war veteran cried himself to sleep. Over a white man.

The next day, he got up and dragged himself to work. On the way to the base, he stopped to pick up supplies in a nearby regional town, Châlons-sur-Marne. In 1963, few French could afford to buy their own televisions. Johnny carries a vivid and symbolic French scene burned into his memory to this day. There was a crowd gathered in front of an appliance store that had a number of televisions on display in the front window. All screens were running coverage of the assassination. Most of the people in the crowd were weeping. Openly and in public. In a land where suffering had been a constant of daily life for so many generations, even weathered old men had tears streaming down their cheeks as they learned the details of America's great loss. Johnny's voice grows husky to this day to speak of it.

So it was, for better and for worse, that Johnny Pail Face made a life for himself in France. He stayed three years. "I loved France," he says in a quiet voice. "They accepted me. They called me The Crazy American, and they welcomed my craziness. It was a good time for me."

At the midpoint of his life, Johnny was, indeed, a "Crazy American" in many ways and not only in France. He had broken out of most of the stereotypes that had imprisoned him in his early years back home in New Mexico and in America. He was a "poor, homeless, illiterate" American Indian who was no longer any of the three. He had many reasons to hate white Americans but did not. He had fought beside white fellow soldiers in Europe to end the same kinds of devastation and even similar concentration camps that white Americans had themselves used to destroy his own ancestors and to take away their lands and livelihoods. Born among the poorest of the poor in America, he never had the chance to go to school as a child. Yet he now held an advanced degree from a respected American university, spoke five languages, the most recent one just acquired at middle-age during his years serving the American armed forces in France.

The list goes on. Johnny had every reason to hate the Germans, but refused to do that as well. Instead he made peace by returning after the war to live among them. He learned their language. He became part of their culture. He fell in love with a German woman. They had a baby together. "Gabriella," he says, still singing her name when he pronounces it. He helped to acquit another German woman who killed her French husband to protect her own child. Arab nomads in Algeria had threatened to cut his throat, but he still found beauty in their religion and honor in the life of their Prophet. He had been through two wars that nearly shattered his mind, but he fought his way through the brokenness.

He could have ended his life staring into a bottle of alcohol, but he chose not only to reverse course, but to pull others back to the surface with him. And then he spent three years in the country on Earth with the highest consumption of alcohol per capita and never drank a drop.

At the midpoint of his life, Johnny Pail Face was a Navajo, a former undertaker's assistant, a whiskey runner, a brothel-owner, a soldier, a two-time college graduate, a weather forecaster, a New Englander, a Mason, a Shriner, a man who spoke Navajo, Spanish, English, German, and French, a man who had lived halfway around the world and back, trying on new identities, new ideas, religions, loves, hates, and friendships along the way.

At midlife, Johnny Pail Face was no longer an angry young mixed-blood Navajo. He was no longer even a man who longed to be respected in a white man's world. He had moved beyond these things.

He was *Le fou américain*, a man French villagers had adopted as their very own "Crazy American." Crazy he was. Crazy like a fox. Crazy like the coyote of Navajo myth and culture. Crazy like the best and the worst in the human story. Yes, Johnny Pail Face was a Crazy American, but it was crazy with a purpose.

In France, that purpose became more clear. "I really became part of a community there," he told me. "I was learning how to do good things, to treat others as they should be treated. It was still a new thing for me. I was learning what civilization is. What it can be. The circle of who I am was growing and expanding. It was finding its own way forward."

CHAPTER 23

Fallen Angels

IN FRANCE, JOHNNY PAIL FACE FOUND MORE of what it meant to become a human being. Nowhere is this discovery and change more evident than in his relationship with Rolande. In their last year together at Vitry-le-François, Johnny gave his Nash Rambler away and used profits from his black market work to buy a red Triumph Spitfire 4 sports car. He ordered it straight from the manufacturer across the Channel in England. After it arrived, he and Rolande took up the habit of putting the top down and touring the French countryside on weekend outings and extended road trips.

When there were no practice bombing runs scheduled at the Suippes Air Base, Johnny often got a week or two of free time. He and Rolande loved nothing more than spending this time with the wind in their faces as they sped along the back roads and byways of France. They went as far south as the Pyrenees Mountains bordering Spain, where they visited the famous religious shrine at Lourdes. They traced the entire length of the French Mediterranean Coast up to Nice and the French Riviera. And they motored their way through the French Alps to explore Switzerland.

So it was that this mixed-blood Navajo man found himself at midlife in a beautiful car beside a beautiful woman sweeping through a beautiful, castle-dotted landscape. It was as distant physically, emotionally, and spiritually from the land of his birth as he could hope to get. "I liked that," Johnny says. "Man, it was a good time for me." On a deeper level, he was equally distant from the angry young man whose first love with Virginia twenty-five years before had been filled with constant jealousy and conflict. A man can change. The road to being a good human being is long, and it can be as filled with beautiful, and dangerous twists and turns as the narrow back roads of France.

But Johnny and Rolande did not need to drive long distances to have good times together. They found constant adventure right in and around the village. Johnny remembers one day when a big storm blew up. Rolande insisted that they jump in the car and go out to the gunnery range. During and right after a heavy rain is the perfect time to harvest snails, she explained. Plus, no one but an American was allowed through the gates of the range, so the snails would have been left undisturbed by hordes of other snail-hunting French. "Oh, they must be as big as rabbits!" Johnny remembers her exclaiming. It was just the sort of thing to grab Johnny's interest. Off they went to harvest snails "as big as rabbits."

Johnny remembers Rolande's cries of delight and her laughter under the falling summer rain as they harvested some of the largest snails she'd ever seen. They filled a large shopping bag to the top and took them home. Johnny explains what Rolande did next.

> *First, she dumped them into a cardboard box about the size of a beer case and filled with salt. When I asked her why she did that, she explained that the salt would make them regurgitate their stomach contents and clean them out.*
>
> *A couple of days later, she put them in a pot of water and gave them a good boiling. Then she poured them out and pulled each one from its shell. She carefully cleaned the shells and stuffed them with lots of garlic and butter.*
>
> *When this was done, she stuffed the boiled escargots back into their shells, put them in a pan, and baked them in the new oven I had procured for her.*
>
> *Oh my God, were they good! I must have burped garlic for the next three or four days, but I tell you that was one hell of a meal!*

Another activity in which Rolande took delight was harvesting fresh fruit from the trees alongside the roads of the Marne River region. Around Vitry-le-François, this was a well-organized activity and one that brought revenue to the local government. City and county employees had attached a metal sticker to each fruit tree and on it was a number. People wishing to pick the fruit simply went to the Town Hall, paid a modest fee, thereby reserving the harvest from the tree with their number on it for their family. Anyone else caught illegally harvesting fruit from the tree they had "rented" for the season faced a stiff fine. Johnny found it to be a good system in a country with far more people than fruit trees.

Rolande followed the seasons and the years carefully enough to know when which cherry, apricot, apple, and pear trees were due for a good yield in a given year. She would go early in the year and pay the small fees for her trees, and then she and Johnny would go out in his red Triumph and fill up baskets of fruit as each crop became ripe. Back at their small, makeshift castle, there seemed to be no end to the ways that the thrifty woman knew how to cook and preserve the bounty of the land. It reminded Johnny of his own childhood lived close to the earth in the American West.

During these times together on long, leisurely road trips or staying close to home for escargot adventures and the like, Johnny learned deeper things about Rolande. Over peaceful picnics on a blanket beside a stream, or after a freshly harvested dinner at home, Rolande shared some of the secret things that had shaped and guided her life. One thing she insisted upon was that she did not want to marry. She had done so before. It had been a terrible experience. It was a part of her life to which she had closed the doors. And she told Johnny no more about the dark things behind those doors. There were plenty of things in his own life on which Johnny had closed similar doors. He had his own battle scars, some of which even a year of constant efforts by army psychiatrists could not get him to look into again. He understood.

As she came to trust him more, she introduced Johnny to her parents, who lived in a town not far from Vitry. They lived comfortably in a small, modest house and seemed to have a good relationship with their daughter. They were friendly to Johnny and appreciated the kindness he had brought into Rolande's life.

Only once did Johnny meet other members of Rolande's family. First, he met her daughter who was in her twenties. Rolande did not mention that she had a daughter until a couple of days before Elsa arrived for a visit. Johnny soon understood that Elsa was part of the things locked behind her mother's deepest doors. She was living with a Tunisian man in Germany and came home for a visit. It was the name "Elsa" that give things away. Rolande's daughter had a German name.

Anyone living in France in 1960 would immediately perceive a painful secret hidden in the simple facts of that name and of a daughter coming from Germany to visit. Rolande's daughter would have been born during World War II under the German occupation of France. Johnny realized that Rolande's first husband or first love must had been with a German soldier. And so he understood how her first marriage left her in a state of devastation. France was brutally unkind after the war to those women who had "fraternized" with German men during the years of occupation. But Johnny did not ask about these things. His own experiences and his Native culture had taught him to respect the secret parts of other people's lives. For her part, Rolande never spoke of Elsa's father nor did she ever offer an explanation as to why her daughter lived in Germany and carried a German name.

During Elsa's time in Vitry, she asked to go for a visit to her uncle and cousins who lived in the outskirts of Paris. Johnny volunteered to do the driving and off the threesome went on an excursion that would reveal another twist in Rolande's past.

Johnny remembers his surprise when they arrived at her uncle's address to find a country estate surrounded by high stone walls and an arched gateway. Johnny and Rolande were squatters in a broken down modest castle. Her uncle's family lived in a real French country castle. It was anything but modest. After they were admitted by a guard through the wrought iron gates, Johnny drove into a large courtyard surrounded by well-kept gardens. At the center of the gardens was the home of an aristocratic family. Johnny looked at Rolande to see if she would offer some explanation. She seemed indifferent to the outward beauty of the world that they were entering. Johnny knew that they were entering her secret. He held his tongue.

They spent the afternoon and evening inside one of the most elegant homes Johnny had ever entered in his life before, or has entered since. Rolande's family seemed pleased to see her and her daughter. They were polite to Johnny. When everyone went to table in the evening for dinner, servants wheeled in a royal meal. It was a nice summer evening and Johnny was seated beside Rolande with his back to an open window. The cool breeze felt nice upon the skin of his neck.

Everything went along fine until dessert. The cook had prepared fresh apricots in a special brandy sauce. Johnny did not know about the brandy until he slipped a nice helping into his mouth. As a devoted recovering alcoholic, he knew that he could not swallow. That put him in a bit of a dilemma.

He could spit the family's elegant dessert into his napkin. Decidedly not an elegant thing to do, particularly as he had a large mouthful with which to work. He could make a run for the bathroom. But he did not know where that was and the dwelling was large. Plus, with a mouthful of apricots and brandy, it would be an added challenge to ask directions. And then he felt the breeze again against his now-reddening neck. Instinct took over. He turned from his chair, lunged to the window, and spewed brandy and apricot chunks a good distance into the royal backyard.

A frozen silence met him as he returned to his place politely wiping his mouth with his napkin. He sat down and looked to Rolande for a solution to the unique cultural situation he had now created. He was surprised to see that her eyes were sparkling with delight and a smile was tugging at the corners of her mouth.

"The alcohol," he whispered to her.

She nodded, took control of her features and turned to the other guests at the table. "My American friend is deathly allergic to alcohol," she explained. "But he is all right now. You need not worry." Then she calmly resumed eating. The others cautiously resumed their meals and no more was said about the incident. The evening ended as it began, on a cool, polite note. Johnny, Rolande, and Elsa stayed the night in a small hotel not far down the road from the family castle.

The next day on the long drive home, Johnny waited for Rolande to explain the stark contrast between her modest life and the place where they had dined the previous evening. He knew that her uncle was the older brother of her father. The firstborn son would naturally inherit the estate. But why had Rolande not mentioned to him that they were going to a chateau when they took Elsa for the visit? Why had she remained so indifferent to that world and to her uncle's family in their time there? What family schisms and ruptures lay under the surface? Rolande never spoke of them and Johnny never asked.

Johnny speaks of Rolande with much fondness to this day. "She took life one day at a time," he explains. "She worked hard, she owned very little and yet she was always happy and content. Anything that she could give, she would give. She took care of herself."

If there is one word that best describes Johnny's feelings toward Rolande, it is "respect." She was an attractive woman, a passionate lover, and a dear friend. She was also one of the most honest human beings Johnny has known in his long life. She never asked for more from him than he was able to give. She never offered him more in return than she had to give. Their days together were filled with laughter, sharing, learning, and growing. Whatever wounds were hidden in her secret places, she had learned to make flowers spring up in the rich, fertile soil of the pain. In this, she mirrored the best in Johnny himself.

As someone born and raised in the mainstream of American culture, I found it hard at first to understand why the relationship that Johnny had with Rolande ended. Harder still to understand is how the two lovers never exchanged a single letter or phone call after Johnny boarded a plane in the spring of 1964 and left that world behind. That was 45 years ago. Still, Madame Rolande du Pont is as alive in Johnny's eyes and as fresh in his words as if it were yesterday. I have little doubt that if I were to find Johnny's Rolande for an interview today, I would find similar beauty in her words about him and fondness would still be dancing in her wise, old eyes.

I make sense of this love by remembering that mainstream America is quite a young culture. I have seen again and again that older cultures do things differently than younger ones. Especially things like love. Johnny's people have been in America for more than 10,000 years, since the most recent ice age. Rolande's have been in Europe for longer than that. Most Americans rarely think about what this means. It means that the Navajo men and French women fall in love for different reasons and in different ways than most Americans do. It means they ask for different things from love, from loved ones, and from themselves when they love. It means that they have worked out long ago many of the things with which people in younger cultures are just beginning to grapple.

For example, in traditional Navajo culture, it would be disrespectful for a man to assume that he had to "take care of" the woman he came to love. The Navajos have a matriarchal culture. It gives women power. They are not inferior creatures. Nowhere does this show up more clearly than in love and marriage. Navajo culture has had a great deal of time to work out male/female roles.

Among traditional Navajo clans, men and women marry as equals. They do not give up their individual identities to make a family. They do not give up their sheep or their lands. And in Navajo culture a woman may possess more of both throughout her lifetime than her husband. In their matriarchal society, a woman inherits material wealth from her mother and from her aunts when their generation passes on. She inherits their livestock, grazing land and water rights, as well as household belongings. If she and her family ever were to decide that she should divorce her husband, she would keep all that she owned, as well as the children.[1] Men likewise inherit their wealth from fathers and male relatives. Their own livestock and other goods remain theirs in marriage and in divorce.

Navajo matriarchy does not empower a woman in a material sense only. It also surrounds her with allies who protect her from male abuse and mistreatment. Throughout their long history, when Navajo couples married, they went to live with the wife's family, not with that of the husband. This provided an excellent environment in which to raise healthy children. The wife had her mother, grandmother, aunts, sisters, etc. nearby from the moment she conceived to the end of her child-rearing years. There was always a babysitter available. There was always help. During her monthly cycle, a woman could retire from daily chores to rest, clean, and renew herself for as long as she needed.

Perhaps more importantly, no man would dare mistreat his wife when she was surrounded by both the women and the men of her own family and clan. This made for a world of much less child abuse and domestic violence than is common in mainstream America today. A woman was not someone to be trifled with. If a romance soured in the years after a youthful marriage, the man was in no position to take his disappointment out on his wife and children. He simply moved on. It was not uncommon for a man and a woman to come together, take stock of a marriage that had turned cold, and to get permission from their families to amicably separate. If they did so, the wife was not left a destitute single mother with few resources for feeding and clothing her children. Matriarchy had worked those issues out over thousands of years.

Matriarchal cultures tend to bring human beings together as equals. In so doing, they often retain more room for honest and open relationships between men and women. In patriarchal cultures when men take for themselves economic, political, social, and even religious and spiritual power, there often seems to be less room for healthy male/female relationships. In the end, women end up being another part of the world that men presume to "own." In this world, rape, domestic violence, child abuse, incest, and other behaviors can easily become common. In Johnny's Navajo world at its peak, such things were extremely uncommon and were harshly punished without delay.

A woman had power through her own material resources and through her family allies to take immediate action against a husband or any other male foolish enough to disrespect her. And males had the same recourse to power through their own separate resources and family support networks. In short, Navajo culture had made important strides in working out ways for men and women to live healthy lives together in its thousands of years of development.

What Johnny discovered through his relationship with Rolande is that French culture had likewise created a world in which a woman had access to power and to equality. That is why the word "respect" defines how he felt for her as much as the word "love." In her own peaceful, cheerful manner, love and respect is what she returned to Johnny. But there was strength in her gentleness and in the independent spirit that filled her life. It is this strength that Johnny remembers most from their final parting nearly half a century ago.

"I was feeling sad," he recalls of the morning that he began his return journey back to the States in the spring of 1964. "I didn't want to leave. I started to get emotional. Rolande got firm with me. 'This is your life,' she said to me. 'You have to be what you have to be. You have to do what you have to do.' I pulled myself together and we hugged goodbye. That was it."

With that farewell, Johnny's life in France came to a close. The U.S. Government no longer needed a "Special Weather Services" man in Vitry-le-François. The Algerian Revolution was over. The insurgents had won their independence. President Johnson was increasingly turning his attention to Vietnam, another former French colony where the U.S. was taking an active role to shape a newly emerging nation.

The U.S. would soon visit upon the Vietnamese the kind of violent devastation it had wrought at home upon Native Americans, but the outcome would be different. In the end, three million Vietnamese died or disappeared in the conflict, but tens of millions more were willing to die to preserve their own culture and autonomy. The U.S. could not kill them all.

In the end, the American forces would prudently choose to withdraw. It would be the first time in U.S. history that the "cavalry" would lose to the "Indians." In another twist of historical irony, Johnny Pail Face would be there fighting on the side of the cavalry to witness key events in this reversal of the American story.

In 1964, however, Johnny was just getting home from France. Upon arrival in New England, he found a very different domestic world than the one that he had left three years before. Mary Elizabeth had shuttered their Laurelhurst Farm when he left. She was not a farm girl. She took her two dogs and moved into a comfortable apartment in Leominster to await his return.

When Johnny came home three years later, he was in significantly different circumstances than when he left. He was no longer a struggling alcoholic who needed his Angel's constant attention and support. Nor was he a poor, beaten-down Indian without resources. After he sold his red Triumph and pulled all of his profits together from three years of a thriving black market career on two continents, he had his retirement assured. He recalls:

I brought home an extra suitcase. It was so filled with American one-hundred dollar bills that I had to sit on it to close it. I got an official note from my base commander to the customs people in New York indicating that they were not to trouble me about my luggage. He told them I was on special assignment from the Air Force. Thank God that they let me right through without touching my luggage. The military could have put me in jail if I told the truth, that the money came from the CIA. It was the CIA fellows who were pouring all that cash into Algeria. My black market profits there were coming straight from Uncle Sam. At this point, Johnny stops and shakes his gray head. *'It's a strange world out there,'* he chuckles. *'Truly a strange world.'*

Mary Elizabeth seemed put off by the independent new spirit that Johnny brought home with him from France. To soothe the transition, Johnny opened the farm back up and made it his home base. Mary Elizabeth stayed at her apartment in town. His new assignment was at Westover Air Force Base in Granby, Massachusetts.

His security clearances allowed him to work behind the scenes at a nearby satellite control center. At the height of the Cold War, the U.S. kept spy satellites over Russia and China to monitor their nuclear arsenals. Johnny's job was to give daily weather updates to the B-52 pilots who were in the air in shifts 24 hours a day, seven days a week with our own nuclear weapons. At the command of the President, they were poised to wipe the capital cities of either Russia, China, or both off of the planet. Again, as Johnny put it, "It's a strange world out there."

Things were becoming a little strange in his domestic world as well. One Saturday, Mary Elizabeth came to visit Johnny at the farm. He could tell something was up by the way she was dressed. She was not wearing farm clothes. She came in a matching blouse, skirt and jacket. Her hair and make-up were done up fine. And she was wearing the diamonds Johnny had brought home from war-torn Germany and had given to her as a gift years before. Something was definitely up.

"How are you doing?" she sang out as she stepped daintily from the car. Johnny had come out to greet her.

They chatted next to the car for a couple of minutes and then Johnny said, "Oh, I've got something for you." While she waited he went to the barn that doubled as his garage. He had stored there a bottle of vodka that he had recently taken from a person who he was helping onto the A. A. bandwagon. A couple of shots had been poured from it, but the bottle was still nearly full and it was good quality vodka. Johnny's frugal side could not bring himself to pour it down the drain.

He came back to Mary Elizabeth with the bottle. "Here's a little gift," he told her. "I know you like this brand."

She took the bottle and smiled. "Looks like you've already started on it," she said.

"Nope," Johnny replied. "Not me."

"You will, though. It's just a matter of time." Then she changed the topic to another of her favorite subjects. "How long before you're broke this time?"

Johnny looked at her for a moment before responding. It had been a long time since he had had one of these "helping" talks where Mary Elizabeth stepped in to save him from himself. Three years to be precise. He'd almost forgotten what it was like. He decided to get right to the point.

Looking her in the face, he said, "You can tell your father, and yourself, that it will take ten to twenty years to break me financially this time."

"Ohhh," she replied coyly, "maybe the IRS would like to know about this."

Johnny smiled. He knew that father and daughter had their own ways of slipping around the IRS. "You do what you think is best," he said. "But I will not take another drink."

Mary Elizabeth grew quiet at this. Things were beginning to add up in her mind. She had spent three weeks with Johnny in France and Europe the previous autumn. He had not touched a drop of alcohol throughout her visit even though she had drunk wine with nearly every meal. He had just handed her a bottle of vodka without taking a sip. There was a resolve in his voice and manner that had not been there the day he left for France. Johnny saw in her eyes something with which he had long struggled. Here is how he describes it.

Whenever I was able to get myself sober and take over the reins of this family, Mary Elizabeth would call Cousin Patricia to fly in from Virginia with her private plane to take her back home to Daddy. He was so powerful that he could have my government benefits stopped and this pushed me to just give up and get drunk again. After a while, he would call to tell me that he was sending Mary Elizabeth back to take care of me because after all she was my wife.

They went into the farmhouse and Johnny made coffee. As they sat at the table talking and drinking the strong brew, Mary Elizabeth had some things to confess. In Johnny's absence, she had fallen in love with a new man. He was another man in uniform, a sailor. He was also another Native American, or more precisely, a Native Hawaiian. The amazing part for her personally was that, for the first time in her adult life, she had not fallen for an alcoholic. She felt like it was a new and important stage of her life. And then she asked Johnny for a divorce.

Johnny agreed to end things. He was no fool. He had sensed the changes underway in their marriage. During his years in France, they had both moved on with their lives. Mary Elizabeth's words were a relief and a confirmation of his own thinking. She told him that she would have her lawyer get into contact with him to work out the details. Then they parted amicably.

A few days later, the lawyer called Johnny on the phone. He and Mary Elizabeth had consulted with the proper people and calculated that her half of the joint property that they owned was worth $167,000. Johnny was aware of exactly what they had paid for the farm and their cars, which was the only joint property that they had. It was considerably less than the sum the man had just given him. Johnny was not one to lose at any bargaining table, legal or illegal. The lawyer was unaware that he was talking to a world-class black marketeer. Johnny Pail Face knew how to negotiate. And so he did.

"My goodness, this is good news," he responded. "Is our estate really worth all that much?"

"Yes, Mr. Sarmiento, it is. I've had it verified by experts in the area."

"Well, I accept your calculations then. When do I get my check?"

There was a long pause. Finally the lawyer sputtered, "Uh, Mr. Sarmiento, that's, um, not what we were intending. Your wife does not want to keep her share of your property. She wants you to buy her out. At the settlement, she wants you to pay her for her half of the estate."

"Oh," Johnny said, pretending surprise. "That puts me in a difficult situation. I'm a soldier, not a farmer. We bought the farm for her. What do I need with a farm?"

Of course, Johnny had devoted several days to hard thinking about what he would do with the farm. He knew exactly what he wanted from the farm.

"Here's what I'm willing to do to make this fair," he told the lawyer. "I'll either take or I'll give $2,000 for our joint property and holdings. Either way I'll walk away from our marriage satisfied that we've done the right thing. Please tell Mary Elizabeth that is my counter-offer."

To the lawyer, it seemed like a strange, even preposterous, response. But Johnny had an advantage. He knew Mary Elizabeth better than the lawyer knew Mary Elizabeth. He knew that she was the daughter of one of the richest families in Virginia, that she was used to getting what she wanted when she wanted it. And she presently wanted to run off with her Hawaiian love back to his islands. What she did not want was to be slowed down by a farm in New England in which she had not even cared to live for the past three years.

Nonetheless, the lawyer persisted in his determination to get the $167,000 from Johnny. About a month later, they met at the courthouse in Manchester, New Hampshire, to finalize the divorce. Johnny planned his strategy around the time of the proceedings. They were to begin at 2 p.m. Johnny arranged with Mary Elizabeth that they would both arrive early, at noon, to have a final talk about things. When she arrived, he put on his best charm, now refined by years of living in France, to invite her to a last lunch together.

Her lawyer was beside himself at the proposal. "You cannot take my client to lunch during these proceedings," he insisted.

Johnny smiled at that. "At this moment, your client is still my wife," Johnny told him. "If she chooses to go to lunch with her husband one last time, I believe that she has the right to do so."

"Let's go to lunch," Mary Elizabeth laughed to Johnny. The daughter of a domineering father, she loved defying authority. Johnny had counted on that too. Away they went, leaving the lawyer standing there with jaws agape.

Over lunch, Johnny said:

Mary Elizabeth, we both know that you do not want that farm. We also know that you do not need the money. I think you know me well enough to know that I will not pay $167,000 for a piece of property that I could not possibly sell for anything near that amount. I've been wheeling and dealing too long for that. Instead of tying yourself to New England for as long as it will take to work all that through, why don't you just take the $2,000 cash I offered and you can be on your way with your new man.

He saw right away that Mary Elizabeth had thought things through as well. "It's true that I don't like that drafty old farmhouse," she replied, "but I might want to build a summer home someday on our property. It is nice out there in summer when the flowers are in bloom and everything is green."

"Okay," Johnny said. How about if I deed a couple of acres over to you for that, plus the $2,000?"

Mary Elizabeth smiled. "And you pick up the tab for this lunch."

It was Johnny's turn to smile. "Deal," he said, and he wrote out a check for $2,000 and handed it to her, and then he paid for lunch.

When they returned to the courthouse at the appointed time, Mary Elizabeth walked into the deliberation room waving the check that Johnny had given her. "We've settled," she announced cheerfully to the lawyers and the judge. "It's all worked out. Where do I sign?" Johnny was sure that Mary Elizabeth's lawyer was going to collapse as he watched his client sign away $165,000 and with it a hefty piece of his lawyer's fees.

A short time after the divorce, Mary Elizabeth's father died and left her 37 million dollars. She took the money and moved to Hawaii with her fifth and what would be her final husband. Johnny took her good fortune in stride with a philosophical note. He says now, "To this day, I tell people at A. A. meetings that this must have been the Creator's way of saving my life because if I had gotten hold of that kind of money, I surely would have drunk myself to death a long time ago."

Johnny wished Mary Elizabeth well and then the soldier/farmer turned to rebuilding his life in New England. He was ready for the change.

What he longed for most would be put into words later in the prayer that would guide his final years on earth. Each day now in old age, he faces West and offers up these words to his Creator:

Let me harvest all that I asked you to take away in the East so that I can serve you better by giving me Patience, Tolerance, Peace of Mind, and all the other things I asked you to take away.

In 1964, as he entered middle age, Johnny Pail Face was ready to begin harvesting some of the best fruits of his years on earth. He soon discovered that the fruits of patience, tolerance, and even peace of mind were waiting for him at a small Tastee Freeze roadside restaurant in Granby, Massachusetts.

At the Tastee Freeze

AFTER THE DIVORCE, JOHNNY DID NOT HAVE A LOT OF TIME to sit around and to stew about things. Uncle Sam needed a Special Weather Services man again, this time in the Dominican Republic. Sergeant Sarmiento spoke Spanish, the language of this large Caribbean island. He was ideal for the work Washington wanted done. But first, they sent him to Langley, Virginia, to receive training from the CIA in covert operations. Then he was parachuted into the mountains of the Dominican Republic to provide support logistics for a possible invasion of the island by the U.S. Marines.

The U.S. leadership had attempted to give the Dominican people a new government on May 30, 1961. That night, a group of assassins supplied with weapons and training by the CIA riddled the limousine of the former President and subsequent military dictator Rafael Leonidas Trujillo Molina with bullets. Mr. Trujillo was on his way back to his wife and presidential palace after a nocturnal visit to one of his more than 20 mistresses. He was killed in the hail of bullets, as was his chauffeur.

There was more than a little historical irony in the U.S. assassination of Mr. Trujillo. The U.S. military had supported his ascension to power in 1930 and successive American administrations had found in him a devoted ally for the next 31 years. In the Cold War focus upon the evils of Communism, there was plenty of room at the table for democrats and dictators to work together in mutually beneficial ways. Trujillo was particularly effective at getting the benefits to flow his way.

By the time that the CIA plot ended his time on earth, he had taken ownership of 20 percent of all the land in the Dominican Republic. He had stolen billions of dollars from the national treasury to fill his personal Swiss bank accounts. He had renamed the capital city, a province, the highest peak, and countless buildings, bridges, and streets in his honor. He had put his name on all automobile license plates. He had erected a neon sign that proclaimed to his citizens day and night: *Dios en ceilo, Trujillo en tierra* ("God in heaven, Trujillo on Earth"). He later changed the order of the phrases to put himself first.

He had thoroughly purged democracy from his land, establishing a single party system that regularly reelected him or his puppet with near 100 percent majorities. He had attempted to purge blacks from Dominican society as well through the slaughter of thousands of people. Shortly thereafter, he had himself nominated for the Nobel Peace Prize by a countryman too prudent to refuse.

Trujillo's unique sense of reality extended to his family. In 1955, he had his daughter proclaimed queen of the "International Fair of Peace and Fraternity of the World," an event he paid $30 million to pull off. He also had his semi-literate wife designated a philosopher and writer-of-note of the nation.

Washington was able to stomach such dictatorial behaviors for far longer than other nations in the Caribbean region and South America were willing to do. Even Cuba's new dictator Fidel Castro was on the list of regional neighbors calling for Trujillo's ouster. For years, the U.S. refused to take action. That all changed when Trujillo began to plot assassinations against other of our dictator friends in South America. Trujillo almost succeeded in killing President Rómulo Betancourt of Venezuela with a car bomb in 1960. The leaders in Washington were outraged at this audacious attempt to kill another head of government in the Americas. So they killed the Dominican Republic's head of government.

In 1964, Johnny was still part of the effort to reestablish stability in the country three years after Trujillo had joined *Dios en ceilo*. Things had not gone as planned for the transition to a new government either for the plotters who had partnered with the CIA or for the country more generally. Five of the assassins were caught by Trujillo's son who returned to carry his father's mantle of leadership. He had them strung up between trees at the family's seaside estate. First they were tortured to death. Then their bodies were dismembered and cut into small pieces. Finally, they were fed to the sharks in the tranquil harbor of the elegant estate.

Such behavior by the second Trujillo did not bring harmony and stability back to the nation. Johnny was part of a U.S. effort in 1964 to make the Republic peaceful again by eliminating yet a third Trujillo, Hector, who had succeeded his unpopular nephew when the younger man was ousted by his own people. Johnny's assignment was to wait in the mountains with disaffected rebel guerillas to assist with the possible landing of 1,500 Marines who would be sent in to "keep the peace" if Uncle Hector did not step down.

Johnny spent three weeks living in the bush, sleeping on the ground, and eating whatever the guerillas were eating from day to day, which generally wasn't much. Then the last of the Trujillo dictators gave in to U.S. pressure, got on a plane and flew into a pre-appointed place of exile before the Marines had to invade. Happily for Johnny, his assignment ended without a shot being fired.

Overall, the experience made for an interesting break from his New England routine. He recalls in particular learning how it was that his guerrilla counterparts seemed to have an edge over him in their ability to get by with little food and little sleep.

I remember some of those guerilla fighters used to carry a pouch filled with green leaves. They would pull some out and stick them in their mouths and just chew on them, swallowing the juice. They offered me some and said it would make me feel good, give me more strength and energy, and keep me awake.

I said, 'No thanks' to that. Later I found out that they were chewing coca leaves from which cocaine is made. Back then, Americans did not know much about cocaine.

After his Dominican Republic assignment ended, Johnny was posted back to his job at Westover Air Base in Granby, Massachusetts. As a weatherman, he returned to briefing the B-52 pilots who were in the air 24 hours a day, seven days a week with nuclear missiles poised to end civilizations in Russia and China should they choose to try to end ours. It was the centerpiece of Cold War policy that the world came to know as "Mutually Assured Destruction," or MAD. This represents a rare instance in modern times when bureaucrats around the world have labeled a policy accurately.

It proved most practical for Johnny to live on base at Westover during the weeks. But he loved getting away to his New Hampshire farmhouse on weekends. He again became active in A. A. meetings in New Hampshire. It was a familiar routine that brought out the best in him. He did what he could to help out at area meetings and reconnected with Alma and friends at Alma's Gateway Lodge in Nashua.

On Highway 202 on the outskirts of Granby, Massachusetts, was located a small drive-in restaurant. The jaunty sign outside read "Tastee Freeze," above the cut-out of an ice cream cone. It was one of those roadside places scarcely larger than a hotdog stand. The French-Canadian family running the place specialized in foot-long hotdogs as well as ice cream cones. Johnny took up the habit of stopping in at the place on his return trips from the farm in Mason, New Hampshire. It was a habit that soon changed his life. Johnny explains.

> *The elderly lady who was there spoke French, so I used to spend a little time with her to practice my French and have an ice cream cone or a foot-long hotdog for 25 cents.*
>
> *Well, one afternoon while I was there, we heard the back door slam and her daughter, Theresa, came in. The older lady asked Theresa if she would get the 'chien chaud,' or hotdog, from the grill and bring it in to where we were sitting.*
>
> *She brought in the hotdog and then just stood staring at me.*
>
> *I finally said, 'Hey, look, that hotdog's gonna get cold if you don't give it to me.'*
>
> *She said, 'Oh, oh, oh, excuse me!' She put it down, turned beet red, and walked away.*
>
> *The old lady introduced her as her daughter and that was the beginning of something with Theresa and myself.*
>
> *Theresa was a widow of about 36 years of age. Her husband had died in his early forties of a sudden heart attack a couple of years before. Theresa told me later that when she brought that hotdog to*

me, she had seen her deceased husband's eyes looking at her through mine.

Johnny soon learned that Theresa had three beautiful daughters. Each day at 3 p.m. when they got out of school, the two younger ones, Sharon and Linda, came to the Tastee Freeze to take over for their grandmother. Little Linda was only seven so she went back to their house with Grandma for the rest of the day while Sharon helped her mother. The hardworking family lived in a modest home next to the Tastee Freeze. Grandmother and grandfather occupied a small cottage behind the main house.

In Theresa's family, after the death of her husband, the women ran everything. The Tastee Freeze belonged to mother, daughter, and granddaughters. They did all the work and managed all the finances. This pattern had begun early in the family's life. As he got to know the family better, Johnny found that the grandfather had never worked in any steady way at any point in his life. Therefore, he had never paid into Social Security, so the old man had absolutely no retirement income. They subsisted on his wife's meager monthly Social Security check and what they could earn from the Tastee Freeze after splitting the profits with Theresa and the children.

Johnny had a number of reasons for taking an interest in Theresa and her extended family. Due to the death of a father and the unconventional personality of the grandfather, the world in which Theresa, her mother, and her daughters lived bore a striking resemblance to the matriarchal world of Johnny's childhood. The women worked hard. They were strong. They did not sit around and wait for men to take care of them. As with Rolande in France, they were the kind of women who had Johnny's immediate respect.

Furthermore, Theresa was a good woman, hard working, and firm in her Catholic faith. Much like Johnny's own mother and sisters, she had withstood many of the larger storms of life and had found ways to make the best of things. She was a devoted mother raising three healthy, beautiful children as best that she could. Johnny admired that. Plus, from the start, he found that he enjoyed Theresa's company. He could use his French to make her laugh and to reignite a light in her eyes that had been dimmed by a painful family tragedy.

He came to affectionately call her Terry. Later, he would put up a new sign at the Tastee Freeze. He had it labeled "Terry's Soft Serve" to honor the person who was at the heart of the business.

Although Johnny had found another woman he could respect and admire, it was not love at first sight for him. There was more to it than that. It was a healthy friendship between a man and a woman who were both beyond the innocent romance of youth. They were two human beings at midlife searching for the best ways to move forward. Both had seen loves come and go. Both had paid the heart-wrenching price that love collects in the long years after the spring-time of romance yields its insistent claims upon our days and nights.

All of this to say, there was a good deal of down-to-earth practicality in the relationship that grew up between this Indian man far from his desert home and a French Canadian widow trying to make ends meet for her extended family. Theresa needed a friend and a husband. Her broken family needed a father.

For his part, Johnny Pail Face also brought some very specific needs beyond female companionship to his relationship with Theresa. He was still dealing with the tricky issue of a suitcase of cash that he had carried home from France the previous year. That money was now stuffed into safe deposit boxes in six different banks. Marriage to Theresa offered him a partnership in an ice cream business. What he really needed was a "laundering business." The shrewd businessman in him saw a chance to combine the two.

This inclination was reinforced with his first look at Theresa's accounting books at the Tastee Freeze. After all debits and credits were added up for the previous year, the family had earned a net profit of $360. Theresa reluctantly explained that they had been living off the life insurance policy of her former husband. That money was almost gone. Johnny knew what he must do. It would be a win-win situation for everyone if he married his laundering business to Theresa's Tastee Freeze business. And so he did.

Johnny and Theresa were united in holy matrimony at his farm in Mason in late 1965 by the town clerk. It was a small ceremony. In addition to bride, groom, and the clerk, the only others present were Theresa's brother Arthur and his wife, Cecile. Just as the wedding was a quiet and peaceful event, the domestic life that Johnny Pail

Face entered afterward was, with the exception of a final posting to Vietnam, likewise quiet and peaceful.

"It was great," he recalls. "They accepted me right away." And so as he entered his fifties, Johnny finally found something that had eluded him time and again through the years—a family. It was the fourth try for this aging warrior at becoming a family man. Johnny had come out a survivor and ultimately a winner in many battles by this time in life. It was far from certain that he would find a path to victory this time.

After the wedding, Johnny moved into the house with Theresa and the girls next to the Tastee Freeze. The "profits" of the small family business immediately experienced a noticeable surge as Johnny began pulling money out of safe deposit boxes and turning it into legitimate income.

Johnny takes care to point out that his overseas income was not "dirty money." He had earned it with the full knowledge and support of military superiors in France. However, when you work in the shadowy margins between nations and peoples and you take high risks for your government, some things are hard to explain. They are especially hard to explain to other branches of the same government where people do not work in the margins, like, for example, the Internal Revenue Service. "Black Market Revenue" is not an official income category that one finds on the U.S. 1040 Tax Form. The Tastee Freeze business offered Johnny a way to translate his overseas earnings into income that the IRS could understand. And so he did.

The same entrepreneurial energy that had led Johnny time and again into overseas black markets resurfaced again before long in Granby, Massachusetts. Ever the restless spirit, Johnny found new opportunities to expand beyond the hotdog and ice cream business. Only this time his work was entirely legitimate. One of the constant problems at the Tastee Freeze was keeping the ice cream freezers functioning properly. When a training course on Refrigeration Maintenance was offered on base at Westover, Johnny signed up. Afterward, he used his newfound skills to keep the Tastee Freeze machines functioning properly, and started a lucrative side business in refrigeration repair as well.

As 1966 sped by, Johnny and Theresa found themselves at the center of a busy and productive family life. They now had the resources to take good care of Theresa's parents. Their two younger daughters, Sharon and Linda, were doing well in school. Donna had graduated from high school and was working as a receptionist at a local business.

With time, Johnny developed a loving relationship with the three daughters that continues to this day. "I respected those girls, as I still do," he says affectionately. "They were my babies." In 1966, Donna was a hardworking young woman who did not drink, smoke, or misbehave. "She was very respectful," Johnny remembers. "She was still living at home after she went to work at the rag-bundling business, so she paid her mother $10 a week for room and board. I was very impressed."

When Donna got married, she asked Johnny to walk her down the aisle and to give her away. About three months after the marriage, Johnny overheard a conversation between daughter and mother. After running her own household for a time, Donna was amazed that her mother had asked only the meager $10 a week for her room and board. "I don't know how you got along with $10 from me," she told Theresa. "I can't even buy toilet paper for the week with $10!"

Johnny found Sharon more introverted and withdrawn than her two sisters. "She was cautious. She was respectful and all, but she would not have much to do with me at first. With time, she warmed up. She became my "Goldilocks." I still call her that. She is petite, barely five feet tall, and has beautiful blonde hair."

Linda was a plump little second-grader when Johnny entered her life. He remembers one day early on when she came running home from school in tears. He calmed her down and got her to tell him what had happened. A group of boys on the playground had been teasing her about being fat. She had informed them with all the bravado her little spirit could muster that, when she grew up, she was going to be a model.

"Yeah, a model for elephants!" the boys had thrown back at her, laughing and jeering.

Sobbing, she had fled to the safety of home where Johnny had "Linda-duty" because he was working the early shift at the base.

Johnny did not quite know how to console his new young daughter. He thought fast and came up with the best counter-argument he could. "There's nothing wrong with being an elephant model," he assured the wounded little soul. "There's that Disney show on TV with elephants in tutus and ballet slippers dancing all over the place. We love watching that show."

"Those aren't elephants," Linda corrected him. "Those are hippos." He noted, however, that her sobbing had quieted and that she seemed to be thinking through what he had told her.

"Well, I think that whatever hippo models can do, elephant models can do better," Johnny said. "Don't you think so too?"

She began to dry her eyes and Johnny saw the faint trace of a smile begin to twitch at the corners of her mouth as she thought about elephants dancing in tutus and ballet slippers.

A few days later, Johnny was sitting in the living room watching TV and reading the paper when Linda called out from the next room. "Close your eyes!" she said. She had a surprise to show him. He dutifully closed his eyes and put his hands over them for added measure.

A short pause ensued, followed by "Okay, you can open your eyes now."

When he took his hands away, he found a plump second-grader standing without shame or self-consciousness before him in tights, a tutu, and ballet shoes. She then danced an elephant dance under his admiring gaze that she had been working on for days.

Forty years have passed and Johnny still remembers that dance. "Those are the things that stay with you," he says.

From then on, Johnny's nickname for Linda became "my model." As the years slipped by, Johnny remembers how well nature worked its magic on pudgy little Linda. The ugly duckling became an elegant swan. The sturdy second-grader became one of the most beautiful young women in her high school class. And the stepfather who had once dried tears that thoughtless boys brought to her eyes found himself chasing off the same boys whose hearts were now at her feet. And so it is that the circle of life cycles on, leaving fathers and mothers with memories that repay the pain.

In his own way, Johnny was ready by 1966 for one of the most important cycles of his life to come to an end. He had put in 30 years with the U.S. military and he decided it was time to retire. Terry's Soft Serve was doing fine and his refrigeration repair business was taking off. Plus he wanted to spend more time with his growing family.

When he applied for retirement, he also requested "Military Privileges." This meant that he would continue to have access to all base services, educational programs, and benefits the same as an enlisted man. Johnny planned to travel with his family in retirement and having privileges meant that they could lodge at military bases, seek healthcare there, and buy groceries and other supplies tax free.

His retirement and the pension he had earned were granted, but his privileges were denied. He did not have enough time in the service to qualify for the added benefits. Johnny asked what he had to do to get them.

> *They said that if I signed up for a One Year Isolated Tour of Duty, they would automatically give me the equivalent of two years of service and that would get me my Military Privileges.*
>
> *I said, 'Okay, where do I sign?'*
>
> *I figured that, as a weatherman, I would be going up to Iceland or the northern part of Canada, or maybe to Greenland to spend my isolated tour.*
>
> *Well, as it would be, they sent me to get jungle training in the bayous of Mississippi, at Biloxi, from July until October. Two weeks after returning to Westover, I received orders to proceed to Saigon, Vietnam.*

It surprised Johnny that, as a family man, he would be shipped off to Vietnam during one of the most dangerous periods of the war. He was able to get 30 days leave to help prepare everyone for his departure. He used the time to go on vacation, one of the first real vacations that Theresa and the girls had ever had. They loaded up the car and drove all the way to Gallup, New Mexico, and Navajo country. They visited with Johnny's family, and he introduced his new family to a world very different from what they had known all their lives in New England.

Then Johnny and Theresa put Donna, Sharon, and Linda on an airplane and sent them back to Massachusetts, continuing on to Mexico for the honeymoon that there had been no time for when they were married the year before. Johnny remembers it as a bittersweet time for the couple. Hanging over their days of travelling and enjoying new things together all the way to the Pacific Coast of Mexico was the constant knowledge of his impending departure.

They made the best of their days together, however, and Johnny knew that when he left, he would be leaving Theresa, her daughters, and her parents in a better situation than when he had found them. He was proud of that. And he looked forward to coming back to them after a year in Vietnam. He had found a world that was not only good for them; it was good for him as well.

But Johnny is honest about the deeper currents that swirled through him during that first vacation with Theresa. "I've never been in love except once, with Virginia," he confesses, "and it was a terrible experience. She was my first and only love and I screwed everything up with my jealousy. I swore then that I would never let myself fall in love like that again. And I didn't, not even with Theresa."

Early in his life, Johnny had set out into the world doing everything he did "for all the wrong reasons." The irony of this approach filled with anger, hatred, and jealousy is that, with the passage of time, "everything turned out right." This reversal is as true in his approach to love as in other dimensions of his life. In the case of Theresa, he married her as much or more for a way to launder a suitcase full of black market revenues as for love.

And yet their relationship turned out right. "I had a family that I loved," Johnny recalls. "That family became part of me. Everything with women and love before that was just a wild ride. I never thought about a family until Theresa."

As Johnny reflects about these statements, he continues:

A. A. has helped me completely with all this. It is because of A.A. that we are able to do this book. I had to sober up before I could grow, before I could start to get responsible for things that I never considered before.

I became a human being, a man with feelings. I can't say that I have a conscience because years ago the doctors said I would commit suicide if I ever got a conscience.

I listen quietly as Johnny explores this thought that he has shared with me dozens of times before. It has been two years and almost three months that we have been working on this book. I have learned when to press forward with probing questions and when to be still. I hold my tongue this time. I sense something working its way to his surface. Johnny has always assured me that he does not have a conscience. And yet in my 53 years on Earth I've never seen a man struggle so mightily with something he does not have.

I don't know, he adds after a pause. *All I can say is that I can cry now and not be ashamed. I wouldn't do anything unkind knowingly because I would have to suffer for it later. The fact remains, if you do something wrong and you know it's wrong, either you have to live with it or you have to fix it up.*

Again there is a long pause, and then the old man adds: *Only someone without a conscience can live with having knowingly done wrong.*

In these statements, what is perhaps Johnny's deepest struggle slips into view. Indeed, how does an Indian who ran booze to other Indians, a former alcoholic, a viciously jealous lover, a warrior who has done things on the battlefield that even psychiatrists cannot induce him to remember, an occupier of foreign lands who traded chocolate for sex with starving women, a father who left behind three families…how does this man *live with having knowingly done wrong?*

As I write up my notes and review the taped interview for this chapter, I find Johnny's answer. It came earlier in our meeting when I pressed him about his feelings for Theresa. This is often the way our conversations work. He has a way of answering his own questions and of working his way out of the impasses that he creates. It is only after I get home and review the transcripts that I find them.

So it was that I found his answer to how a man like him could live with himself and even eventually lay claim to a conscience. It had come earlier in response to a question I asked about how he felt for Theresa if he would not call it love. His response:

> *Let me put it this way. The Lord God Creator of Mother Earth and the Universe brought me to that point and to that lady. I found out later that she was very sick with pernicious anemia. The Creator knew that her eyes were going to go. The Lord Creator knew that she would be affected by Parkinson's disease. So He put me in her life so she could be taken care of.*

Johnny is very clear that his attraction to Theresa was, at the outset, largely based on his need to legitimize a suitcase full of cash. Yet something else began to grow up in their relationship, something that legitimized their very marriage. There is an element of compassion in Johnny's words that one cannot miss. Others have pointed out in words more eloquent than I do here that compassion is simply love in a different form. Some might even argue it is a better form, one that is gentler on both the bearer of love and the recipient. And like the best of loves, it can lift the lives of those who it touches.

In Johnny's words about Theresa, then, comes the answer to the dilemma summed up in his statement: Only someone without a conscience can live with having knowingly done wrong. Johnny not only found love in his compassion for Theresa. He found a conscience.

If a conscience is a difficult thing to find in a troubled life, it is equally difficult to keep, especially for a soldier called to war. War is a place where innocence is lost, not gained, and where conscience is generally the first casualty when bullets begin to fly. In November, 1966, Johnny Pail Face was still a soldier and his country turned to him once again to do the necessary evils that soldiers do on battlefields. So it was that he took leave of the first family that had introduced him to a world of peace and plunged back again into the dark side of the human story for 22 months in Vietnam.

CHAPTER 25

Hemorrloids in Vietnam

THE LIFE OF JOHNNY PAIL FACE SHOWS US HOW VERY DIFFICULT it is for a man to fight his way out of alcoholism. But there are other intoxications in life, many of them less obvious. In some ways, war and violence can be as alluring and as addictive as strong drink. In any of our wars that have lasted a long period of time, we read about soldiers who reenlist and return again and again to battle. In the two wars raging in Iraq and Afghanistan as Johnny and I worked upon this book, the media told us often of men and women who had done two, three, and four tours of duty to the frontlines.

We shake our heads in wonder at such things. Why would someone do this? Is it for the money? Soldiers earn but little. There are many other ways to get money and in larger sums. Is it for glory and honor? Do some soldiers come to enjoy being shot at? Do they become addicted to the adrenaline of the battlefield or even to killing itself? And why do we heap glory and honor them for doing things elsewhere that would land them in prison or bring the death penalty at home? These are, of course, the swirling complexities that have forever surrounded the work of the soldier.

But it is not just soldiers who become intoxicated by war. It also happens to journalists, photographers, and government contractors. Careers are made as war correspondents, battle photographers, bodyguards, supply truck drivers, camp cooks, and the list goes on. What people intoxicated by war have in common is that they choose to go. Johnny Pail Face is among those who have made the choice again and again. Over his years of service, he chose to do four tours of duty in three different war zones. As Johnny and I began this chapter, I was determined to find out why.

The first thing I noted is that when Johnny left for his third war in as many decades, he took with him a useful collection of survival skills and abilities. Among his most valuable resources was an ironic sense of humor. This teased out when he first began to speak of his time in Vietnam. He was a different storyteller than when he had earlier described to me his experiences in World War II and Korea. He laughed more. He chuckled at things in passing. He made me laugh. A man changes from war to war.

Johnny seems to have developed a finer sense of irony from war to war, and from extended contact with the way a large organization like the U.S. military works. For example, he smiles and shakes his head at an experience that happened even before he arrived in Saigon. His plane stopped in Japan for refueling. It was late November and cold as ice when he stepped from the plane. The Air Force had equipped him from head to toe for the jungle assignment where he was headed. So all he had to cover up over his tropical shirt and thin pants was a cheap, plastic military rain coat. Before he could reach the warmth of a hangar with a heater, the rain slicker not only froze solid in the frigid air, but the bottom part of it actually broke off and fell to the ground. As he puts it, if that layover had lasted much longer, they could have cut him into small cubes and used him to chill drinks in Vietnam upon arrival.

The arrival itself likewise leaves him smiling. He recounts:

> When we came in over Saigon, we were at high altitude, about 30,000 feet. The Captain told us to tighten our seat belts and he nosed the plane down into a steep dive. Let me tell you, that was quite a ride down into Tan San Noot Airbase. I thought we were going to crash, but as we came close to the ground, he straightened it out and we landed beautifully.

> When we were safely on the ground, the pilot explained that this kind of landing was necessary to avoid the persistent ground fire around the outside of the base.

Johnny had assumed that the main airbase outside of Saigon would be a secure area, a place where one did not risk a bullet in the head when walking from sleeping quarters to breakfast. He had also been told that he would only be in Vietnam for a year. That turned out differently than expected as well. It would be 22 months before he would board the flight that would take him back to Theresa and his girls. It's good to have a sense of humor in such circumstances, particularly if you are determined not to return to strong drink. Johnny was determined.

Stepping off the plane in Saigon in the late November weather was a radically different experience than having his raincoat freeze and break in Japan. "It was hot, humid, miserable, and shitty," Johnny recalls. "It was like opening the door to a furnace."

The first thing he did was to go for a haircut as a way to ease the discomfort of the heat. He had a Vietnamese barber cut his hair down as short as his clippers could take it.

Among the survival skills that Johnny had picked up in his military career was the ability to speak foreign languages. The French he had picked up with Rolande in Vitry-le-François was most valuable in Vietnam, which had spent most of the previous century as a French colony. As he recounts, he put his French skills to immediate use.

> When I got to my assigned quarters, there was a Vietnamese woman there, so I asked her if she spoke French. She said she did, so I asked her if she would do some housekeeping for me if I paid her. She readily agreed.
>
> The other guys, when they saw this, were pretty put off. They asked me if I spoke her language and said that they couldn't get her to do anything for them. I told them that we spoke together in French and that was the breaks.

Johnny also quickly learned the limits of cooperation with the local people regardless of the language spoken. On his first night, a lot of shooting and fireworks erupted around the base. "I just stayed in bed and rode it out," he recalls.

In the morning he got a look at the damages. There was a sobering shock awaiting him. "There, hanging on the barbed fence around the base was the dead body of my barber. It seems he was one of the Viet Cong who had attacked the night before. I learned right off that you couldn't trust anybody who was Vietnamese."

Johnny and two other weather services men were soon given an assignment to parachute into a forward position in the jungle at a strategic location where the U.S. military had decided to build an airbase for continuing operations against the enemy. Johnny recalls:

> *They had assigned two younger guys to assist me. I remember one was called Porky Dog and the other was a Jewish kid. They were okay. I was the old-timer at 50.*
>
> *When we got our orders, we drew portable weather equipment from the supply line. Then we were flown in a C130 transport over the east coast of central Vietnam, and parachuted into a place about 35 miles east of Quinyan with all our equipment.*
>
> *I came down in the middle of a Vietnamese cemetery. This was Phou Kát, where the U.S. was going to build the largest military airbase in the country.*
>
> *Our job was to determine the direction of the prevailing winds so that the engineers could line up the runways in the right places. So we set up our equipment on a knoll and began to take our readings and radio our reports in.*

One day about three weeks later, Johnny was sitting on his knoll watching a U.S. Navy Corsair fighter bomber that was bombing something three or four miles away over the tree tops. A couple of hours later, he and his team heard troops coming through the brush towards them. They dived for cover and grabbed their weapons. Soon, however, they could make out distinctly British-sounding voices cursing the "Yanks" as they made their way through the undergrowth. They were upset that the American bomber did not know where to place his bombs and that they had very nearly ended up as the victims of the Corsair.

When the squad in blue-gray uniforms walked into the clearing where Johnny's team was set up, their commander asked, "What are you blokes doing here?"

"We are collecting weather data and radioing it in to prepare for the construction of an airbase," Johnny told him.

"Where is your perimeter?" the commander asked in surprise. The perimeter is the line of defense around a place where soldiers dig in and protect it from attack.

"We don't have one," Johnny replied. "There's just the three of us here."

"Are you guys crazy?" the New Zealander burst out. "You blokes must really be out of your minds! There's Viet Cong all over the area! How long have you been here?"

"Oh, about three weeks."

The commander shook his head in disbelief. "All I can say is that you're very lucky."

The squad of New Zealanders had no pressing mission so they set up a perimeter for the three Americans and kept them safe until they were replaced by U.S. Army Military Police and the South Korean Tiger Division. The South Koreans were ferocious fighters and they cheerfully took over guarding the perimeter. Their main role deep in the jungle was to go out and hunt down Viet Cong and to bring them back alive for interrogation. As Johnny would find out in time, they were brutal interrogators who could and would do things that the Americans were not officially allowed to do.

Johnny had been in the military long enough to know how to get most of the things that he wanted from the vast supply depot that Uncle Sam always sets up near a war. At Phou Kát, he wanted a nice, safe, and comfortable place to sleep at night. So he ordered a classy, twenty-four foot aluminum trailer to be flown in on one of the large transport planes. The trailer was nice and comfortable, but he soon found that it was anything but safe. "The trailer was beautiful," he remembers, "but it made a great target because it was so visible." The shiny aluminum reflected the sun in the day time and stood out nearly as bright as day under the moon at night. Johnny got some soldiers to help him and they soon solved the problem. "We had to completely cover it with sandbags so it was not obvious to the enemy that a trailer was even there," he chuckles.

Johnny remembers another interesting experience that occurred on his first New Year's Eve in that country. This time, however, he ended up laughing at himself. He had gone to bed for the night in his snug trailer when all hell seemed to break loose outside. He recounts the rest.

I jumped out of bed, grabbed my weapon, and carefully went outside. Stuff was exploding in the air and there was quite a racket. I realized that I made a real good target standing there in just my undershorts under a full moon, so I dove under the trailer for cover.

I could see in the light of the exploding rockets that I was among a bunch of scorpions, so I bolted out of there and went back inside to bed.

The next morning, I found out that the engineers had fired off all those rockets to celebrate the New Year, 1967.

Johnny still shakes his head and smiles at the memory of that night.

There are other memories, though, that defy humor. Because of Johnny's lively, outgoing spirit and his knack for getting what he wanted and spreading it around black market style, he was often in the thick of things. He soon took up the habit out in his rapidly-expanding jungle encampment of bartering stuff other people couldn't get for stuff he wanted. He would have booze, cigarettes, and candy flown in with weather supplies and then he would circulate out through the firebases that were set up every half-mile around the airport area and trade with the Army guys out there protecting the site. The soldiers in combat positions got the best food, things like fresh milk and steaks. "The milk was a welcome change from that powered stuff that the Air Force gave us," he recalls. And the steaks were better than meals out of a tin can.

It was on forays around the air base site that Johnny came into contact with the ugliest side of war. He shares an example of that.

I remember one time I was walking along a path toward one of the fire bases. I was following two other guys who were quite a ways up ahead of me, when I heard a terrific explosion.

I ran up to where it happened and saw that the first guy was cut in half from the back and lying dead face down on the ground. The second one was down on his back, still alive, trying to hold his intestines in. There was blood all over him and the ground.

When I asked what had happened, he said that his buddy had stepped on a 'Bouncing Betty,' an anti-personnel mine that jumps out of the ground when it explodes, and that he was full of shrapnel in the stomach.

I just stayed with him and talked to him while I cradled his head.

He pulled his wristwatch off, handed it to me, and said, 'Here, you better take it before Charlie gets it. I've only got fifteen or twenty minutes left.

We stayed that way, quiet, and fifteen minutes later he was gone. When I looked down at the watch, I saw that it was a Rolex. I still have it.

When I got to the firebase, I told them what had happened to those two men. They said that they had heard the mine go off and that somebody would be along to 'pick up the meat.'

There is no hint of humor in Johnny's voice when he talks about such experiences. He closes the story with "My faith in 'mankind' really hit bottom after that."

And yet Johnny did not stop trying to make the best of the war, for himself and for others. As time went along, a lot of new personnel arrived, including a captain and a number of weather equipment operators who joined Johnny's team. One day, Johnny was replacing sandbags on top of his trailer, which required pushing the heavy bags some eight feet up on the trailer roof. As he exerted himself, he felt an awful pain shoot through his chest. "It felt as if my chest were ripping out," he recalls. He went to his knees and dropped the sandbag.

He was taken by helicopter to Quinyan and then on to Cam Ron Bay. He spent a few days there and then was moved again, this time all the way to Tachikawa, Japan, where the U.S. had a first-rate military hospital.

In Japan, the doctors informed Johnny of what had happened inside his body.

They told me that I had torn the muscles around my esophagus where it passes through the diaphragm, which is called a hiatal hernia. They said that they could remove three or four of my ribs to go in and repair it or that, if I could manage the discomfort with antacids, I could get by without surgery.

Johnny spent 45 days in the hospital. Humor helped him get through the days. One of the soldiers he met there was a very young fellow whom the others came to call Junior because he had enlisted in the U.S. Army at the age of 14 by lying about his age. Junior had a nasty wound in his butt cheek from shrapnel. Johnny took a liking to the boy and tried to help out as best he could.

It must have been very painful for him because whenever he tried to move, his face just twisted up and he would scream and moan. When I saw this starting to happen, I would grab my camera that I had there and start shooting pictures of his face to distract him.

I'd say, 'Come on Junior, give me a smile so I can get a good picture!'

It seemed to help him get his mind off the pain.

Another time, a troupe of young Japanese doctors in training came by for a visit. When Johnny learned the purpose of their tour, he could not help himself from having a bit of fun. The adventure began when he asked one fellow who seemed to be the guide what they wanted.

He said, 'We doctors. We doctors.'

I asked, 'What you look for?'

'We look for 'hemorrloids,' was the eager response.'

'Oh!' I said, 'You're looking for hemorrhoids!'

'Yes!' he said, 'Hemorrloids! You know, the behind.'

I said, 'Oh, yeah, that's easy! That guy in that bed, that guy across the aisle and that guy in the bed in the corner…' I must have pointed out a half dozen, maybe eight men.

Then those Japanese doctors just charged right in and started examining those poor guys.

The rest of us had one hell of a charge out of that one!

It was at that hospital in Tachikawa, Japan, that Johnny smoked his last cigarette. It was on his last night there as he prepared himself to return to the war. He went to his quarters early because his flight left back for Saigon at 5 a.m. In those days, he "smoked like a chimney," averaging two to three packs a day. He had gravitated from Camels to the more potent Pall Malls that did not have filters.

Once in his quarters, he discovered that he was completely out of cigarettes and would have to get dressed to go across the street to get more. Johnny was in a bad mood in the middle of a bad war which he was about to rejoin back on the front lines. He needed a cigarette, and he needed it badly.

I was getting more and more uptight, and I began to curse and raise hell in my room in my underwear.

One of the guys came by and asked me what was wrong.

I told him that I had run out of cigarettes and that I was just too goddamn lazy to get dressed and go across the street to buy a pack.

He pulled a pack of Winstons out of his shirt pocket and said, 'Here, keep the pack.'

I pulled one out of the pack and lit it. I didn't realize that I had lit the filter end until I was taking a big drag on it. Man! That was god-awful! I threw that one away and proceeded to take three or four puffs from another one. Even smoking them in the proper way did nothing for me.

Finally, I just took the pack, twisted it up, and threw it away, still feeling miserable. The idea that I could be so hooked on these lousy things really got me down. When I had stopped drinking I guess I told myself I could just smoke to fill in the void that alcohol used to occupy. It was the lesser of two evils. Now, I never wanted to see another cigarette. And I just quit smoking.

As with any addiction, the desire does not leave when the mind decides that it must end. There is always the final working out stage. As soon as Johnny was settled on the airplane back to the war the next morning, he started facing down his addiction. Once the plane was airborne, the "No Smoking" light went out, a signal Johnny had always responded to in the past by immediately lighting up. Not this time. He held firm.

Soon the stewardess came by on her rounds, informing the people around him that they could now smoke. When she got to Johnny, he announced his new resolve. He had quit smoking.

"When?" the stewardess asked.

"Last night," Johnny responded.

She smiled. "When you're climbing the wall for a cigarette, I'll come running with one." And then she added, "Wow! Good luck!"

When Johnny was getting off the plane at the end of the flight, she again wished him good luck. "She had the most beautiful smile," he still recalls, over four decades later.

Johnny thanked her for her encouragement, but assured her, "For anything else, I'd welcome the luck. For giving up cigarettes, I won't need it."

And there he was, back in Saigon. Back at another ugly war and headed for the front lines. But he kept his vow. He never smoked again.

There was just one major addiction left in Johnny Pail Face's life—the addiction to violence. It is important to note that Johnny was never personally a violent individual. Perhaps it was because he grew up in a world so filled with violence and potential violence, especially toward a young Navajo boy, that he knew he could never win at anything through his own use of violence.

From the beginning, his motto was, "If I have to learn your language to beat you at your own game, that's what I'm going to do." And he did, again and again. By the time he found himself in Vietnam fighting in his third war in as many decades, he spoke five languages. He would have learned a lot more Vietnamese as well had his French not solved the communication problem for him in this former French colony.

Johnny used words, not his fists. I asked him once if he ever got into fights and brawls in the many, many bars throughout the American West and much of the world where he regularly hung out during his drinking days. "Nope," he replied with a wide smile. "I'm a lover, not a fighter." And yet he was drawn to war. And while there, he regularly demonstrated a reckless abandon that took him into some of the darkest places of human violence. Upon his return to Vietnam from the Japanese hospital in 1967, this side of his personality revealed itself clearly and often.

From Saigon, he caught a ride with a convoy back to Phou Kát Air Base. Upon arrival, a superior officer told him to drive the 35 miles or so over to Quinyan to pick up a newly-arriving captain. Johnny went looking for someone to "ride shotgun" with him for the journey. He recounts.

> *I spotted a heavyset, sloppy looking kid and asked him if he knew how to handle an M16 assault rifle.*
>
> *He said, 'Yeah, I was trained on it at the base I came from. Why?'*
>
> *I said, 'Good! You're coming with me to Quinyan. We have to pick up a captain.'*
>
> *He said, 'No way!'*
>
> *I said, 'What? Why not?'*
>
> *He said that they had to fly him in to our base by helicopter because there was so much Viet Cong activity along the roads, and that he just wasn't going to go.*
>
> *I said, 'Bullshit! They had to fly here anyway, so they just took you along.'*
>
> *He still wouldn't get into the jeep.*
>
> *I pointed my weapon at him and calmly asked what hospital he would like to be sent to because I was going to shoot him if he continued to refuse my order. I was his sergeant.*
>
> *He dropped his head and climbed into the jeep to ride shotgun.*
>
> *Well, we got to Quinyan with no problem and picked up the officer. On our way back as we neared our airbase, we heard some loud explosions in the jungle alongside us.*
>
> *The heavy kid, his name was Mullins, like in the 'Moon Mullins' comic strip, jumped out of the moving jeep and rolled down the embankment on the side of the road. He was yelling, 'They're shooting at us!'*

I stopped the vehicle and backed up to where he was crouching. I said, 'No, no, no! Get back in the jeep! That's just the Koreans trying to dig some V. C. out of their holes. It's got nothing to do with us.'

He sheepishly got back in and we arrived at the base without any further incident.

The next day, as I was walking past his tent, I heard a lot of sobbing and crying. When I looked inside there's another sergeant and this fat Mullins kid. Mullins was sitting on his cot bawling away.

When I asked what the matter was, he said that he was going to have another nervous breakdown. He said that when they refused to allow his fiancée to be with him during Basic Training he just broke down and was treated in the hospital.

I told him, 'Look, I'm going to take a walk over to the mess tent and have a cup of coffee. That should take me about half an hour. Then I'm gonna come back here, and if you haven't straightened yourself out by then, I'm gonna have them throw you over the barbed wire fence, and you can have your nervous breakdown when the Viet Cong come for you.'

I turned around and left.

That fat kid not only straightened out, he became one of my most dangerous troopers.

But all was not struggle and strife as the months of Johnny's days in Vietnam slipped by. At one point, he and a few of his men were given a week of "Rest and Recuperation" time that they spent in the safe world of Hong Kong. Johnny chose to spend his free time quite differently than had been his custom in previous respites from war. He recounts.

When I got there, I checked into a fine hotel, The President, and went down to the nearest bar. I ordered my ginger ale and thought to myself how great it was to be here.

It wasn't long before a beautiful Eurasian woman came over and sat next to me.

She said, 'Hey, you buy me a drink?'

I said, 'You want a drink? Look here's ten dollars Hong Kong,' and I put it on her lap. 'Buy yourself a drink if that's what you want.'

She looked at me and took the bill, folded it up, and put it in her purse, saying to me, 'No, I just sit and talk to you.'

I understood that she needed the money much more than the drink, so I said, 'Okay.'

Every time the bartender came over to see if I wanted to order a drink, I'd just push another ten dollars over to her.

Finally it was time for the bar to close and she said to me, 'Come, you go to my home with me.'

I said, 'No thanks. I no want to. I don't want anything from you.'

She said, 'I go to your hotel!'

I said, 'No, thank you, but no.'

'You queer, or what?' she asked.

'No, I'm not queer.'

She said, 'I'm good! I give you everything!'

'I don't want everything,' I said.

'You come! We go bed!' she insisted.

I said, 'Nope!'

'I think you queer,' she said.

After again insisting on going to my hotel and my refusing her request, she took out a little card out of her purse and wrote something in Chinese on it. She handed me the card, saying, 'You decide you change your mind, you give taxi driver this card. He take you to my home.'

I just said 'Okay,' and went back to my hotel.

By his third war, Johnny had outgrown his habits of drinking hard and carousing with women in his free time. He was a quieter man. He was a husband and a father to three beautiful daughters.

The next day in Hong Kong, he decided to go out to the "New Territories" to do some shopping for his family. He had heard this was the best place to find good bargains. The New Territories was a part of the city that had expanded into a new area immediately adjacent to the Chinese border. This was a time when Communist China and the U.S. were not on good terms due to the Cold War and the U.S.'s willingness to invade nations far from home and close to China, like Vietnam.

Johnny made the mistake of falling asleep on the train to the New Territories. When he woke up, he found the train stopped at a station in Canton, China. When he stepped off the train in his U.S. military uniform, there was suddenly a lot of excitement around him. Station employees in their uniforms came and quickly dragged him into the station offices. There they put him in a cramped bathroom and locked the door. One of them told him in accented English, "You wait!"

Johnny did as he was told. There were not a lot of other options.

Finally, the door opened and the station personnel quickly ushered him to an outbound train headed for the New Territories. "You lucky," one of them smiled. "The police no get you!"

On his way back to safe territory, Johnny reflected on the simple kindnesses that people often offer each other when they have every reason to do otherwise. If only governments could do likewise.

When Johnny got to the New Territories, he found beautiful jade earrings for his two younger stepdaughters who were still living at home with Theresa back in New England. They have them to this day.

After a week of rest and relaxation in Hong Kong, Johnny and his men returned again to the jungles of Vietnam and their lives there. One of the most intriguing and revealing aspects of Johnny's time in this, his final war, was that he not only followed orders that took him into danger, he regularly courted close contact with lethal violence by choice. He did not have to do this. He was a weatherman, not an infantryman. He was no "grunt soldier." He held a Master's Degree from a first-class American university. His role was to predict weather conditions as part of the day-to-day planning of operations at Phou Kát Air Base. Furthermore, he had proven his mettle in two previous wars. He had faced death more times than he could remember, more times even than psychiatrists could get him to remember. And yet he often left the relative safety of the large air base on forays into the heart of the war. It was on one of these ramblings that he lost two comrades to the "Bouncing Betty" land mine. Even after witnessing the horrible deaths of those two fellow soldiers, he continued his trips into the jungle. Here is another example of what he found out there.

As I was telling you, I used to go out to the firebases to do some trading so that my guys could have some good things to eat, and so forth. I would check out a pickup and put sandbags up on its roof to take a 50 caliber machine gun or an M60 cannon and get one of the Koreans to stand up in the back to man it. If, while we were driving along I thought I saw anything like a booby trap or explosives, I would have him open up on it.

So we went way up on the top of this high hill to one of the firebases. I brought them several bottles of booze and we had a great cookout. They grilled some steaks and we just really enjoyed them. They tried to get me to stay the night, but I said, 'No, I've got to get back to my job before I'm missed.' It was starting to get dark so my Korean friend and I took off.

When we were about halfway back we suddenly saw a lot of tracer fire arching up and coming down. It was a real firefight. The next day they told me that the firebase we had just left was attacked and overrun by the V. C. All the men the Korean fellow and I had barbecued with the night before were wiped out.

Johnny always pauses after sharing events such as these. He shakes his head slowly and I know where his thoughts go in the silence. He has told me more than once. It is only natural in the face of the deaths of others to wonder why he was spared. In similar circumstances, we all do it. Was it fate? Has God determined it this way? Is there some reason that one is spared when others are taken? Many find reasons and a higher sense of purpose in life after a brush with death. Johnny does likewise, and understandably so. His brushes with death are many and serve to multiply the urge to do good things with a life that has often been spared. But this does not answer the mystery of why he consciously and unconsciously chose not only to be in wars but to be in those specific parts of war where death is in full view in its most ugly, brutal state.

This did not always require Johnny to leave the safety of the air base. Occasionally he would go visit the Korean troop compound after they came in from a raid on enemy positions in the jungle. One of their primary roles was to capture the enemy and to gain intelligence to feed to the Americans. If facing death oneself is a traumatic experience, watching another human die can be equally traumatic. Johnny chose not just to tempt death with his own life, but he also chose to watch other men die. He shared one incident that goes to the heart of this mystery.

One day when Johnny was in the Korean camp, they brought in a Viet Cong prisoner who they had reason to believe could tell them about enemy plans, troop strength, weaponry, etc. So they tied him upright on a bamboo frame and began the interrogation. One of the Koreans was an expert with a knife. He began to cut the skin from the prisoner's back in strips an inch wide that ran from his shoulders to his buttocks. What Johnny found amazing was that the skinner never actually drew blood. He took off just enough skin that you could see beads of body fluid seep up in the wake of the knife. Then another soldier would rub salt into the fresh wound. This would cause the Vietnamese prisoner to scream uncontrollably for a time. Once his voice weakened to a whimper, the interrogator would go at him with his questioning. When the prisoner refused to answer, another strip of skin would be taken from his back, and the process would repeat.

I asked Johnny how he felt while watching this torture session. He said that it just pissed him off. "That Vietnamese fellow was a damn fool," he says. "Why wouldn't he just divulge the information? Why wouldn't he just tell the Koreans what they wanted to know? Then they would have had mercy and killed him right away. He had to know that." Instead, the ordeal lasted until the next day when the prisoner died from dehydration and trauma, still hanging on the bamboo frame.

I pushed Johnny to try to express what it was that drew him to such horrific scenes of war. He thought for a while and then said, "It's an incredible human drama to see someone skinning another person, while a third person rubs salt into the wounds. When you watch something like that you have to feel something. Even I felt something there, watching that."

And so the deeper secret began to come out. I do not pretend to understand it. You may struggle as well. Johnny Pail Face continued to go to war long after others turned back because he wanted to feel again. There is certain logic, even poetic justice, to this. It was war that took away his ability to feel. By war I do not mean only World War II and the horror of what happened the day that the Allies took Monte Cassino, a horror so complete that Johnny locked it up in his psyche and has never found it again. I also mean the war that Johnny faced from the very beginning of his awareness of what had happened to his mother to make her bow her head in shame at who she was as a Navajo woman raised in a Catholic Mission in white America.

Is it too much to suggest that the priests took their knives to her little girl identity? Did they not cut it away as skillfully and as painfully as the Koreans skinned their unfortunate prisoner under Johnny's eyes decades later? Was Refugio Perez's life not lived out in a war zone? Even if we chose not to label it so, of one thing we can be sure: Refugio Perez's world was able to strip her Navajo son of his ability to feel. To regain his humanity, the last obstacle Johnny faced on his struggle out of the many wars of his life was finding a way to feel again.

When speaking of the horrific deaths that he witnessed, particularly in his last war, Johnny says with a note of wonder in his old voice:

> *I became a human being. I began to feel. If you had known how I felt! It could have been me. Why did God put me ahead of them? The Creator was giving me room and examples so that I could understand what life is all about.*
>
> *Look at me. I spent the first 42 years of my life raising hell anywhere and everywhere. And then I changed. I got to a better place in life.*
>
> *Look at me now. I spend my days feeding birds, squirrels, and rabbits in the back yard. I offer up my daily prayers and try with*

everything in me to be a human being. Don't tell me there is no Creator!

After talking like this with great energy, Johnny stops, looks at me, and laughs. "Do I sound like a preacher, or what?" he asks.

"A good one," I say.

"I learned to feel," he says with an air of closure. "I was ready to come home to my babies and to my wife. I would be able to feel them now. That's what Vietnam gave me."

Johnny Pail Face with daughter Lorraine in Santa Fe, early 1970's.

Part Four

Prayer to the North
(The Last and Longest Road)

Oh Lord, Creator in the North, I know that the trail from the South to the North is very long, as is life very difficult, difficult because when you blew the Breath of Life into me, you gave me free will. I have used, abused, and misused that will and now I am ready to do your will. I pray for the Knowledge of your will for me and the Power to carry it out. I know that every day that I open my eyes to the East, I have one more day to redeem myself. Please let me keep this day. Every day I take one step toward the day that I will be with you. My body will be in Mother Earth and my spirit will be with you. Let me keep this day so when I am called I can come to you with Clean Hands and Straight Eyes. So that when my life fades as the fading sunset, my spirit can come to you without Shame.

CHAPTER 26

The Long Road Home

ONE OF THE MOST COMPLEX JOURNEYS ONE CAN TAKE IN THIS LIFE is the one that leads home from war. It can be a long road to travel. Some soldiers never finish it. These are the ones who take to the streets. They become drifters. They sleep under bridges in summer and over heating grates in winter.

Johnny's homeward journey from World War II included a year in a mental institution. Doctors there told him that he had lost his conscience. They told him that if he ever found it, he would likely kill himself for the things he had been through and the things that he had done.

When he left the institution, these revelations haunted him. They lurked on the edge of his consciousness like a predator at a high desert watering hole in Navajo country. Years later, he realized that he had never returned fully from his first war. He became determined to finally "come home" from his third war.

As the end of his one-year tour of duty in Vietnam neared, he went to his commanding officer to begin arrangements for repatriation. However, in the summer of 1967, things were heating up for the Americans in South Asia. Boots were needed on the ground. Johnny found himself among thousands of soldiers who were "held-over" beyond their enlistment agreements. It would be ten more months before he began the journey home to his girls and Theresa.

It wasn't until April of 1968 that Johnny made himself eligible for release by taking his 60-day accrued leave time. Again his Air Force superiors tried to keep him on. They offered a hefty bonus if he would spend his leave time right there at Phou Kát Air Base.

Johnny laughed at the officer who made the offer. "No way, buddy. I am going home," he told him straight out. They had to let him go. Within days he had his orders in hand and hitched a ride on an outgoing plane to Saigon.

Johnny arrived in Saigon with four days to spare before his flight back to the States. He looked forward to doing some souvenir shopping for family gifts, getting some good food, and catching up on his rest. He soon found his plans turned upside down.

After I landed at Saigon, I got my sleeping quarters and everything seemed okay. When I went to bed that night, all of a sudden all hell broke loose outside with explosions everywhere and shrapnel flying in through the screens.

A guy comes running in and says they're shooting all around us.

I asked, 'Where's the weapons room so we can get ready?'

He said, 'We don't have a weapons room. We don't keep any weapons here!'

I said, 'In that case, don't bother me, buddy.'

I rolled out of bed and pulled down the mattress from the top bunk and grabbed the one that I had been on. Over by the wall on the side of the room there were some steel lockers, so I crawled in between the lockers and the mattresses to get some protection from any shrapnel that might come in. I fell asleep that way.

In the morning after what had been an all-night firefight, I got up and went out to get a cup of coffee.

Everything was quiet when Johnny went outside. He found the Air Force mess tent on fire and abandoned, so he kept walking until he came to an Army mess tent. There he was able to get his morning coffee.

As he was sitting in the quiet of the new day, a lieutenant came over to where he was sitting. The young officer asked if he knew how to handle a 50 caliber machine gun.

Johnny's response, "Sure can!"

The Lieutenant asked, "You mind taking these four guys and setting up a bunker so that we can protect these helicopters that we have here?"

"No problem!" Johnny told him. And he went to work with his new team.

I got a bunch of barrels and we filled them with sand. We filled sand bags and put them up so that we could mount the weapons. Then I found some mattresses that were still good in one of the destroyed barracks so that the guys would have a place to lie down when they weren't on guard duty. Then I sent one of the guys up to the mess hall to get some C-rations.

Johnny and his crew of four hunkered down in their bunker for the next three days. They saw a lot of action at night when the Viet Cong came out shooting. Johnny remembers the images of the heavy weapons firing in the darkness as they kept the enemy away from the helicopters. Both sides in the fray had tracers on their heavy caliber bullets so that they could better see where they were shooting in the night.

Johnny remembers the Viet Cong bullets came buzzing in with white streaks behind them and their return fire went out with red tracers. The night was lit up in this way with deadly fireworks as men fought over control of a small piece of ground with helicopters sitting on it like ducks in a shooting gallery.

On the fourth day of this back and forth of calm in the daytime and intense fighting at night, a jeep came by and the driver asked if anyone was headed for the States.

"Yeah, me!" Johnny called out.

The driver responded, "You better jump on this jeep then. A Japanese airliner just landed here by mistake and I don't imagine he's gonna stay for more than ten minutes. You better hurry!"

Johnny scooped up his few belongings that he had with him at the bunker, tossed them into the jeep, and climbed aboard.

When he got to the air strip, he was confronted by a fellow in another bunker surrounded by sandbags. "Hey, hey, hey, where are you going?" he challenged as Johnny started to run for the JAL plane.

Johnny told him that he was going to catch that plane for home.

"Have you got orders?" he asked.

Johnny responded that he did.

"Well you better give me a copy or you'll have to be listed as Missing in Action," he responded.

Johnny gave the soldier what he needed and then ran for the plane. "I had to jump over three or four V. C. bodies and then sprinted up the tail ramp of this green JAL airliner," he recalls.

> *I got into one of the seats and strapped myself in. I was breathing hard. When you run and jump into a plane like that, it's pretty exciting. Three minutes after that the ramp came up. It wasn't more than ten minutes later that the plane cranked up and was on its way.*
>
> *I looked down after we took off and I could see the Mekong River falling away. This was in the middle of the Tet Offensive, and I just said, 'Bye, bye Vietnam!' I had escaped the Tet Offensive. It felt good to be alive that day!*

Those who Johnny left behind were not so lucky. The U.S. and its allies (South Vietnam, Korea, Australia, and New Zealand) suffered 28,176 killed, wounded, or missing in action during the eight-month Tet Offensive. The long battle was named after the Asian lunar new year, or *Tết Nguyên Đán* in Vietnamese, because it began as a surprise attack on the first night of the New Year holiday.

The North Vietnamese took an estimated 82,000 casualties. All major cities and hundreds of regional towns in South Vietnam were attacked. Many were devastated. The human cost was high. By the end of 1968, one out of every twelve people in South Vietnam was living in a refugee camp. Historians now tell us that it was the turning point of a war that Vietnam would win.[1] The will of the Vietnamese people to decide the direction of their own country was greater than the willingness of leaders in Washington to kill them for doing so.

In the midst of this test of wills between the most powerful nation on Earth and the fourth poorest nation on Earth, Johnny Pail Face left Saigon in a Japanese airliner rather than in a body bag. In his own mind, this made him a victor. To this day, he suspects that to military bureaucrats in Washington, sending him on an isolated tour of duty to Vietnam immediately before his retirement was a shrewd bureaucratic decision. "It's easier to pay $10,000 in a death benefit to a man's family than to pay retirement benefits for the rest of his life," Johnny sums up. "That's government thinking. But I beat the bureaucrats at their own game. I lived."

These were the thoughts running through Johnny's mind as he sat on a Japanese airliner and watched Saigon and the Mekong River drop out of sight below him in 1968. But when he left his third war, he was a long way from home. Vietnam is twelve time zones away from Massachusetts. It is almost exactly on the other side of the planet. Johnny's inner world was about the same distance from home. He did not rush back to Massachusetts to sweep his "babies" and wife up in his arms. He took his time. He made the journey long. He took it carefully. He wanted to be sure to get all the way there this time.

His first stop was at Manila in the Philippines. He stayed several days poking around, looking at the sights, finding a gift here and there. Then he caught a TWA flight to San Francisco. His first order of business was to turn in his retirement orders at a base there and quietly end his professional career with the U.S. military. And then, once more, he did not go rushing home.

Instead, he spent a few days in San Francisco. One morning while reading the newspaper, he came across an ad asking for a driver to chauffeur a 1957 Corvette convertible across the country to Boston. Johnny called up and took the job.

His next call was to Theresa. Would she fly out and join him for the long drive home? He wanted to stop by Gallup and visit with his family. He could pick her up in Albuquerque. They could tour the country. Would she come?

To this day, Theresa is a model of New England reserve. Winters are long in this part of the country. The soil is rocky. Eking out a living has always been a struggle. Yankee New Englanders are survivors. They work hard. They do what needs to be done. They don't complain. In fact, if Theresa is taken as a character model, they don't even talk that much, especially about how they feel. The husband/wife relationship between Johnny and Theresa was always respectful, cordial, honest, and largely unemotional.

Theresa showed emotion that day, Johnny remembers. She was happy to hear his voice. Yes, she would come. Right away. She would try to meet him the next day in Albuquerque. She looked forward to it. She looked forward to having him home again.

All Johnny could think to say in response was that she should be sure to bring warm clothes. They would be driving in a convertible. It could get cold with the top down. He did not want her to catch a chill. And with this simple gesture of kindness, the kind of thing a soldier would never say to another soldier, he hung up the phone. He was on his way home.

Johnny got in the red Corvette and drove all that day to Gallup, New Mexico. It was the third time he had returned from a war to this home town. He had a lot on his mind. Foremost was that he did not want to stay in or near Gallup. He was eager get away from Gallup after short visits to relatives and to move on to Albuquerque where Theresa would be waiting. Then they would hit the road in a convertible with the top down and New Mexico behind. They would have the wind in their faces and the open road before them all the way to Massachusetts.

He kept his mind focused on their new home in New England. There were positive things awaiting him there. There was a hard-working, gentle-spirited wife and three healthy daughters. Together, they had the "Terry's Soft Serve" ice cream business to run. He also had his refrigeration repair business to get up and going again. They had all the cash they needed to move ahead. Johnny still had a couple of hundred thousand dollars from his French/Algeria black market profits sitting in safe deposit boxes. He could resume putting that cash back into circulation.

He looked forward to seeing how much his daughters had grown and changed. He hoped that the Chevy work truck and his 1963 Ford Galaxy 500 XL were still in good condition. There was much to be done in New England for a newly retired man who had abundant energy and who now had time to do with it what he wanted.

Johnny spent the night with his sister Luisa in Gallup. She barely recognized him, not because she had forgotten who he was, but because she remembered what he had once been. As they sat at the dining table that evening, she gave him a long, pleased look and said,

"If I didn't see you sitting here before me, I would not believe you are my little brother Johnny. If I close my eyes, I do not recognize your voice or even the normal way that you are talking to me and treating me."

Johnny laughed. "You used to forbid me to enter your house. Why were you so hard on me in the old days?"

Luisa shook her head at the memory. "When you were drinking and you and our brothers would come to visit me, they would open the screen door when they came in. You wouldn't! You would walk right through it just to show that you didn't give a damn. That's why I didn't want you coming around here. You were such a hell-raiser."

"I'm sorry about that," Johnny told her. "I was not a good human being in those days."

"You've changed so much, Johnny," Luisa said. "If I weren't sitting right here looking at you, I would not believe it. I'm so glad. It hurt me to see you like you used to be."

Brother and sister talked on like this through the evening, friends again, at peace again. They had been very close long ago. Luisa had assisted in Johnny's birth. She had been a second mother to him throughout his childhood. Now they were close again. Life had come full circle for a big sister and a little brother. Johnny came home to Luisa that night.

The next day, he picked up Theresa in Albuquerque. She greeted him cheerfully with a hug and a kiss. Then their cross-country journey was on. Theresa was becoming increasingly frail with anemia at this point in her life. The warm April weather of the American Southwest and the fresh air rushing by in the convertible seemed much better for her than the chill that grips New England, often until early summer. She was in good spirits.

They drove 400-500 miles each day and then found a place to eat and to sleep. Johnny remembers how good it felt to have a real American hamburger again, and a T-bone steak. Such simple pleasures helped him make the transition back to the life he'd known before Vietnam. The long drive home gave him and Theresa time to talk through their plans for their businesses and for going on with life. When Johnny had entered her life, the Tastee Freeze business was on its last legs, the family home was in need of serious repairs, and the future looked bleak. They had come a long way in turning all that around. Johnny was eager to continue moving forward as a family.

It was late April after they delivered the convertible in Boston and made their way to Granby. Springtime was beginning to green the earth. The first leaves were unfurling on maple forests. Daffodils were peeking from the ground. There was the smell of new life in the air. Johnny and Theresa were met in the front yard by three daughters and Theresa's parents. His step-daughters gave Johnny big hugs to welcome him home.

As soon as they had their luggage in the house, Johnny was out the door again. He started up his Ford Galaxy 500 and his work truck. Both turned over without any trouble. Then he went next door to the ice cream and hotdog stand. It had been shuttered for winter. He started up the refrigerators and took the shutters off the windows. The place smelled musty and a winter's worth of dust had settled on every flat surface.

Johnny opened the doors and windows to let fresh air blow in. He grabbed a rag and wiped down the counter and table tops. They cleaned up quickly with a little elbow grease. Then he sat down and took a deep breath. He was in a good place, a safe place. Any loud noise on the road out front would just be a truck backfiring or the horn of an impatient driver. There were no bombs, no landmines, no incoming machine gun fire. There was a wife and a family next door who needed him. He was retired. He had a lot of things that he wanted to do. Now he had time. He had resources. He had people about whom he cared. He had what he needed to move forward with life. This was home. He was home.

After being gone for three wars, Johnny Pail Face was home.

Retiring into the Circle of Life

JOHNNY PAIL FACE WAS 51 YEARS OLD when he returned from Vietnam in 1968. He was a newly retired man, but still young and in the prime of life. At first, he poured his energy into his family and their businesses. Before his first summer of retired life was over, he had the ice cream stand on good footing and his refrigeration repair business bringing in nice profits.

Underneath the day-to-day business of making a living, Johnny began to focus more and more upon a deepening philosophy of life that had long been sitting quietly at the edges of his thoughts. From boyhood, he had been taught by his family and by the old shaman Victor about the circle of life in which he lived. Johnny had now lived long enough to begin to take more seriously the implications of this way of looking at the world.

When I got back to New England, I had a chance to start over. It was like in my younger days when all my feelings were about accomplishing things, about doing what had to be done. I had always wanted to do the best that I could to feel good, to feel right, to feel that I was a part of civilization. It took me a lot of new starts to learn how to do that.

In Granby with Theresa, I had taken on the responsibility of finishing some things that a deceased husband had started. There was a house to pay for, a business to run, a family that needed a man around, two grandparents who were facing some hard times.

After I brought Theresa into my circle of responsibility, it was all about carrying through, about being responsible. My main purpose became to get ahead so that a family that another man had started would not have to suffer later. I had started some families myself and had seen everything fall apart under my feet. It was my turn to step up and to try to redeem myself if I could.

I worked hard, but it was not for the riches. I didn't want the money. I was buying a better future for a family and for myself too. They were good people. Helping them was a way to become a better human being. That was important to me.

With this new understanding of where, what, and who he was in his circle of life, Johnny spent his days working on becoming a good family man and provider. He joined the board of the school where his youngest daughter, Linda, was a student. He accepted a position as a loan officer at a local credit union. He became a stockholder in a bank. He became involved in Alcoholics Anonymous again, got active in Masonry, and gave his support to the area Shriners Hospital network.

At the core of things, he spent his days working hard at the family's two businesses, cheerfully wheeling and dealing much as he had done in other places around the world as a black marketeer. Ever the shrewd businessman, he would barter goods and services rather than work in cash whenever he could. "This saved on my taxes," he explains.

The company that sold him liquid ice cream mix soon became one of his refrigeration repair clients. After he did refrigeration work for them, he would accept bags of mix as payment. The company, in turn, would write off the mix as goods that had been given him to replace supplies that had gone bad or had been damaged. Everybody benefited when there were no cash transactions to put on balance books. Of course, the greatest benefit to Johnny was that he was able to pull cash regularly out of his safe deposit boxes and to pour it into his two businesses.

By fall, 1968, Johnny had bought a new utility truck for his refrigeration business, a brand new Dodge station wagon for the family, plus a 19-foot two-wheeled camping trailer for extended family outings. The first big outing came during the winter of 1968-69.

With their daughters in their teens and grandparents living next door, Johnny and Theresa decided to experiment with a new approach to life. Theresa was becoming increasingly frail and Johnny had a good deal of wanderlust left over from his military postings around the globe. Instead of facing another winter in the bitter chill of New England, they decided to seek a warmer climate during the harsh winter months.

Johnny had long wanted to explore the Pacific Coast of Mexico. As is always the case with him, he had a number of reasons for wanting to do so. In addition to taking Theresa to a climate more suitable to her health, he was keen to return to a trade he had learned as a boy—Navajo jewelry making. Making traditional jewelry had just been an interesting craft to Johnny when he was young, but when he returned to it as a retired man, he brought a different perspective and a different kind of energy to the work.

When I was six years old, I learned how to craft rings, pendants, bracelets, belt buckles, and all kinds of things using silver and semi-precious stones. The first thing I learned was how to take a silver quarter and to pound it into a ring. But in those days no one had money to spend on jewelry, not even a quarter. There were hard times and then the Depression hit. People were starving to death where I lived. They were not buying jewelry.

But making Native American jewelry is like riding a bicycle. Once you get back on, you're on your way again. You may be a little rusty, but it all comes back to you.

In his old age, Johnny no longer thinks of jewelry making as a craft or trade. He calls it his "spiritual hobby." Each piece that he makes in his small silversmithing workshop is done using imagination and vision. Sometimes he will set aside an unusual piece of turquoise, onyx, or other semi-precious stone for a year or more as he waits for a clear vision of how to work it into a piece of jewelry. The end result will usually be artfully surrounded by silver feathers or arrows or other designs, or perhaps by bear or eagle claws, all drawing together the power and the beauty of the natural world in a single bold piece of jewelry.

One afternoon, Johnny took me and two young friends from Korea out to his jewelry-making shop. M. J. and Jenny were college students of mine who Johnny insisted upon meeting when I spoke to him about them. He wanted to practice his Korean language skills to see if he could still make himself understood. He could. He charmed the young women from the first moment that they met and made them laugh with delight as he teased them playfully in their own language. Jenny and M. J. were the guests across the table from Johnny that night at the Korean restaurant when he blurted out the tale of his days with Suko.

As the months of their student exchange in America went by, they came to call him "Grandfather," and his friend Nancy, "Grandmother," a gesture of kindness and respect that made the eyes of both elderly souls dance each time they heard it. One day Johnny gave a beautiful Navajo ring he had made to M. J., the more outgoing of the two young Koreans.

For Jenny, he decided to make a new ring. "That way you can see how I do it," he told them. So out to the barn we went. It is where Johnny parks his cramped six feet by ten feet, two-wheeled jewelry-making trailer in winter.

We watched in wonder as the old gentleman worked. It was immediately obvious not only that he had been making silver jewelry by hand for decades, but that he had been doing it in the same tiny work space. Every one of the dozen or so hand tools that he needed to heat, bend, ply, and turn strips of raw silver into a ring was exactly where he wanted it. His hands moved so quickly that it was visually hard to keep up. Gas torch, clamps, pliers, cutting tools, ring sizer, and more flew in and out of his nimble fingers. He seemed not even to look as each tool leaped into his hands, fulfilled its purpose, and then was just as quickly replaced where it had been.

It took less than twenty minutes for a beautiful turquoise Navajo ring to come into the world between Old Johnny's fingers. After he burnished it on an electric wheel, he took Jenny's hand and carefully slipped the ring onto her finger.

As he did so, I saw tears forming at the corners of her eyes. "Today is the most wonderful day I know," she whispered as she looked at the delicate splash of Morenci blue turquoise cradled in polished silver that now decorated her hand.

Johnny later told me that when he had first looked into Jenny's eyes that day, he knew instinctively that he would need to make a new ring for her.

"There was a wonderful, beautiful new person just starting to come to life in that girl," he said. "It seemed right to honor that with something new. And I knew that she would understand the ring better if she watched it being made before her eyes. She had to see it being made to understand that the ring is the same as her heart."

For old Johnny, the beauty of the ring was not separate from the beauty of the young woman herself, a beauty that was just then coming into the world as she made her way forward on her own in America, the hopes and dreams and fears of youth shining as freshly in her eyes as the new ring on her finger. For Old Johnny, it's all connected now, rings and people and journeys and dreams. These are not separate pieces of the world.

On our drive back to campus after a delicious Korean dinner that the students had cooked to share the beauty of their home culture with us, M.J. said to me, "I think we have seen a part of America now that no Koreans ever see. We are so fortunate to be friends with Johnny and Nancy."

I smiled and nodded. "I think you have seen a part of America that few *Americans* ever see." Then I agreed, "Yes, we are fortunate to be friends with Johnny and Nancy."

As Johnny began his journey back into Navajo silversmithing as a newly retired soldier in the late 1960s, he realized that a trip to Mexico would allow him to pick up raw silver, turquoise, and various other supplies at rock-bottom prices, as well as to see the work of other artists. But there were other things that pulled Johnny to Mexico. He loved the idea of exploring the wild, rugged terrain of the Northwest part of the country. He had heard interesting things about the Huichol Indians who lived in the Sierra Madre Mountains there. He wanted to know more about them and about their ways.

And finally, there was a family connection. He was interested to look up his long-lost sister, Manuela, the one who had been taken before he was born. She was now a grandmother living in the state of Chihuahua. The last he had heard, she had raised a dozen or more children. Johnny had a lot of family south of the border to catch up on. He wanted to explore that part of his circle.

So Johnny and Theresa loaded up the camping trailer, hooked it to a brand new Dodge pickup, and drove all the way to the state of Nayarit on the Pacific Coast of Mexico. Theresa was amazed at the beauty and tranquility of the warm, Pacific beaches. She immediately fell in love with beachcombing for the great variety of sea shells that were to be found in abundance. It would become one of her favorite pastimes for years to come.

The adventuresome couple soon drove further south along the coast to the resort town of Puerto Vallarta. In 1968, the hordes of tourists, college students on vacation, and Hollywood stars had not yet discovered this quiet beach town. It had a population of some 2,000 people and the beaches were wonderfully isolated and little used. Theresa and Johnny soon made great use of them on their beachcombing walks and long lazy days passed within the sound of the waves. In the evenings, they went out for peaceful dinners and met other couples seeking in similar ways to escape the hustle and bustle of life.

On one of his walks along the beach one day, Johnny came across a couple of boys climbing palm trees and harvesting coconuts. They said that they would sell him the coconuts for 10 pesos apiece. The price seemed a bit steep for the wheeler and dealer, so he decided to get his own coconuts. He made the mistake of starting up a coconut tree in nothing but his swimming trunks. Here's how that adventure turned out.

Well, I got about halfway up the tree when all of a sudden my feet slipped and I slid all the way back down to the ground. Man did I skin up my chest and belly! Oh that hurt! My skin was full of sharp bits of coarse sand and splinters. I guess those coconuts were really worth the ten pesos that those kids were getting.

As the months of winter went by, Theresa's good health and a warm circle of friends confirmed the decision to leave New England for the warmth and hospitality of Mexico. Johnny's fluency in Spanish made their integration into the local population smooth and full of adventure. In restaurants and other public places, he would often interrupt his own meal or conversation to help other American visitors communicate in Spanish. A first helpful conversation often provided the launch point of a new adventure.

For example, one evening Johnny and Theresa were dining in a favorite restaurant next to a table of men attempting to negotiate in English and Spanish. An older, English-speaking man was in charge and seemed to be getting frustrated with the others. He was obviously wealthy and wore a gold flower over one ear. Johnny hated to see people struggle to communicate, so he got up and started to approach the man with the gold flower. He was immediately stopped by a large, redheaded male bodyguard.

"What do you want?" the big man asked Johnny in English that was tinged with a Boston accent that Johnny knew well.

"I would like to help these people communicate with each other," he said, gesturing towards the group at the table.

"Let him through," the man with the gold flower said, waving Johnny over. "What can I do for you?" the man asked Johnny.

"Maybe I can help your people here talk to each other," Johnny said. "It looks like they are having problems."

The man nodded and explained that his two guests were lawyers he had hired to work out a deal. One spoke English and the other spoke Spanish, and neither spoke both languages. Johnny jumped into the negotiations and soon had everything smoothed out. Then he went back to his table and finished eating with Theresa.

The next night, the man with the gold flower was back again. Johnny stopped by his table to offer a greeting and the man asked him to sit. The bodyguard spoke first. He asked Johnny where he had learned to do what he did.

Johnny asked what he meant.

"Where did you learn to translate like you did last night?" the redhead asked. "The Spanish lawyer said your Spanish was perfect and we all found your English to be perfect too. Where did you learn that?"

"I was raised speaking both languages, and then I learned a couple more during my years in the service," Johnny told him.

The older man was impressed and took a liking to Johnny. They ended up eating together and formed a friendship. The older man had an Italian name and Johnny soon understood that he was a Mafia boss. He asked Johnny about his war experiences and his ability to handle a gun. He was impressed by what he learned. When he found out that Johnny lived near Boston, he gave him the names and addresses of his two nephews who lived there. He told Johnny to look them up if ever he wanted extra work. They could always use a fellow like him who could both provide protection and help facilitate communication with foreign clients.

Johnny was intrigued enough by the adventurous thought of working for "the family" that he did, in fact, look up the nephews back in Boston the next spring. They had heard of him from their uncle and were happy to have him help out on a couple of projects. They gave him the title of "Financial Advisor." However, his only duties were to get a legal gun permit and then to stand behind them with a large pistol in a holster under his arm while they met with clients. After a couple of guard sessions, Johnny moved on to other things.

Back in Mexico during the winters, he regularly made similar connections with people who valued his talents and he took up the habit of following through on the most interesting ones to see where they would lead.

When March rolled around to end that first winter escape to Mexico, Theresa and Johnny were eager to get back to New England to catch up on their girls and the grandparents. At the same time, it was also hard to leave the peaceful paradise they had found in Mexico. The journey home went smoothly enough until they reached El Paso, Texas. There, Johnny stumbled into something that would shake up the rest of his years with Theresa. He recounts.

I was looking over the ledger that Theresa used to list all our expenses. I couldn't read her writing. I asked her what in the world was going on that I couldn't make out what she was writing.

She said, 'I can't see. Everything is blurred.'

I said, 'Oh my God!' I headed the truck straight for the military hospital at Albuquerque, New Mexico. Driving straight through, a good 700 miles, we got to the hospital at about 10 p.m. They took her right in and called an ophthalmologist.

At first he was saying that she needed to be flown back east because he couldn't see anything due to the amount of blood in the left eye. They even had a T38 fighter/trainer plane warmed up to make the trip. It was the fastest way to get there.

Then it was decided that there really wasn't anything that could be done because she had ripped the retina. She later told me that she had struck her head on one of the cabinets in the trailer when she went to get up from the sofa one time and that this must have been the cause of the injury to her eye.

Theresa was going to become blind.

Johnny and Theresa took this sobering news in stride as best that they could. It would be years before Theresa became totally blind, so they continued their new seasonal cycle of working from spring to fall at their businesses in Massachusetts and then spending the winter months on the Pacific Coast of Mexico. Johnny was able to put more and more time in winter into collecting supplies for his silversmithing work and to making jewelry. Theresa got into her own rhythm of working hard during the warm months in New England and then walking the beaches, reading as best she could, and enjoying life in Mexico during the cold months.

The couple eventually traded the camping trailer in for a motor home, making themselves even more nomadic in their wanderings around Mexico. Here is how Johnny describes their annual pilgrimage to the warm country.

When we took our winter trips to Mexico, we would leave the Northeast and go down to Tennessee for the first stay over. Then we would pick up I-40 straight out to Albuquerque, New Mexico, rest the night, and then head due south to El Paso, Texas, to visit with old friends. We would cross into Mexico there and go to the city of Chihuahua. There we would stay in the beautiful Hotel Victoria. The hotel had been built by a man who had been the police chief of Los Angeles, who had absconded with a large amount of city money. He spared no expense because he built it for his wife, Doña Victoria, or Madame Victoria. We loved to stay there for a week or ten days as we made our way down to Puerto Vallarta.

Johnny's long-lost sister Manuela lived in a remote part of the state of Chihuahua. He had never met her because she had been stolen before he was born. At age thirteen, she had been kidnapped either by Commanches or Utes who sold her to a man in Chihuahua. Johnny was to learn that he eventually took her as his wife. In 1936, twenty years after her disappearance, a hand-delivered letter had come to Johnny's mother from the long-lost daughter. She was living in a small village near Copper Canyon in the state of Chihuahua, Mexico. She had given birth to sixteen children, thirteen of whom had lived.

Johnny had tried a couple of times to find her, once before World War II and again afterwards. He had gone to the address on the 1936 letter and found one of her sons living there with his family. Manuela herself lived in a small village 80 to 100 miles away in a remote area of the state. There was no regular bus and no phone system for contacting her.

Johnny had tried during his visit in the late 1940s to hitch a ride on a truck, but after waiting all night at a freight depot for the truck to leave, the driver cancelled the journey. Johnny was not able to wait around for days until another truck was scheduled to run, so he returned home without having tracked down Manuela.

In 1970, Johnny decided to try again to reach her when he and Theresa were in Chihuahua City. This time, he went with his nephew, Arnulfo, to the city's radio station and paid to put an announcement on the air. In the announcement, he informed Manuela that he would be waiting for her at Arnulfo's home in Chihuahua at a certain time a few days later. He also communicated that he would pay her train fare if she would come. Then he and Theresa spent the time visiting Arnulfo's family and a couple of other of Manuela's children who lived in the city. On the appointed day and time, Manuela showed up. Her neighbor had heard the radio announcement and rushed over to give her the message.

So it was that Johnny found his long-lost sister who had been stolen over 50 years before. "She was tiny and full of piss and vinegar," he remembers. "She had a lot of energy and had lived through a lot of hard times. It was good to finally put a face and a person with the stories from my family about her."

After that first reunion, Johnny made a habit of stopping in to visit Manuela and her children each year as he and Theresa passed through. Manuela was a poor country grandmother with few resources. So Johnny took up playing a game with her in which he would hold a dollar bill in his fingers and she would put her open fingers just below his hand. When he dropped the bill, she would try to catch it using just her fingers. This is quite hard to do, especially for an older woman. But Manuela became rather good at it. The game would entertain them both for quite some time because Johnny would keep increasing the dollar amount of what he dropped. When Manuela caught a dollar bill, she could keep it or she could trade it for a chance to catch a five dollar bill. Once she caught the five, Johnny would let her trade it for the chance for a ten, and from there for a twenty. In the end, Johnny always made sure to leave her with a crisp, new twenty dollar bill, which was a large sum of money in her world. Only one time did Johnny break this tradition with Manuela.

One year when I went through Chihuahua, I was angry at my sister. The year before, I had lent $350 to her. Her son who had migrated to Gallup had promised to pay me back in turquoise stone when I came through the following season. When I returned as agreed, my nephew laughed at me and said he had already sold the turquoise to someone else. He cheated me and I got angry at my sister for raising a crook. When I got to Chihuahua, I told her that if she wanted any more money from me, she could get it from her crooked son.

She asked if we could at least play the dollar bill game. I said 'No way!' When I drove away, she ran after my car, begging for the money that I gave her each year.

About fifty miles later, I started to feel bad. It wasn't really her fault that her son had turned out bad. I decided that when I came back through in the spring, I would give her double what I normally did.

When I stopped at her son Arnulfo's home the next spring, Manuela had died during the winter. Oh man, that has eaten at me ever since.

After leaving Chihuahua on their way to the Pacific Coast each late autumn, Johnny and Theresa's annual voyage to Puerto Vallarta on the Pacific Coast entered another stage of adventure. To get to the ocean, they first had to drive down the "Devil's Spine," which is what people of the region call the high, mountainous country of the Southern Rockies that shoots up 13,000 feet and divides Mexico into Atlantic and Pacific watersheds. The rain and snow that falls on the eastern side of the mountains flows to the Gulf of Mexico. The moisture on the western side drains into the Pacific Ocean. Driving over 13,000 foot mountain passes on narrow gravel roads takes a great deal of nerve and self-control.

Johnny and Theresa would begin their climb into the towering Rockies at the city of Durango, which, at 9,000 feet elevation, is itself nearly two miles above sea level. They would wind their way up endless switchbacks and narrow turns to the 13,000 foot pass. Then the real excitement would begin on the long descent to the sea. Johnny explains.

> *You must travel one hundred miles of very steep, curvy dirt road with no guard rail. There was no sense in putting up guard rails because the traffic going over the edge would have just taken them right out again. On your way down the winding road, you can see the tiny wrecks of cars, trucks, and even buses lying down at the bottom. They look like toys way down at the bottoms of the steepest ravines. I don't think anyone even tried to recover the bodies from them in those days. This is why you should make sure you've got at least six hours of daylight to make the slow descent 13,000 feet down to sea level at Mazatlán.*
>
> *About two-thirds of the way down the Devil's Spine was a Swiss-style chalet that we liked to stop at for dinners and a few nights' stay. It was owned by a person of French-Swiss heritage and the food was very good. The scenery viewed from the top of the cliffs at the chalet which were a couple of thousand feet above the forest below was beautiful beyond description. Also, there were many, many crystals that you could simply find along the walking paths.*

From the chalet stop, the couple would descend another fifty miles down to the city of Mazatlán and then drive twenty miles to pick up the Pacific Coast Highway. This led them to the town of Tepic, where both the Huichol and the Cora Indians lived. They generally stopped there for a day or two to shop for Indian artwork and handicrafts, then pushed the final hundred miles to Puerto Vallarta, their home base for the winter.

There was only one year that Johnny and Theresa took a different route to their winter paradise. In the fall of 1969 on their second pilgrimage, they drove all the way to the Pacific Coast of Southern California and entered Mexico at Baja. Johnny remembers this journey with particular fondness, his eyes sparkling as he recounts the details. He wanted to explore the Baja Peninsula along the Sea of Cortez. He and Theresa also wanted to take in the views of the Pacific side of the peninsula where whales do their winter calving in the safe shelter of what was then one of the most isolated places on earth. Johnny recalls what was behind such ramblings.

I guess I wanted to go to the end of the earth just to see what was there. I sure wasn't disappointed in Baja. It was very, very wild. The place was completely untamed. There were no towns for hundreds and hundreds of miles. There were no villages, no farms, no people. It was wonderful! There weren't even roads. We were just following dirt tracks with our four-wheel drive pickup most of the time. Sometimes they turned into animal trails that we'd follow for miles. We'd left the trailer in Puerto Vallarta the previous winter, so we were free to wander wherever the four-wheel drive could take us.

Many times, I'd run the pickup to the top of a hill, stop, get out, and walk over the top to see if we could go down the other side or if we were headed straight over a cliff. A few times, all I found was cliff over there.

One of our first destinations was a big, sheltered bay where the whales did their calving. We sat on the rocks above the bay for hours and hours. With binoculars you could see up close the mothers and the babies when they surfaced. The mothers were carrying the smallest ones on their backs. They seemed to be pushing the little guys up to the surface to make sure that they got plenty of air before going back down again.

I remember how peaceful it felt to be out there, just the two of us all alone on the edge of a huge ocean, watching God's largest creatures doing what their Creator intended for them to do. I thought about how many times over the years I'd sat and watched my own kind do things I was pretty sure the Creator never intended. But who knows. That's all what my old friend Victor used to call 'the great mystery.' Sitting on a windy outcropping above whales caring for their young makes a man think about such things.

I went back to that bay years later when the roads were paved and it was easy for people to travel there. I soon learned from other travelers that the whales were almost all gone. The Japanese whalers had found the bay. They waited in the waters just outside the mouth of the place and killed the mothers and the babies when they began their migration back toward the North Pacific for summer feeding.

After we left the Pacific Coast and the whales and headed inland across the Baja, Theresa and I came to a place that had once been inhabited. It was a big, open-pit granite quarry where they had been pulling out building rock and countertops and things like that. When the operation went under, whoever had been working the place must have decided that it was just too much expense and trouble to try to get their equipment back to civilization. Old vehicles and machinery were sitting around everywhere but they weren't rusting like you might expect. It was just too dry in that country. The trucks were so old that they did not have driveshafts, just chains running from the motor back to the rear wheels. Talk about stumbling into an antique collection.

We found one old stone building still standing, and camped inside for a night. The building had a corrugated tin roof. It also seemed almost new because it hadn't rusted in the desert air. What a strange, wild, lonely place that was. It was like being on another planet. I loved it.

When we finally made it to the east side of the Sea of Cortez, we stopped for a while at a hot springs. The hot water came pouring out of some of the most rough, volcanic rock you could hope to find. I guess it was coming up from down where the lava was still bub-

bling and the earth was on fire. The way the hot water flowed into the cool water of the sea allowed you to pick places as hot or as cold as you wanted by staying close to the shore or going out further.

Theresa loved to hunt seashells and boy did she get the chance to do it there. We found the most amazing big seashells, the rare ones shaped like triangles and such. It wasn't hard to find them. They were piled six to eight feet high for miles along the beach. It was a little overwhelming. It was like walking chest deep in gold coins or some other kind of treasure.

And there were NO people around anywhere to collect them. Except for the track of a road that we were following and the occasional road sign, you wouldn't know that there were humans on the same planet. The road signs weren't the normal things you'd ever find in civilization. Every two or three days, we'd stumble across one. It would be some old junked wreck of a vehicle with an arrow painted on the side pointing in the direction we were supposed to go. Under the arrow painted in rough letters would be the name of the next crossroads or ghost town.

We only came to one tree in the whole trip through Baja. It was more of a big bush. It was near the end of the journey not too far from Cabo San Lucas. It was covered with women's panties. I'm not sure why. Maybe because after wearing them for so long without a bath, the women were eager to get rid of them. Theresa disappeared behind the pickup for a few moments and then added her own pair to the collection.

After two weeks in the Baja country with just the one bath at the hot springs, we were happy to see a motel on the outskirts of Cabo San Lucas. We were dirty and smelled so bad we had to keep the windows of the pickup open for fresh air. A good, hot shower has never felt so good before or since.

The Baja adventure was the wildest one that Johnny and Theresa had in what would become years of exploring the remote parts of Western Mexico. It was also one of Johnny's most memorable journeys. With it, he seemed to have found "the end of the earth" enough to backtrack towards civilization again.

Men, and perhaps women too, who come home from bloody wars or other traumatic events sometimes seek such solitudes. I've known of others like Johnny who fled for a time from the world of men and commerce and jobs and even of families in the aftermath of war. They often seek refuge in the wildest places that they can find. That may be under a freeway overpass in California or in the misty woods of the Smokey Mountains of Tennessee.

My own stepfather, a fighter pilot who saw and did horrific things in the South Pacific during World War II, ran away from his home and his alcoholism in California after the war. He went to Idaho where he met my mother. He spent years as a bush pilot flying alone into the wildest parts of the Idaho backcountry before he was ready to move on with life. What former warriors like him were looking to find precisely, I cannot say. I have never been in their shoes. But I do know what Johnny found. He told me.

> *I loved the solitude. I loved the wildness and the isolation of that beautiful, beautiful, uncivilized piece of Mother Earth—because it was me. I was trying to find the part of me that was brought up in the wild, a time when there was nothing but me, my family, Mother Earth, and the Creator, a time before I knew how broken the world is. Nature is always whole. Only the human beings are broken.*

After Baja, Johnny and Theresa did not venture again into the most uninhabited and wild regions of Mexico. They kept to safer haunts. For the first few winters, they either stayed in their motor home or rented an apartment in Puerto Vallarta. Then Johnny learned that there was a law in Mexico allowing you to take official ownership of a piece of property after two years of occupancy. Ever the shrewd dealer, Johnny saw opportunity knocking. He looked around the area and soon found what he was looking for. He tells what happened.

> *In 1976, I found this little brick cottage in a village beside the sea called Busarias. It was a one bedroom place in a huge grove of palm trees that was surrounded by a brick wall. It had two porches, one facing the orchard and one facing out to the bay. It had four rows of*

palm trees on the bay side and an orchard filled with orange, lemon, grapefruit, pomegranate, and six types of mango trees. So I sold my apartment in Puerto Vallarta for $3,000, making a $1,500 profit, with which I leased the cottage.

So it was that we moved over to the little town of Busarias about twelve miles north of Puerto Vallarta. We had the best of all worlds. We had three miles of beach and were close enough to Puerto Vallarta to go there whenever we wanted.

In Mexico at that time there was a law that if you paid the taxes and the utilities on a place that you leased for two years, you could declare ownership of it. After two years, I declared ownership of the cottage. It was quite primitive. The iguanas would just come in and stay under the corrugated roof tiles. It was like living in heaven.

Although many people might not consider living with an iguana colony under the same roof to be "heaven," Johnny and Theresa were quite content in their beachside paradise. Perhaps it was Johnny's Native heritage of living close to nature in the Southwestern desert that put him at ease in the earthy life of the cottage. He recalls rising early one morning and going to drink his coffee in the leather chair facing out the bedroom window toward the sunrise. Despite the shadows of dawn, he could tell that the seat of the chair was much higher than it should have been. As he got closer, he recognized the coils of a large snake. There was a mature boa constrictor sleeping on the warm leather seat. Johnny began talking to it, encouraging it to go back outdoors where it belonged. The big snake yawned and then slowly left the chair to slither out the open window beside it. The creature was nearly ten feet long.

Johnny and Theresa found a healthy balance of life in this world that blended a unique closeness to the earth and to nature with the fruits of civilization. They spent their nights out on the town at good restaurants with live music, with village festivals, street markets, and a new place to explore almost every week. Morning would find them combing the beach to see what the previous night had washed ashore. Lunch might be a flavorful meal at a little Mexican cantina run by a family that they knew well enough to call "friends." In the afternoon would be a visit to some old ruins or to an outdoor crafts market. If it were a weekend, they might travel to a nearby village festival to enjoy the music, the traditional costumes and parade, the dances, and the good food that always came with a small town celebration of life.

It was a good life for a retired couple. The winter months flew by each year in their own private Shangri-la far from the struggles and routines that they had left behind with retirement.

Then one day in the mid-1970s, an urgent phone call came. Johnny and Theresa's daughter Sharon was spending a few weeks of her own vacation with them in Puerto Vallarta that winter. She took the call. Johnny was out somewhere on the beach. Sharon wrote the message down, then immediately went looking for Johnny. She found him sunbathing not far away.

"Your daughter called from Albuquerque," she told him, out of breath from hurrying along the sand.

Johnny looked at her for a moment. "Lorraine? You mean my daughter Lorraine?"

"Yes," Sharon replied. "She's in trouble. It sounds serious."

Lorraine's Story

WHEN JOHNNY HAD BEEN DIVORCED FROM HIS FIRST WIFE LENA in 1946, she had left him while carrying their unborn baby. Lena gave birth to a daughter a few months later and named her "Lorraine."

Lena's family was Spanish-speaking and staunchly Catholic. Johnny had known from the start that the marriage was their way of avoiding the shame of an illegitimate birth. What they had wanted from Johnny was a legal father who would provide a last name for the baby. That's all. To make this abundantly clear, they wrote a legal clause into the divorce that forbade Johnny from having any future contact with his daughter until she became an adult.

Johnny broke that law many times over the years.

From the start then, the marriage between Johnny and Lena had been built on the rockiest of terrain. In 1946, Johnny was a patient at a mental hospital in Santa Fe recovering from shell shock. That was the year that he turned 30. Lena was 17 and wild. Johnny met her brother Phil first. They worked together at the New Methods Cleaners where Johnny spent his days away from the Bruns Hospital. His outpatient work in dry cleaning there was part of his recovery program.

As the staff at Bruns came to trust Johnny more, they allowed him greater freedom to come and go on his own. One of his favorite places to spend his newly acquired free time was in front of the old governor's building near the center of Santa Fe. The structure was a left-over relic from the days when New Mexico was a territory. It was a large, weathered building with a long porch out front that the Indians of various Southwestern tribes had come to use as a street market for their arts, crafts, foods, and such. The Indians would sit up against the wall of the building under the porch, out of the sun or the occasional rain, and sell their wares.

Johnny enjoyed spending his off-hours among the people and the crowds that came and went around the Indian market. One could hear a half-dozen different languages besides English and Spanish being spoken in the short walk it took to get from one end of the market to the other. Johnny felt at home among the crowds of people like himself. Every one of them seemed to be broken or wounded in ways he recognized and understood. He found something familiar and comfortable and safe in their midst.

They all lived in the margins of America. Even the ones who only spoke English. In fact, the English-only speakers were often the most broken. Among the English-speakers, you could see from the colors and shades of their skin, eyes and hair that they did not come from ancestors who spoke English. Their features were Native or Spanish or some mix of red, brown, and white. Not only could they never belong in the white world of the 1940s, but, like Johnny, they no longer had other worlds to fall back on.

And yet the market was not a place only of hopelessness or despair. Quite the contrary. The miracle of the human spirit was as much in evidence there as anywhere else on the planet. "Oh man, there was always something going on at the market," Johnny says, shaking his head at the memory. "I'd go there on the weekend to hang out, to meet people, to buy booze cheap, and to fool around with the Mexican guys."

As one might expect, the Mexican guys were mostly interested in fooling around with Mexican girls. Or Indian girls. Or any other females who happened by.

Phil from the New Methods Cleaners often spent time with Johnny, passing the time laughing, drinking, and flirting with the women. Johnny remembers the homemade "Sneaky Pete" wine that they used to drink. In those days, it was against the law for Indians, even 30-year-old war veterans, to drink alcohol. So they had to sneak it through the streets.

One day Phil's little sister, Lena, came by the market. She had a lively personality and, as a girl who had learned early to deal with big brothers, she was fearless around men. "She liked to drink and to cuss and to raise hell just like her brothers," Johnny recalls. "But she was much prettier to look at."

Johnny was soon hooked on the fiery young woman, and Lena was soon pregnant.

That's when Lena's parents got involved. As Lena was only 17 years old, her father told Johnny he had two choices: marriage or jail. Johnny chose marriage.

As soon as he was released from the Bruns Hospital, he and his young bride went back to Gallup. In Gallup, Johnny was known and could always find work. His former employer at the Deluxe Dry Cleaners was happy to have him back.

But Lena was not happy away from her family and friends. She lasted three months. Johnny came home from work one day to find her clothes missing and a short note on their kitchen table.

Lena had returned to her parents and was filing for divorce.

When their baby, Lorraine, was born, her family was afraid that Johnny might remarry and one day seek joint custody of his daughter. So they went to court and requested a permanent restraining order. Johnny had a public reputation as a hard drinker and hell raiser. He did not bother to contest the court proceedings. The restraining order was granted. Johnny was forbidden by law from seeing or visiting his daughter until she reached the age of 18.

The first time Johnny met Lorraine, she was in elementary school. He had kept tabs on her through her Uncle Phil, who remained his friend despite the family upheavals. One day six or seven years after the divorce when he was in Albuquerque, he decided to drive on to Santa Fe to see if he could meet his daughter. He just wanted to know how she was doing and if she was being well cared for. He knew from Phil that Lorraine regularly stopped by his house on her way home from school. So he drove to Phil's for a visit.

Lorraine showed up for a snack shortly after Johnny arrived. She had no idea who the strange man was until her auntie told her.

Her eyes lit up, she looked him right in the eyes, and asked, "Where you been, mister?"

She said it with a smile. Johnny knew right then that they were going to be all right.

"So I got to hold my baby on my lap for the first time," Johnny says. "I told her I couldn't visit her much because her mother would not allow it."

"Why is Mama so mad at you?" Lorraine asked.

"Because I drink a lot and I'm trouble," he responded.

"Oh, that's a good reason," the young girl said. And with the simple logic and resilience of childhood, she accepted the situation.

Before he left, he gave her $50 so that she could buy clothes and other things that she might need. She and her aunt said they were going to go out and buy a winter coat that very day as the weather was already turning cold.

After that, Johnny dropped in at Lorraine's uncle and aunt's place for a visit whenever he was in Santa Fe. Lena was not happy about this and she eventually found a way to put an end to it.

One day when Johnny was visiting with his daughter, a police car came roaring up to the front of the house. Johnny kissed Lorraine and ran for the back door. Phil went with him as far as the backyard, then took Johnny's car keys and circled around the block to where Johnny had parked his car. While the police were in the house looking for the man who was breaking his restraining order, Phil got in Johnny's car and drove to where Johnny was waiting to make his getaway.

The ruse worked and Johnny avoided arrest. But he did not see his daughter after that until she was no longer a minor.

The woman Lorraine became was a lot like her father. She was smart. She knew how to get what she wanted in the world. And she was deeply angry at the brokenness of her own life and the world around her. Where her father had gone into the military to escape the injustice and discrimination against people like himself, Lorraine went into politics. She worked for a number of local and state politicians over the years, rising to the point of running for state senator herself by age thirty. That's when the sky caved in on her world.

Johnny describes Lorraine as an outgoing person. She had a strong will and loved to be at the center of whatever was going on. Like her father, one of her most pronounced traits is that she refused to let anyone disrespect her. Because of this, she had gone through a couple of marriages by age 30. If a man raised his voice to her, he was gone before he could finish the sentence. If he chose to stick around, he risked leaving in an ambulance.

It was this anger and determination to be respected that was at the core of the emergency phone call that Lorraine made to her father in the mid-1970s. He remembers well the return call.

> *When I got her on the phone, she told me that she was in jail and that she was almost certainly headed for prison. She just wanted me to hear about it from her personally, not from the papers or through the grapevine.*
>
> *I asked her what she had done.*
>
> *'I shot a man, Daddy.'*
>
> *'Oh, God. What happened?' I asked.*
>
> *She then explained that a fellow she knew had wrecked her car. He was a drug dealer and a bit of a lowlife, but Lorraine had befriended him. He borrowed the car one day without asking. He knew where she kept an extra set of keys. That evening, he came by her house to say that he had accidentally wrecked the car.*
>
> *She wasn't too mad at first. 'You're gonna have to pay for it,' she told him.*
>
> *Then she said that the man made a big mistake. He laughed in her face and told her he wasn't going to give her a cent for the car. If she was too dumb to have insurance on it, then she was just going to have to eat the loss.*
>
> *'I had a .38 pistol in my purse,' Lorraine said. 'I pulled it out and shot him three times in the chest. I wasn't going to let any man treat me like that.*
>
> *We were out in my yard when I shot him. I dragged his body into the house to make it look like a burglary, but that didn't work out so well. When the police saw all the blood in the yard, they brought charges of manslaughter against me.'*

After talking to Lorraine, Johnny's next call was to her lawyer. He asked if he should come to Santa Fe for the trial. He was willing to do anything he could to help. The lawyer told him not to bother.

It was an open and shut case. His goal was only to get Lorraine as short a sentence as possible.

He got her 10-15 years in the state penitentiary.

There was one small benefit to penitentiary life for Johnny's relationship with his daughter. He knew where to find her when he wanted to come for a visit. Lorraine had lived an active and chaotic life up to that point. She moved a lot. She drank a lot. She divorced a lot. And she had three children to chase after. Johnny remembers the first time he visited her in prison.

First I went to see the warden. I let him know that I was a retired military man and that I was a veteran of three wars. I also told him that I lived most of the time in New England and only came through New Mexico a couple of times a year.

He was very understanding and told me right away that he could give special permission to let me see my daughter more than once a month, as the prison rules said. He and I got to be friends after that and he treated me real well, even though my daughter gave him lots of trouble in the next few years.

Then I went to the visitors' room to wait for Lorraine. I was there on time, but she kept me waiting and waiting.

Finally I heard her voice. She was yelling at a guard, saying, 'What the hell is wrong with you? Can't you open a door for a lady? Has this prison ruined your manners as much as it has your looks?'

Then she made her grand entry into the visitors' room. She was not wearing the typical orange colored prison garb. She was in a beautiful blue pants suit. She gave me a big hug and said, 'Hi Daddy. Do you like my outfit?'

I told her I did, that she looked really great.

Then she explained that she was late because she was not about to let her dad see her in prison clothes. She had to make a fuss before they would let her dress properly. But in the end, she won out, as she generally did.

Three weeks later, Johnny went back for a second visit. This time he was told he could not see his daughter. He went back to see the warden.

The warden explained that Lorraine had been "a bad girl." She had beaten up a guard. She was now in isolation and wouldn't be allowed to have visitors for a while. Johnny promised to call before he came again to make sure that she could have visitors.

After he left the prison in Santa Fe, Johnny and Theresa went to Albuquerque where they had friends and family to visit.

A few days later, they learned that isolation had not agreed well with Lorraine. They learned this on a special news bulletin that interrupted their evening television show. Lorraine had broken out of prison taking four other prisoners with her. They were on the run.

"Boy, that was just like Lorraine," Johnny says now with a note of admiration in his voice. "She never let the world push her around. Not even in prison."

Within hours, another news flash reported that three of the five women had been recaptured.

The next day, a Texas state trooper was killed and the two women on the lam were listed as suspects. A week later, one of the pair was apprehended. It wasn't Lorraine.

Days later, Lorraine called Johnny from hiding. The first thing he told her was that she had to turn herself in. Especially after the trooper was killed.

"Daddy, we didn't kill that trooper," she told him. "And I won't ever turn myself in. The man I did kill deserved what he got."

Johnny did not hear again from Lorraine for ten years. When the call came, he was in Oregon with a friend working at her family newspaper to liven up his retirement.

His secretary buzzed him to say that he had a caller on line two.

He picked up the line and a voice said, "Do you know who this is?"

He knew.

"Where are you?" he asked.

"I can't tell you," Lorraine said.

"What are you doing?"

"Not much. I'm just lonely for my family and had to finally call someone to find out how everyone is doing."

"How is everything going for you?" Johnny asked.

"Well, I don't want to say much, but I've just returned from Hawaii. I'm back in politics. I found a job working for a U.S. senator. Things are okay. But I miss my family so much I can hardly stand it. Especially the children. I'm thinking of turning myself in, Daddy. What do you think?"

Johnny thought it was a great idea.

The next thing Johnny heard through the family in New Mexico was that Lorraine had made a deal with the authorities. She would fly into Albuquerque, be driven by a friend to Santa Fe, visit with her family, and then she would report to the court and turn herself in.

Lorraine had worked for years in state politics. She knew who to talk to and she still had friends in the right places. The result was that not only did she get approval for the deal, but she was immediately let out on bail after turning herself in.

When she returned for the court hearing of her case, she was met with very good news. She would not have to return to prison. A friendly judge determined that she was no longer a threat to the community and gave her parole. She was required to report regularly to her parole officer for an amount of time equal to what remained of her original prison sentence. The primary stipulation was that she could not leave Santa Fe.

Johnny fears that this proved to be Lorraine's ultimate undoing. "She had a lot of hard memories in that town," he says. "Sometimes the best thing you can do is just to put a lot of miles between you and the memories."

Following in her father's footsteps earlier in life, Lorraine became a hopeless alcoholic as the years went by.

I tried again and again to get her into A. A. She couldn't do it. She ruined her life. She gave up. She drank herself to death.

The last time I saw her alive, she was very tiny. She was lying in a fetal position in a hospital bed. She was so shriveled up that you could hardly tell there was a person in the bed. She died a day or two later.

He is quiet for a moment and then shakes his head as he says, "My baby was 44 years old. Just 44. And then she was gone."

Subsequent events would suggest that, in fact, she was not entirely gone.

Lorraine had been firm in her final instructions to her family. She wanted no church services or memorials or anything like that. She wanted to be cremated and for her children to have her ashes, if they wanted them. That's all. She was adamant about this. As soon as she was cremated, her half-brothers and sisters decided that they needed to hold a nice, traditional church service for her.

"When I got the invitation," Johnny recalls, "I knew we were in for trouble." But he went to the ceremony anyway. "It seemed the right thing to do," he says.

The service was held at a funeral parlor in Santa Fe. Johnny was asked to sit in the front row beside Lorraine's half-brother Danny. In proper Catholic and family tradition, there was a large, framed picture of Lorraine beside the podium, with flowers all around.

When the funeral director indicated that it was time to begin, Danny stood and began to make his way to the podium. As he did so, Lorraine's portrait crashed to the floor.

"It was a very solid floor," Johnny says with a shake of his head. "It was made of concrete. It wasn't like Danny somehow shook the floor and made that portrait fall."

Danny's wife turned to Johnny and asked in shock, "What's going on?"

"She's here," Johnny told her. "And she's pissed. She told us not to do this."

But the rest of Lorraine's family bravely soldiered on. Danny and the funeral director picked up Lorraine's picture, now with the glass broken, and placed it back on its stand. Then Danny delivered a heartfelt tribute to his sister.

Other members of the family followed, each adding to the stories and remembrances of Lorraine's vibrant life. They referred to her as something of a legend in her own ways, a bright, dynamic young woman who conquered the statehouse and ran for the state senate by age 30. Family members remembered her best qualities, her cheer, her sense of humor, her willingness to work hard for what she wanted and her way of speaking her mind openly and fearlessly.

They also recalled how she could walk into a room and immediately become the center of attention.

Johnny smiles at the thought of that. "She always wanted to be at the center of things and to stir things up," he says, "and it didn't take her long to do just that even at her own funeral." Johnny recounts what happened next.

After everyone had blah, blah, blahed about how great Lorraine was for quite some time, all of a sudden a gal from the back of the room stood up.

'I've got something to say about Lorraine,' she said. And then she went to the podium and started in.

'Lorraine was nothing but a fucking whore,' she told us. 'She fucked everybody in the state legislature trying to get herself a senator's job.'

Lorraine's half-sister Mary Lena cut the woman off. 'You'd better get down from there right now,' she called to the woman. Mary Lena was a large woman and, like her sister, she was used to people doing what she said.

The woman at the podium said she wasn't going to sit down until she had told them the truth about Lorraine. She started speaking again and so Mary Lena went to the podium and grabbed a hold of her.

The woman was too little to give Mary Lena a fight, so she grabbed onto the podium and kept trying to speak. Mary Lena took hold of her hair and dragged her and the moveable podium down the aisle and to the back of the funeral chapel.

As the struggling pair went past us, I turned to Danny and said, 'Now Lorraine is happy. This is what she likes.'

Danny agreed.

Most everyone in the room seemed to be coming to the same conclusion because we were all laughing and cheering.

When Mary Lena got the woman to the back of the place, the stranger's boyfriend jumped up and pulled out a gun.

'No one is going to do that to my woman!' he shouted.

Before he could get a shot off at Mary Lena, a couple of fellows jumped on him and took the gun away. They called the police and a squad car came and took the trouble-makers off to jail.

So then we all left and went to the house of another of Lorraine's half-sisters, Caroline. We gathered there to talk and drink coffee and to remember Lorraine. As we were all visiting, I suddenly heard a crunch and a cracking sound. You can believe this if you want to and you can disbelieve it if you want. But right there before our eyes, a cuckoo clock started coming off the wall. It fell right down on the floor and shattered. We all just sat in amazement and surprise for a moment.

Then Caroline said, 'That was a gift to me from Lorraine.'

'You're damn right it was,' I told her and everyone else. 'She's still here and she is still pissed off. She told us that she did not want this whole memorial service. When Lorraine tells you not to do something, it's best not to do it.'

The party did not last long after that. We all went home hoping that Lorraine would cool down without any more trouble to the living.

The End of Paradise

EXCEPT FOR THE UPHEAVALS CAUSED BY LORRAINE, life for Johnny and Theresa had a peaceful rhythm to it throughout most of the 1970's. In the warm months of the year, they spent their time raising three girls in Granby, Massachusetts. When the weather turned cold in New England, they escaped to the Pacific Coast of Mexico. There, they found no end to the interesting experiences of day-to-day life. They spent the warm winters poking around the region as they explored out of the way places and made friends along the way.

But all earthly paradises come with time limits and it was no different for the healthy winter refuge the couple had made. Johnny speaks of the end of their annual pilgrimages to Mexico with a heavy voice.

> One day when I came in, this must have been around 1980 or so, Theresa said that she was scared because there was something moving in the magazine that was on one of the small end tables. When I went over to investigate, I discovered the biggest scorpion I had ever seen under it. At this time in order to read anything, she would have to hold the printed page a couple of inches from her face. I could just imagine what might have happened had she picked up that scorpion with the magazine.
>
> With that, I said that it was time that she went home.

The couple knew by now that the best "home" for Theresa was not in New England. Theresa had long held a romantic, childhood attraction to New Mexico. It had started in elementary school when a boy from Albuquerque had joined her class one year. She had befriended the newcomer and he delighted her with tales of the desert and the wonderful things he had experienced growing up there.

Perhaps some of her attraction to Johnny came from the same happy childhood memories of friendship and sharing. The two of them regularly passed through Albuquerque on their annual pilgrimage to Mexico and Theresa had quite fallen in love with the place. It was a natural choice for a place to make a new home for Theresa as her sight dimmed and her health grew more and more frail.

They had been planning to relocate to Albuquerque for some time before the scorpion incident. An old friend of Johnny's by the name of Jack Pickard had helped move their plans forward. Johnny had known Jack since his days as a dry cleaning employee after World War II. Jack had been in the same line of work and they had grown close over beers and long talks in the evenings as Johnny was recovering from shell shock. Johnny and Theresa had taken up the habit of visiting Jack and his wife each time they passed through Albuquerque.

On one of their visits, Jack had told Johnny about a big financial disappointment he'd had recently. He'd had a chance to buy a great little resort property up in the mountains behind Albuquerque. A historic hotel with trailer sites had been offered to him for just $29,000. Because of a bankruptcy on his record, he was not able to scrape together the capital to buy it.

"Why didn't you call me?" Johnny had asked his old friend.

Johnny remembers Jack giving him a surprised look. Then he said to Johnny, "Of all the people in the world, I would never have thought that you would have $20,000 in your possession at one time."

Johnny laughed.

The next time a property came up for sale that Jack felt was a good bargain, he called Johnny. It was a nice home on the same block as his own. Johnny jumped in with the cash and came to own his first home in Albuquerque. The second house came soon, but with tragedy attached.

Jack was an alcoholic. He had tried over the years to dry out, but he was not as successful at it as Johnny. For a time, Johnny served as

Jack's sponsor in Alcoholics Anonymous. But then Jack came across another fellow who lived in the area who claimed to have 18 years of sobriety. He was eager to become Jack's sponsor and Jack soon let him replace Johnny in this role. After meeting the fellow, Johnny told Jack that he didn't have a good feeling about him.

Jack brushed off his concerns. "You're just jealous because I took a new sponsor," he told Johnny.

Johnny shrugged the exchange off. He wasn't going to let such a thing interfere with their decades-long friendship.

A bit later, Jack paid a surprise visit to his new sponsor at home one afternoon when Jack was passing through the man's neighborhood. He found his sponsor on all fours in his house. He was too drunk to stand. Jack was so disappointed and angry that he swore off A. A. and went back to the bottle himself.

Johnny did not hold it against his old friend. He'd seen it happen too many times before. Then one late spring day as Johnny and Theresa were leaving Mexico to make their way to Albuquerque, things came to a head. On their way up the Devil's Spine, the car overheated and the transmission fluid drained out on the road. Johnny was able to get the car to the Chalet resort but was held up a day as he got the car fixed.

Jack and his wife were expecting them. Johnny later learned from his stepdaughter who lived on the corner that Jack had been wandering around the neighborhood waiting for their arrival. He was terribly drunk and kept asking for "the gypsies" as he fondly called Johnny and Theresa.

The next day when they knocked at Jack's door, they learned what had unfolded during the night. During his drunken stupor, Jack had fallen down in his own bathroom, lodging his head between the toilet and the bathtub. Lying there too drunk to rise, he had drowned in his own vomit. Jack was dead.

And he had left his widow in a difficult situation. The house was not paid off. Jack had died owing Johnny some $6,000, and there were other debts that had to be paid. Jack's wife wanted to sell the house and to move to Texas to be with her children. Johnny gave her market value for the three-bedroom home, forgave the $6,000 that she owed him, and paid off the rest of her mortgage so that she could leave free and clear and with a good nest egg to be with her family.

Johnny and Theresa then moved into Jack's house that year, 1980. Their daughter Sharon and her husband had already moved into the corner house next to Jack's, so there was family nearby. For a few months, they all lived side by side, with Sharon helping with Theresa as needed. Later, Linda moved down to join them in the warmth of the Southwest, and Johnny bought yet another house in the neighborhood to keep everyone close. It was an ideal situation for an ailing mother to have two daughters and her grandchildren next door. Everyone was well-settled and happy. Everyone, that is, but Johnny.

Albuquerque was a difficult place for the aging Navajo to live. Just being in New Mexico itself wore upon him. Everywhere he went and everything he saw reminded him of hard times and dark days.

When I was a boy, we were treated like animals. The first time I read a sign above the entrance to a bar that said 'No Dogs and No Indians Allowed,' I almost regretted that I had learned how to read.

I grew up angry at that kind of stuff. I grew up hating people who would treat me like that. I decided to get even, to beat the 'white eyes' at their own game.

I did a lot of bad things to people. I became an alcoholic. I went to war and saw and did more bad things. I came home to find my mother dead and my mind messed up. I had children I didn't even know and divorces I didn't care about. All that happened in New Mexico.

Johnny thought that he could go home again with Theresa and the girls. He thought he could create a new and better world back in New Mexico, one that he could stand to inhabit. But in the end he couldn't. Theresa's impending blindness was part of the problem, but there was more.

Theresa now needed a lot of care and I knew that if this was what my life was to become that I would most likely return to drinking. I was afraid that I would most likely end up like my friend Jack, dying in some god-awful way in a pool of my own vomit.

And it wasn't just my past that bothered me. In 1980, New Mexico was still a strange place for a Navajo to live. My brother Pete worked at a lumber yard. It was right near a social services office for the Indians. Every adult Indian who reported in sober each day was allocated a certain amount of money. After X number of days, they could collect a check for what they had earned by staying sober.

As soon as they had their check, they would come over to the lumber yard and buy a small bag of nails or something so that Pete would cash the check. Then they were off on a long drunk until the money ran out. Once the hangover was over, they'd be back to the social services office to earn more money by being sober just long enough to get drunk again.

You can call the Indians uncivilized fools, if you want. I won't argue with that. But what do you call the educated white people who were giving them the money?

That's the kind of thing that I wanted to get away from. You become ashamed of seeing these guys on the curb drunk. It works on you after a while. It makes you sorry that you're a sober alcoholic because they are exactly what you were and you can't help them. There's nothing you can do, especially when the people who are supposed to help them have found such a crazy way to keep them down and, at the same time, to feel real good about doing it.

Johnny was both old enough and young enough not to sit in Albuquerque and let despair take its course. He had seen too much of the world and other ways of life to go down that road again. And he was young enough to want more of life before he died.

Ironically, it was a feature of his early life in Navajo country that directed the course he would take at this crossroads. Johnny had come from a nomadic world. His Native ancestors had long moved around the land from season to season in natural rhythms of hunting, gathering, and raising sheep. Part of him remained a nomad.

I had returned to a bit of a nomadic experience with Theresa in 1968 when we first started travelling to Puerto Vallarta for the winters. In 1980, I decided to become fully a nomad. At that point, I was finally beginning to find me, my purpose in life.

I found I was a man who didn't like being tied to a house. You have to have a place you can call home, but you don't want to have to be there all the time and to become sour. In 1980, it was once again time for me to go off on my own.

For starters, I went back to New England as a base because it had become my home. I had found sobriety here. To this day, I feel great here. It's wonderful. I don't have to worry about getting drunk. I don't have to worry about the strange world of New Mexico. I have found my place in the sun here.

In 1980, Johnny Pail Face became a full-fledged nomad. He would remain so for the rest of his life. He turned the titles for the family's two Albuquerque houses over to Theresa and Sharon, climbed into his motor home, and returned to New England.

Not long afterward, their youngest daughter, Linda, decided that she wanted to live near her mother and sister as well. Johnny bought another home in Albuquerque next to Theresa's. Sharon and her husband then moved into Theresa's three-bedroom place, Theresa moved into the smaller house, and Linda and her family took up residence in the house on the corner. And Johnny turned the title of a third house over to the people he loved.

When Johnny returned to New England, he was not entirely alone. His eldest stepdaughter, Donna, still lived there with her husband. Theresa's parents had moved to a home for the elderly a couple of years before as their health deteriorated. Johnny and Theresa had sold their businesses and the house they owned in Granby shortly after Theresa's parents moved out.

They sold the house to Donna and her husband for $25,000. The young wife and husband later sold it for $135,000. Johnny also sold his bank stock to Donna's husband for $8,000. The fellow sold it for $87,000 a few years later.

Johnny remembers such transactions in detail. They mean a great deal to him. They show that he has taken care of the people in his circle even if he, himself, chooses to follow the life of a nomad.

For a time, Theresa insisted that they should get a divorce, but Johnny argued against it. If he divorced her, she would lose the healthcare benefits that came with his military retirement. They both knew that this would be devastating because in addition to the onset of blindness she had been diagnosed with Parkinson 's disease. On top of this was the pernicious anemia that had plagued her throughout her adult life.

In the face of such health issues, Johnny was determined to keep her safely in his circle. "That's the reason I married her and took on her little family in the first place," he says now.

So they were not divorced. At the time of this writing, it has been over 30 years since they separated. Theresa remains in Johnny's circle. And Johnny remains a nomad.

In many ways, Johnny Pail Face has lived a delayed life. His has been a "dream deferred," as the poet Langston Hughes once wrote. It was not until his early 60^s that the "good part" of his life fully began. Everything before that was a long struggle first to figure out what civilization was and then to join it as best he could.

Underneath the struggle was an insatiable curiosity about the world, about people, about life itself. Once this curiosity was no longer tied up in working out his own inherited struggles, it was free to roam more broadly in the world. And it did.

"I wanted to see whatever I could see, wherever I could see it," Johnny muses now. "I wanted adventure. I wanted to meet new people. I had spent half a lifetime doing stupid things. I wanted to do smarter things before I died."

And so it was that at the point where many people are slowing down and coming to the ends of their lives, Johnny Pail Face's life was building toward a unique and unexpected crescendo. In 1980, as he entered his mid-sixties, the adventures began to hit like the magnificent summer storms that descended with great energy and renewal upon the New Mexico desert of his youth.

Healing Kit Among the Huichol

AMONG THE BEST STORIES THAT JOHNNY SHARED with me about what his life became after age 60 is one that was difficult at first to come to grips with. It helps that I teach a college course on world religions that includes treatments of alternate spiritual paths from various places around the world. It also helps that I am a life-long admirer of physics, as my mother was before me.

Astrophysicists tell us that there are as many as eleven different dimensions of existence in our universe. We see three of these dimensions (height, width, and depth) when we look out at the world around us. We can also perceive a fourth dimension, time. That leaves seven that we can only reach through complicated experiments in the laboratory or through mathematical calculations.

It is instructive to note that through the four dimensions that we can experience directly, we only perceive about five percent of all the matter and energy that is in motion around and *through* us and through every part of our world. Ninety-five percent of the universe seems to be composed of dark matter (25 percent) and dark energy (70 percent). These are the things that we cannot see.

Physicists only know about dark matter and energy because of the tremendous influence that they exert upon the things that we can see, things like suns, planets, rays of light, atoms, and the small particles that make up atoms. These are details of our world that now show up in every high school physics course. You can find them in greater detail with a computer search or can even meet the scientists and see their findings on educational television.

To appreciate the influence that the invisible world exerts upon the visible, it is important to know that the entire universe is expanding at an increasing rate. Physicists tell us that every one of the billion galaxies in the heavens is moving away from all the other galaxies at increasing speed despite the fact that they should be doing just the opposite. The forces of gravity should be pulling them together. But there seems to be a force more powerful than gravity out there. Dark, or better to say "unseen," energy is winning out in this cosmic struggle.

Such things help me to make sense of one of Johnny's most interesting adventures in Mexico later in life. The experience took him into the unseen ninety-five percent of the universe. It took him into the world of a Huichol *Ma'arak'ame*, an Indian medicine man among the indigenous Huichol people who live in the Sierra Madre mountains of Northwestern Mexico.

The Huichol encounter was part of the rich mosaic of stories that Johnny experienced during this stage of his life. He led me into the Huichol experience slowly, with smaller stories leading one by one to the big one. Here is how the story flowed in his telling.

After he left Theresa and his girls to their lives in New Mexico, Johnny returned to the annual nomadic rhythms at the heart of his retirement years. In summer, he made his home base in Massachusetts. He devoted himself to his spiritual hobby of making Navajo jewelry and traveled to Native American powwows up and down New England to sell his handiwork.

During the long, cold winters, he could be found back on the Pacific Coast of Mexico gathering craft-making supplies, exploring around, and making new friends.

Midway through the 1980s, he met a woman by the name of Kit. Their paths crossed at a gathering of mutual friends. They formed an instant bond when Johnny learned that Kit came from Hopkinton, Massachusetts, to spend her two-week vacations at Puerto Vallarta. Hopkinton is a short drive from Johnny's own Massachusetts refuge in Granby.

Kit had a nomadic spirit and shared Johnny's love for travel, for exploring new places, and for meeting new people. The two spent much of her short vacation together. When they parted, Johnny promised to look her up when he got back to Massachusetts in the spring. He held true to his word and their friendship deepened.

When summer came, Kit joined him on weekends on the pow-wow circuit throughout New England. She took delight in helping him to sell his Navajo jewelry and other Indian crafts.

When the end of summer approached, Johnny asked her to meet him again in a place near Puerto Vallarta called Zihuatanejo for her two-week autumn vacation. She accepted.

Johnny rented a cottage on the beach and they had the seashore stretching for miles to themselves during the days that they spent there. To liven things up, they decided to hit the road for a "round robin" tour of a large section of Mexico.

First on the agenda were the Pyramid of the Sun and the Pyramid of the Moon at Teotihuacan, about 25 miles outside of Mexico City. Johnny had climbed the Pyramid of the Sun with Theresa the year that he turned 50. That had been during their first vacation, just before he left for Vietnam in 1966. He had promised himself to come back and do it again when he turned 75. He did so with Kit.

The city of Teotihuacan is a place capable of changing in a single afternoon the common stereotypes that many people of America today retain of the "savages" who lived on this land before the arrival of the first Europeans. It covers some fifty square miles and was, at its zenith in 500 A. D., larger and more developed than any city in Europe—London and Paris included. A more accurate comparison would be to Rome at the height of the Roman Empire.

The Pyramid of the Sun is the most imposing structure of the city, measuring 738 feet along its base and rising 246 feet into the sky. It is the second highest pyramid in the world, behind only the Great Pyramid of Giza in Egypt.

After a visit to Teotihuacan, it is hard to continue to assume that the Native peoples of the Americas were all simple, backward hunters and gatherers who knew nothing of the fruits of civilization. For Johnny Pail Face, the place is a personal confirmation of the best that he saw and experienced among his own people in the American Southwest where ancient stone townships, wide roads, and skillful-ly-engineered cliff dwellings are common.

There are 365 steps to the top of the Pyramid. Kit dropped out after about the first 40. She didn't have the energy to keep going, plus she was afraid of heights. Johnny laughed as she sat down and began to scoot from step to step to make the descent back to ground level. "She slid down that thing the whole way on her butt," he says, shaking his head at the memory. "It had to hurt." Johnny kept going up.

After he reached the top, he explored around the sacred site where Aztec priests once carried out human sacrifice as part of their religious rites to honor their deities and to call down blessings upon the people.

"It was a lot like that old Jewish fellow Abraham tried to do with his son Isaac, only no angels stopped the killing in the nick of time." Johnny chuckles as he adds. "I guess you have to be Jewish to get those kinds of breaks."

At one point, Johnny lay down on the altar himself to try to experience the place more deeply.

I wanted to feel what it might have been like to be on that huge granite block as a sacrificial victim centuries before. The stone was dark with old blood that had forever stained right into the granite.

I lay there for a while letting myself feel how a prisoner might have felt as he or she saw the knife coming, saw it piercing the breast and then removing the heart in the same long motion I had read about in books. I wondered if you might still be conscious enough to see your own heart as it was pulled out. Probably not. The blood supply to the brain would have been cut off by then and the eyes just glaze over.

There is still a bit of movement though, and gasps and groans. What always got me were the smells when the person's body functions opened one last time and he messed himself while his spirit was leaving this world.

I wondered how those Aztec priests dealt with that. If the victim shit on the altar on the way out, would the sacrifice still be good with the gods?

I smiled at the thought of that for a moment as I lay there. Then I imagined how I might escape the knife back in the day by pointing at my butt and saying to the priest, 'Not now! Not now! I feel a really big one coming on! It'll curse the land for years if you stick me now!'

I chuckled some more at that. I realized that I was having very sacrilegious thoughts and that I should expect lightning any minute. I also realized that thinking like this had probably kept me alive and mostly sane despite the ugly stuff I'd been through in my own life.

As soon as Johnny came down from the Pyramid of the Sun, he hiked over and climbed the Pyramid of the Moon.

"It was easier," he recalls. "Only 280 steps." Then he adds with dancing eyes, "And I'm going to do both of them again when I reach 100!"

Next on the itinerary for Johnny and Kit was a stop at Oaxaca in the South of Mexico. It is known as the "city of 365 churches" because a Christian *Conquistadore* by the name of Hernan Cortés took it as an inspired mission to slaughter vast numbers of "heathens" upon his arrival in the Americas and then to build Christian churches in all of their sacred places. Tradition has it that he vowed to build a church on every Native temple site that he found in the region around Oaxaca.

No one can question the seriousness of the man's devotion. He seems to have identified 365 sites and then went on a building spree using the labor of whatever "pagans" survived his first coming into their lives.

As he implemented his church-building program, he soon found it better served his spiritual purposes to have indigenous peoples die slowly building churches rather than to die quickly under the sword and pike. When one looks closely, what modern societies consider "civilization" often comes down to such minor shifts in thinking. The "civilized" ones are generally better equipped to kill more people than the "savages," but they do so in ways that leave lasting testimonials to themselves.

In the case of Cortés, one of his crowning achievements is the magnificent cathedral at Oaxaca with its dome covered in 24 carat gold—all plundered along with vast quantities of human labor from the Native civilization. Johnny and Kit found it still gleaming in the midday sun all these centuries later, a testament to Spaniards and their "civilizing" practices.

"Everybody seems to remember the terrible human sacrifices of the Aztec," Johnny ruminates as he shares his and Kit's journey through the region with me. "No one talks about the human sacrifices that men like Cortez carried out. It's like he ripped the heart out of every Indian that he met, not just a handful each year on the altar. But he was smart enough to get them to build amazing Churches the whole time he was killing them."

After Oaxaca, the pair travelled due west to the Pacific on the southern border that Mexico shares with Guatemala. They were travelling in a van that Johnny had come to call "Black Beauty," which he subsequently shortened to "BB" or simply "the Beeb." It's a 1978 Chevy van that he bought used in 1980 for $1,000 and then customized to make into a comfortable touring vehicle. It has logged over 370,000 adventure-filled miles and is still driveable over thirty years later. After making their way along narrow, mountain roads with dizzying drop-offs to the ocean below, he and Kit finally reached a trailer camp where they could rest for the night on Mexico's southern border with Guatemala.

The first thing that they discovered was that the entire camp of three dozen trailers had been vandalized by bandits. A frightened local informed them that one person had been shot in the leg during the robberies. A lapse in the availability of federal police officers during a change in the government in Mexico City was allowing the bandit population to run rampant. Most of the residents of the park had fled inland for safety. The few who remained warned Johnny and Kit to turn back and to head for the nearest large city before they, too, ended up robbed. Or worse.

But the courageous duo was not so easily frightened away from a good adventure. They took off all of their jewelry and hid it, along with their cash, in a special place Johnny had designed for such purposes in the back of the van. Then they pushed northward up the coast following narrow jungle roads. Johnny recounts what happened next.

Somewhere on a back road near a town called Colima, we came around a bend to find a big tree trunk lying right across the road. There was nothing to do but stop. From the jungle on the sides of the road a half dozen men emerged and surrounded us, pointing weapons at us. Their jefe, or leader, approached my side of the van.

I rolled my window down and called out in Spanish, 'What can I do for you?'

He laughed, saying, 'What you can do for us is give me your money.'

I said, 'We are not carrying any cash. I only use my credit card from city to city when I travel.' I pulled the credit card out of my wallet and showed it to him along with the empty wallet. I said, 'We are returning from our vacation in the South where we spent our money on food and lodging.'

While I was giving him this explanation, he noticed the gold chain that I had forgotten that I was wearing. He said, 'Isn't that chain gold? Give it to me!'

This was the chain on which I wore my Alcoholics Anonymous pendant. It is a gold circle about the size of a quarter in which an equilateral triangle of the same metal is set. When I pulled this up out of my shirt to show him, I pleaded, 'Oh, no, no, no! Please, friend, I can't give this up! It has too much importance for me. It is the symbol of Alcoholics Anonymous and it is a token of my twenty-eight years of sobriety. It was given to me long ago.'

Upon hearing this, he said, 'You are an alcoholic?'

I nodded gravely.

'And you are a member of Alcoholics Anonymous?' he asked.

'Yes I am!' I said.

'That is a very fine organization, señor,' he answered.

My relief was palpable. He had called me 'sir.'

'I, too, am an alcoholic' he continued, 'and I have been sober for five years now. I attend the A. A. meetings in our village in the hills.' Whereupon he removed his hat, bowed to me respectfully, and then waved to his compatriots to remove the roadblock.

As they did so, he said to me, 'It is a pleasure to have met you and have a very good trip, sir. Please travel carefully. There are many bad people around here these days! A Dios!'

He then waved us on and we continued our journey all the way home without further incident.

After Kit's vacation weeks ended, she returned to New England with many such tales to tell her friends and family. The following summer, she and Johnny again travelled the powwow circuit together in the Northeast. Then Kit became proficient enough at selling Native crafts that she struck out on her own to powwows that Johnny was not attending.

They drifted apart for a couple of summers. Then one day Johnny decided to drop in again on his friend.

He was surprised to discover that Kit had fallen quite ill. At first, the doctors had feared that she was suffering from lupus. She had many of the symptoms of that illness, such as exhaustion, difficulty walking, and disorientation. She was also suffering from a great deal of pain in her back and stomach.

The doctors tried two exploratory surgeries, one on her shoulder which had also become very painful, and on a lump in her breast. They found and removed a small, benign tumor from her breast and changed their opinion about the lupus. Nonetheless, the debilitating pain in her stomach and back continued. They cut her open a third time, looking for cancer in her stomach or other internal organs. They found nothing.

At that point, Kit was ready to try a different approach from what modern medicine was offering. Among the Native crafts that she and Johnny sold at powwows was the magnificent beadwork of the Huichol Indians of Northwestern Mexico. Johnny had told Kit as much as he knew about the Huichols. They were renowned not only for their beading of ornamental and decorative items, but for the unusual healing powers of their *"Ma'arak'ame,"* or medicine people.

One day Kit came to Johnny and asked if he would be willing to take her back to Mexico and to help her find a Huichol healer. After months of medical attention, three exploratory surgeries, and a huge stack of bills, she was ready to try a different approach.

Ever the adventurer, Johnny was pleased to take on the assignment. He told her that it seemed like a long shot to fix her problems, but then, she had nothing to lose either. Johnny tells what happened next.

Off we went to the state of Nayarit, arriving in the city of Tepic. She had heard of a certain medicine man that lived near there. We took a motel room and began our search for this man. We looked all over Tepic for days.

We were about to give up on the idea when we stopped in at this small museum. We inquired of the staff person there if he knew of a medicine person, a 'Ma'arak'ame,' among the local Indians.

He said, 'Oh, you are looking for a Ma'arak'ame? *Why don't you go over to the Office of Indigenous Personnel? They take care of all the tribes in the area.' He gave us the address and we caught a cab.*

When we got there, it was about two in the afternoon. There was a lady standing with her back to us talking with another woman seated at her desk. I excused myself and blurted out to them that I understood that I might find a medicine man here, or nearby, that they might suggest.

The woman who had been standing turned around and said, 'Oh! I guess the Creator kept me here longer than I should have been, because I have been off work for a half an hour. He must have kept me here for you!' She then asked, 'You want to see a Ma'arak'ame?'

'Yes, I guess that's what you call him,' I said.

She said, 'Look, just tell me where you are staying and I'll pick you up and take you to one in the morning.'

The next morning she was outside our motel room driving a white Dodge pickup. We got in and she headed up into the mountains. Although the truck was a four-wheel drive, I still had to get out to guide her past the huge craters and ruts in the dirt track that was the road.

Finally, we made it to the top of the mountain. A man came out of a small house and introduced himself as José Benitez Sanchez. He said that the person we were seeking was not there, but that he, too, was a Ma'arak'ame *and could he help us?*

I said, 'I don't know. This lady here has an awful lot of trouble walking and she seems to think that you can cure her.'

Turning to Kit, he said, 'Well, do you have faith? Because if you do not have any faith, there's nothing I can do for you.'

I translated this for her into English. She replied, 'All I have left is faith.'

'In that case then I will be able to help you,' he said. 'But I can't do anything right now because the sun is already up. If you will return before the sun comes up tomorrow, we will start in the morning.'

We agreed to return before sunrise. The Ma'arak'ame *told us to bring three lengths of ribbon one and a half meters long, one black, one red, one white, plus three plain white candles and one five-peso coin of the old style, if we could find one.*

So we drove back down to Tepic and ran around getting the items that he had called for. In the morning, our gracious lady guide was there waiting for us before dawn, at the first light. We made the difficult ascent once more.

José Benitez Sanchez was outside waiting to greet us. He said, 'I have been waiting for you. Have you brought the things that I asked for?'

Kit showed them to him. He was pleased.

Our lady driver said that if this was going to take much time, she would not be able to stay because she had to get back to town for an important meeting at eight a.m.

The Ma'arak'ame *said that that was no problem. When we were done, we would all just walk down to the main highway, where Kit and I would be able to catch the bus back to town.*

I asked him in surprise, 'How can we do that? She can hardly walk ten feet without having to stop and rest.'

He replied, 'I don't know how, but we'll be able to make it.' And looking at me this time, he asked, 'Do you have faith?'

'Yes,' I answered. I couldn't let Kit down after all that I had done to get her to this man.

He said, 'All right. Let's go.'

He took us inside a small church. It was a round building at the center of which was an altar. On the altar was a large cross with the crucified Jesus wearing a lady's skirt around his waist. At his feet were offerings of fresh, raw lamb and deer meat. Around the sides on the curved walls of the room, I could see deer antlers and other sacred objects that I did not immediately recognize.

Then he took us outside across a yard to a little chapel called a cálihue in the Huichol language. On the pathway to the cálihue we stopped before a dish-like flat stone that was the cover for a hole that contained other ribbons and ritual objects used for the cleansing of the air. After lifting the cover and explaining this to us, he returned the cover to its place and we continued on toward the altar in the cálihue. This little chapel was no larger than ten by twelve feet, all in all, covered by a straw thatched roof. The roof was maybe six or seven feet high. He seated me in one corner where I could watch the entire proceedings.

He then placed a small milking stool in the center of the chapel. The altar now on the far end consisted of a small pyramid built of adobe mud and comprised of three steps. Impaled into the top level of this adobe altar was a lance that served as a staff to which were tied many, many of those different colored ribbons.

The Ma'arak'ame seated Kit on the milking stool, placing the three lighted candles upright between her separated feet, with the five peso coin centered inside the candles so that their wax could drip onto the coin. I had no idea why this was done, but I never questioned it.

He tied the three ribbons that we had brought to the staff. Then he gave the ends of them to Kit and instructed her to hold them. Under no circumstances was she to let them go.

She grasped the ribbons tightly with both hands.

He pulled her blouse out of her waistband and rolled it up, tucking it under her brassiere all around, exposing her midsection. Then the Ma'arak'ame commenced to mumble and to sing chants in his Native language. After a time, he went to the altar and took from a small, bowl-shaped basket what looked like a bar of candy and had Kit bite off a piece and chew it up, without letting go of the ribbons.

After feeding this bar to her, he returned to the altar and scooped up a handful of black, gooey, ugly-looking mud that was in another bowl set into one of the adobe steps. He applied it in spots to her chin, around her neck, behind her ears, and in other places.

Then he went over to the altar and picked up a number of movediz, which are slender wooden sticks that are wrapped in colored yarn with a bunch of feathers tied into one end, like a feather duster with two more feathers attached by a string hanging to the ground from the cluster of feathers on the end of the stick. He placed one of these movediz carefully between each of the fingers of both of his hands with the feathered ends hanging down beneath his fingers.

He then began to sweep the feathers repeatedly over the black-daubed mud spots that he had put on her body while continuing his chanting. Occasionally he would reproach himself for having 'missed it,' referring to something that only he was aware of. When this would happen, he would start the process of brushing over again from the beginning, until he was satisfied that it was done correctly. It must have been about noon when he finished the movediz work.

At that point, he began to suck on Kit's abdomen. He pulled a white piece of cloth, like a hand towel, out of his belt and started to spit into it large, ugly masses that appeared to be old blood clots.

I saw this with my own eyes, but I could not believe it! I know he didn't have anything in his mouth, certainly no blood clots. He managed to keep up the singing and chanting between expelling the huge blood clots. He did this procedure from one side of her stomach to the other, showing her and me each of the clots as he removed them. How or where he was getting them was a complete mystery to me. All I know is that I was there and I saw what I saw.

When he was done, he was completely washed out. He was drip-ping with sweat, exhausted. When he had composed himself and Kit had restored her blouse to its proper place into the waistband of her skirt, he asked, 'Well, are you ready? Let's walk down!'

And would you believe it? We three walked the three miles back down the mountain to the main highway. That woman couldn't walk ten feet without stopping to rest before this was done. I still can't believe it!

The Ma'arak'ame *instructed us to return before sunrise again the next morning and we were grateful to our lady guide who brought us back up the mountain once again.*

The next morning before he started his work, I asked him how much I should pay him. He looked at me and I'm not sure if he was shocked or offended. He answered, 'Oh, no. We are not allowed to charge anything for what we do. This work belongs to the Creator and only to Him. No señor! Un Dios, solamente!' *One God only! Like many Native peoples I'd met throughout my travels, he refused to mix spirituality with money. He added that God allowed them to do this work for Him and that if, when it was done, I wished to give a gift in thanks, he could accept that.*

When he went back to work on Kit, this time he applied the black mud behind her ears, down her neck, under her shoulder blades, and on the small of her back. He repeated the process of brushing with the movediz, *singing and chanting and humming until he was again satisfied. Then he began the sucking again, but this time over the area of her kidneys and the small of her back.*

I don't know how or from where, but he began to spit out kidney stones! I mean kidney stones! And I know what they are because I passed them when I was in France. I know damned well what they look like. Nobody can fool me about that! He pulled out three of them from her back.

'This, again, is what was hurting her,' he said. 'This and the old adhesions from her past surgery many years ago had swollen and affected the nerves, making it difficult for her to walk. This is what has been giving her so much pain.'

I remembered then Kit telling me about her 'boo boo belly.' When she was younger, she had gone to the doctor with stomach problems and he had told her to go home and take a laxative, only to find that by morning the whole right side of her abdomen was black and blue and purple. They rushed her to the hospital by ambulance and found that her appendix had burst, poisoning her entire abdomen. She said that after they opened her up, they kept the incision open for three months while they continued to flush out the poison. The adhesions had formed inside during this long process of surgical cleansing of her insides. She was left with a huge scar across her belly.

When the Ma'arak'ame completed this part of the healing, he told us that we would have to return for the next six Fridays for him to finish with Kit's cure.

I said, 'Oh no, I'm sorry. That's not possible. We are only here for a short time. We are only on vacation.'

He answered, 'Well, that's too bad. I guess we'll have to do the next best thing.' He went over to the altar and removed one of the movediz *and a length of the black ribbon. He tied the ribbon to the end of the stick. He picked up a wad of cotton and fashioned six little cotton balls. He affixed the cotton balls to the ribbon by forming six knots to hold them. He rolled these up and gave them to Kit with these instructions.*

Every Thursday night, Kit was to place the movediz *above her head on the pillow before going to sleep. On Friday mornings as soon as she woke up, she was to remove one of the cotton balls and throw it away. AND HE WOULD BE WITH HER IN JUST A FEW MINUTES.*

Well, needless to say, I still can't understand how this could happen. On Friday mornings for the next weeks while we were sitting and having our coffee, Kit would just start twisting and jerking back and forth, saying, 'Oh, damn. He's back at me already! He's here!' Then she would squirm for about half an hour to forty-five minutes because he was there in spirit, I suppose.

I really don't know, but I can tell you that she wasn't just putting this on. Something was there. Anyway, we continued on our trav-

els around Mexico and Kit claimed that her pains were gone. She was certainly able to walk about and to enjoy herself from then on.

Kit's good health continued after Johnny brought her home to New England. In the weeks and the months after their experience with the Huichol *Ma'arak'ame*, Johnny recalls, Kit was "as healthy as the day that she was born." A couple of years after the healing, Johnny saw her again in Puerto Vallarta. She was still going strong. Later, in the 1990s, he lost track of her when one of her parents died and she moved into the family home back in Rhode Island.

Twenty years have passed. Johnny has had time to reflect on what he and Kit experienced in the mountains above Tepic, Mexico, long ago. He has passed through the region again many times. He has met again with the *Ma'arak'ame* Jose Benitez Sanchez and counts the man among his friends. He even has a photo from the Guadalajara newspaper in 2001 with himself and the well-known spiritual healer standing side by side. Here is how Johnny views Kit's healing all these years later.

I saw things that the Ma'arak'ame *did that under our civilized way of life are impossible. Being able to withdraw blood clots from somebody's body as he did is hard to believe and even harder to understand.*

And yet I believe everything he did. You either accept those things or you don't accept them. It's up to you, to the individual. I've seen too many things in my years on Earth for me not to believe that there is something higher than our own individual minds.

Why am I still here? Because I belong here. Why do I belong? Because the Creator doesn't want me yet. He has things for me to do.

I live one day at a time. Every day, I live as if it was the last day of my life. One day it will be. Maybe then I'll better understand what that Huichol Ma'arak'ame *already knows.*

The healing experience with Kit was a foreshadowing in many ways of the direction that Johnny's life has taken in the years since, as he nears the end of his many years. Nowadays, his journeys are less physical, less focused upon seeing new places, meeting new people, and doing new things. More and more, they turn toward the unseen world, toward the world of the spirit.

Guiding his path on these inward-looking adventures is a quote that sums up how he sees and understands the human story from the mountaintop of old age. The quote speaks to him, and of him, on many levels. It comes, aptly enough, from a chapter entitled "Misplaced Indian," in the book *The Red Road to Wellbriety in the Native American Way*. It comes from his Alcoholics Anonymous readings and has served as a sort of bible to keep him on the road to sobriety. He read to me in a quiet, firm voice a short passage that he had marked about halfway through the 300 pages. It is:

> *Let me look beyond that which I know and that which I see. Let me allow you to be what you are and nothing less. Hopefully, you will look at me and allow me to be what I am and nothing more.*

In his final years on Earth, Johnny spends much of his time looking beyond what he knows and what he sees in the material world. Nowhere is this more apparent than in what promises to be the final great friendship of his life. It is with a woman with whom he has a beautiful, tender, respectful, and loving relationship that the above quote describes well. Her name is Nancy. In her company, Johnny Pail Face has finally found something that he could never have known in advance nor have seen clearly as it unfurled. He has found the meaning of his life. It came in the form of a prayer.

It is to this final story that we now turn.

Final Prayer

THE BEST THINGS IN LIFE RARELY ANNOUNCE THEMSELVES. They arrive unexpectedly, unbidden, unplanned. As he approached age 80, Johnny Pail Face was taking things one day at a time. He had learned to enjoy the simple events of day-to-day life peacefully and with gratitude.

He liked the feel of the sun on his face in the mornings as he drank his first cup of coffee. He lived in a comfortable motor home that was plenty big for a person who required little. He enjoyed making Navajo jewelry and selling it on leisurely summer days at powwows up and down New England. He took pleasure in continuing conversations with old friends and in starting conversations with new friends. The jewelry stand that he moved from powwow to powwow provided an ideal meeting place for doing both.

When the cold weather came, he spent his winters among another group of friends in Puerto Vallarta enjoying the warm weather there, roaming the beaches, and enjoying good food and good company. It is these simple rhythms of an elderly man's life that create the context for a final story to close this book. In many ways, it is the best story of all.

In the 1990s, Johnny had found a place to park his motor home during his New England stays in Granby. A family there had a trailer space with water, sewer, and electricity hookups that they were not using. They were happy to rent the facilities to Johnny.

Julie was the sweetheart of a young man in the family and the couple lived there with his parents. Johnny noted that a woman in a gray jeep regularly visited Julie. He learned that the woman's name was Nancy. She was Julie's mother. He also learned that Nancy came from French-Canadian heritage and spoke French.

When Johnny spoke to the man of the household about wanting to meet Nancy, he warned Johnny to stay away. He told him that Nancy was married and her husband was an unpleasant fellow. However, Julie had developed a warm affection for the old Indian and Johnny enjoyed chatting with her on a daily basis in her comings and goings. Now and then, Nancy would be with her and would join in on their talks.

When Johnny tried out his French on Nancy, he found her quite fluent with a delightful old-country French-Canadian accent. In their three-way conversations, Johnny soon learned that Nancy had divorced her husband a couple of years before. She was a private person and had not made this information general knowledge.

One day in June during a conversation with Julie, Johnny asked if she thought it would be appropriate for him to invite her mother out for a cup of coffee or maybe lunch. Julie not only thought it was a wonderful idea, she offered to put up the money for the date. She knew her mother was going through a lonely time and she thought that Johnny's company might be just what she needed to bring a bit more cheer back into her days. Julie's encouragement cemented Johnny's resolve. But, he assured her, he could afford to pay for the date.

For that first date, he chose the lunch option. He had learned that Nancy liked Chinese food, so he invited her out for lunch at a small Chinese restaurant. They laughed and talked in English and French, sharing stories of their lives and enjoying each other's company. After that, Johnny began to call her on the phone regularly for long chats and they went out again for Chinese food many times. Johnny smiles at the memory. "Nancy never tired of Chinese. She could eat it every day. We ate a lot of Chinese food that summer."

As the months slipped by, Nancy was the one to take the next step. On Labor Day weekend at the start of September, she asked Johnny if he might like to go with her on a weekend retreat to a Catholic priory in the countryside in Vermont. The priory and Benedictine monastery is located four miles north of Weston in the beautiful countryside bordering the Green Mountain National For-

JOHNNY PAIL FACE BECOMES A HUMAN BEING

est. It was founded in 1953 by an abbot who came to the rich forests of New England from Dormition Abbey in Jerusalem.

The monks of the little priory have made a regular outdoor mass a unique and valued feature of religious life in that part of Vermont. People from all faiths and walks of life can be found gathered there on Sunday mornings during the temperate months of the year as they take in the liturgy performed in Latin by the monks. Adding to the charm of the service, they perform the hymns in English and other languages with beautiful guitar music. The sound of the monks in their long, brown robes tied with rope at the waist, their voices echoing across the meadow in a celebration of God and of life never fails to transport Nancy to the clouds.

So it was that Nancy had taken up the habit of attending the Sunday mass at the priory whenever she could get away from daily life in Granby. Knowing that there was a small group of Guatemalan Indians who also live at the priory with the monks, Nancy decided to invite Johnny along. She thought that Johnny might enjoy speaking to them in Spanish and learning more about their culture and the reasons that they had taken refuge in Vermont, so far from their homes. Johnny was quick to agree and accepted the invitation with enthusiasm.

Nancy picked him up at 6 a.m. on a beautiful September morning just as the first colors of autumn were beginning to transform the leaves of the forests that lay along their route. Nancy had brought along a pork roast with all the fixings for their Sunday dinner in a closed roasting pan in the back seat of the jeep. Around midmorning, they stopped at a small summer cabin owned by her son on their way to the priory. It was where they would have their Sunday dinner after attending mass. Nancy opened up the windows to let in fresh air and slipped the pork roast surrounded with vegetables into the oven. Then they drove the few miles on to the priory.

They arrived in time for the 10:30 a.m. mass. Johnny found it a wonderful experience. They sat on blankets on the lawn outside the chapel as the Benedictine monks performed the mass outdoors. Johnny especially enjoyed that they chanted the liturgy in Latin. Furthermore, he had a particular affinity for the Benedictines. He had spent time at the original monastery founded by St. Benedict

1,400 years ago in Italy. It was the monastery devoted to peace that he had helped the allies reduce to ruins at the top of Monte Cassino during World War II. Stumbling across a peaceful and intact Benedictine priory tucked away in the quiet New England countryside gave him a better sense of what St. Benedict had intended long ago.

After mass, Johnny met a couple of the Guatemalan visitors and chatted with them in Spanish. They were wearing their native costumes and were eager to share stories of their lives and the struggles that their own indigenous people faced in Guatemala. After that, Nancy introduced Johnny to Brother Dan, a native of Mexico City who had taken up residence at the priory. Johnny was impressed with how well the man spoke both English and French in addition to Spanish.

As Nancy and Johnny were heading for the parking lot to return to the pork roast simmering in the oven, they walked past a building with a blue metal circle and the letters A. A. hanging on the door. Johnny knew immediately what it meant.

"There's an Alcoholics Anonymous meeting going on in there," he said to Nancy. "Do you mind? Could we just peek in for a moment and greet people?"

Nancy was happy to do so.

They found a young lady named Gail in charge. She seemed pleased to have special guests and immediately asked Johnny if he might like to chair the meeting. Johnny accepted her offer. They spent the next hour sharing in the stories and struggles of people fighting the same struggle that had consumed nearly half of Johnny's life.

Johnny was among those who spoke. It was the first time that Nancy heard him speak publicly.

"I cried," she remembers. "I just cried."

When it ended, he and Nancy rushed back to the cottage to salvage what they could of the pork roast.

"It was very well done, but still edible," Johnny remembers. "We were an hour late and Nancy's roast was bone dry. The flavor was good but you had to drink a lot of liquid to wash it down."

"But the A. A. meeting was worth it," Nancy adds. "I would not change a thing in that beautiful day."

When Johnny pushed back from the dinner table that night, he was in a good mood. It had been a good day for someone devoted to living one day at a time. From the early start in the freshness of a new day, to the drive along small New England highways bathed in the fading colors of summer, to the mass in Latin, to meeting people from other lands, to running an A. A. meeting, to dinner with a beautiful friend, it couldn't have been better. Or maybe it could.

"I was thinking romance as Nancy and I sat there across the table from each other that afternoon. 'Why did you bring me here?' I asked her. I'm sure she saw the spark in my eye when I asked that question."

"To show you the mountains and the trees and to take you to mass at the priory," she answered.

"It that all?" he asked.

"Yes, that's all," she told him. And she meant it.

"Nancy is a devoted Roman Catholic," Johnny explains to me as he tells the story. "When you are married, you are married for life, even after divorce. Our friendship started out strictly platonic and it remains so to this day."

After dinner, the couple drove home to Granby in the early evening on small, winding blacktop roads through the forests. "After that first outing," Johnny recalls, "we became better and better friends. I kept hoping that things might turn to romance, but Nancy's devotion to her faith kept things at the friendship level."

A month later, in late October, Nancy and Johnny returned a second time to the priory. Both remember how especially breathtaking the leaves were that year. They provided the perfect setting for a friendship that was springing up in the autumn of two long and well-lived lives. Though Nancy would protest otherwise, it would take another book equal to this one to begin to get at the richness, the beauty, and the struggles of her own life.

As a young woman, she chose nursing as her career. She rose to the top of her profession as a nurse practitioner and finished her years of care-giving as a highly respected teaching nurse at an outstanding regional hospital. She was also a loving and devoted mother who raised three beautiful children. Like many women of her generation, she took time out from her career during the early years of motherhood to give her children a good start in life.

Once her own children were off to school, she remembers fondly how she turned the small family farm on the edge of Granby into a daycare center to help the family budget. She took seven or eight children at a time, charging the parents only a dollar an hour for her services. Those services included lunch and a day-long array of learning activities that few other daycare centers match. On the family farm was a huge back yard and barn filled not only with room for the children to run and play, but it was filled with life in the most beautiful, basic ways, ways that are magic for small children.

Scarcely a week went by without the arrival of a newly hatched brood of chicks, or a newborn calf, or some baby pigs, or perhaps a baby lamb for the children to meet and to help care for. Nancy remembers how excited the mothers would get sometimes when they arrived to drop off their children in the mornings. Nancy would tell them if the children would be experiencing something special that day, like chicks breaking out of their shells or the birth of a new animal. Sometimes the mothers would stick around all day to share with the children the birth of a batch of baby pigs, or kittens, or some chicks.

One hen was too old to get alarmed around children. Nancy and her family called her Henrietta the School Chicken and took special care of her. The pre-school children took delight in admiring and petting her each day as she sat on an egg or two and clucked contentedly. There were two bantam roosters that they named Bert and Ernie after *Sesame Street* characters who strutted around the back yard but were too wary to be petted.

Then there was Sting Ray, the family goat. He was a gentle old soul who took for himself the role of guard dog when the children were present. Nancy laughs to remember how Sting Ray would follow her and the children any place that they went on the farm. If they sat down for a picnic or began to play in an area, Sting Ray would lie down close by and keep an eye on everyone, cheerfully allowing the children to pet him and to crawl around and on him in their affection for their furry guardian.

Patches, the family pony, was equally a favorite of the children. Each day, Nancy would set aside time to take each child on a pony ride around the farm. As she walked them with a guide rope on Patches past a little pond, the turtles would dip out of sight in the water and the frogs would jump and splash at the sound of approaching footsteps.

In addition to this natural paradise, there was an endless supply of stray cats who came to stay in the shelter of the barn and who thereby became part of the family. And of course, there was the faithful family dog, a large German shepherd named Prince that helped Sting Ray with the work of guarding and protecting Nancy's young charges. All in all, there was an amazing world on Nancy's small family farm filled with animals for the children to learn from and to care for.

It was the "caring for" that Nancy emphasized. She took advantage of life on the farm to teach other people's children what she and her husband had taught their own youngsters. They had taken the time to instruct them in the proper ways to treat and to care for the animals around them at their home. When Nancy was running her daycare, it was her own three children who would rise at 5:30 a.m. to feed and water their pets, to clean out stalls and cages, and to make sure that every one was good for the day. Only then would they come to breakfast, take showers, and head off to school like other children.

The lessons Nancy taught her preschool charges each day weren't just about how to feed and water the animals, but how to respect them, when to give them affection, and when to leave them in peace. Nancy also regularly took the children on group walks and picnics in the forest around the two dozen acres of the farm. She encouraged the natural instinct in each child to explore the world of dirt, grass, trees, flowers, and plants, as well as the cacophony of insects, birds, and animals that infused the farm and forest with life.

It is, without doubt, Nancy's own deep, instinctual connection to the earthiness of the world that carried her through her years as a mother, as a unique teacher of children, and as a highly-skilled nurse. This down-to-earth side of her nature also makes her a person who would welcome a weathered, nomadic old Indian into her life.

As Johnny and Nancy took their second journey to the outdoor mass at the priory, Nancy announced that they would not need to rush back to Granby as they had before. She had a Sunday dinner planned, after which they could spend the evening and night at her son's cottage. There was just one bedroom, so she would make up a bed for Johnny on the couch in the living room. She made the point very clearly so that Johnny would know where the borders of their friendship lay. Little did he suspect that, on the couch in the small New England cottage, he was in for one of the most intense and life-changing nights of his life.

It was the weekend of October 12, 1994. Early the next week, Johnny was to head off on his annual pilgrimage to the Pacific Coast of Mexico. After attending another uplifting outdoor mass at the priory, Johnny and Nancy had dinner again at her son's cottage. This time the roast was not overcooked. "Beef," Johnny recalls. "With all the fixings cooked right in the pan with the meat and broth. It was delicious."

After dinner, Johnny put a fire in the fireplace to chase away the October chill. There was no TV, but the couple did not need it. They spent the evening talking. Nancy told Johnny of all the memories she had of the cottage and the surrounding woods. It had been a favorite getaway place for her and her three children when they were little. They had a tape player and Johnny shared some of his favorite Spanish music. "Julio Iglesias and Placido Domingo," he smiles. "Romantic stuff."

The romance ended at bedtime, however. Nancy got Johnny comfortably settled on the couch and went off to her room.

Then it happened.

Around midnight, Johnny awakened from a deep sleep. When he looked at the dark ceiling above the couch, words began to form in a line and to move across the ceiling.

I didn't know what to think at first. The words were so clear and intense. It was amazing. I started to read them. They were a prayer to the Creator. I don't know if they were really there on the ceiling or just coming from my own mind. Anyway, they went on and on. It was a pretty long prayer. I just kept on reading and reading.

Then, when the prayer ended, it immediately started again. I realized that I was supposed to memorize it. So I started repeating the words as they appeared and ran across the ceiling. This went on and on. Each time the prayer ended, it would start again. Finally I had it memorized and it did not start again. It must have been around four or five a.m.

I knew I was not going to be able to go back to sleep after that, so I got up and went outside to get some fresh air and to think. It was a frosty morning, just before dawn began at that really dark part of the night. When I looked up at the stars, I couldn't believe how bright and beautiful they were. The whole Milky Way seemed so close that I might be able to touch it. Well, I couldn't let that go by without sharing it with Nancy, so I started yelling for her to come outside.

When Nancy woke up and heard Johnny calling for her out in the yard, her first thought was that he must have gone out to relieve himself and fallen in a hole or something. There was a bathroom in the cottage but she was learning new things about this old Indian every day. She thought maybe he preferred doing his personal business at night in the old way. Then it occurred to her that he might be in trouble with a bear. There were plenty of them around in the forest. She threw on her robe and went scrambling to help.

She burst out the front door and found Johnny standing there in the yard with no bears or holes in sight. "What is it? What is it?" she asked in near panic.

Johnny smiled and pointed upward. "Look," he said.

And she did.

Then they stood there together marveling at the heavens. Johnny began to point out the constellations and various star formations like the Big and Little Dippers. He directed her attention to the North Star and talked about how it helped guide his people in the old days.

After a time, the first faint rays of dawn began to show to the East. When Johnny saw that, he knew what he had to do. "Listen to what came to me during the night," he said to Nancy. Then he turned to the East and began a ritual that has been a part of his daily rhythm of life every day since. As Nancy stood and watched with amazement and awe, Johnny offered up his prayer for the first time.

The next day, the couple drove back to Granby. Nancy dropped Johnny off at the place where his motor home was parked. He packed up his 1978 "Beeb" van for the long drive to Mexico and then stopped by Nancy's place to say goodbye for the winter. She cried when he left. "It was such a spiritual, great friendship," she says now. "I knew even then that I was going to miss him."

With a twinkle in her eye, she recalls, "He called me a lot after that. He called from Pennsylvania, then from Ohio, then from Illinois, and so on. I teased him about being the Energizer Bunny because it seemed he was just hopping across America so fast. Every few hours I'd get a call from a new state."

"I'd found a partner," Johnny explains. "She was a good companion, even by phone. She was someone I could talk to, someone I could depend on, someone I could love. She understands about the things in my life, the good and the bad. She gets me. No one has ever gotten me like Nancy."

It is a good thing that Johnny Pail Face has lived a long life. When any life is cut short, it is a tragedy. In Johnny's case, had he died early, the tragedy would have been greater, for the best did not come in the beginning or somewhere in the middle. Johnny Pail Face saved the best for last. The best friendships, the best love, the best laughter, the big adventures, the greatest kindnesses, the greatest giving—they all came most fully near the end.

There is no accident in this. It is no grand trick of fate that caused Johnny's life to flow as it has. It is by choice that a Navajo boy who once hated who he was has become a gentle, old Indian who loves who he is. It is by choice that he has taken the ugly brokenness of life and transformed it into beauty and wholeness.

Johnny Pail Face planted seeds of kindness and understanding and caring and beauty in the dung heap that the world offered him long ago on an Indian reservation of the American West. And the Creator, or life, or fate, or all three have been kind enough to let him live to see the harvest.

When his last day arrives, when his life "fades as the fading sunset," he will look Northward with "Clean Hands and Straight Eyes," as his prayer puts it. When his life circle comes round to its ending place, a bitter, angry youth who has become a kind, cheerful old man after nearly a century on earth—this human being will return to his Creator.

Without shame.

THE END

Epilogue

Johnny Pail Face left this earth at 9:30 on a Tuesday night in early February. It was one week to the hour after his book came into the world. The previous Tuesday night, I had been doing the first public reading to share his life story at Bay Path College in Longmeadow, Massachusetts, with a supportive crowd of brave souls who had come out on a bitter cold January night. As I was signing copies after the reading, Johnny called on my cell phone.

He was in good spirits. His voice was so loud that I had to hold the phone away from my ear. "I'm sorry I can't be there, J. J.!" he called out.

It sounded like I had him on speaker phone setting. I didn't.

"Too damn cold outside for a poor, homeless, illiterate old Indian like me. Nancy is keeping me in tonight. I told her that she better kiss me if she's going to keep me home." He then shifted to a whisper that carried the same volume as his normal voice: "J. J., I think she might do it!"

I laughed. This was Johnny in his nineties. I sometimes thought of him as a rough-hewn oak barrel of aged red wine. I had seen barrels like this on out-of-the-way farms in southern France as a young man. They always held the wine that the farmers found too good to sell. Old Johnny was non-alcoholic of course, but no less full-bodied and with flavors that made you want to stop whatever you were doing and do more of him.

He didn't mention that he was now on oxygen constantly. He didn't bring up how hard it was to drag oxygen tanks along whenever he left home. Johnny did not dwell on the unpleasant things in his life.

In the next breath he got to the point of his call. "Do they like my book?" he sang out.

I smiled while keeping the phone a safe distance from my ear. His call had caught me halfway through signing a book for a student. There was a long line of people behind her. I thought quickly then held my cell phone out to the young woman.

"This is Old Johnny," I said. "Could you tell him what you think of his book? Do you mind?"

Her face flushed with surprise. "Of course! Yes. Thank you." Then the phone was in her hand and their conversation went racing off while I went back to signing books. I noted that she, too, was holding the phone a safe distance from her ear.

When they finished, Kevin, Johnny's stepson who represented him at the reading, came to my rescue and picked up with Johnny. He spent a long time giving his "pop" a rundown on the event. Every time Kevin stopped speaking, I could hear Johnny prodding him for more detail. He wanted to know everything that was going on with his book.

That was the last time that I heard Johnny's voice.

The next time that I saw my dear old friend, he was no longer talking. He was lying in a beautiful four poster log bed. The king-sized bed was in an equally large and comfortable log home. Nancy and Johnny had relocated to the ranch of Nancy's son Tommy a couple of months before. They were living in a cozy "in-law" apartment above a three-car garage.

When my wife, Jasmine, and I arrived, Johnny was in a light coma. He seemed to be sleeping. Four days after the book launch, he had lost consciousness. His life partner, Nancy, is a retired nurse practitioner. Together, she and Johnny had carefully planned every detail of how he wished his life to end. Nancy had spent the last year and a half at Johnny's side preparing for what was now taking place.

"I followed everything we set up together," Nancy told me a few weeks later when I returned for an interview. "The one thing I didn't want was for him to gasp for breath and to be in pain at the end. I'd seen so many people go through that in my work. I loved him so much. I did not want him to suffer at the end."

Johnny came into this world during a cesarean section on a kitchen table in a Navajo hogan in one of the poorest parts of America. It's hard to imagine a more violent or bloody way for a new life to begin. He left this world in opposite circumstances. The last gift that Nancy gave the man she loved as completely as I have seen a person love was to send him out of this world peacefully.

The thing that she was most firm about was keeping Johnny at home for his final days on earth. People who knew and loved him came each day to sit beside his bed. We shared our favorite Johnny stories. His son, Kevin, played a Native flute. We took turns holding his hands. When he would become restless or agitated in his deep slumber, Nancy would give him pain medication. That always calmed him. We found that Jasmine, who is from China, had the same soothing effect when she massaged his chest and hands as she had learned to do from the ancient traditions of her homeland.

Nancy's son Tommy, his wife Mary Ann, Nancy's granddaughter Michelle, and her great grandson Aiden were ever present. Other members of Nancy's family came in and out to say farewell to a gentle old friend who had been in their lives for over twenty years. There were Julie, her daughter Emily and son Curtis who made a quick trip home from the college near Boston where he is a first-year student. Granddaughter Courtney and her husband Kyle came from another state. In all, four generations gathered around Old Johnny in his final days. The youngest was little Aiden at just eleven-months. It is a thought-provoking sight to witness an old man dying at the same time as a small baby laughs and plays beside and occasionally right on the same large bed.

"It's Johnny's Circle of Life right there," I said to Nancy as I motioned to Aiden and Johnny side by side. Johnny was sleeping his final sleep. Aiden was smiling his first smiles.

Nancy smiled and nodded.

"He's been telling us for weeks now that his dying wish is to be cremated," Kevin said. There was a pause while we waited for what would come next. We all had heard Johnny tell us this part of his "last will and testament." Kevin continued, "And after we cremate him, he wants us to flush him down a toilet in Holyoke."

There was a round of chuckles and knowing smiles from the people in the room. It was one of Johnny's earthy jokes that, as was often the case with him, was more than a joke. Holyoke has a large minority of Spanish speaking citizens. Johnny had told us again and again in the previous months that he had been born in an earthy place where people spoke other languages and it seemed fitting to him to return to one when he died.

"Flush me down a toilet and I'll be right where I belong," he would say with a big smile. This would of course get Nancy agitated. "Oh, Johnny, don't talk like that. Be nice," she would scold him.

"I am nice," he would protest cheerfully. "I am being me."

Nancy would heave a sigh, shake her head, and then start fussing over him in one way or another while Johnny beamed.

We remembered such pithy sayings and experiences in Johnny's life to pass the time. Stories alternated between the humorous and the serious, between the mundane and the earthshaking. There seemed to be an endless supply of Johnny quotes to be shared and an abundance of memories to sift through. Each time a new group of visitors arrived, the best stories and quotes would be repeated.

Later, when I interviewed Nancy to write this final Johnny story, she told me that she knew very clearly when the end was drawing close.

"He had two nights of hallucinating and crying out in his sleep about two weeks before he left us," she told me. "The visiting nurse said his time was near. I knew she was right. I had seen it before. We started giving him medication to calm him so that he could sleep peacefully at night after that." In the little time that they had left together, Nancy did not bother to tell Johnny what she knew. He knew it too in his own way. There was no point in bringing it up.

Johnny began failing on a Saturday. He slept all day in his easy chair and scarcely responded to Nancy when she talked to him and rubbed his joints. That night, she had to call on Tommy to help put him to bed. He was able to walk from his chair to the bed with them supporting him on each side.

"I'm tired. I'm tired," he said quietly to her as she tucked him in.

The next day, Nancy kept him in bed all day. She spent much of her time holding him in her arms and caressing him as a mother might do to calm a restless child. She told him over and over how much she loved him.

In the middle of the afternoon, he regained consciousness enough to respond. His eyes opened slightly and he mouthed the words, "I love you too." Those were Johnny Pail Face's last words.

On Monday, Johnny remained unconscious the entire day. Tommy brought an eagle feather from a wounded eagle that he had rescued and released a couple of years before. Kevin used the eagle feather, considered sacred in many Native cultures, to do a traditional smudging ceremony. It is a purification ritual that prepares one spiritually for a special event. Death was Johnny's special event. Along with birth, it is among the most sacred of events. Each happens once in a lifetime.

After Kevin completed the ceremony, Tommy beat a simple rhythm on an elk hide drum and Kevin played the flute. Johnny slept peacefully with the eagle feather resting on his chest while the two younger men filled the room with sounds that would have been familiar to Johnny's ancestors for a thousand generations.

Tuesday was Johnny's last day on earth. Nancy and Johnny's family drew close. There were no outside visitors. There was good reason for dear friends to stay at home that day. The region was under a major winter storm warning. A late winter snow was about to sweep through New England. Weather announcers on all television channels were encouraging people to stay home, and to bundle up if they needed to go out. School closings were starting to appear in a ticker-tape scroll flowing across the bottoms of screens. Above them, weather forecasters showed swirling images of clouds and winds inching their way across multi-colored maps toward our region.

At 9:30 that evening, Johnny stopped breathing. Nancy was lying at his side, holding him in her arms.

"His breath became erratic for about an hour," she told me. "Then he took a last weak breath and that was it. I waited to make sure and then I said 'He's gone,' to everyone in the room."

Nancy described the moment vividly. The eagle feather was still resting on Johnny's chest. Little Aiden grew quiet in his mother's arms at the bedside. Everyone in the room rose and came to the bed. There were six of them on vigil at the time. They all hugged and caressed Johnny for the last time. They all cried.

After a few moments, Tommy said, "We should open the door," In one motion, the family rose and went to the kitchen door that opens out to a big balcony. Without planning to do so, all six, including baby Aiden in his mother's arms, went out into the dark night and stood on the balcony, leaving the door open behind them.

"We felt it would help his spirit on its way," Nancy said simply and then was quiet.

After a short pause, she continued. "We could feel the big storm coming. Clouds were coming fast but you could still see a star now and then between them." She paused again after this and I watched her thoughts drift to another place and time.

"All I could think about was the night at the little cabin in Vermont when Johnny got his prayer. Afterward, he went outside and started calling me to come join him. He was so excited when he called to me that I thought there must be a bear after him. I was really worried. When I went out, he took me by the hand and pointed at the sky. The sight took my breath away. The stars were so bright that it was like you could just reach up and touch them."

"'I wanted you to see this, Nance,' he told me." Again a short pause as she gathered her words.

"Now I was standing under the same stars and I was thinking that the love of my life was somewhere up there among them. Before I could think much about that, Tommy said we needed to take Johnny to the funeral home right away. He said with the big snow coming, we might not be able to get him there for days if we didn't do it right then."

Tommy made a couple of phone calls and people were immediately on their way to help. The visiting nurse arrived first and pronounced Johnny dead. She and Nancy washed him and then dressed him in his favorite red scrubs. Nancy gently pulled his favorite wool socks on his feet. "I didn't want his toes to get cold," she said. "It hadn't occurred to me yet that he wouldn't feel the cold."

Then a man and a woman from the funeral home brought a gurney up the stairs to the apartment. They wrapped Johnny in the bed sheet and lifted him onto the gurney. Tommy and the man from the funeral home carried him down to the hearse with Nancy following close behind. She did not weep. She had been a nurse for nearly four decades. She had trained herself to save her tears for when the work was done.

Just before they loaded the gurney into the hearse, Nancy asked if she could kiss Johnny again. The funeral services man understood. He let Nancy unwrap the sheet from Johnny's quiet face. She kissed him on the lips. She gave him a long hug.

"It was our last kiss," she said quietly. "Then they covered him again and began sliding him into the hearse. I reached out and squeezed his toes. When they closed the doors, I could not touch him anymore. I watched as the hearse drove down the drive toward the highway. It's a long driveway, over a quarter of a mile. I watched until the hearse disappeared. I went back into the house just as the first snowflakes began to fall."

At this point, Nancy excused herself and went to the bathroom to gather her emotions. I sat thinking about the story that she had just told me. I had heard so many of Johnny's stories over the previous seven years. Nancy had given me his last one.

My first thought was that it had to be among the most beautiful of them all. It also seemed to be connected in symbolic ways to the stories of his childhood. Things often come full circle like that, but the circle seemed especially intense in Johnny's case. The symbolism common to his life's beginning and to its ending was both religious and historical.

The woman who had just told me Johnny's final story is a devoted Christian. She comes from a long heritage of French Canadian Catholics. Many times, as Johnny had shared his stories with me at her dining table over the years, I had noted her moral indignation. Occasionally she became so agitated at what other Christians had done to Johnny and to his people that she would rise and leave the room. If she did not leave, she would shake her head with a dark look and say that she just could not believe what some people had done to other people in the past.

But Nancy's response to the ugliness of the past went beyond words and expressions of disapproval. I heard her say on more than one occasion when Johnny finished a painful story, "No one will ever treat you like that again." And she made sure that they did not. She had taken Johnny into her home two decades before after he had an operation on his leg and could not do his own shopping or cook his own food for a time. After he healed, she kept him. She made her home his home. She shared all that she had with him. They travelled together. They went to powwows together. They never tired of going out for Chinese food and having long talks over dinners filled with laughter and tenderness.

Nancy's most common way of referring to Johnny in their final years together was "the love of my life." And Johnny used the similar words to describe how he felt in return. "She 'gets' me," he confided to me. "She really 'gets' me."

The relationship between Johnny and Nancy was more than a tender love between a man and a woman that brought a warm glow to their "golden years." There was something important and symbolic in the fact that Johnny found the truest love of his life in the arms of a Catholic woman. His mother's Catholicism wounded him at the start of his life. Nancy's Catholicism healed him at the end of his life.

And it was no accident that Nancy found the love of her life in the arms of an Indian. Her love laughs openly and boldly in the face of one of the darkest chapters in American history. It unveils the great lie behind the sense of inevitability with which white Europeans systematically destroyed almost to extinction the original owners of America and then hid the horror from themselves with noble-sounding phrases like "Manifest Destiny" and *e pluribus unum*.

Johnny and Nancy's love shows us that things did not have to go this way. Genocide was not the inevitable result of Christian civilization "clashing" with Native civilization. Human events are never unavoidable. We always have a choice. Our lives are the sum total of our choices. And so is our history.

At that point in my reverie, Nancy returned from freshening up and took our conversation in a new direction.

"Johnny is back now," she said.

"He's back?" I asked, caught off guard.

She nodded. "I keep him over there between those two Native statues." She pointed across the room to a sturdy paper sack with the name of the funeral home in gold letters. It rested between two Native American statues that blended human forms with trees and wolves and eagles and nature scenes.

"There is an urn inside with his ashes. I like to hold them in the evening while I watch our favorite TV shows. I even talk to him as I watch. Our cat Spirit sits on my lap and purrs the whole time."

Spirit was sitting on the floor near Nancy as she said these things. It was early evening and it looked as if he were waiting for their evening ritual to begin.

"When I sleep at night," Nancy continued, "I put the urn beside my pillow. I love having Johnny close to me. And Spirit sleeps curled up with us both."

"Will you keep his ashes here with you?" I asked.

"Just a few of them," Nancy replied. "I promised Johnny I would put a little of him in a locket that I would wear around my neck and close to my heart. I will do that soon. He wanted the rest of his ashes scattered in a special place. When the weather warms up, we will do a gathering on the other side of the meadow near the big pine trees. Kevin will do a Native ceremony to honor Johnny's spirit and to send him on his journey. Johnny's wish was for Tommy to ride his pinto horse carrying his ashes. There is an old Indian burial ground under the pine trees. Johnny asked if Tommy would scatter his ashes on the wind as he rode past the burial grounds. He said that would put his spirit at peace. That's what we are going to do."

Our interview ended soon after Nancy talked about spreading Johnny's ashes. Jasmine and I did not linger. I could tell that it had taken a lot out of Nancy to tell me all that she had. We hugged and said our farewells.

As we drove away from the large ranch house to begin the trip home, I looked across the dark meadow and saw the tops of the burial ground pines in the night. I imagined the final goodbye that we would offer to Johnny when spring brought warmth and life back to New England.

As I drove, I had a vision of Johnny's spirit resting beneath the trees in that ancient burial place. I imagined him preparing to meet his creator. I imagined that he was in no hurry to leave. Then it became hard to distinguish his spirit from another one in my daydream of a vision. Two spirits began to overlap and to blend in the dance of my headlights along the dark dirt lane.

One was the spirit of an Indian man. One was the spirit of a Christian woman. They were standing before their maker. They were standing before tumultuous events in a great nation's history. They were standing before their consciences. They were standing before me and you.

In my vision, they have Clean Hands.
In my vision, they have Straight Eyes.
In my vision, they are without Shame.
I leave you with my vision.
It is my gift to you from Johnny.
It is my gift to you from Nancy.
It is a gift of love.
Aho.

—John Jarvis, March 30, 2014
Longmeadow, Massachusetts

Acknowledgments

It takes a "tribe" to make a book such as this.

In addition to the three people in the Dedication, I am grateful to Bay Path College leaders and dear friends Carol Leary and Bill Sipple who believed in Johnny's story enough to give me a sabbatical to begin the writing. I thank the Bay Path Board of Directors for generously approving the released time.

I am grateful to Old Johnny, who, among many other lessons, has taught me how to respect women, how to grow old gracefully, and how to die with dignity. The three things are interconnected, by the way. Disrespect mothers like Johnny's or my own and the other lessons quickly unravel.

I am grateful to Kevin, who brought Johnny and me together, and to Nancy, who sustained us on the journey.

I am grateful to Ellie, who loved me enough to let me go.

I am grateful to Jill and Jake, who are in my bones.

I am grateful to Hannah, who leads me to the top of mountains and keeps us going through places that could break us.

I am grateful to Chanhui, whose mother departed this life for love and whose father stayed in this life for love. They guide our careful steps now.

I am grateful to my brother Sherrod, to Dusty, to Aidan, and most recently to Neacko. They taught us to feel the way slowly through stories that fall on us like mountains being made low.

I am grateful to Neena's Lori who has become caretaker and guide to the new generation.

I am grateful to Edward Joseph Osterman and to Glenna Sanderlin Evans. As spouses and step-parents, they gave us all love, hope, and stability when mountains came tumbling down left, right, and center.

I am grateful to Rod Ariwite, Roseanne George, and Danny Ariwite, who planted seeds of Shoshoni kindness in our childhoods. The seeds now bear fruit in this book 45 years later. I'm sorry that it took so long. I had a lot to learn.

I am grateful to Princess Yvonne Webb, Chris Webb, Aaron Webb, Jo-Ann Jose, Ethel Seubert, and Old Andy and Mrs. Jackson, who watered the Shoshoni seeds with Ni mii poo rain.

I am grateful to Mary Ellen Bollman Parker who helped me learn to walk a traditional path and who remained my friend when I took a side road.

I am grateful to Bob Egbert, who has been my friend through all the changes and who still points me towards the best in myself with every word that we share.

I am grateful to Birdie (Green) Barrett who came back after 40 years of quiet just now as I finish this book. She was often on my mind and ever in my heart.

I am grateful to Dick Adams and to Bob Schultz. As with my Uncle Mike, they chose careers in teaching. Generations of students benefitted from their goodness.

I am grateful to Sonia Hussa who always walked her own path and helped me discover how to do the same.

I am grateful to Diane Deerheart Raymond, Loving One Swenson, Kind Warrior White, Tall Pine White and to the Nipmuck Chaubunagungamaug People who live near their ancestral homeland at Lake Chagogagogmanchogagogchaubunagungamaug, Massachusetts. They opened their lives to me and I opened my heart to them in a fair trade that deepens my journey day by day. I note that the film we made with twenty-six Bay Path students led me to Old Johnny and to writing this book.

I am grateful to "Bookstore Bob" Greene and to Acoma Pueblo poet Simon J. Ortiz for giving most valuable feedback on the manuscript along the way.

I am grateful to agent and book editor Sandy Chmiel, who worked tirelessly to help me harvest Johnny's story.

I am grateful to Steve Strimer and his team at Levellers Press who brought the project beautifully together.

I am grateful to Kathy Bourque and Susan Mattei for helping to set up the scholarship fund and for working with Kathy Wroblewski and Briana Sitler to get this story out to readers. A special thank you to Xiaotai Chai who joined the publicity team as well.

I am grateful to Suzanne Strempek Shea who has graciously accepted to peruse and to write a review of this book.

I am grateful to Aurora Foxx who is adding her elegantly simple artwork and he simply elegant self to the success of this project.

And finally, I am grateful to the many students who have enriched my Native History classrooms, my life, and this book-in-progress over the past five years. Their heartfelt input has breathed new life and better energy into each page.

All of these make the tribe that has made this book.

I honor them.

John Jarvis
Longmeadow, Massachusetts
November, 2013

Appendices

Johnny Pail Face
Daily Prayer to the
Four Sacred Directions

PRAYER TO THE RISING SUN IN THE EAST

Oh Lord, Creator of Mother Earth and the Universe, I have opened my eyes to another day. Please help me by taking away all that is negative. Take away my Impatience, Intolerance, Resentments, Denials, Anxiety, and any other things that are negative within me.

PRAYER TO THE SUMMER SUN OF THE SOUTH

Oh my Lord, Creator in the South, where the sun never sets and everything grows, please help me by letting me grow in Eye Sight and Hearing, so I can hear and see the beauty you have created. Let me grow in Courage to be able to fight the battles that come before me. Let me grow in strength—not to be greater than my brother, but to fight my greatest enemy, Myself. Please let me grow in Wisdom, so I can pass it on to others. Thank you.

PRAYER TO THE SETTING SUN IN THE WEST

Oh Lord, Creator in the West where the sun sets and the harvest takes place. Let me harvest all that I asked you to take away in the East so that I can serve you better by giving me Patience, Tolerance, Peace of Mind, and all the other things I asked you to take away. Let me have them in the Positive so I can redeem myself in your eyes.

PRAYER TO THE WINTER SUN IN THE NORTH
(THE LAST AND LONGEST PATH)

Oh Lord, Creator in the North, I know that the trail from the South to the North is very long, as is life very difficult, difficult because when you blew the Breath of Life into me, you gave me free will. I have used, abused, and misused that will and now I am ready to do your will. I pray for the Knowledge of your will for me and the Power to carry it out. I know that every day that I open my eyes to the East, I have one more day to redeem myself. Please let me keep this day. Every day I take one step toward the day that I will be with you. My body will be in Mother Earth and my spirit will be with you. Let me keep this day so when I am called I can come to you with Clean Hands and Straight Eyes. So that when my life fades as the fading sunset, my spirit can come to you without Shame.

CHAPTER NOTES

CHAPTER 1: NEW ENGLAND REFUGE

1. "Holyoke's History," retrieved 2 Jan. 2008 at http://www.holyoke.org/history.htm.

2. Information on the Connecticut River Atlantic Salmon Restoration Program (CRASR) is from the following three sources: David Howard, "Here Come the Salmon, At Least a Few," New York Times, 3 Aug. 1997, retrieved 31 Dec. 2007 at http://query.nytimes.com/gst/fullpage. html?res=9D01EFDD1E3AF930A3575BC0A961958260&sec=&sp on=&pagewanted=all. "Slow Salmon," Connecticut Fishing Tips and News, June 1, 2007, retrieved 1 Jan. 2008, at http://ctfishing.blogspot. com/ 2007_06_01_archive.html; See the Massachusetts public health warning in: "Public Health Fish Consumption Advisory," retrieved 1 Jan. 2008, at: http://db.state.ma.us/dph/fishadvisory/ SearchResults.asp? Action=WATER

3. For an ecumenical Native blend of four directional prayer symbolism, see *The Sacred Tree*, Phil Lane, Jr. *et al.*, Lethbridge, Canada: Four Worlds Institute, 1984.

4. Irwin M. Wall examines the complexities of the U.S. role in the Algerian War in *France, the United States, and the Algerian War*, Berkeley, University of California Press, 2001. For CIA activities that undermined French success, see especially pp. 97-98, 140-48.

5. For a useful overview of red/white relations and U.S. governmental policies over time, see James Wilson's *The Earth Shall Weep: A History of Native America*, New York: Grove Press, 1998. An exceptional treatment of Indian boarding schools can be found in David Wallace Adams' *Education for Extinction: American Indians and the Boarding School Experience, 1875-1928*, Lawrence, Kansas: University Press of Kansas, 1995.

6. Margaret L. Archuleta, Brenda J. Child, and K. Tsianina Lomawaima, *Away from Home: American Indian Boarding School Experiences*, 1879-2000," Phoenix: Heard Museum, 2004: 78, 87.

CHAPTER 2: SUNRISE OVER SHEEP SPRINGS

1. Iverson, Peter, *Diné: A History of the Navajos*, Albuquerque: University of New Mexico Press, 2002, p. 66.

2. Ibid. p. 67.

3. Sumrak, Dennis, "Navajos Will Never Forget the 1864 Scorched-Earth Campaign: Soldiers Destroyed the Peach Orchards in Canyon de Chelly," *Wild West*, September, 2012: 22-23. See also Iverson p. 55.

4. Locke, Raymond Friday, *The Book of the Navajo*, Los Angeles: Holloway House, 1976 & 2005: 358.

5. Alfred W. Crosby, The Columbian Exchange: Biological and Cultural Consequences of 1492, Praeger Publishers, 2003.

6. Johnston, Denis Foster, *An Analysis of Sources of Information on the Population of the Navajo*, Bureau of American Ethnology, Bulletin No. 197, U.S. Printing Office, Washington, D. C., 1966, p. 23.

7. Ibid.

8. Weatherford, Jack, *Native Roots: How Indians Enriched America*, New York: Fawcett, 1991, p. 132.

9. Ibid., p. 133.

10. Ibid.

11. Ibid., p. 134.

12. Ibid., p. 135

13. Casas, Bartholomé de las, *The Devastation of the Indies, A Brief Account*, New York: Seabury Press/Continuum, 1974: 41.

14. Bordewich, Fergus M., *Killing the White Man's Indian: Reinventing Native Americans at the End of the Twentieth Century*, New York: Random House, 1996, pp. 50-51.

15. Ibid., p. 51

16. Weatherford, pp. 145-146.

CHAPTER 3: LEARNING TO HATE

1. For a thorough overview of this piece of American history, see David Wallace Adams, *Education for Extinction: American Indians and the Boarding School Experience 1875-1928, University of Kansas press, 1995.*

2. See especially Lenore A. Stiffarm with Phil Lane, Jr., "The Demography of Native North America, A Question of American Indian Survival," in *The State of Native America: Genocide, Colonization, and Resistance*, M. Annete Jaimes, Ed., Boston: South End Press, 1992: 23-53.

3. Minnie Braithwaite Jenkins, *Girl from Williamsburg*, Richmond, VA: Dietz Press, 1951: 283.

4. In Adams, *Education for Extinction*, 274.

5. In addition to Adams, *Education for Extinction*, see especially Margaret L. Archuleta, Brenda J. Child, and K Tsianina Lomawaima, Eds., *Away from Home: American Indian Boarding School Experiences*, 1879-2000, Phoenix: Heard Museum, 2004.

6. Adams, *Education for Extinction*, pp. 58, 320.

7. Carlos Montezuma in Peter Iverson, *Carlos Montezuma and the Changing World of American Indians*, Albuquerque: University of New Mexico Press, 1982, p. 112-113.

CHAPTER 4: *CHI'INDIE*

Bartolomé de las Casas. *The Devastation of the Indies: A Brief Account*. New York: Continuum, 1974: 40-41.

CHAPTER 7: DOWN THE ROAD AND BACK AGAIN

1. Iverson, Peter. *Diné: A History of the Navajos*. Albuquerque: University of New Mexico Press, 2002, p. 203.

2. Ibid. "Voting Rights and Freedom of Religion, 1945-1962," pp. 201-204.

CHAPTER 8: LOVE AND WAR

Bataan Memorial Museum, New Mexico National Guard. http://www.bataanmuseum.com/bataanhistory/

CHAPTER 9: BAPTISM IN BLOOD AT MONTE CASSINO

1. In Richard Holmes, "World War Two: The Battle of Monte Cassino," searched 2 July, 2008, at <http://bbc.co.uk/history/worldwars/wwtwo/battle_cassino_04.shtml>.

2. There are many, many books and articles available on the details of the Battle of Monte Cassino and on the irony of St. Benedict's monastery of peace being destroyed by war. See especially John Ellis' *Cassino: The Hollow Victory*, London: Aurum Press, 1984.

3. For an in depth study of the destruction of St. Benedict's Monastery and the controversy surrounding this act of war, see David Hapgood's and David Richardson's *Monte Cassino: The Story of the Most Controversial Battle of World War II*, Cambridge, MA: Da Capo Press, 1984.

CHAPTER 10: CROSSING THE PO

1. John W. Mountcastle, "Po Valley: U.S. Army Campaigns of World War II," p. 16. Searched 24 September, 2013 at http://www. history.army.mil/html/books/072/72-33/CMH_Pub_72-33.pdf

2. United States Holocaust Memorial Museum, "What Is Genocide?" p. 1. ushmm.org. Searched 23 March, 2014 at http://www.ushmm.org/wlc/en/article.php? Moduleld=10007043.

3. David Livingstone Smith, *Less Than Human: Whey We Demean, Enslave, and Exterminate Others*, New York. St Martin's Griffin, 2011: 4-51.

4. Ibid., p. 13.

5. Ibid., p. 14.

6. Mountcastle, p. 19.

CHAPTER 13: IN THE WAKE OF WAR

1. Elfrieda Berthiaume Shukert and Barbara Smith Scibetta, *War Brides of World War II,* New York: Penguin, 1989, p. 132.

2. Ibid., p. 135.

3. Hsu-Ming Teo, "The Continuum of Sexual Violence in Occupied Germany, 1945-49," *Women's History Review,* 1996, 5:2, pp. 207-208.

4. Claire Duchen and Irene Bandhauer-Schoffmann, *Women, War and Peace in Europe,* 1940-1956, p. 82.

5. Ibid.

6. Shukert and Scibetta, pp. 127 and 134.

7. Ibid., p. 133.

CHAPTER 22: LE FOU AMÉRICAN IN FRANCE

Historical overview of Vitry-le-François from: *Vitry-le-François (Municipality, Marne, France),* retrieved 16 Feb. 2009 from <http://www.crwflags.com/fotw/flags/fr-51-vf.html

CHAPTER 23: FALLEN ANGELS

For a summary of Navajo matriarchal culture, see "The Beautiful Rainbow of the Navajo" in Raymond Friday Locke, *The Book of the Navajo,* 5th edition, Los Angeles: Mankind Publishing, 1992: 13-32.

CHAPTER 26: THE LONG ROAD HOME

For a text, photo, and video overview of the Tet Offensive, see: http://www.history.com/topics/tet-offensive

The Johnny Pail Face &
Nancy L. Roberts Scholarship Fund

Fifty percent of royalties from *Johnny Pail Face Becomes a Human Being* are being dedicated to student scholarships at Bay Path University in honor of the following persons:

Johnny Pail Face Sarmiento
Nancy L. Roberts
Carla Ellen Hicks
Michael Colin Hicks
Anita Janece Jarvis Smith

If you would like to make an outright donation
to this fund, please contact:

The Johnny Pail Face and Nancy L. Roberts Scholarship Fund
The Development Office
Bay Path University
588 Longmeadow Street
Longmeadow, MA 01106

Please note that a maximum donation is deposited in this scholarship fund when you order copies of the book directly from Levellers Press at www.levellerspress.com/.